THE PRENTICE HALL SMALL BUSINESS SURVIVAL GUIDE

A Blueprint for Success

PRENTICE HALL EDITORIAL STAFF

PRENTICE HALL
Englewood Cliffs, New Jersey 07632

Supervisory Editor
Richard M. Turitz, Esq.

Contributing Editors

Michael Cross
Robert J. Hard
Jo-Ann Heyer
Jeff MacCallum

Joanne Mitchell-George, Esq.
Alan Rubin
Rhonda Silver, CPA
Kelly Reilly Wiessner

Production
Louise Rothman
Joanne Anzalone

Library of Congress Cataloging-in-Publication Data

The Prentice Hall small business survival guide : a blueprint
for success.
    p.   cm.
    Includes index.
    ISBN 0-13-045329-3
    1. Small business—Management.
HD62.7.P72   1993   93-6514
658.02′2—dc20   CIP

ISBN 0-13-045329-3

PRENTICE HALL
Career & Personal Development
Englewood Cliffs, NJ 07632

Simon & Schuster, A Paramount Communications Company

With the rocky economy, the 1990s are likely to be difficult years for many businesses—large and small alike. That's why *The Prentice Hall Small Business Survival Guide* is so valuable. In tough times, it takes all of your efforts and ingenuity to keep your company moving ahead. The *Survival Guide* helps you do this by giving you proven strategies for cutting costs, operating your business more efficiently and, ultimately, more profitably.

Here's a closer look at the types of cost-cutting, profit-generating information you'll find in each of the *Survival Guide's* four sections:

Section One—Boosting Your Sales and Increasing Your Profits: This section focuses on power-packed sales and marketing strategies that can help your company win bigger orders, land new customers, and tap new markets. You'll find strategies for improving your sales—and profit—picture, and how to find and develop new product ideas. You'll also see how small companies like yours are getting in on the growing overseas market. This section also shows you how key customer service techniques can put—and keep—your company on top. Finally, it shows you how to establish an effective credit and collection policy—which will become increasingly important as more customers and clients have trouble meeting payment deadlines.

Section Two—How to Improve Employee Productivity and Lower Your Benefits and Compensation Costs: This section offers a comprehensive guide to help small business owners get top productivity from their employees. You'll learn how successful companies build a high-quality workforce and how to get consistently superior work at low cost. You will also learn how to get the most from your employee benefit dollar. This section features innovative management and compensation strategies to motivate your sales force to bring in more sales.

Section Three—How to Reduce Operating Costs in Production and Office Management: This section brings you techniques for squeezing costs out of your operations. You'll find advice on how to buy computers to fit your company's needs—at the most cost-effective prices—and how to get the most out of rapidly advancing technology. Finally, this section shows you how you can be a more effective executive by managing your time more efficiently and making better use of your subordinates.

Section Four—Financing and Accounting Strategies for Greater Profits: This section brings you practical, down-to-earth explanations of the pros and cons of the various forms of doing business (i.e., sole proprietorships, partnerships, corporations). It also features expert advice on how to raise financing for your business plus key information on accounting techniques and business finance methods. And it shows you, step by step, how to read and analyze financial statements.

We hope this book will help you enjoy many successful and profitable years.

SECTION 1

SECTION 2

How to Improve Employee Productivity and Lower Your Benefits and Compensation Costs..........167

SECTION 3

How to Reduce Operating Costs in Production and Office Management...277

SECTION 4

Financing and Accounting Strategies for Greater Profits

SECTION 1

Boosting Your Sales and Increasing Your Profits

CHAPTER ONE
STRATEGIES FOR IMPROVING YOUR
SALES AND PROFITS

CHAPTER TWO
HOW TO USE LEADING-EDGE MARKETING
METHODS TO MAXIMIZE PROFITS

CHAPTER THREE
HOW TO TURN YOUR SALES FORCE
INTO A PROFIT FORCE

CHAPTER FOUR
HOW CUSTOMER SERVICE
CAN PUT YOU—AND KEEP
YOU—ON TOP

CHAPTER FIVE
HOW TO ESTABLISH AN EFFECTIVE CREDIT
AND COLLECTION POLICY

This section of the Guide will show you how to bring your sales and marketing efforts into sharp focus around a long-term profit plan. It will tell you how to:

- Forecast sales accurately so you'll have an early warning if current sales head south;
- Analyze the marketplace to detect changes that can be translated into big profit opportunities;
- Find growth areas where risks are relatively low, and reduce them even further;
- Develop a new product or service and give it a strong send-off into the marketplace;
- Determine the right marketing mix in order to maximize profits;
- Boost your sales by giving your customers the service they want—at a price they can afford;
- Hire, train and motivate the best sales, marketing and service team possible; and
- Use credit to boost sales and profits.

CHAPTER ONE

STRATEGIES FOR IMPROVING YOUR SALES AND PROFITS

"If you don't plan for success, then you plan to fail." That's the way one entrepreneur explained why his business had been so successful. Unfortunately, small business owners forget this essential key to success far too often.

As a result, many businesses that should be experiencing strong growth merely plug along. Instead of looking ahead to find the right path to high, long-term profits, their owners spend their energy on day-to-day operations and improving their bottom-line return today. The idea of developing a strategic business plan is set aside. In too many cases, the long-range profit plan is forgotten completely. The business ends up reacting to changes forced on it by competitors, economic conditions or other external factors. Without a clearly defined profit plan, business owners lose sight of their real goals.

SELECTING YOUR PROFIT PLAN

Marketing experts point to three main strategic options that are available to all businesses, regardless of size:

• **The least-cost strategy:** Under this option, businesses sell uniform, standard products. Demand for these products is usually very elastic. An increase in price invariably triggers a sharp drop in sales volume because (1) demand is price-driven and supply is high or (2) there are plenty of competitors who can supply substitutes at lower prices. Customers seek out lowest-price producers, so companies pursuing a least-cost strategy put special emphasis on constantly increasing productivity and lowering per-unit costs.

• **The differentiation strategy:** A company using this approach attempts to offer products that are clearly different from the competition. This difference can be a matter of better quality, more features for the money, exceptional customer service or anything else that makes the product or service significantly more valuable to the customer than competitors' products or services.

Goods are priced well above production costs, which leaves the business with the cash necessary to invest heavily in product development. The key to success with this strategy is to stay closely in tune with the changing wants and needs of customers.

• **The niche strategy:** By selecting the right niche, or highly specialized market, companies concentrate on providing high-priced products or services to a very limited number of customers. Unit costs are high because output is low and production costs are almost always very high. But, by focusing on a niche, companies often avoid serious competition because the market is too small or too specialized to support more than a few suppliers. Customer satisfaction and brand identification are the keys to success here.

In picking a way to go, most small businesses opt for a differentiation or niche strategy, or a combination of the two. The least-cost strategy really doesn't work for small companies. And there's a simple reason why.

Per-unit costs almost inevitably decline as the company gains experience in production. Shortcuts are discovered, building and plant expenses are spread over more and more units as production goes on and raw materials can be purchased at ever lower prices as orders grow in size. As a business grows to dominate its market, costs are continually whittled down. In other words, the larger the market share, the lower the costs.

Thus, the dominant producer in a market is in the best position to pursue the least-cost strategy. It and others with significant market shares are also in very strong positions when it comes to keeping new players out. Big manufacturers will chop profit margins to shreds—or even sell at a loss for a short period—to drive out new competitors.

Avoid facing off against established players in a market for basic products dominated by a small number of producers—unless you're prepared for a long and costly business battle. *Better:* Concentrate on your company's strengths. Use differentiation or superior service or some other edge to gain an obvious advantage over the competition. Focus on appealing to the customer that isn't buying strictly on price. You can do this by:

- Developing a new product;
- Designing your product to appeal to a market audience where you have the most experience; or
- Finding a highly fragmented market where there are no clearly dominant competitors.

We'll look at new-product development later in this chapter. For now, let's take a closer look at ways of improving sales of your existing products.

HOW TO IMPROVE SALES OF EXISTING PRODUCTS

Concentrate on your strength. As long as possible, stick to the main part of your core business. If your company manufactures a product, put your energies into improving the manufacturing process. And beware of the growth trap. As your business grows, more and more peripheral services are needed. These support functions can easily sap your strength. Increasingly, the answer to this problem is to contract with specialists for these services and functions.

For one thing, it's often cheaper to contract out for support services than to hire additional staff. Also, each distinctive business function has its own tricks, short-cuts and hidden pitfalls. In starting an in-house support operation from scratch, you'll be committing time, money and energy to an effort that may not pay off for years.

SELLING QUALITY TO THE END-USER

One way to break away from the pack and make your product stand out from the competition is to sell it on the basis of obviously superior quality. Once the perception of quality is firmly established in the mind of the consumer, it's a simple matter to convince distributors and retailers to stock your products. The trap is that until the public is clamoring for your goods, stores aren't likely to gamble shelf space on new items that may or may not match the sales (and profits) of currently stocked items. Above all, says the president of FireKing International, Inc., you can't afford to lose your good image with consumers. At the same time, find ways to make your product attractive to wholesalers and retailers because they're the ones who will do the actual selling.

Case Example _____

FireKing is a good example. The manufacturer of fireproof filing cabinets started off with one big advantage: Users of the company's cabinets agreed that the quality was significantly better than that of competing products. But that didn't equal the disadvantages that retailers saw. FireKing cabinets are much heavier and bulkier than competitors' models, creating added costs and warehousing headaches all along the distribution chain.

To counter these complaints, FireKing's president came up with a series of proposals aimed at easing the distributors' burdens:

- First, he set up a prepaid-freight program that spared distributors the extra shipping cost.

- Second, he dropped the lowest-priced model from the line. This reduced the number of items dealers had to stock from four to three and emphasized the company's commitment to quality.

- Third, he offered to take back any FireKing product that rusted while in the warehouse. This strategy was a two-way winner. (1) The deal was unlikely to cost anything because FireKing cabinets really were rustproof; and (2) at the same time it pointed out a flaw in many of the competition's products.

Once dealer objections had been overcome, FireKing concentrated on growing its business with consumers. By keeping close tabs on what end-users were thinking, FireKing was able to bring out new products that filled specific niches well ahead of the competition.

For example, when market research showed that consumers wanted a smaller fireproof cabinet, the company came out with one that was 25 inches deep instead of the standard 31.5 inches. When some consumers complained that the metal cabinets were ugly, FireKing introduced a line of fireproof cabinets with wooden exteriors that sold well even though they were *priced two-and-a-half times* higher than metal ones.

By keeping in touch with both sets of customers (end-users and dealers), the company was able to increase its lead over its competitors. A trap many small business owners fall into is that they forget there are different levels of customers—wholesalers, retailers, consumers—and all must be satisfied for a product to sell well.

FIVE WAYS TO HELP THE MIDDLEMAN SELL YOUR PRODUCT

The more satisfied a distributor or retailer is with the manufacturing company, the better effort it will make to move the goods. Here are five ideas on what to offer the middlemen.

- *Offer a short line and wide variety of case-pack sizes:* Distributors don't want to clutter up their shelves with lots of varieties of the same product.

- *Offer a variety of point-of-sale (POS) displays:* For bigger dealers, tailor a unique POS display with the store's assistance. Also, consider tailoring displays to meet regional differences.

- *Offer co-op advertising deals:* While these are common with larger retailers, they should be provided to small stores, too. Reason: The added money from the manufacturer may be the only way to get the store to advertise at all.

- *Offer special price or credit terms:* Use these special deals in addition to regular discounts for prompt payment. For new products, consider extending credit (at no cost to the dealer) until after the goods are sold.

- *Offer incentives to dealers' sales staff:* Bonuses are great motivators for keeping your products at the top of the sellers' thoughts. FireKing, for example, offers free trips to distributors who attain certain sales levels.

DIVIDE AND CONQUER FOR NEW SALES FROM OLD PRODUCTS

You may be able to differentiate an existing product from the pack simply by aiming it at a number of new markets.

Case Example _____

At first glance, thermal underwear (or "Long Johns") wouldn't appear to have much potential appeal for today's fashion-conscious consumer. For years, sales had grown at an unexciting 2% to 3% annually. But that didn't stop the president of J.E. Morgan Knitting Mills from revitalizing the company's sales pitch for its Long Johns. The result: A 38% sales increase— from $40 million to $55 million—in one year.

Instead of continuing to sell thermal underwear as a basic item with a single sales pitch, the company diversified its underwear into three categories: Working Johns, Super Johns and Active Johns. Packaging was also changed to zero in on specific climatic conditions. Thermals are now available for "cold," "very cold" and "extremely cold" conditions. The change has been so successful that the company now has plans to introduce an "Executive" line of thermal underwear.

NEW PACKAGING CAN GIVE SO-SO SALES A SHOT IN THE ARM

Every business owner dreams about boosting product sales without spending a ton of money on advertising. Advertising dollars frequently are something that small companies just don't have. However, there's a way to get more attention for your product without spending a fortune on ads. Try redesigning your product's package for maximum effect. The smaller your promotion and advertising budget is, the more important your packaging. Packaging is the "silent salesman."

There's never been more competition among packaged products in the marketplace than there is today. Shelf space everywhere is at a premium. Your package isn't just competing against the packages next to it, but also against the fancy advertising campaigns your biggest competitors use.

For small businesses, the package could be all you've got—it's the key to all the things advertising can do for you. Here's how to go about changing your packaging for maximum sales effect:

Take a fresh look at where you stand. First, assess how your package compares with the competition, as well as whether it portrays the image you want and fits your overall marketing and profit goals. For example, a contemporary product should have a contemporary look; the packaging for an informational product should have good information on it; and so on. It's also vital to determine whether the package works properly or can be improved, and whether it can be produced more economically.

Is your package environmentally sound? Would a different material be easier to dispose of or recycle and be less costly for your customers? Surveys show environmental considerations are becoming increasingly important to consumers. Your choice of packaging material should reflect these concerns.

While you want your package to be attractive and eye-catching, you can get an additional advantage from having a structural expert check out your packaging and your packaging process. There may be more efficient ways to make the package. A better structure could lure more consumers, as well. A special feature—an unusual texture, a fancy closure—could help your product stand out.

Even big marketers are discovering the value of packaging gimmicks such as these. For example, Procter & Gamble offers a measuring cup as part of its leading laundry detergent package. Including something extra like this as part of the package can make a big difference when the product itself is virtually identical to the competition's.

If you produce your own packaging, you can take satisfaction in the fact that production-line changes needed to make packaging changes are often easier for small companies to carry out than for your large competitors. Changes are typically difficult and costly for big production lines, while small company production lines are far more flexible.

When one successful firm redesigns a package, it conducts tests of the new design right on the shelf to gauge market reaction and interviews consumers to find out if they see an improvement. Even if your market research is conducted informally, you can get a pretty good sense of how successful a change may be. And don't forget to be sensitive to possible negative reactions to a change in your packaging.

The potential boost a new package can give sales is enormous. For example, a small Puerto Rican brewery facing stiff competition from the big boys saw sales jump 30% a mere six months after its containers were redesigned.

Of course, you can't always be sure how much of any sales improvement is due to a change in packaging alone. Other factors, such as distribution or advertising changes, may also play a role. Even a new sales manager can help tip the scales. But in general, a carefully redesigned package almost certainly results in a stronger market presence and stronger sales.

There are times, however, when there's nothing wrong with the package at all. Your sales problems could be due entirely to your pricing policy, an inferior product or a shortage of shelf space at the point of sale. A good package design firm can probably design a package to sell any product once, but if your product's not up to snuff, it won't sell again—whatever the package looks like.

TEN WAYS TO IMPROVE YOUR PRODUCT PACKAGING

A principal at a Chicago-based package-design firm recommends that you follow these 10 steps to determine when and how your packaging should be improved:

1. **Examine whether your package matches your product goals.** What does your package communicate, how does it communicate and to whom? Do package graphics and text connect with your intended buyer?

2. **Examine your overall graphics.** Over time, small changes may have crept onto the package. Promotional messages and other clutter may now undermine your original design and the impact of the package.

3. **Study the packaging material and structural design.** Technology doesn't stand still. There are likely many ways your package could be improved. New materials or a new shape could add up to cost savings for you, a bigger impact on consumers and more protection for your product.

4. **Check out all opening, dispensing, and closure features.** Consumers complain more about problems with these features than about any other element of the package. Anything you can do to improve convenience can only build loyalty among your customers.

5. **Review the back panel.** Fewer than one in ten products makes the best use of the back panel. Typically, it's where you provide instructions or list ingredients. But you can also use it to enhance your product's image by including quality statements, product updates or product-use suggestions.

6. **Study your package sizes and configurations.** A look at how consumers use your product often will suggest alternate package sizes and configurations than what you currently offer. A broader range of sizes or "multipacks," for example, may better match consumer needs.

7. **Review your package's manufacturing quality standards.** These may have been altered over time. Making sure standards are maintained will give you a better-quality package, reflecting well on the product inside.

8. **Examine how your package fits into your promotional plans.** Use a little creativity to build loyalty. For example, can consumers use your packages after the product has been used up? How about offering a "free trial" size?

9. **Analyze your package development plans.** When planning your marketing strategies, always consider how future packaging changes might be used to serve your marketing goals. Alterations in your package should never be on an "ad hoc" basis.

10. **Build packaging expertise.** To maintain a quality package, you need to develop a team of packaging experts (ideally both internal and external) who stay abreast of the latest trends and advances in packaging. The best packaging requires experienced and creative people. You can never stop looking for them.

RELOCATE YOUR PRODUCT TO BOOST THE BOTTOM LINE

Another way to give an existing product new profit life is to "relocate" it to a distribution channel where it will be unique. In effect, you create a new product from the ashes of the old.

Case Example _____

In a risky move that now promises to pay off in big new profits, a New Jersey hardware manufacturer is moving into the retail market. Up to now, the $10 million company had sold its brass fixtures exclusively to door manufacturers and other commercial users.

Recently, the company has been receiving a growing number of requests to sell its products at the retail level. So, the company decided to test the waters. The test was a success, mainly because company executives took a long, hard look at packaging before going into stores. Each brass fixture was individually packed, which allowed different stores to stock and display the items in the most effective manner for their customers. It also allows retailers to keep close track of inventory.

GIVE CUSTOMERS MORE THAN THEY EXPECT

One way to sell more of your product is to convince end-users that it's a better buy than the competition. To do this, find the competition's weaknesses and then capitalize on them by stressing your product's strengths.

Case Example _____

When M. Caparrelli took over as president of Servus Rubber Co., the safety-footwear manufacturing company had been devastated by foreign competition based on price. Despite repeated price reductions, the company just couldn't compete on price with offshore manufacturers whose production costs were drastically lower. The company was losing market share and profits were taking a beating from panicky price cuts.

Although Servus' lines of industrial boots were bought mostly by safety directors, Caparrelli reasoned that their decision-making process was much the same as consumers went through. So, he raised the same questions that consumer marketers ask: How can we differentiate ourselves? How can we present our product as a better value to people who purchase on the basis of a mix of price and quality?

Caparrelli disagreed with the sales force's recommendation that prices be cut even further to encourage new accounts. Instead, he opted to become a "quality leader."

For each line of industrial safety boots sold by Servus, the company created a flagship product. This was a top-of-the-line boot of the highest quality. These flagship boots created a prestigious image that also boosted the image of lower-priced boots in the rest of the line.

Caparrelli also instructed the sales force to "demonstrate" the quality of its products to customers. So when salespeople made calls, they brought with them cut-up samples of Servus boots showing their high-gauge felt lining, waterproofing, seamless construction and rust-resistant buckles. Competitors' boots had all these features, too. The difference was that competitors didn't talk about them.

Also, by emphasizing *hidden benefits*, the company was able to demonstrate how the higher cost of its boots was more than made up for by savings the user would achieve. For the safety boots, for example, better protection of workers' feet resulted in fewer, and less-severe, industrial accidents, which reduced the number of lost workdays.

The company then took competitors' boots to an independent laboratory. When tests showed one boot's steel toe collapsed under less than 75 pounds, this became part of Servus's sales pitch. Salespeople took the poor test results to purchasing agents and distributors. This lowered their opinion of the competitor's boots and further boosted the image of Servus' products. Caparrelli's marketing efforts were rewarded by a substantial increase in sales and market share.

Selling Your Time-Tested Reliable Products

Is there a way for your company to "sit tight" with the products it already has, withstand the challenge of your competition's innovations and take in profits while your competitors take on expenses? Yes, if you use the right approach.

Sell your customers on the advantages your product offers because it does *not* incorporate the competitor's so-called improvements. Don't panic and push your company into producing a new model every time your competitor adds a new gimmick. Instead, market your product as a simple, less-expensive, *time-tested* alternative.

Here are some counterarguments you can use to maintain sales of "unimproved" products in the face of advertised changes in your competition's items:

- *More automatic*—"The more automatic a machine is, the greater risk you run of expensive breakdowns and downtime. Let's look at all the new downtime traps you would be buying—one by one . . ."

- *More functionality*—"The more elaborate a device gets, the more it's going to cost. Before you spend the extra money, let's see, dollar for dollar, how much more these added functions are going to cost compared to the system you're using now. . ."

- *More stylish*—"The higher a product rides on the crest of a fad, the faster it will lose its appeal. Do you remember what happened to tail fins on cars?"

- *A radical new principle*—"You can always tell the pioneers from the arrows in their backs. While there are certainly some significant benefits from this new development, we still see a lot of work that needs to be done. Our company isn't ignoring it; just the opposite. We're testing and refining the concept before we'll be willing to sell it. We think too highly of our customers to saddle them with something new until we're sure it works perfectly."

Learning more about the competition

You can get information on competitors and their products from the following sources:

- Trade association directories and trade shows
- Articles in trade or professional journals dealing with your competitors' products
- The competition's price lists, specification sheets, catalogs and new product announcements
- Test evaluations of competing products
- Reports from independent laboratories and rating services

On every sales call to a company where a competitor's product is currently being used, find out why. End-users will go on at great length about products they appreciate.

Compare your product with the information you've gathered. Then work out sales strategies that maximize your advantages and minimize possible disadvantages in your line.

A Florida company puts facts on competing products in binders for its sales team. Each sales rep has a binder. When a prospect points out, for instance, that a competing product has a new time-saving feature, the rep can turn to the binder page that documents how much downtime or other problems the new feature causes.

HOW TO EXPLOIT A LUCRATIVE NICHE

Profitable niches are often found in markets where there's no clear industry leader. But finding the appropriate niche can take patience. And once you find it, it's vital to cultivate customer loyalty and confidence.

Case Example

Novus Windshield Repair makes a product that, at first glance, looks like a sure winner. It's a kit that repairs cracked car windshields so well they look like new. But the president and founder of Novus quickly discovered that marketing this sure winner was no easy matter. For one thing, the repair kit is not a do-it-yourself item. "Even with sophisticated equipment," he explains, "it would be virtually impossible for most people to repair a windshield."

Novus first decided that the natural buyers for its repair kit were firms with large automobile fleets and car dealerships. This was a readily identified customer group with a clear need for the item. Sales immediately took off, but repeat business never developed. It turned out that only 15% of the products sold over a five-year period were actually used; the other 85% were sitting unopened in garages.

The president then decided that Novus couldn't just *sell* the product to a select group of potentially big users—it also had to provide strong support to the customer.

First, Novus began selling its repair kit directly to auto repair shops. Orders weren't as big as those from car dealership and fleet operators, but there were a lot more of them. Then, to make sure the repair kits were used—and reordered—it offered a free training program on proper repair procedures to purchasers. The training program cemented customer loyalty to Novus. It also enabled the company to expand its line of repair products. Now Novus has franchises around the country and is the global leader in automotive windshield repair.

HOW CURRENT CUSTOMERS CAN HELP YOU SELL TO NEW PROSPECTS

Almost all companies claim that their customers are their best salespeople. But not many firms have put this slogan into action as aggressively as GMIS Inc., a manufacturer of specialized computer software for the health-care industry.

By going the extra mile for its customers, the company has been able to use current customers as references to help land new sales. And the results have been remarkable: After struggling for 15 rough months to make its first sale in 1985, GMIS now has 25% of the Blue Cross/Blue Shield market and does business with five of the ten largest commercial health insurers nationwide, according to GMIS President and CEO Michael M. Nightingale.

The key ingredient is good old-fashioned customer service, including personal attention from the company's president when customers have problems. It also includes ongoing customer communications and feedback to ensure that the company stays tuned in to the needs of both purchasing people and the actual users of the company's products.

Here's a look at how GMIS has tapped the selling power of one of its biggest assets—its customer base.

- GMIS salespeople give potential customers a list of existing customers to call for a reference. The company also encourages potential buyers to visit current customers to see how GMIS software works in actual use. Seeing real-world applications is usually far more effective than watching a salesperson demonstrate a product.

- The company makes it a point to ask new customers for permission to use them as references before it starts giving out their names. No one has ever said no.

One reason these references are so effective is that the company makes no attempt to refer prospects only to fully satisfied customers that it knows will give glowing accounts. Some of the customers on the list have had problems with the software. GMIS doesn't try to discourage them from speaking candidly about their experiences with the company. These may, in fact, be some of the company's most impressive sales references because they can describe the after-sale service and support that GMIS provides when problems arise. One example of that support is personal attention from the president.

When you're selling computer software, follow-up service is vital. Some users are bound to have problems operating almost any program. That's why Nightingale calls customers personally when they have problems with GMIS software to make sure the company is doing everything possible to solve the problems. "I tell them if they don't feel they're getting the right service to call me." And in case something comes up after business hours, Nightingale gives customers his home phone number.

While no one has called him at home yet, Nightingale feels it's important to extend the invitation. Doing so helps reassure customers that they've made the right purchasing decision, and they appreciate the high-level attention. And chances are they will mention it when a GMIS sales prospect calls to ask for a reference. "It's a small world when you treat customers badly," notes Nightingale.

GMIS stays in touch with customers through focus groups and newsletters. In the focus groups, GMIS brings in customers to meet with the company's managers and product designers to identify and evaluate new product opportunities and discuss how existing products are performing and how they can be improved. These groups, which usually meet only when there are plans for a new product or significant changes in an old one, provide feedback on the company's sales techniques and help the company fine-tune its marketing strategy.

> **IMPORTANT:** Before embarking on a marketing strategy that uses current customers, remember your company's commitment to customer service must be absolute. If even a few customers feel they're being slighted in the service area, the word gets out fast. And one talkative dissatisfied customer can quickly cancel all the good will you've earned from a thousand contented customers.

Even highly satisfied customers can hurt a company's sales if you're not careful. One New Hampshire computer systems integration company gives prospective clients a list of *all* current and past customers. The company's president is so certain his firm's services are above reproach that he feels anything less might smack of dishonesty.

Unfortunately, some customers that give the integrator rave reviews focus only on solutions to those business problems that have troubled them. If prospects are looking for answers to different problems, they may choose another integrator because the reference talked about only a small area of the integrator's services. Be sure to match prospects with references who have similar needs.

HOW TO KEEP CUSTOMERS—YOUR MOST VALUABLE ASSET

Always keep in mind that the key to the success of any business, new or old, is its customers. That may seem obvious, but often new manufacturers and service providers become so wrapped up in their products or services that they forget that simple fact. And that can be a costly disaster.

For example, Stew Leonard, a supermarket operator in Norwalk, Connecticut, knows just how costly. A customer once complained to him about a 65-cent carton of egg nog. He tasted the drink, told the customer there was nothing wrong with it, but refunded her money anyway. The customer left in a huff, vowing never to shop in the store again. After calming down, Leonard considered just how expensive the episode was. He calculated that each shopper spends about $100 at the store each week—and most shop there for 10 years or more. His 65-cent error really cost him $50,000 in sales.

That's why it's so important to keep these rules in mind—no matter what your sales methods or marketing strategies may be:

- Always put yourself in the customer's place: If you or your employees can see something wrong or something that needs changing in a product, your customers are sure to be aware of the same flaw.

- Encourage customers to talk to you: When users of your product believe you're willing to make changes based on their requirements, they'll be much more loyal to your company.

- Listen to your own employees: They're involved with the product every day and often see problems that users experience—and, more important, simple solutions to these problems. If they feel management will support them, they'll come up with good suggestions on how to improve the product.

- Be open to change: There's no product that can't be improved upon. By constantly working to make a product better, you'll develop a reputation for quality that will translate into future sales. When a product has been significantly modified, repackage it and sell it as a new model. Not only do you pick up new sales, but your established customers will buy the new version to replace an older one.

- Serve *all* your customers: There is almost always more than one group of customers involved with the buying of a product. Wholesalers, distributors, retailers and end users all have different needs. Where possible, serve them equally. Pay particular attention to the middlemen—if they believe you're helping them as much as possible, they'll be a lot more aggressive in moving your goods. (For more on how effective customer service can help you achieve your profit goals, see Chapter 4, "*How Customer Service Can Put You—and Keep You on Top.*")

HOW TO PRICE FOR MAXIMUM PROFITS

Price is the most important marketing decision you make. It's also the one that's most sensitive to customer demands and competitive forces. At one time or another, your pricing policy may have to take all of the following factors into account:

- discounts for volume, prompt payment, trade status, etc.
- the need to reduce inventory
- the need to unload obsolete (or near-obsolete) items
- the desire of salespeople to negotiate on price
- competitors' price moves
- inflation
- the frequency of past price changes

    IMPORTANT: While you must be prepared to react quickly to competitors' moves and changes in business conditions, today's pricing decisions can reduce your future flexibility. For example, you may encounter buyer resistance to a product priced above a competitor's product if the rest of your line is priced below competing products. Similarly, once you lock your company into a low-price strategy, you may find it very difficult to increase prices without making obvious improvements in quality or design.

Of course, taking a low-ball approach to pricing to overcome a temporary decline in sales or other business setback can quickly make your company the price leader. But after that, any change from this new—accidental—market position is likely to create confusion in the minds of consumers and have a strong negative effect on the company's bottom line. That's why it's best to keep your options open.

It pays to establish a general price policy or strategy, follow it closely and—when possible—leave the door open to return to it if you have to adjust to meet some short-term need. Here are some techniques for maintaining a consistent and profitable pricing policy:

- *Discounts:* Your price list can state the full price of a new product or product line, while also offering an introductory discount. The discount is then dropped when the new product has gained customer acceptance. Or you can make strategic use of discounts to get more mileage out of your current sales force and selling season, as in the following example.

Case Example _____

Following the seasonal pattern in his industry, Al Denton's sales force sold hard from June 15 to September 15, booking orders for merchandise to be delivered to retailers by the end of October. In those 13 weeks, his sellers would book most of the year's business. Denton wanted to stretch the normal 13-week season to 15 weeks. But, he thought, "If we call on the average retailer as early as June 1, he's going to say it's too early."

Denton used a price discount to get around this obstacle. Here's how he did this.

- *Step 1:* In early April, he had his sales staff do some checking. First, they were to list the 10 retailers who gave them the biggest orders the previous year. Then they were to check back and determine the buying patterns of these big buyers over the preceding three years.

  From the original list, the sellers were to select the five who had averaged the largest orders over the last four years. (This was done to weed out one-year "fluke" orders and new customers.)

- *Step 2:* Denton had each of his sales reps call on their big five starting in mid-May, weeks ahead of the traditional starting date. As Denton anticipated, these retailers already knew what they would be ordering, and how much. To offset their reluctance to place orders this early in the season, Denton's sellers offered the customers a 1% discount on purchases made before June 1. (The company also made this offer in sales literature sent to all customers in late April.) As a result, nearly 85% of Denton's biggest customers placed their orders then and there.

- *Step 3:* Denton then had his sellers start calling early on other accounts. In many cases, they were able to land sales a bit earlier than usual by showing retailers the big orders that had already been placed.

- *Step 4:* As the traditional selling season got underway, Denton encouraged his sellers to prospect vigorously for *new* customers. Previously, they'd had little time during the busy season to do much cold calling. And drumming up new business during the off-season was next to impossible. The extra weeks of active selling enabled Denton's sales force to rack up record-setting sales for the company.

• *Balanced pricing:* The general strategy here is to price products as a group rather than individually. This has the effect of spreading out increases that are too large for one product to absorb. You may price one product as a loss-leader. This product is sold at or below cost, but the revenue is made up through increased prices and profit margins on the rest of your product line.

• *Razors and blades:* In a variation on the traditional strategy of giving away the basic item (the razor) and then getting the profits from essential accessories (the blades), absorb all cost increases in the prices for supplies, replacement parts, accessories and service connected with the product's use and leave the price of the basic item alone. Customers are much more tolerant of small increases in these items than they are for obviously raised prices for expensive items.

• *Long-term contracts:* These are particularly important if production lead times are long or you must invest heavily in equipment and raw materials. The contract prevents buyers from continually shopping around and then canceling the moment they obtain a better price. *Customer benefit:* Buyers can lock in current prices for the future. This makes the long-term contract an easy sell.

• *Extended payment terms:* During periods of tight money and sluggish sales, extended credit terms can be as effective as a price cut in winning market share. However, you'll need to toughen your requirements for granting credit in the first place and should be prepared to drop weaker customers. (For more information in this area, see Chapter Five, *"How to Establish an Effective Credit and Collection Policy."*)

- *Prevent price shading:* It's important to have a unified discount policy that prevents salespeople in the field from negotiating whatever price cuts they feel are necessary to make a sale. Price shading can raise havoc with gross profit margins and may convince customers that your products are low-quality. Give your sales force firm guidelines on what discounts to allow based on the customer's industry, location, delivery date, volume, etc. Be careful. There is always a danger that once your salespeople start selling off the price sheet, customers will demand the added discounts forever.

RAISE PRICES FOR A QUICK PROFIT SPURT

There's a golden rule for putting across a price increase: Do whatever you can to soften the blow, but don't apologize. Here are some ways to do it:

- **Lead from strength.** When you must boost prices for two or more products, you can make the news easier to swallow if you first announce the price increase of the best-selling product in the group. The increase is least apt to stir up resistance on this product.

In the price-hike announcement, simply state that increases for other products in the line "are in line with the increases already announced for (the top seller)." This makes these increases appear routine.

- **Provide a window of opportunity.** Give buyers a chance to beat the price hike. A 30- to 60-day period during which customers can continue to buy at current prices can be an effective promotion tool that blunts the immediate impact of the price boost. It can also generate a surge of orders from customers who are stocking up and from customers who have delayed buying.

Another approach is to give the price hike immediate effect, but extend your payment terms from one month to three. Example: "Customers who buy at the new higher prices effective October 1 do not have to pay until January." This can work well if the cost of money is low. You get a surge of orders in October, increased collections in January, and start the new year at a higher price level.

- **Cash in on a product change:** If you offer a new model or make any improvement in the product, emphasize this when you announce the higher price.

For example, one company headlined two new features of its redesigned office equipment, with the new price barely mentioned. Another announced three new sizes in its line, with price increases spread across the entire line. The key to this tactic is to keep the increase in price purely incidental to your main news.

• **Sell à la carte.** If most of your products are sold as part of one low-cost package, unwrap the package and charge more for the individual items. This tactic can have the same effect as a direct price boost on the package itself.

For example, an East Coast chain of family restaurants offered a complete hamburger dinner—including the hamburger, french fries, and beverage—at a basic price of $4.65. The price of the same dinner on the new à la carte menu was $5.35. Patronage dropped a little, but sales volume is actually up. The reason is that customers are ordering more large drinks and large orders of fries—sizes that weren't available under the old fixed-price menu.

• **Drop the low end.** Dropping your low-priced products altogether and concentrating production and sales efforts on top-of-the-line products can produce the profit equivalent of a price increase without any fallout from customers. The key requirement is that you must be able to quickly recoup lost sales volume through increased sales of higher-priced products.

A less risky tactic has been used by companies that produce both brand-name and private-label (or generic) goods. They increase prices on the brand-name products only.

• **Get distributors involved.** If you've improved a product, involve your distributors in a public relations push. Encourage them to expand cooperative promotions, emphasize the improvements and compare the price increase favorably with the industry average or with the wholesale price index.

• **Get fresh mileage from quality features.** Your sales force may have dropped some of the product's quality features from their sales presentations. Price increases are the ideal time to do the following:

• Recheck the benefits your product provides;

• Recheck your advertising to see that it presents these benefits effectively; and

• Recheck your sales force's presentation to make sure that the product's benefits are being emphasized.

Have your sales force "sell" your own buyers. They're traditionally a hard sell and can usually spot flaws in a presentation.

- **Put new accents on service.** One way to do this is to step up service calls. Following a price increase, the president of a Raleigh, North Carolina, firm had her people call on customers ten times a year rather than eight.

HOW TO ANSWER A COMPETITOR'S NEW PRICE

You don't have to match or respond to every change in competitors' prices. Sometimes you can sit tight and profit handsomely. But it's important to find out the motive behind the price change. Answer the following questions.

- Is the competitor acting aggressively?
- Does it have a new cost advantage?
- Is it angling for a larger share of the market?
- Is it acting defensively—for example, selling off excess inventory, struggling to raise cash or improve profit margins?
- Finally, is the price change part of a change in its product line or does it reflect a change in the target market that you haven't caught up with?

When a competitor raises prices, you should check the replacement cost of your own inventory. This means estimating future costs, since there may be new cost pressures that your past experience will not reflect. If your costs are not rising appreciably, you have a choice between raising prices and profit margins yourself or becoming a lower-cost producer and increasing sales volume.

If a competitor cuts prices aggressively with the apparent objective of grabbing a big piece of your market share regardless of the cost, you may have to follow suit immediately. But don't slavishly follow suit—if your sales don't drop precipitously, it's foolish to panic. Keep close tabs on sales in order to spot warning signs of a sales slowdown. But until all the evidence is in, there's usually no need to cut your prices.

If the competition's actions are affecting your sales, then it's time to act. You may want to cut prices on established products or start up a new low-priced line that will compete head to head on price. On the other hand, if your competitor's motive for cutting prices is simply to move goods out of the warehouse, your best move may be to hold the line on prices but strive for better service and delivery times.

Is your price right? The answer lies in what a price increase or decrease will do to your gross profits. To determine this, keep your eye on the number of units that have to be sold to maintain profits. Looking at just sales-dollar volume can be deceptive. The example given in Figure 1.1 shows why.

XYZ's current gross profit percentage is 30% and its product sells for $10 per unit. Figure 1.1 shows how XYZ's gross profit percentage will vary at various levels of price increase and decrease (column D). Columns E and F show how sales volume must change to maintain XYZ's current gross profit. Columns G and H show how many more, or fewer, units XYZ will have to sell to maintain profits given a change in price.

The changes required in sales volume can, taken by themselves, be misleading. For instance, if XYZ reduces prices 10%, sales volume must increase 35.1% to maintain current profits. But of more interest to XYZ's salespeople is how many more units they will have to sell. That increase is 50%. They must sell 50% more units than they do now to maintain gross profits if the price is cut from $10.00 to $9.00.

XYZ Price Analysis
(30% Gross Profit Percentage)

A	B	C	D	E	F	G	H
			Price Decrease				
0%	$10.00	$3.00	30.0%	$1,000	0%	$100	0%
−5	9.50	2.50	26.3	1,141	14.1	120	20
−10	9.00	2.00	22.2	1,341	35.1	150	50
−15	8.50	1.50	17.6	1,705	70.5	200	100
−20	8.00	1.00	12.5	2,400	140.0	300	200
			Price Increase				
+5%	$10.50	$3.50	33.3%	$901	9.9%	85.7	−14.3%
+10	11.00	4.00	36.4	824	17.6	75.0	−25.0
+15	11.50	4.50	39.1	767	23.3	66.7	−33.0
+20	12.00	5.00	41.7	719	28.1	60.0	−40.0

Key to columns:
A—% Price Change
B—Sales Price Per Unit
C—Gross Dollar Profit
D—Gross Profit %
E—Sales Needed to Earn $300 Gross Profit
F—% Increase/Decrease in Sales Dollar Volume
G—Units Needed to Earn $300 Gross Profit
H—% Increase/Decrease in Units Needed

Figure 1.1

After you have worked up a price analysis, get together with your salespeople. They know, perhaps better than anyone, how customers will react to a price change. And they're particularly reliable when you're talking in terms of units sold, rather than dollar volume, before and after a price change.

On the facts above, a 15% price cut is feasible if it will enable the sales force to at least double unit volume. On the other hand, a 15% price hike is feasible if unit orders will not decline by more than 33%. If neither of these outcomes is likely, a price change of this magnitude won't improve gross profits.

Of course, a smaller change in price may be a profitable move. This should be carefully checked, however. It may help to get three different unit sales estimates at each alternative price—optimistic, most likely, and pessimistic. If possible, test each price at trade shows or in test mailings of new price lists. By comparing these results with historic sales results, you will be able to refine your estimate of sales at the new price.

HOW MARKET-WISE PRICING CAN IMPROVE THE BOTTOM LINE

More and more companies are abandoning, or at least de-emphasizing, *cost-plus* pricing. Cost, of course, will always dictate a base selling price. But beyond this, aggressive companies seize every opportunity to use price to boost sales volume or enhance profit margins.

The owner of a small business needn't have a new or unique product to price aggressively. But you do have to be sensitive to how customers perceive value. The most profitable price may depend on one or more of the following effects:

• **The unique value effect.** Naturally, if your product has a feature or benefit that customers *perceive* as unique, you can charge a premium over competitors' prices with little or no effect on sales volume.

For example, American Express charges more for its traveler's checks than most of its competitors. It can do so because of a unique advantage, one that is not overlooked in its print and broadcast advertising: The company will arrange refunds anywhere in the world. Even though the number of traveler's checks that are lost or stolen each year is minuscule, purchasers willingly pay a premium for peace of mind.

• **The substitute/awareness effect.** You develop a product that is the best on the market: fewer parts, better design, *and* lower price. It's the kind of product that should sell itself. But when it hits the marketplace, sales bomb. Why? One possible reason is the substitute/awareness effect—or more precisely in this case, the lack of customer awareness that you are offering a cheaper substitute that's of comparable quality to the product they're accustomed to buying.

A customer's "zone of awareness" can be very narrow. Even within the same store, a seller can influence buyers' awareness of substitutes by the method of display.

For example, when generic grocery products first became available, some stores placed them among the corresponding brand-name products, while others placed all generic goods together in a separate aisle or display area. Generic sales were much greater, and brand-name sales correspondingly less, in stores where generics were interspersed among the brand-name products. The reason was that shoppers quickly became aware of the more economical substitutes.

Beware of putting *too* low a price on your product. Consumers have bottom limits on what they'll pay for an item, just as they have top-end ones. If a price is too low, customers won't accept quality claims, regardless of how true they are. Determine the price range for similar products and set a price for your product toward the bottom of that range.

If you have a quality product that can be made and sold for less than the competition, there's a chance you can set off a profit explosion. But you need more than the product. You need a cost-effective way (that is, one unencumbered by heavy advertising costs) of penetrating your target customers' "zone of awareness."

Case Example _____

In just a few years, *Medco Containment Services, Inc.* became one of the fastest-growing major health-care services companies in the world. Its New Jersey-based business is built on the sale of prescription drugs by mail.

By and large, prescriptions can be filled more cheaply by mail than through a pharmacy. Medco's challenge, however, was to make consumers aware that a high-quality, economical alternative to pharmacy purchasing was available. Diabetics, for example, while well aware of the cost of insulin at different pharmacies, were almost totally unaware of the general level of insulin prices.

Medco's highly cost-effective approach was to sign up big companies, labor unions, and other large groups for its mail-order service. Working with employee and retiree medical plans, the company provides medications at big discounts to plan members. Savings were even greater when generic drugs were substituted for much more expensive name brands.

• **The shared-cost effect.** This effect is becoming more important in the health care industry as third parties, such as the government, businesses and insurance companies, increasingly share the cost of purchases with end-users. That's because customers are sensitive only to the portion of the price that they actually pay. For example, business people and professionals are less sensitive to the price of publications, educational courses and travel related to their businesses or professions because, in many cases, the entire cost is absorbed by the company. Even where that's not true, tax deductions are available that, in effect, pay part of the cost.

Direct price discounts don't work when there's a shared-cost effect. The reason is that the discount "comes off the top." Thus, it primarily reduces the payment or reimbursement made by the *third party*—not the buyer's out-of-pocket cost. Yet a price cut can still give a big kick to sales volume if it's structured as a *purchaser rebate*.

For example, *Boots Pharmaceuticals* realized that low introductory pricing of its antiarthritis prescription drug, Rufen, would not work because insurance reimbursements covered much of the drug cost. So the company took a different tack. It attached a coupon to the bottle that a buyer could send in for a $1.50 rebate. Customers got the full benefit of the low introductory price, even though insurers paid a substantial part of the cost. The result was that Rufen captured a 6% market share in just four months, an unusually swift rate of penetration in the pharmaceutical industry.

However, once rebates and bonuses become universal—and expected—most of the sales-improving benefit is lost.

For example, frequent-flyer programs were started by a few airlines to boost sagging sales in the early 1980s. The programs worked so well that all major carriers followed suit. Today, many travelers demand the bonuses and won't use an airline that doesn't offer them. Now air carriers are increasing mileage awards and reducing the number of trips necessary to earn free flights in order to keep sales up.

CHAPTER TWO

How to Use Leading Edge Marketing Methods to Maximize Profits

As anyone with a full-time sales force knows, sales brought in by a company's in-house sales reps don't come cheap. The average in-person sales call costs about $300—regardless of whether or not the rep lands an order.

That's why more and more companies today are turning to so-called direct marketing methods such as telemarketing, direct mail and consumer advertising to reach more customers. Such methods can provide a more cost-effective way to boost demand for your product or service.

Devising a Marketing Plan

What's the difference between sales and marketing? A marketing consultant—admittedly a biased witness—may have described it best: "Sales-oriented companies try to fit their customers to their products; market-oriented companies try to fit their products to their

29

customers." In other words, companies that emphasize marketing understand that their greatest asset is the customer.

Both approaches are, of course, needed. If salespeople don't press hard to sell the product line, a business will not survive long. Nor will it thrive if it fails to respond to competitors' challenges. But it also pays to deal sellers the strongest hand possible. This means innovating to beat the competition, defining types of customers and customer segments, anticipating new needs and tailoring your products to enhance their perceived value to customers.

A market plan lays out what products to develop and sell, and how to package, price, promote and advertise them. It also establishes the types of buyers you're trying to reach and how to persuade prospective buyers to buy. Moreover, the market plan determines how your product or service will be distributed and what kind of customer service you will furnish.

FIVE KEY FACTORS THAT WILL DETERMINE YOUR MARKETING PLAN

The answers to five key questions will dictate your marketing plan:

1. *What is your firm's "competitive edge"?* Does the competition fear your product's superior design, reliability, durability, or price-to-quality ratio? Do you have low-cost production capacity, specialized expertise or resources not available to competing firms?

2. *What are your sales goals?* Start with your long-range objective for the next five years. Where do you want to be at the end of that time? Then lay out the short- and medium-range goals you must reach first. The goals should be realistic, measurable and affordable.

3. *What is your product strategy?* Start with those who are, should be or could be end-users of your product or service. What are their needs and requirements? Next, what are the needs and requirements of distributors, wholesalers, retailers or other intermediaries? How will your product line age in the next five years? What products will have to be redesigned, replaced or discontinued? What new products should you be developing to sell to what customer segments?

4. *What are your marketing strategies?* What tactics will you have to adopt to achieve your long-term sales goal? Advertising, sales promotion campaigns, direct mail and telemarketing may have

to be used. You may also have to increase the size of your sales force.

5. *What's the best pricing policy?* In many instances, buyers do not dictate a "competitive" price. Pricing above or below competitors will yield very different results; not just on the bottom line, but throughout your organization. While you must be ready to respond to competitors' price challenges, you should have a general policy that emphasizes increased market share and gross sales—or maximum profit, return on investment and good cash flow.

WHERE TO GET MARKETING DATA

Accurate marketing data is essential when estimating the demand for a new product and the sales volume you can expect. Here are the most commonly used sources:

• **Business and trade publications.** These can give you information on customer demographics, buying patterns, competitive activities and new technology. Newspapers, magazines and radio stations that collect data for their advertisers can also be a useful source of information. Many banks, colleges and universities publish business and economic research reports for the areas where they operate.

• **The federal government.** Federal agencies publish reams of statistical data. Much of this information is made available at little or no cost through the Government Printing Office, or by the agencies themselves. Among the most useful resources are:

— Business service checklist—a weekly guide to publications of the Department of Commerce.

— Population census—detailed information on social and economic patterns.

— Census of housing—number of residents, occupancy rates, ethnic makeup and other housing patterns.

— National business patterns—marketing data compiled by state and county. Covers agriculture, construction, manufacturing, wholesaling, retailing, finance, insurance and real estate.

— Survey of current business—a monthly guide listing national, regional and statewide income figures.

- **State and local governments.** Every state and a growing number of cities and counties publish industrial directories containing economic data by city, business and product lines.
- **Public utility and transportation companies.** These businesses are a super source of data on state and local conditions. They're constantly updating demographic and marketing information in their economic development reports.
- **Business directories.** Dun & Bradstreet, Moody's Manual and Thomas' Register of American Manufacturers are available in larger libraries. These provide company profiles that include trade name, headquarters, address, functions, annual sales, number of employees, Standard Industrial Classification (SIC) number and names of chief executives.
- **Market research services.** Professional services offer market data for a price. The common sources are:

  - Multi-client surveys—done on behalf of a group of businesses or a trade group with an interest in one market segment.

  - Omnibus surveys—done monthly or more frequently for a wide variety of sponsoring companies. Each company receives the results of its specific questions only.

  - Focus-groups—group interviews with a dozen or fewer target customers, usually concerning a specific product, service or ad campaign.

HOW TO DEPLOY A NEW MARKETING MANAGER

If you've decided that your business could profit from more marketing expertise, the next question is where to fit a marketing adviser into your organization.

Put the new marketing expert on your personal staff. From this spot he or she can act as liaison between top management and the sales department. Your visible support will increase the new executive's acceptance and power. But because the exec is on your staff, he or she will be less of a threat to your sales managers.

From this strategic position, the marketing manager should be able to take over tasks such as planning, forecasting, budgeting and sales analysis that many sales managers find tedious and generally don't have the training to do well. The marketing manager can also direct your sales force's efforts to gather focused sales data that will be more useful in making profitable decisions. By doing so, you can get answers to key questions such as:

- Is the sales force getting through to those with buying power?
- Are territories apportioned according to sales potential and salespeople's abilities?
- Are salespeople making the best use of their time by giving priority customers the most attention?
- Are sales calls coordinated with advertising and promotion efforts?
- Is sales working effectively with credit, collection and customer service people?

It's important to impress on everyone involved in the sales effort that *profit* is the goal, not *volume* for its own sake.

CASHING IN ON THE MULTI-BILLION-DOLLAR EXPORT MARKET

Small firms increasingly are looking overseas for new sales and growth opportunities. If you're not checking into the profit potential of the many markets opening up around the world, you could be missing the boat. With the opening of the Soviet bloc and the commercial unification of Western Europe, this is a particularly opportune time to get into overseas markets.

While more small and medium-sized companies are exporting today than ever before, many more small firms that *could* export are sitting on the sidelines, according to a recent Dun & Bradstreet survey of 5,000 U.S. companies. They're afraid of the hurdles they might encounter abroad—language and cultural differences, customs headaches, legal and other trade barriers—and of tying up capital in risky undertakings that could take many years to pay off.

Another recent survey, however, suggests that the hurdles may not be all that intimidating, nor the payoff so remote for many small exporters. Half of the small and mid-sized exporters responding to a survey by *Inc.* magazine and Price Waterhouse said they encountered no legal problems in doing business abroad. Most important, 61% said their attempts to crack foreign markets produced profits within the first year.

The government in recent years has launched a number of programs to help small companies expand into international markets.

Federal agencies offer everything from market research and other support to help with financing. We'll tell you about some of these programs and how to get more information. But first, here are some tips from various government trade agencies to help you decide whether you should consider selling your products or services abroad, and how to go about it.

Where to begin

Obviously, the first step is to figure out if your product or service has export potential. Is there an existing need for it overseas that isn't being met? Or can you *create* a need through clever marketing? The following businesses have the best prospects for foreign sales, according to government trade agencies:

- Computer and telecommunications hardware, software and services
- Electronic components, production and test equipment
- Medical instruments, equipment and supplies
- Analytical and scientific laboratory instruments
- Industrial process control instruments
- Aircraft and automotive parts, equipment and accessories
- Regional products not available in overseas markets (for example, citrus juices, ornamental plants, quality food products)

The next step, after you've decided that your product is something foreign buyers might want, is to figure out where the best place is to sell it. In other words, do some market research.

Federal agencies such as the Commerce Department, Census Bureau and Small Business Administration provide export statistics and other economic data you can use in assessing potential markets. You need to look not only at current exports to your target countries, but also at export trends, economic and demographic data. Identify five to ten large and fast-growing markets for your product, as well as several smaller but fast-emerging markets that may provide ground-floor opportunities. These up-and-coming markets may yield faster sales growth and higher profits because competition tends to be less than in established markets.

Many business publications and international trade newspapers, such as *The Journal of Commerce* in New York, run regular listings of export opportunities. Not only do these publications provide specific sales leads, but regular analysis of these needs can give you a good idea of what the business trends are in specific countries where you may be considering entering the export market.

Next, target three to five of the most statistically promising markets for more in-depth assessment. Take a closer took at these countries, following this step-by-step guide developed by the government:

Step 1: Examine sales trends for your product or service, as well as trends for related products that could influence demand. Calculate overall consumption of the product and the amount accounted for by imports.

Step 2: Figure out who your potential competitors are—both inside and outside the country.

Step 3: Analyze factors affecting marketing and use of the product, such as end users, channels of distribution, cultural idiosyncrasies and business practices.

Step 4: Identify any foreign barriers to imports of your product, both tariff and nontariff. Also, be sure to check whether the U.S. government restricts exports of your product. For example, U.S. export controls bar sales of certain high-tech products to many countries for national security or political reasons.

Step 5: Identify any U.S. or foreign government incentives to promote exports of your product or service. Under the Foreign Sales Corporation Act, for example, U.S. exporters that set up qualified foreign sales corporations (FSC's) can obtain a corporate tax exemption ranging from 15%–30% of export earnings. The FSC must be incorporated and have its main office in a qualified foreign country or U.S. possession, among other requirements. It can be either independent or related to its parent company, and can function as a principal (buying and selling for its own account) or as a commission agent.

After you've analyzed the potential markets, you may conclude that your overseas marketing efforts would be more successful if you targeted just a few markets initially. In general, companies that are new to exporting should aim for 10 or fewer markets at the outset; one or two may be sufficient to give you a feel for what it takes to succeed in the international arena. Of course, the scope of your effort will depend on how much capital and other resources you're willing to venture.

FOUR APPROACHES TO EXPORTING

Keep in mind that exporting doesn't necessarily require large capital outlays and personal dealings with foreign governments and customers. Government trade experts note that there are four basic approaches to exporting. Only one of them requires you to become totally involved in the process. The four approaches are:

1. Filling orders from domestic buyers who then export the product: These sales are indistinguishable from other domestic sales. You may not even know your goods are being exported.

2. Seeking out domestic buyers who represent foreign end-users or customers: Many U.S. and foreign corporations, general contractors, foreign trading companies, foreign governments and foreign retailers and distributors purchase U.S. goods for export. With this approach, you know you're tapping foreign markets, but you assume none of the risk.

3. Exporting indirectly through intermediaries: With this approach, a company engages the services of an intermediary firm capable of finding foreign markets and buyers for its products. Export management companies, export trading companies, international trade consultants and other intermediaries can provide expertise and overseas contacts. The exporter retains considerable control over the process and assumes more of the risk. At the same time, the potential profits are higher.

4. Exporting directly: This approach requires a major commitment of time, money and other resources. Typically, the exporter controls the whole process—from market research to distribution. This is the riskiest of the four options—and potentially the most profitable.

Financing your exports

The recent *Inc.* Price Waterhouse survey indicates that the vast majority of small and medium-sized exporters finance their expansion into overseas markets out of available internal capital. Among the advantages of internal financing are greater control over the process and the fact that you don't have to share the profits.

There are a variety of other options, however, for companies that don't want or can't afford to go it alone. Among them: bank loans, joint ventures and state or federal loans or loan guarantees.

Avoid the ten common mistakes new exporters make

If direct or even indirect exporting seems like the best approach for your company, it's important not to underestimate the risks and difficulties you face. As with any new venture, you need to proceed slowly and carefully. Be alert to the pitfalls that other companies have encountered in international trade. The ten most common mistakes new exporters make, according to the government, are:

1. Failure to obtain qualified export counseling and to develop a master international marketing plan before starting an export business.

2. Insufficient commitment by top management to overcoming the initial difficulties and financing requirements of exporting.

3. Insufficient care in selecting overseas distributors.

4. Chasing orders from around the world instead of establishing a basis for profitable operations and orderly growth.

5. Neglecting the export business when the U.S. market booms.

6. Failure to treat international distributors on an equal basis with domestic buyers.

7. Assuming that a particular market technique and product will automatically be successful in all countries.

8. Unwillingness to modify products to meet regulations or cultural preferences of other countries.

9. Failure to print service, sale and warranty messages in locally understood languages.

10. Failure to provide readily available servicing for the product.

WHERE TO GET HELP

Federal agencies offer support services and, in some cases, direct financial assistance to help small business exporters meet the challenge of competing in the international market place.

Be careful when relying heavily on U.S. government agencies for direction in selecting target countries. A Greenwich, Connecticut, international market research analyst notes that these agencies often place *political* considerations ahead of economic ones. It's best to back up government suggestions with independent research from the private sector.

The small business administration

The SBA offers an array of services ranging from export counseling to loan guarantees. It also offers a number of programs specifically designed to encourage closer contacts and relationships between small manufacturers and exporting specialists. These include the following:

- The matchmaker trade delegation program, an ongoing project co-sponsored by the Department of Commerce that helps small exporters build relationships with agents and distributors overseas. SBA sends product literature to these potential distributors and pre-arranges meetings with those that show interest. Some financial aid is also available under this program.

- Publications and educational materials on exports, as well as one-on-one export counseling by SBA district offices and free advice from international trade experts who volunteer their time as part of SBA's SCORE program (for Service Corps of Retired Executives).

- Free legal advice on exporting under an SBA agreement with the Federal Bar Association.

- Free market research on overseas markets under SBA's export information system.

- A revolving credit program that provides up to $750,000 per company in loan guarantees to small businesses trying to enter the export market.

- Special conferences and seminars on topics such as how to develop an international marketing plan. Foreign trade expositions feature representatives from foreign countries, a trade fair, workshops and policy sessions designed to produce recommendations to Congress on ways the government can foster more small business exports. In preparation for these events, the SBA conducts computer match-ups to identify U.S. companies with foreign agents and distributors interested in their products.

Department of Commerce

The United States and Foreign Commercial Service, a part of the Commerce Department's International Trade Administration, provides export counseling, foreign market statistics and information about foreign trade barriers, regulations and competition. USFCS can also help you find sales leads and contacts in foreign countries, among other services.

For more information about SBA programs and other federal assistance for small business exporters, call your nearest SBA district office or (800) 368-5855.

BEEFING UP SALES WITH TELEMARKETING

Sales and marketing experts suggest that you can get more mileage out of your investment in a full-time sales force if you supplement your reps' efforts with telemarketing. Let's take a look at some of the advantages—and disadvantages—of this approach.

Telemarketing offers a number of benefits that simply can't be obtained through any other sales technique. For one thing, selling by phone puts you in contact with far more prospects in a day than personal sales presentations ever can. A good telemarketer will complete about 20 presentations a day out of about 100 calls made. Even if *no* sales are closed, you'll get instant feedback from the marketplace and can fine-tune your sales pitch and pricing strategy to adapt to what customers want daily.

Another advantage is cost. Compared with the $300 average cost of an industrial field sales call, closing the average telemarketing sale costs about half that much. Some marketers claim sales costs are as low as $20, but they ignore the cost of the hundreds of calls that result in no answer or no sale. Still, it's easy to see why companies want to sell by phone. It is essential to integrate telemarketing into your overall sales and marketing plan. It won't work by itself.

Use telemarketing to complement your field sales team. Telemarketing can be most profitable as a tool for canvassing sales leads and qualifying prospects—in other words, to help your field sales force set up better appointments and cut down the number of cold calls your field reps must make. Telemarketers can also check up on dormant accounts and help with account management by maintaining contact with current customers.

Lead off with a direct mail campaign, follow up with telemarketing efforts and close the sale in person. When possible, structure this combined marketing effort around a special deal or promotional offer.

The more easily understood a product or service is, the better suited it is to telemarketing. Complex or expensive products or services are often impossible to sell over the phone.

For example, a New Jersey magazine publisher attempted to sell advertising space in a new magazine by using telemarketing first and then following up with direct mail. The magazine's distribution plan was sophisticated and advertising charges were high. After months of contacting hundreds of potential advertisers, not a single ad had been sold.

In fact, when the publisher tried to give away *free space*, the response was equally bad. The campaign failed because the magazine's concept was too difficult to explain without a personal presentation.

Another company tried to sell high-priced, high-tech home security systems over the phone instead of through its sales force to save on commissions. Even though the company lowered its price (to reflect the lower commission structure), it wasn't able to move the product nearly as effectively. Some products just won't sell unless the customer sees them in operation and can ask questions of the salesperson.

A product's price is also a key element in telemarketing success. Products priced above $1,000 are virtually impossible to sell over the phone. Items priced below $100 are prime candidates. One of the biggest telemarketing success stories is the selling of newspaper home-delivery subscriptions where quoted prices seldom top a few dollars per week. (Of course, that weekly price quickly escalates past $100 over the course of a whole year.) Generally, anything in between $100 and $1,000 is risky.

Do it right or not at all. As recently as a decade ago, telemarketing was touted as an easy way for companies large and small to rack up miraculous sales gains. Back then, professional telemarketers were few and consumer resistance was low. Consumers today are bombarded with telephone sales calls and resistance to telemarketing sales pitches is growing stronger.

As a result, small companies are having a much harder time in this marketplace, simply in terms of getting any attention at all. Large, name-brand companies have the easiest time getting through potential customers' screening devices. Thus, if you're going to take the telemarketing plunge, you shouldn't do it halfheartedly.

WHAT IT TAKES TO BUILD A PROFITABLE TELEMARKETING OPERATION

Telemarketing can make your sales dollar go farther. But putting together a profitable telemarketing program means more than simply buying a few extra phone lines and hiring a few people with pleasant speaking voices. You can't do it on a shoestring if you expect to be successful.

Recruiting is tough

Telemarketers need to bear up well under pressure and bounce back quickly from rejection. The job requires a special kind of person, and you'll be looking for people constantly. Most telemarketers burn out fast, and those who don't are prime candidates to be lured away by businesses willing to pay them much more money. It has been said that two months of telemarketing is like two years in a normal job.

Thus, you should face the fact that you may not end up with the cream of the crop. But you can find good people who—if you treat them right—can bolster your sales effort at a reasonable cost.

To help your people overcome the resistance they're sure to encounter at the other end of the line, it's vital to develop a telephone sales pitch that will cut through all the other telemarketing noise around today and *immediately* grab the prospect's attention. Then you've got to train your people to deliver the pitch effectively. But be forewarned:

Training is expensive

It can cost $1,000 or more to properly equip and train each telemarketer. And that's a big investment for small businesses—especially if the person is likely to walk away from the job after a few months.

But training is vital for your sales success. Poorly trained telemarketers misuse the telephone by talking too loudly or slurring their words, misuse the script by merely reading it and not treating it as a guide, and can *permanently* turn off potential customers not only to the product, but to everything with your company's name on it. Good training will teach your people how to project a positive image of the company with their voice, emphasize the benefits the customer will receive by using the product and turn customer objections into selling points.

Pay competitive salaries to make it attractive for telemarketers to join—and stay with—your company. You don't want your training dollars to be wasted on mediocre employees who wash out quickly. Base earnings on a flat rate plus incentives for each call completed and each closed sale. Even if the call only generates a lead for an in-person presentation, give the telemarketer a small bonus.

Telemarketing alternatives

Hire a telemarketing firm to provide services to you. This is a good way to find out if your product or service can be sold over the telephone. Monitor the firm's efforts closely to ensure the right message is getting out and that the response (in terms of closed sales) is what you're seeking. If the program is successful, then weigh the costs (these firms charge by the hour and completed call) with what it would cost you to set up a comparable system in-house. It may make more fiscal sense to leave it with the outside contractor.

A second possibility is using computer-generated calling systems. These systems can reach the largest audience at the lowest cost.

A potential drawback is that computerized calling systems are highly impersonal—some say intrusive; but they have been effective for some companies.

HOW TO GET FREE PUBLICITY IN TRADE MAGAZINES

Many modest-sized businesses are gaining valuable sales-building space free in the *editorial* pages of trade magazines. So can you. Magazines can always use articles and story material. And it's extremely rare that a magazine will turn down a good story or refuse to use a new-product release just because you don't advertise.

Editors are always on the lookout for information about new products and good feature material and ideas. It's important, though, to know what makes a good story.

A good feature article must offer information that other business owners and their technical staffs want to read about. Such facts come from answering the questions: who? what? where? why? and how?

The "how" question is the one editors look for most carefully. How does your product lead to faster production? How does it cut maintenance costs? How does it eliminate machine downtime? How does it improve accuracy and performance? Here are three tips to help get your story in print:

- Use the reader's point of view: It's absolutely essential to understand—and keep reminding yourself—that editors don't care how good your product is. They're only interested in information that is useful to their readers. If your product or service is used by a magazine's readers, there's a good chance it will be mentioned in the magazine's stories—but only as it relates to the readers' businesses.

- Make sure your story has something new: "We're always interested in new ways a product is used," says an engineering magazine editor.

- Keep advertising out of the story: "If a story is loaded with obvious puff and unsubstantiated claims, it'll end up in the wastebasket," says the editor of a magazine for motel owners.

Tell about your best-known customers. You'll have a better story, as far as the editors are concerned, if the article deals with an industry leader. This doesn't mean that articles about small, less-well-known outfits are ruled out. But, generally, the bigger the customer's company the greater the chance your story will be printed because it's more likely to be a company that others in the industry look to for ideas.

How do you get story material? Here's an idea from a manufacturer of chemical instrumentation systems in St. Petersburg, Florida. A key part of the company's low-budget drive to get publicity is a mail questionnaire that asks customers how they're using the company's equipment.

Information obtained for the questionnaire helped get 43 pages of mention in the nation's trade magazines. "We sent out 35 questionnaires and received usable information from 25 respondents," says the advertising and publicity manager of the Florida company. This material was boiled down to show trends in the industry—information trade editors are always interested in.

Here's another way to a good story: Invite the editor of the publication to have a reporter visit the plant that uses your products the next time a reporter is in the neighborhood. If the editor likes the story idea and can see how the information would be useful to the readers, there's a good chance he or she will arrange for a writer to make the visit.

"One advantage of this technique," observes an experienced advertising manager, "is that the story, in most cases, will be used." And because most writers don't take their own pictures, offer to provide a photographer when setting up the visit with the editor. (A good person to use is a photographer for your local newspaper. He or she probably does freelance work as well.) Even if the editor declines the offer, you've gained by showing your willingness to assist the magazine with its work.

Another suggestion is to contact the magazine editor by phone. Though headquarters for most of the largest trade publishers are located in either New York, Chicago or Boston, many have regional bureaus. Check the page in the magazine that lists the magazine's staff for the office nearest you. If you see listings only for advertising offices, call the editor at the main office. *Note:* Never suggest story ideas to advertising people: They're not interested and, usually, won't pass the information on unless they think they can sell you advertising space. Also, don't believe advertising salespeople who say they can guarantee you editorial coverage if you buy an ad—in almost every case, they can't.

HOW TO GET THE BEST RESULTS FROM YOUR ARTICLES

Once you've written a feature article or press release, what results can you expect from placing it in the trade press? A small but solid number of inquiries, most advertising managers believe. This is because the feature article deals with a specific fact that selects its audience. When you get a response, you can feel pretty sure that the respondent is interested in doing business.

Capitalize on name-building value. If a reader sees your company identified with advances in technology, chances are that your company name will sink in. The reader will remember this next time he needs a product that your company manufactures.

New-product releases bring in the greatest response of all types of publicity copy. Here, however, competition for space is keenest. Editors are always being flooded with releases. To give your release a better-than-even chance, do the following:

- *Give the writing job to a writer.* The engineer or whoever else helped develop the new product may end up writing an overly technical article. Look for someone with writing ability in the office. But have that person work hand-in-hand with the engineer.

   If you have a public relations or advertising agency writing your releases, carefully check what they turn out. According to one editor, these agencies assign their most inexperienced people to new-product releases. Only if the product seems of great interest, editors tell us, will they rewrite or check back with the company for additional facts.

- *Start off right to the point.* Editors like to know at once what you're talking about. If they don't get the main point right away, they're apt to discard the release.

- *Stress the "how" and "why."* Have your release emphasize not what the product can do but how it can do it, and how the consumer will benefit from it (by saving time, money, etc.).

- *Include a photograph.* You can help "sell" the release by including a photo showing how the product is used in an actual work situation. Include people—not as personalities, but to put the equipment in proper scale and show its usefulness.

- *Aim at the right publication.* Sending your release to a magazine with the right readership is the best way to get it published. Check directories in the trade and technical field for profiles of readership. Ask your customers what trade publications they read.

  Never imply that you will advertise in a magazine on the condition that the release is published. "Anytime I read 'we are considering advertising in your book, but first we want to see how the release pulls,' I throw it away automatically," says one editor.

- *Consider "free offers."* Manufacturers tell us that the rate of inquiries from a *free-offer* new-product release is much greater than a feature story. Of course, you have to take into consideration that certain people write in for anything as long as it's free. But, by and large, an inquiry has a good chance of being turned into a sale.

  Don't make your free offer too appealing. An offer of literature gives you a better chance of hearing from potential customers than one of a ball point pen or a slide rule. Of course, if you're just looking for names, the slide rule giveaway will help you more.

KEEPING UP WITH THE NEWEST ADVERTISING TRENDS

Most companies know it pays to advertise—not only to gain new sales but also just to hold on to the customers they've already got. But your ad campaign—particularly if you market directly to consumers—could be a real turn-off if you don't keep up with the latest advertising trends and methods.

MAKING YOUR AD CAMPAIGN CLICK WITH YOUR CUSTOMERS

You need to look no further than your TV to see that advertising has gotten more sophisticated to appeal to ever more sophisticated consumers. You can't simply hawk your wares and expect to win over today's buyers. Whether you use TV, newspapers, magazines, trade journals, radio, direct mail or telemarketing, your ads need to connect with consumers on a personal level to convey a powerful image of your product and company.

If you want your ads to pull in a lot of business—and not just take up high-priced advertising space—they've got to establish a bond with your customers, emphasizes the chairman and CEO of a New York-based ad agency. Three of the most effective types of ad messages for creating such bonds are those that appeal to consumers' aspirations, tap deeply felt memories and honestly evoke real-life situations, he says.

Consider using humor

While advertisements are growing more serious today, there's still a lot of room for a humorous approach. This doesn't mean the ad should fail to pass along a powerful message for consumers to buy. And while potential customers may not accept ads that are too cute or foolish, sophisticated consumers may also be turned off by ads that seem to take the product they're selling too seriously. Thus, for the right products, ads with a sense of humor can be quite powerful.

On the other hand, you've got to be careful not to overdo it or to overreach. With a humorous appeal, you run the risk that the joke will fall flat or that your ad may give the impression that you don't take your product seriously.

Today's most effective ads make the emotional connection with consumers first, and then sell the product.

Show how to solve a problem

Probably the best ads for the business customer are those that show an answer to a business problem. That's why one computer company's recent ads were so effective. They demonstrated problems that were common in companies of almost any type and size, and then showed how the product (one of the company's computers) solved those problems better than the competitors' machines.

One device marketing experts use to help make the crucial connection between consumer and producer is *interactive* advertising—ads that solicit consumer feedback or responses through business reply cards, toll-free 800 numbers, free product samples, giveaways and the like. Marketing surveys show that asking consumers for input makes them more responsive to your sales pitch. And the feedback you get provides an excellent source of market research.

Do your homework

You can't develop an effective ad campaign until you've done the market research to find out what consumers want. But even more, "You really have to know what consumers care about," says the CEO. "The only way to know that is to study consumers' lives and what they think about themselves."

Review your current media advertisements, product literature and brochures to see how well they measure up. If they fall short, it may be time to rethink your company's ad campaign.

WHEN TO LET YOUR CUSTOMERS' FINGERS DO THE WALKING

When you're planning your advertising efforts, don't overlook the benefits of an old standby—listing in your local Yellow Pages. Shoppers who consult the Yellow Pages have already decided to buy something. And in most cases, they're looking to buy it from a business close to home. Since this is the case, you may not need to spend top dollars to reach your target customers.

To bring in more sales, consider advertising in more than one directory. Since the AT&T breakup, many alternative phone directories have sprung up and joined the smaller yellow guides published in many areas. (Call your local Better Business Bureau to check the publisher's track record, especially if the directory is new to your area.)

Business customers, too, are increasingly turning to specialized directories aimed at them. These "business-to-business" directories are available in a growing number of large cities. If you sell a product that many businesses use and operate in an area with a specialized business yellow pages, it probably makes sense to advertise in it.

How many ads do you need? If you operate a retail business, your potential customers probably live close by. So your best investment is an ad in the Yellow Pages that circulates in your immediate area. But if you offer a hard-to-find, unusual or exotic product or service, you'll also want to advertise in directories outside your immediate area, and perhaps under more than one category. The same holds true if you have a toll-free 800 number for order-taking. Advertising in the toll-free directory may be useful in reaching far-away customers.

Beware of Yellow Pages salespeople working on commission who will try to talk you into buying more and bigger ads than you may need. Ads are placed on the page according to size—the largest first—and then either by advertising seniority or alphabetical order, depending on the local phone company's policy. In most cases, ad location isn't as important as the location of your business.

FINDING AND DEVELOPING NEW PRODUCTS AND MARKETS

Your company can move in on the giants if you exploit new product breakthroughs and new markets. But where do you get the ideas for new products or find new markets to explore? There are a number of low-cost sources, including your customers, your sales reps, distributors, suppliers and your own employees.

HOW TO GET HELP FROM CUSTOMERS

Many small business owners agree that current customers are a top source of new-product advice. Customers are usually happy to cooperate when you show them you're interested in helping them.

• **Ask how they use your product.** Sales people should find out if any of your present customers are using your product in an offbeat manner. You may find your product has a market much broader than you think. With some redesigning or repackaging, you may be able to sell a new version of the product in a lucrative new market.

For example, a manufacturer of hair care products for beauty salons had concluded that it did not have a consumer-oriented product. The reason was a lack of convenience. Two lotions had to be stored and applied in sequence and then quickly dried. Then it found out that several salons made occasional sales of the product to their patrons. The manufacturer reformulated the product for greater safety, repackaged it and began selling it through retail channels as a hair care "system."

• **Require your sales force to share survey information.** There's no immediate reward for your sales force in doing person-to-person customer surveys. And a memo isn't going to change their minds. You may have to demand results *in person*.

For example, *Black Machine Company* of Virginia makes a precision machine that measures the dimensions of surgical instruments during the manufacturing process. The market was good, but growing at a snail's pace. At a sales meeting, the company's president demanded that his marketing and sales people give him an answer to a single question: "What other markets need quick precision measurement and quality comparison inspection?"

To find the answer, sales and marketing took two steps: First, they analyzed sales records. The company checked its customers and pinpointed those sales that were outside its usual market. These sales had been made to companies that, on the face of it, had no use at all for instrument measurement.

Next, the company contacted the offbeat customers and asked them what use they made of the company's product. The result: Black found a host of new markets for its precision machine—including the growing robotics industry.

Ask customers what they really want. Have a specific place on the sales report for customer suggestions. When salespeople get a turndown, they can spell out what *would* have sold had they been able to offer it.

• **Don't overlook ex-customers.** Go directly to former customers and ask why they dropped you. Many of the reasons you uncover won't help you find new markets or develop a new product. But if you can get a few solid ideas, you're ahead of the game. Along this line, don't forget to check records of returns, allowances, adjustments and service or repair records.

Tap Distributors and Suppliers for New Product Ideas

Your distributors and suppliers also are a good source for helping you find and develop new products and markets.

Cash in on your distributors' experience. A good way to get information from distributors is through a questionnaire. Because distributors like to be "in the know," they pay close attention to new-product surveys.

You should ask questions such as these:

• Have you had any requests for _____ product?

• If so, approximately what percentage of your customers has inquired?

• Approximately how many units of _____ do you think you could sell per month?

• Do you think this product could be profitable for you?

- What would be the best way to promote this product, and to whom?

Take advantage of suppliers' knowledge. Suppliers generally have a very strong idea of what the market wants. If they don't, they often end up buried in their own inventory. What's more, any new product that produces more sales for you means more business for those who sell to you. So you're likely to find suppliers glad to help.

Case Example _____

> P. Kelly is the owner of a new retail clothing store in Chicago. When he opened for business, he was well aware that the merchandising trend was toward small, upscale specialty stores and away from discounters and department stores. It was taken as common knowledge in the apparel industry that the hot items in men's wear were suits costing $350 and more. But to get a better understanding of the "trend," Kelly went to clothing manufacturers to see what their sales figures were like.
>
> To his surprise, Kelly discovered that suits with high price tags accounted for only 15% of the market. Suits costing between $200 and $299 accounted for 21%. Yet, in the area where this store was located, there was very little competition in the $200 to $300 price range.
>
> Kelly tailored the line of men's clothing he carried to meet his customers' budget. Suits, shirts, ties—everything—were priced just below top-of-the-line to meet the second-tier demand. The store has proven highly profitable.

Use employees to market-test. It can cost $4,000 or more to have a marketing consultant set up a consumer test panel of a dozen people. You may be able to use your employees to get the same results, at much lower costs. Do the following:

- Use employees and their families on consumer panels. Most will be willing to go along if it is pointed out that the results might be bigger sales for the company. You might offer a gift to the spouse for helping out or combine the test sessions with after-hours dinners.

- Have your workers test your new product. Let them use it for a couple of weeks and then conduct a roundtable discussion with them to evaluate it.

HOW TO PRE-TEST YOUR NEW PRODUCT

Once you have your new product prototype, ask yourself: Does your idea work? Does it do what you and your customers, dealers or distributors thought it should do? Don't put the product on the market and hold your breath. Have it tested first.

- See if it will pass laboratory tests. The services of commercial testing laboratories are used by thousands of companies to test new products. These laboratories put a product through grueling tests and, usually, the bugs are eliminated before it hits the consumer market. You can also direct a laboratory to compare your new product with the products of leading competitors and tell you how your product must be improved to meet the competition (if yours comes off second-best).

- See if it will stand up under actual use. Many products can be tested under actual-use conditions as well as in a laboratory. If yours is one of them, you can put your product to actual use and detect flaws that don't show up in a laboratory.

Here are some ways of testing your new product in actual use:

- Display and demonstrate it in retail stores so company representatives can get consumer reactions. You yourself should be part of the research team. This way, you can see your target customers with your own eyes and hear them with your own ears.

- Test it on visitors to the company. Large food companies often use this method.

- Place it in homes of company executives or employees. The disadvantage of this method is that employees are generally biased in favor of their own products.

- Test it in nearby homes and offices. This procedure can be expensive and may require a large number of models.

- Let your current customers use it. In most cases, if a new product will improve the customers' operations, they'll be more than happy to try it out and report back on potential problems and possible improvements. Be cautious. *Only* approach your best customers—those you can trust not to leak information about the new product.

HOW TO ENSURE COST-EFFECTIVE PRODUCTION

How will a new product affect the fixed and variable costs of your business? To find out, you must estimate the extra investment required to manufacture and distribute the new item, the extra working capital you will need at various sales volumes and the cost at these volumes to manufacture and sell the product.

The difference between your total costs with and without the new product can be allocated to it and form the basis for computing a unit cost. Here's a look at the primary cost categories involved in the cost of a new product—direct labor, production materials, outside purchases, special equipment, overhead, and sales expense.

Direct labor

This can be estimated three ways:

- by comparison with past operations;
- by developing a mockup; or
- by applying predetermined time estimates based on motion research.

After including all times for the complete operation, multiply the total direct labor time by the appropriate labor rates.

Production materials

Make a list of all requirements, jot down the specifications and costs and total it up. Include any extra costs for customized or nonstandard materials and make reasonable allowances for waste.

Outside purchases

Get competitive bids on any parts supplied by outside sources. If there's a substantial volume of purchased parts, add your receiving, handling and storing expenses to the cost of the parts themselves.

Special equipment

Determine whether you need special tools to produce your new product. Get an estimate for the cost of this special equipment as well as the cost for "retooling" your current equipment. Again, competitive bidding might be an effective cost-cutting technique.

Overhead

Overhead may be estimated as a percentage of direct labor, machine utilization or some other factor determined by your accountant to be the most sensible basis. Make sure your accountant doesn't overlook any indirect changes in overhead that could be caused by the new product.

Sales expense

Pin down the added sales expense traceable to the new product. Consider the following items:

- Salaries, commissions, travel and entertainment expenses,
- Salary payments to technical specialists,
- Training,
- Labor costs of customer services,
- Carrying costs of parts and inventory,
- Shipping, warehousing and packaging,
- Advertising and sales promotion,
- Bad debts, billing losses and collection costs, and
- Sales overhead (office expenses, insurance, depreciation, etc.).

HOW TO HOLD DOWN NEW PRODUCT COSTS

The biggest opportunity to hold down a new product's cost occurs before it passes beyond prototype stage.

Have a team of engineers, designers, production, marketing and sales people sit down and think carefully and creatively about the product's entire function. Tell them their role is to see if the product should be altered—not whether or not it should be killed. (You, of course, will make that decision based in part on their conclusions.) Their job is to identify and eliminate potential costs by comparing the current way the product fulfills its necessary function with other means of accomplishing that function.

Cost out the product's basic function in terms of materials, parts, labor, etc. Then list its secondary functions.

Often a product's secondary functions cost a great deal more than its primary function. Can these functions be eliminated? And if they're needed, can secondary functions be performed by the primary parts at no additional cost?

Get a firm commitment from customers to buy *before* you put a new product into production. That was a motor manufacturer's key to cost control when it brought out a line of fractional horsepower motors.

The company's salespeople favored introducing 12 different horsepower ratings at the start of production. They felt an across-the-board offering would create a strong market presence for the new line.

Other people at the company weren't so sure. Finance worried about financing the increase in inventory and accounts receivable. Production was concerned about hiring and training new workers. With so many models to produce, it would be five to six months before production could get up to current quality and time standards.

The company's president decided to let customer acceptance answer the questions. Engineering developed prototypes of the new motors. Sales located 14 customers who placed early orders for the new motors. Production then swung into action. But only those *five models* for which customers had already committed to buy were scheduled for production.

With firm orders in hand and reduced parts requirements, purchasing was able to negotiate favorable terms with vendors. Finance found it easier to obtain the funding to support the scaled-down effort. And as sales generated additional demand, the company was able to move finished goods out the door almost as fast as they were produced.

NEW PRODUCT PRICING STRATEGIES

There are as many ways to price and promote a new product as there are for an existing product. But for a new product, the first question is: "What range of prices can be supported by estimated demand?" Once that range is determined, the exact price will depend on which of the two basic pricing strategies you adopt.

Measure the total potential market and estimate your share of it. Then judge the probable sales volume at two or three possible prices within the price range you feel is competitive. You can do this by examining closely the sales volume and prices of similar products bought by customers like those you want to attract. You may also want to test market your new product at different prices.

Last but not least, consider how your competitors will react. If they are hurt badly, you can expect a quick response in the form of competing products. If your new product does not have a proprietary element such as a patent or trade secret, it can be quickly copied by the competition. When this happens, you can expect a very quick shakeout in prices.

On the other hand, you may be able to sustain a high price if any of the following conditions exist:

- You sell to industrial customers who are fast-growing, profitable and dependent on your company.

- Your customers can easily pass their costs through to their customers, or they regularly sell on a cost-plus basis.

- Maintaining a relationship with your company is very important to buyers because of your consistency, service, prestige and the like.

- Your product is essential to the customer but accounts for only a very small fraction of his total costs.

- Your new product is part of a system that would be expensive for buyers to change.

Two approaches to pricing

The reaction you anticipate from competitors may be the most important factor in choosing between "skim" pricing and "penetration" pricing.

• *Skim-pricing advantage:* With skim pricing, you combine high price and low volume. You bring your new product to the market at a high price and expect a low sales volume to start. The high price helps you quickly recover development and promotion costs. You can channel part of the profit back into added promotion so sales volume will gradually increase. Skim pricing works well if your new product does the following:

- Is different from anything now on the market

- Fills a new need

- Appeals to buyers for whom price is no object

- Has so much appeal it can be sold despite the high price

Skim pricing is a short-term strategy. It assumes that competition *will* emerge. If it doesn't, prices will still have to be reduced in order to expand the size of the market. Many of the products introduced with skimming strategies, such as hand-held electronic calculators, have relatively short life spans for top-dollar pricing.

• *Penetration-pricing advantage:* With penetration pricing, you aim at mass volume with a low price tag. Your profit margin per unit is lower than with skim pricing, but this is offset by the greater number of units sold. Economies of scale keep your per-unit production costs low. Consider this strategy when your new product is:

— Easy to imitate, so the competition will be on your heels in a very short time; or

— The same as, or only a slight variation of, a product that is already on the market.

If either of these conditions exists, penetration pricing is almost certain to be the best policy. A low price designed for mass sales can establish the product. On the other hand, a high price in a highly competitive market probably won't bring in enough volume for your product to pay its way.

Penetration pricing is a long-term strategy. Until a following for the product develops, profits may be small or nonexistent. But profit margins can be adjusted upward as market share increases. Often, the upward adjustment doesn't require a price increase, but rather a gradual elimination of introductory discounts, sales promotions or other special deals.

HOW TO TURN YOUR SALES FORCE INTO A PROFIT FORCE

An effective sales force may be the key that helps your business open the door to big sales and profits. Unfortunately, finding, training and retaining dynamic and successful salespeople may be one of your toughest challenges.

Hiring and training a high-quality sales force takes time and patience. And coming up with ways to compensate your sales force so that you and your business—and your salespeople—profit is a tough job that requires constant reevaluation.

This chapter explains:

- How to plan for more—and bigger—sales, and get the message across to your sales force

- How to sharpen your company's sales effort by hiring top achievers—and making sure your current sales force is doing the job

- How to train your salespeople so that their sales message is irresistible

- How to compensate salespeople so you get the most profit for your dollars

TECHNIQUES TO IMPROVE YOUR SALES FORCE

A sales expert maps out how you and your sales force can plan for more successful sales. The small business that prepares for its sales calls is able to:

- talk about those benefits that relate directly to the needs of the buyer
- bring proper materials to the interview so that it progresses efficiently
- set realistic call objectives, and develop a sales strategy around them

Get your sales force to prepare for their sales calls by using a "Sales Planning Guide" (see Figure 3.1). By assembling a file on each prospect, your sellers can move smoothly from pre-call research to a closed sale on the final call-back.

Research is the key to successful sales. Initially, have your sales force concentrate on determining: (1) whom to contact, (2) their possible needs, (3) their financial status, (4) when they want to buy and (5) who your competitors are.

Your company is an excellent source of information. If the prospect is a former or present client of your company, a file will already exist which can provide some of the information needed.

It is imperative that your salesperson meet with someone who is in a decision-making position. Preferably, this person is someone with knowledge of the subject matter of the salesperson's presentation.

If your salesperson discovers that the person he or she is meeting with does not have the authority to buy or to make decisions, your salesperson should diplomatically find out how the system works and who is the right person to see. Have the salesperson ask: "Would you give me an idea of your company's decision-making process for a purchase such as this?"

> **IMPORTANT:** Your salespeople should try to arrange to meet with *all* parties who are influential in the decision-making process—such as managers, technical advisers and buyers—at one time. That way, they can make their sales pitch, answer all questions and persuade all parties at the same time. It's a timesaver for all concerned.

PREPARING YOUR SALES PLANNING GUIDE

A carefully designed worksheet or checklist will assist your sales force in their research. The design of the worksheet or checklist must be suitable for your company's needs and adaptable to different sales situations. *The benefit:* After completing the worksheet, your salespeople will know exactly where they stand with potential clients.

Let's look at the basic areas that your sales guide should cover:

• *What is the prospect's current situation?* Your salesperson should get a feel for the prospect's business by asking something like: "Tell me a little bit about your business." This is a safe, non-threatening opener which can lead the way to more in-depth probing, such as "What's happening with sales?" or "Are you encountering any special problems with your present product or service?"

The salesperson must adapt these questions to your particular business or industry. Some delicate probing can identify needs that might otherwise have remained hidden.

• *What are your prospect's goals?* Aside from making money, what are your prospects trying to accomplish in business? Your salespeople will be showing the prospects that they are interested in their business and well-being, in addition to making sales.

Have your sales force get a grasp of the overall picture. Tell them to forget about your product or service for just a moment. Once your salespeople understand a company's primary purpose in the marketplace, they'll be able to relate to it in a more relevant way.

• *Does your prospect have potential problems and needs?* Have your salesperson look to see if a "need gap" exists. This is a situation where the prospect's current situation is not living up to or accomplishing desired objectives or end results.

The greater the need gap, the greater and more immediate the need for the prospects to change what they're currently doing or purchasing. And, the greater the need gap, the greater the chance your salesperson will make a sale.

• *What are your call objectives?* Your salespeople should have a reason for making the call every time they see a client. If the sale has not closed, the reason for stopping by should be one of the action steps that will move your people closer to making the sale.

• *Ask probing questions to uncover needs:* Your sales reps should have a "questioning strategy." However, pre-determined, specifically worded questions will probably not help ferret out the client's needs. Instead, it's a better idea for your sales force to have a *general* idea of what they would like to ask in order to get the particular information required.

• *What are the decision-making criteria?* In general, your people know that *executives* are interested in the long-term goals of their companies and in increasing overall sales and profits. *Middle managers* will base their opinions on the cost-effectiveness of your product, while *first-line supervisors* will be concerned with installation and operation. Have your salespeople gear their presentation to the different perspectives and decision criteria of each contact. Have them show everyone how your product or service will benefit them. If they show all levels of management how they will benefit, your people will be strong contenders in the race for their business.

• *How will you have to prove yourself?* Most prospects will want your people to prove their claims about your service or product. Prior to the call, your people should find out the best ways to prove themselves, and concentrate on preparing effective proof that's appropriate to the prospect's needs.

Have your sales reps demonstrate your product or service for the client. Have them offer testimonials from other satisfied clients. Have them provide phone numbers of long-standing clients for the prospect to call for a reference about your product or service. (Of course, make sure you first ask permission of your clients to do this.)

• *What is your competitive edge?* Is there something about your company that is unique? Something which gives you the advantage over other companies and salespeople? If so, use it to your advantage. Often a minor detail will tip the balance in your direction. Many sales have been made based on the salesperson's statement: "In addition to the product, you also get me. I come with the package. I'll be here when you need me to make sure that everything runs smoothly and that you realize the full benefits of the product." That kind of enthusiasm and sincerity makes your salespeople winners.

This also is an excellent time to admit a *limitation* in your product. Customers will find out anyway. So your reps might as well score points by being the ones to enlighten them. Contrast any weak points with your products' or services' strengths. For example, if you sell dictation machines, your rep might say, "It's true that my machine will not take a standard cassette. The microcassettes are, however, much easier to store and take up less room in your briefcase. They're actually easier to carry with you." That's honest selling which shows that your sales rep is different from the rest.

• *What commitment will you ask?* It is essential, at the end of the sales call, to know what action will follow. Regardless of the commitment you seek, before your people make the call, they should have a specific end result in mind for the meeting. This is the most important objective of the call.

Attempt to reach a verbal agreement with the potential buyer. Ask for more information, a referral, permission to make a demonstration, or best of all, the order itself!

Figure 3.1
SAMPLE SALES PLANNING GUIDE

Here's a sample sales planning guide for your sales force to use:

1. Company _____ Type of Business _____

2. Location _____ Phone _____ Date_____

3. Key Contact _____ Title _____

4. Who is the decision maker? _____
   (a) Current Situation?
   (b) Goals and Objectives?
   (c) Potential Problem(s)/Need(s)

   _____

5. What objectives should I seek to accomplish with this account?
   (a) Next call:
   (b) Overall:

   _____

6. If the key contact is not the decision maker, how can he/she influence the objective(s) I am trying to achieve?

   _____

7. What questions can I ask to uncover, clarify, or amplify prospect problems, needs, and/or goals?

   _____

8. What decision-making criteria are important to this prospect?
   (a) Possible benefits and proof materials prospect is seeking
   (b) Features that provide those benefits
   (c) Letters, testimonials (to be used if necessary)

   _____

9. How can I be of more benefit to this prospect than anyone else who has called on him/her?

   _____

10. Possible prospect objections   Potential answers

   _____

11. Based on my objective(s), what specific commitment will I ask this prospect to make?
    (a) Why should the prospect want to make this commitment?

---

12. By what criteria will the prospect judge whether or not my product/service/company was a satisfactory solution to his/her problem/need?

13. What methods, procedures or forms can I use to measure whether or not the actual results did, in fact, meet the above criteria?

EVALUATING YOUR SALES FORCE

In order to boost sales, one of the first things you should do is evaluate the strengths and weaknesses of each of your salespeople. Then use your findings to make the most of your sellers' strengths—and make improvements where you've discovered weaknesses. Among the questions you should consider are the following:

• **Do your salespeople find new product uses?** Salespeople who constantly boost their own sales by finding new uses for your products show creative flair. Highlight how important you feel these new uses are by publicizing them to the rest of the sales force. As an added incentive, offer a cash bonus for each new idea a salesperson employs successfully.

• **Do your salespeople upgrade present customers?** Many old, reliable accounts plod along buying products at the same price and quantity year in and year out. The proficient sales pro, however, gains the reliable customer's confidence and encourages the customer to move up to more and better products.

Assign successful "upgraders" to as many steady accounts as possible, instead of having them waste their talents on one-sale trial customers. Then have these salespeople instruct the rest of your sales force on how to convince buyers to go for something bigger and better.

You may be able to build this emphasis on upgrading customer accounts into your normal sales procedure. For example, when one garden tool company receives a mail or phone order for its low-markup standby—a hedge shear—*two orders* are written up. One is for the shear, the other for an expanded complete-line deal.

The hedge shear order goes to the warehouse for shipping. The complete-line order goes to a branch sales office. A salesperson then visits the dealer who placed the hedge shear order, explains how well the whole line is selling at other outlets, and tells the dealer: "If you change your mind, just send this to me. I'll see that it's shipped immediately." The result is that, on average, 15% of contacted dealers upgrade to complete-line orders after the sales call.

• **Do your salespeople resell customers?** You can easily tell if your salespeople are servicing their customers—helping them work a new product into their operations for maximum effect—by how well they are doing in the way of repeat sales.

Periodically stress the importance of servicing accounts in your memos and other communications. You can also drive home the point by including a column on sales report forms that requires your salespeople to indicate when they last called back on a sale.

• **Do your salespeople manage themselves?** You can tell how good your salespeople are at self-management by keeping track of the time they spend traveling, their promptness at appointments and meetings and the time they spend in prospects' waiting rooms.

Have your salespeople keep a time log in which they detail the time spent for each portion of the selling day. Then review each log and question them about time that appears to be wasted.

HOW TO HIRE TOP SALESPEOPLE

A veteran sales pro once quipped that top salespeople could be spotted by one anatomical similarity—their thick skin. The best salespeople sell more because they make more calls. And they make more calls because they handle rejection better than most people.

When you're looking to hire a new salesperson, look for evidence of a competitive nature. Does the applicant want to excel, prove something to someone, or impress others? Did the applicant progressively move up in former jobs, win awards or other forms of recognition? Has the applicant experienced defeat of any kind? If so, did he or she recover quickly and go back for more? In short, look for persistence and tenacity.

Don't oversell the job: Once you've decided that an applicant possesses the skills and qualities you're looking for, it's imperative to give the applicant an accurate picture of the job. Don't exaggerate money or the opportunity for advancement. If the job has drawbacks—for example, plenty of travel and repetition of a canned pitch—be up front about this. Inflating the job will only create false expectations—and high turnover.

Top salespeople will quit the moment they realize they can expect to earn no more than, say, $30,000–$40,000 working for you. What's more, they may sue you for breach of an implied contract if you suggested during the job interview that the position paid considerably more.

SIX TECHNIQUES TO GET MORE MILEAGE FROM YOUR SALES REPORTS

Using sales call reports is a simple and effective way to get your sales staff to close more sales, generate new leads, and gather vital information on customers and competitors. According to one study, 90% of companies that have a direct sales force require *daily* sales reports from their sellers. All too often, however, the information in these reports is too sketchy to be of much use.

You can boost your sales volume in the months and years ahead by using your sales reports to pinpoint hot markets, new buyer needs, and your competitors' latest tactics. But your people will have to say more than just whom they saw and what they sold in their reports. You're going to have to overcome seller resistance to filling out *any* report that cuts into selling time. Here are some ways to do it:

1. **Streamline the reporting process.** A compressor manufacturer follows this rule of thumb: Keep reports short and simple. The company decided that it shouldn't take a salesperson more than five minutes to fill out a report. To speed things up, it designed a form using symbols and number codes, which quickly gained the staff's support.

2. **Get it on tape.** A fishing tackle company reasoned that, while salespeople don't like to write, they'll gladly talk up a storm. So, the company arms its sales force with a Daily Call Report form and portable cassette tape decks. Using the form as a guide, sellers dictate their daily reports. The tapes are transcribed overnight by a typing service.

3. **Develop sales energy.** Using the weekly call report turned in by each salesperson, an Ohio company compares how each seller did on the basis of the number of closed sales and number of presentations. Since the group is compared against itself, half the salespeople will always be rated "below average" in their weekly sales energy rating.

The company knows that salespeople are competitive and sensitive to their standing in the group. It firmly believes that each member of its staff works to make more calls and close more sales to avoid the hated "below average" rating. The fact that half the staff will inevitably receive the inferior ranking each week keeps the pressure on.

4. **Bring in hot leads.** Salespeople often tend to forget that *customers* are an excellent source of leads. One company encourages its staff not to forget by paying a bonus for each customer-generated lead that results in a sale. To qualify, the lead must have been recorded in a call report.

5. **Keep tabs on the competition.** Losing an order to the competition is bad news, both for the seller and your company. But timely reports on lost sales can help you counter competitors' moves before they dig deeper into your customer base.

A California-based specialty clothing operation has salespeople report a loss of regular business the day it occurs. This lost-order report contains basic information: customer name and address, competitor's name, and the reason why the customer is switching.

The report is sent directly to the company's headquarters, bypassing branch offices that get weekly sales reports. As a result, the company starts reacting in days—rather than weeks—to a competitor's tactics. This kind of damage control is particularly useful in highly competitive markets characterized by short selling seasons and "fad" items.

6. **Other uses.** You can also use sales reports to improve customer relations and refine the company's marketing strategy. Depending on your needs, the report can ask sellers to assess customer response to a new product, estimate future demand, collect credit information, and schedule future sales calls.

   IMPORTANT: The more "bells and whistles" you hang on a sales report, the more salespeople will resist filling out the report accurately. Your salespeople should be required to add details only if the details can give information that will fill the particular need you've decided to emphasize. Information that you can get just as easily from other sources (for example, customer service reps, product specialists, or engineers in the field) can be left out of your sellers' call reports.

HOW YOUR SALES FORCE CAN TURN PROSPECTS INTO "DONE DEALS"

11 TIPS FOR TURNING COLD CALLS INTO HOT PROFITS

The owner of an aggressive East Coast company cited these startling facts and figures: "Even in the best of times, we lose between 4% and 7% of our customers—for reasons that are simply beyond anyone's control."

An unusual case? Hardly. Other company heads agree that customer attrition makes profit growth an uphill battle. But what is unusual is the East Coast exec's way of winning that battle. He continually acquires new customers by making his salespeople experts in the *cold call.*

The first step in this direction, according to this owner, is to use top level pressure to overcome the reluctance of salespeople to make cold calls. He requires that one out of every seven sales calls his people make be made on someone who is not now a customer. He calls this the "one-out-of-seven rule."

Sellers aren't given the opportunity to stand still. They're forced to go after bigger profits for the company—and bigger commissions for themselves.

Cold calls aren't sales. So the owner follows up on his one-out-of-seven rule by drilling his sales force on the steps that turn cold call opportunities into sales dollars. They can help your sales force rack up big profits and take home big commissions, too.

1. **Let your business card run interference.** When calling on a company for the first time, don't lose valuable time introducing yourself and the company to the customer's receptionist. Simply hand your calling card to the receptionist and ask: "May I see the boss, please?"

   Since the receptionist knows better than you who has the authority to buy, chances are your card will get to that individual a lot faster. And you can be sure the receptionist will get your name and that of your company right the first time out.

2. **Look for clues to possible uses for your product.** From the moment you enter the new prospect's premises, keep a sharp eye (and ear) peeled to pick up clues that indicate possible uses for

your product. How do other firms in the same line use your product? For example, a look at the type of machines on which clerical workers and secretaries are working, and at the wastebaskets near their desks, could give an alert seller some idea of the customer's needs for paper, office machines, and the like.

3. **Put the clock on your side.** Create a favorable first impression when you call on a new prospect by demonstrating that you're a "right-to-the-point" salesperson who's not there to waste time.

"I let the prospect know how much of his time I want," says one salesperson. "I have a wrist alarm that I make a point of setting when I start my pitch, and I state that when the alarm sounds—say in ten minutes—I'll have completed my sales pitch."

4. **Educate the prospect on what your product can do.** When calling on a prospect who is not familiar with your type of product, come up with a dramatic idea of what your product can do. A salesperson who sells a line of computer printers, for example, stresses not only their speed, but their quietness as well.

5. **Point out the prospect's need for the product.** If new prospects can use your product, they have a need for it. But the prospects may be unaware of that need, and have to be shown it exists. For example, the printer salesperson casually looks over the type and quantity of correspondence being produced in a prospect's office. Often, he finds internal reports and memos being produced on dot matrix computer printers, while external correspondence is done on electric or memory typewriters.

The salesperson is quick to display to the potential buyer samples of letter-quality documents produced by his top-of-the-line laser printers. He points out that one or two printers could service the prospect's entire area, making word processing available for all—instead of just part—of the firm's document production.

6. **Demonstrate on the spot.** The best way to show prospects that your product fills their needs is to let them see it work on a typical job. For example, a salesperson who sells smoke-eliminators finds prospects who recognize the need—but doubt the effectiveness—of her product.

She demonstrates the smoke-eliminator by plugging it in the prospect's office and then lighting a cigarette. She then goes on with her pitch, the central point of which is that the eliminator can cleanse the air in an enclosed area of smoke without "tying down" an employee to within a few feet of it.

7. **Sell your expertise.** When dealing with a prospect who uses a product similar to yours, it's particularly important to sell the expertise that only your company can provide. But when you're calling on new prospects for the first time, it may not always be apparent that they are users until they say: "I've already got a copier (if that's the product you're selling) and I'm satisfied."

   You should answer: "Good, I won't have to take up your time telling you of the benefits a copier can offer. But I may be able to help you save time, money and effort, and to give you an opportunity to make the kind of copies you can't make now."

8. **Look at the user's equipment.** The people who buy the equipment usually aren't the people who use it. And that means they're probably not fully aware of any shortcomings the present equipment may have. So you have to press for an opportunity to see the equipment in action, note the things it can't do, and point them out to the buyers.

   Ask to see the prospect's equipment in action. Determine quickly what it is being asked to do and how well it's doing the job. (You may only have a few minutes to do this!) Then show how your product can do more, or do the same work better, faster, cheaper or with less effort.

   One salesman sells office copiers. On a visit to one prospect's office, he noticed that the person using the copying machine was constantly changing from one size of paper to another and at the end of the job had to sort the copies by hand.

   "Would you like a machine that saves time by changing paper sizes at the flick of a switch; automatically sorting the copies into sets at the flick of another switch; or feeding pages automatically at the flick of another switch?" he asked. "I have machines that can offer any one of these benefits or all of them, plus a number of others." And because he could offer a benefit the customer wanted, he made a sale.

9. **Keep your briefcase with you.** When you go into a prospect's shop to look at the operation, take your sales material with you. Use your brochures or other display material to let prospects size up your equipment against what they've got. Meanwhile, keep your order pad out and if an opportunity comes up to close a sale, you'll be ready to write up the order.

10. **Don't throw in the towel.** If you can't close on the third call, count it as just a temporary setback. Leave literature, put the prospect's

name on your mailing list and call again in six months. Literature left behind sometimes brings surprising results.

The person who said "no" several months ago may now be having trouble with old equipment. There are many cases where a deal was closed because there was a name and a phone number on a piece of literature pulled out of a file six months after the salesperson made his or her pitch.

11. **Make call-backs selling calls.** Don't skip a firm that gave you a frosty reception the last time. With good information on your prospect card, start a call-back with: "I've been thinking about your problem ever since I saw you. I think I can help you by..." Then start selling all over again. Be sure your prospect card has complete information regarding the buyer's problem and application. It's impossible to remember names, titles, or the small details of every call. Write it all down.

HOW TO TURN SALES INQUIRIES INTO HOT PROSPECTS

Handling sales inquiries the right way can give your company a direct line to top profits. Here's how one Midwest manufacturer of electronic parts gets maximum sales mileage out of inquiries. "We zero in on the inquiries," explains the company's top exec, "by using a technique called key questions screening. We try to weed out the catalogue collectors, browsers, curious competitors and other 'duds' by looking for the answers to four key questions:

1. Are you interested in a particular product from our line?
2. Are you considering a purchase within six months?
3. Do you have the authority to buy?
4. Would you like a salesperson to call?

"Naturally," says the Midwest exec, "some inquiries already contain 'yes' answers to those questions. And we relay them to our sales force at once, as hot leads." However, most inquiries don't answer these questions. So the electronics firm goes out and gets these answers.

"We mail appropriate literature, a standardized cover letter and a business reply card containing the four key questions to each interested party."

"The returned cards save us a lot of time and money," says the exec. "The leads we relay to our sales force are live prospects with decision-making power and the intent to buy. Then, to make sure an excellent lead doesn't wither on the vine, we take this follow-up action: "We keep track of the leads forwarded to individual salespeople. If we don't receive a sales call report on a lead within two weeks, the salesperson had better have a good reason."

HOW YOUR SALES FORCE CAN MAKE GREAT PRESENTATIONS

There is only one way to reach the top in selling—you must know how to give a great presentation. Here are some proven-in-action techniques you can relate to your salespeople to help them create highly effective presentations.

Outline your presentation

The best way to organize your material into a logical, orderly and convincing presentation is first to make an outline. Outlining organizes your thoughts and enables you to make the best use of the facts, benefits and sales features that you want to present to your prospect. Through an outline you can see how all your material is going to fall into place, and you get a clear idea of what the actual presentation will be like.

Whether the outline is simple or detailed will depend on what you sell, and on your personal preference. For most people, making a detailed outline gives them a better understanding of what they must say, and how they will say it. A detailed outline also simplifies the actual writing of a word-for-word presentation.

These steps, which are the natural outline of almost any sale, provide a framework that will enable your sales force to develop your own presentation outline:

1. Introduce yourself.

2. Get the prospect's attention and keep it.

3. Make the prospect desire your product.

4. Convince the prospect with proof.

5. Get the prospect to take action (close the sale).

By arranging the elements of your own sales story under the appropriate headings, you will see your outline fall easily into place.

Take pains to make each step connect smoothly with the next. This will be of particular importance when you put your presentation into words, following the outline.

However, there are *three exceptions* to this established selling sequence:

1. Steps can be combined. For example, you usually get prospects interested by describing benefits *after* you have their attention. But if you can make outstanding benefit claims, you can use them to capture their attention at the start. You would then be combining the attention step and the interest step. Most sales, however, are made by leading prospects through each step in turn.

2. Convincing is not always handled as a separate stage. Some salespeople include facts, figures, testimonials and similar convincers *throughout* their presentation, making convincing a constant process.

3. Close the sale at the earliest opportunity. Don't wait until the end of your presentation to sew up the order *if* the prospect is ready earlier. *Trial closings* should be placed at intervals in your presentation to feel out the prospect's buying readiness.

Putting your presentation into words

When your outline is completed, the next step is to write out the presentation just as you intend to give it. Simply take the information you have already decided upon, in the shape or form that your outline gives it, and put it into words.

1. Introduce yourself. Almost all initial personal interviews begin with your salespeople introducing themselves and stating what company they represent. Since this is the natural beginning, it should be the first thing you write in your presentation.

The importance of the first few seconds of an interview justifies a little thought about your initial introductory words. The opening is to show prospects that you know their names, and at the same time to further impress their names on your own memory. You can amplify this effect by stating the prospect's name as a question and then confirming the name:

Salesperson: "Mr. Brady?"
Prospect: "That's right."
Salesperson: "Mr. Brady, I'm Al Franklin..."

You then explain what company you represent.

2. Get your prospect's attention. As soon as you have properly introduced yourself, you must get the immediate and complete attention of the prospect. Just because you are standing there does not mean that the prospect is paying attention to you. Your first sentence must be one that is an attention-getter.

The following types of opening remarks have all been used as attention-getters by successful salespeople in one field or another. Select one that will do the job for you, having in mind your product or service, your personality, and the prospects with whom you deal.

- State an emphatic benefit.
- Promise to solve a problem you know the prospect has.
- Ask the prospect a thought-provoking question.
- Use the "no-name" approach to win more sales.
- Begin with an exhibit.
- Use an item of related and interesting news.

Both your words and your manner should tell the prospects that something important brings you to their offices. Never use the "I just happened to be in the neighborhood" opening. The remark reflects thoughtlessness of your own time and little regard for the prospects and their businesses—and doesn't gain attention.

- *State an emphatic benefit.* Prospects want to hear benefits that satisfy their buying motives. If you can offer a substantial benefit that will be sure to interest a prospect, use it as your opening remark.

A statement of benefit as an opening must meet these four tests:

1. The benefit should be one that the prospect wants.
2. The claim must be thoroughly substantiated by your presentation.
3. It must be a benefit that you are sure you can deliver in full.
4. The claim should be specific. A dollars-and-cents offer is far more effective than a sweeping generality as a means of getting attention.

Here are examples of statements indicating buyer benefits used as openers:

"Mr. Carlysle, what I stopped in to tell you about is a new type of truck rental service that will save you up to 15% on your present delivery costs."

"Mr. Worth, we have a new process that can cut operating time in your lithography department by one-third."

"Miss Upton, we are offering a special this month that enables you to have your typewriters and other office machines completely reconditioned at 25% less than the usual charge."

- *Solve a problem.* If you are in a position to solve a prospect's specific problem, you have an ideal opening. This, too, is a statement of benefit. But it's a special kind because it is personal and specific. A person who is wrestling with a problem is eager to listen when someone offers to help solve it. For example,

"Mr. Prospect, it took me four minutes to reach your office from the street, and the return trip would double that. Multiply eight minutes by the number of your employees who go to the corner drug store for coffee every morning. Then add the time they spend waiting for it, or drinking it. The total time consumed, all *nonproductive,* is amazing, as you probably realize. Our on-the-spot coffee service recovers that lost time and puts it back to work for you."

- *Ask "How am I doing" without really saying it.* The most valuable information a salesperson can have during the presentation is to know "How am I doing." Of course, it is ridiculous to ask such a blunt question outright. But there are more subtle ways of asking and finding the information without phrasing the actual question.

(1) You might pause in your presentation and ask, "Isn't this a good value for the money," *before* you have brought up the subject of how much your product costs. If your prospects nod in agreement, you know immediately you have lost them. They're not listening.

(2) You might leave some obvious "loopholes" in your presentation so that an attentive listener will be left with an obvious question to be asked. If the question does not come, you know that your prospects have their minds elsewhere.

(3) If you think your prospects are not listening, but aren't quite sure, try this. Try to be vague in clarifying a particular feature of your product. Then ask, "Do I make my point clear?" If they are listening, there's no problem. They'll either say "No" or ask a question. If their answer is "Yes," you know you're in trouble and you should be prepared to adjust.

- *Use the "no-name" approach.* Many salespeople have the idea that when they introduce themselves to a buyer for the first time, they must race in with their hand extended and say, "I'm John Jones with the Ajax company." What they fail to realize is that prospects—especially prospects whom salespeople call on regularly—are not really interested in their name, or in anything they have to say. They are only interested in one thing—themselves. Start right there, telling prospects what you're going to do for them. For example, if you're calling on a car dealer to talk to him about an advertising program, begin with "Good morning, Mr. Prospect. I have an idea that will put twice as many people into your Buicks. I'm with the Ajax Advertising Agency."

  Later, when you *show* the prospects how you can serve them, they almost always say, "I'm sorry, what did you say your name was?" Now they're interested in what you have to say. So smile and tell them your name.

  Practice this technique of introducing yourself until it feels natural to you. You'll be on good, solid ground because you'll be thinking in terms of your prospects' interests—how you can serve them, and what they'll get out of the sale.

- *Start with an exhibit.* One way to get attention is to catch the prospect's eye with an exhibit or visual attraction of some kind. Some companies provide their salespeople with scale or cut-out models, blow-ups, and the like, and in many cases these can serve to get the interview going. Salespeople who have these aids, or who sell a product that stirs curiosity by its appearance, can often get under way by simply saying something like:

  "Mr. Prospect, this is the newest and fastest-growing home appliance on the market."

  Remember that the *eyes* are a person's quickest and sharpest point of registration. Your prospects' eyes work for you if you have something interesting on which they can focus.

- *Use an interesting news item.* News of something new and big in the industry, or of something out of the ordinary that has a bearing on the interview, will help you get your prospect's attention. The closer the news affects prospects personally, the more closely they are likely to listen. The effectiveness of this method is increased if you present an actual article or newspaper clipping for prospects to look at.

These examples illustrate how news can serve to launch the interview:

"Mr. Prospect, perhaps you saw the amazing results of Fortune magazine's recent survey of the petrochemical industry and its future. Let's look at this figure in particular, the one that concerns you most..."

"Ms. Prospect, it isn't often that a new product is exciting enough to deserve a major article in two leading trade magazines in the same month. But our new machine is that exciting, and here are the articles..."

- *Build interest.* You have to change your prospects' state of attention into favorable interest. Do it by telling them what benefits they will gain from the purchase of your product or service. Remember that it is *benefits* that they want and will pay for.

3. Turn interest into desire. Making prospects want what you offer narrows the important gap between interest and a signed order. While interest is mainly a mental reaction, desire is an emotional one that incites prospects to take action.

People want: (1) whatever answers a strong need, and (2) whatever gratifies a personal buying motive, such as comfort or amusement. You must, therefore, dwell on the need which you can answer, to make it seem like a strong one, and *personalize* your offering in every way possible.

Here are means by which to accomplish these goals:

- Build up your prospect's needs, pointing them out if necessary.
- Show in what way your product or service is the best answer to that need.
- Point out your prospect's personal stake in the matter.
- Emphasize the satisfaction that the benefits will bring.
- Add glamour or fascination to your product.

- *Build need for your product or service.* You must remind most prospects how important their needs are to get them to want what you are offering. In some cases you have to point out a need or needs of which prospects are unaware, before your story can strike a responsive chord.

No matter how obvious you feel the need for your product or service may be, restate that need to amplify your prospects' awareness of it. Then they'll begin to actively want the benefits you promise.

If, for some reason, average prospects do not realize that they need your product or service, or why, then you've got to point out the need to make them want what you're selling.

- *Show your product as the best.* Create desire for your product by presenting it as the best one for your prospects' needs. Make it stand out in their minds as the answer, and they'll want it. This is especially important when you have close competition.

To do this, make full use of exclusive product or service features—whatever your product or service can do that others can't. Even a minor point seems important when it is presented as the only one of its kind.

Knowing all about your product and its market, and where your prospects fit into that picture, helps you to portray your product as the ideal one. You know what features to stress, what changes or new ideas in the industry you can capitalize on, what will make your offer sound most up-to-date. If you run a close race with competitors, the more you know about your competition the better you can make your product appear as the best one for your prospects.

- *Point out personal stake in the sale.* You may sell to buyers for large corporations or people who otherwise have little personal connection with the materials or services they are purchasing. If this is the case, you can give your sales talk special appeal by pointing out how the prospects are personally involved.

If the prospects are purchasing agents, for example, they probably try to do the best job they can, regardless of the nature of their purchases or their individual feelings for the things they buy. Make them want your product by connecting it favorably with success and good judgment in their responsible positions. If headaches such as returns, short shipments, and incorrect billings are usual problems, emphasize the relief from them if they buy from your company.

This is not to suggest that a purchasing agent, or anyone else, will buy flattery or an easy deal instead of a good product. The point is to combat the impersonal remoteness of some purchasing situations by highlighting the aspects of the sale that concern the prospects as individuals. Your prospects are more likely to want what will benefit them.

The following examples illustrate how this personalizing can be done after you've been specific about the benefits.

"Mr. Prospect, you have a responsible job and I know you are intent on doing it well. That's why I'm sure you will be enthusiastic about this service. It takes a large burden off the shoulders of your office staff. Equally important, it assures you of putting your money where it will do the most good."

"Isn't that important to you, Mr. Prospect, knowing that placing your orders with us will give you the comforting assurance of full-order deliveries every time, thanks to our large stock?"

"Mr. Prospect, my product not only does its job better than others, as I've shown you; it also tells the people who use it that their purchasing agent knows his stuff."

In each case the idea is to promote personal enthusiasm for your product or service by searching out ways in which the prospect will benefit as an individual.

- *Make benefits sound personally satisfying.* Elaborate on the happiness, the enjoyment, the pride, the admiration or whatever other personal satisfaction you can offer your prospects. If their work will be made easier, urge them to picture the physical comfort and pleasure that less work will mean to them. If it will help them make more money, stimulate thoughts of how that extra money will provide enjoyment or supply their wants and needs. Stir their imagination into envisioning personal satisfaction, and you will succeed in making them want to buy.

  As you write out your presentation, try to picture each benefit as bringing personal satisfaction to your prospects, no matter what their product or service is. It's this kind of touch that makes your proposition sound more desirable to prospects than others they hear.

- *Add glamour.* A touch of the romantic or glamorous gives your product a special appeal. If there is an intriguing angle you can weave into your story, use it to create desire.

4. Make your presentation convincing. Conviction is "a firm belief founded on evidence," says the dictionary. That firm belief is what prospects must feel before they make the decision to become a customer. Your presentation must therefore do far more than convey information; it must create conviction in your prospect's mind.

The most essential ingredient in the formula for a convincing sales presentation is evidence. Include all you can of these three kinds: (1) a demonstration; (2) visual aids, especially testimonials; (3) facts and figures.

Almost as important as the evidence is the manner in which you present it and your attitude during the interview. To carry conviction, you must:

- Have enthusiasm.
- Be confident.
- Speak forcefully.
- Be sincere and willing to serve.
- Show loyalty to your company and product.
- Make only those promises that you can keep.
- Be thorough.
- Speak on the prospect's level.

When do you trot out the convincer in your presentation? At the beginning? At the end? Do you always follow the old adage that there are two sides to every story? Or do you leave out some of the facts, some of the time? Or all of the time?

Where do you find the answers? Your prospects provide the best clues. They're the ones who will determine for you just what road you should take. Let's look at the immediate approach. If your prospects have reluctantly agreed to see you, or they've given you a deadline, give them the punch line pronto and hope that one point will make the sale for you.

The prospects are already convinced that your product or service won't do. You must shake them immediately to gain their attention. If you start the orthodox way, you'll lose them before the start.

There are certain types of prospects where it's important to tell all of the facts. For example: (a) the educated prospect; (b) the prospect who counters one of your first points with an argument; and (c) the prospect who hears arguments against your product from competing salespeople.

You show (1) educated prospects that you respect them for their knowledge; (2) argumentative prospects that you aren't afraid of any point they can make, and (3) exposed prospects that you're ready to deal on a product vs. product basis with them.

You should hold back when your prospects are just the opposite of the ones cited above. When dealing with these prospects, you already have them sold or even if they're not totally sold, they wouldn't dream up the arguments you could put into their heads by stressing some of the negative values.

This isn't deceptive selling. For example, if your stapling machine can bind 500 pieces of paper in three minutes, why should you mention that a competing firm's machine can do the same job in 2:38? On the other hand, if the prospect mentioned the time factor, you would have to acknowledge that point and then play up another strong factor of your machine.

- *Be thorough.* Most salespeople can turn to their company for facts and figures to back up statements that are made to convince a prospect. The company is usually in the best position to secure data from its own laboratories, sales offices, outside sources, and so on. The experienced salesperson can often add facts acquired in his selling efforts.

  Your presentation is more likely to be convincing if it tells a complete story than if it is sketchy. Suspicions that you have left things out or are slighting important points put prospects on their guard. You should be thorough, even to the extent of bringing up disadvantages of your product if their omission would suggest you are afraid of prospects' knowing them. When prospects see you lay all your cards on the table, they know that you have confidence in what you are selling. This gives them confidence that your statements are valid and, therefore, convincing.

  Your presentation can tell a complete story even if it omits some of the selling points that you hold in reserve. You must be selective of selling points in order to keep your presentation within time limits.

- *Speak on the prospect's level.* Prospects prefer to do business with a salesperson who can speak their *own kind of language.* If your speech is too formal for prospects to understand easily, they will miss part of your message and resent your attitude. If, because of their education or the nature of their work, they expect a more refined or technical presentation than you give them, you will fail to earn the respect necessary for conviction. Write your presentation to suit the level of the average prospect upon whom you will call.

  The following statement, for example, is used by a drug salesperson to sell an injected tranquilizer to doctors:

  "This product has proven its effectiveness in alleviating symptoms of anxiety, tension, psychomotor excitement and other manifestations of emotional stress. It is also a highly effective antiemetic agent for the symptomatic control of nausea and vomiting due to a wide variety of causes."

To a doctor, this is "talking his language." It would be utterly unsuitable for anyone else.

When you are done, reinforce your advantage by summarizing. The repetition enhances the effect that your sales points had when first made.

5. Make a firm bid for the order. Your presentation must include as an integral part a *final close*—the attempt to get the order after the story is told. (Later in this chapter, we will show you how to recognize closing opportunities and come away with signed orders.) You will be more successful closing the sale if you know just how to go about it, and remember that the prospect expects you to do so.

The trial closings you include at intervals in your presentation are tentative, but there must be nothing tentative about your *final* effort to get the order. A sales interview should have as a logical conclusion a buying decision by the prospect. Don't rest until your closing words are *ACTION* words that move prospects to where you want them...the dotted line.

HOW YOUR SALESPEOPLE CAN NEGOTIATE THEIR WAY TO BIG SALES DOLLARS

A sales trainer and consultant has some timely advice on the power and importance of flexibility and good negotiation skills:

> In recent years, the art of negotiation and compromise has entered the sales picture as a vital element. The reason is that buyers are becoming much more skilled. They have to look more closely at the bottom line, they have to understand marketing and they have to be able to recognize sales techniques.
>
> At the same time, there is a growing recognition between buyers and sellers that they need each other to succeed. There is little tolerance for gamesmanship, but plenty of room for professionalism.

The salesperson as negotiator

Most salespeople receive little training in negotiations. Usually, a few reminders given them by you, your sales managers or other veteran sales personnel are their only real guidelines. For instance:

- Aim high—if necessary, adjust down.
- Keep the whole offering in mind. Avoid splitting it up.
- Keep searching for variables and alternatives.
- If you are turned down, give yourself time to think before you go back.
- When you desperately need a delay, excuse yourself to go to the restroom or make a telephone call.
- Allow the buyers to *feel* they are in control, even though you're actually in control of the situation.
- Never make a concession without getting a purchase order or something significant in return.
- If you start backing down, it's a tough job climbing up.
- Take notes of the discussion. They come in handy if you want to review the past actions and reactions.
- Never make an offer your company is not willing to stand behind.

While these reminders are helpful, they will prove more successful if your sales rep works to create a win/win attitude. You want both sides—the potential buyer and your salesperson—to come out of the negotiations feeling like winners. Generally, that means that both sides feel that they would have preferred a more advantageous arrangement, but both are satisfied with the results.

In win/win negotiations, both sides take the time to look for the best arrangement. Each party tries to improve the other person's position and profit without hurting his own.

Some areas where both sides can profit from a win/win approach are:

1. **Technical specifications:** If the prospect should reduce or change some of the technical requirements of the specifications, it may be less expensive to manufacture and test. This could reduce the cost and sales price.

   Conversely, if the manufacturer designs a better product than required, it will last longer. This could also be a point to negotiate.

2. **Equipment, schedules, shipments, and service:** The cost of engineering, manufacturing, testing, storing, shipping and service is all part of the selling price. If the potential buyer is willing to negotiate changes in preliminary requirements, it could affect the sales price.

Some examples follow:

- A customer wants design drawings in eight weeks; it suits your schedule to make them in six or ten weeks. If the customer changes, can you?

- The prospect wants the equipment in six months; you would prefer to ship in five or eight months. This could be a negotiation point.

- The customer wants exclusive truck shipment; you prefer rail. Which is best?

- The prospect prefers special packaging—cardboard carton shipment, one to a box; you prefer barrel shipment, three to a barrel. How is price affected?

- Installation time and on-site training programs can vary. This is a negotiable point.

- What portion of total cost will be charged to the buyer if he or she cancels before shipment? It can range from a minimum cancellation charge to 100 percent of the order, depending on engineering, design, manufacturing and testing completed.

- Will shipping costs be paid by the seller or the buyer?

- For territorial protection, you may agree not to sign any additional authorized distributors or representatives in a particular territory.

- The prospect may require instruction manuals in different quantities than you normally supply. This may be a small item, but a negotiable one nonetheless.

- Isn't order placement time the best time to get a replacement parts order? It sure is—a good parts order can be very profitable.

3. **Terms of sale:** All the terms of sales are items that can be negotiated. For example, consider the following:

- Basic price: If there are any "gives" in this area, you must get something in return, such as a change in shipping schedule, payment schedule, parts order, specifications and/or purchase order.

- FOB point: Ownership of material can pass at the shipping or receiving point. Processing claims for possible shipping damages between these points takes time and effort and must be initiated by the owner at the time of damage.

- Special warranties and guarantees: The length of time a product is guaranteed can vary. You can consider extended periods of coverage following the normal guarantee. Does your standard policy cover only the repair or replacement of the defective part? What about cost of removal packing and reinstallation of the defective product? Is it feasible to supply a "loaner"?

- Package offer: You may have many products you are offering for sale at one time. Will it be to the buyer's advantage to buy them all from you at a better package offer? Are there items in your total offering that you don't want taken out of the package?

- Payments: When will payment be made? At shipment, upon receipt, ten or thirty days after installation, after six months? Is there a discount? On large projects or major purchases, should progress payments be made? What's the schedule?

- Delays: If the project is delayed beyond the shipping date by the seller, buyer or someone or something else, how will the cost be handled? What about storage—who will pay? How much for how long? What about extra handling or loss of revenue by the buyer?

- Patents: There may be a unique feature that the buyer wants built into your products, and buyer wants patent rights. Your approval, preparation for filing a patent and development costs are negotiable.

- Cancellation charges: When capital equipment is ordered, many actions begin prior to manufacturing. Materials must be ordered, designs started, tools set aside, financing arranged, etc. If order is canceled, the seller has a right to recoup expenditures.

These are just some of the areas that offer room for negotiation. If the proper rapport is present, both the buyer and the seller will consider as many alternatives as possible to consummate a sale that benefits both sides.

EIGHT WINNING WAYS YOUR SALES FORCE CAN TURN PRICE OBJECTIONS INTO MORE SALES

Tell your salespeople to take the offensive when they're hit with price objections. Give your sales force winning lines that turn "your price-is-too-high" objections into closed sales. The secret to this kind of turnaround selling is to prove that your high price is actually lower than the competition's—when prospects consider the value they're getting for their money. By showing that your product is the best buy on the market, even at the higher price, your salespeople should be able to move right into the close.

According to the national sales manager for a large Eastern manufacturing company, there are eight basic responses to price objections:

1. Your price is justified by quality of materials, superior workmanship, construction, durability, built-in convenience, and so on.

2. Your price is actually lower than your competitor's when economics of quality and service are considered.

3. Your company could produce a cheaper product. But years of experience show that the current product is best for the job.

4. A cheap product can cost more in complaints, mishaps, breakdowns, and the like.

5. High-grade performance—the result of superior command of "the basics" plus specialized know-how—is worth a few pennies more.

6. Your company produces a quality product at the lowest possible cost and sells at a fair markup.

7. If a less expensive method of quality production were developed, your company would be the first to apply it.

8. When selling to dealers, remember that higher-priced products are prestige builders for the dealers *plus* there's more profit in it for them. National advertising of your company helps the dealers sell your product. An inexpensive product costs more in loss of customers and in customer dissatisfaction.

Admit the fault, and win the sale

Adapt the turnaround strategies that best suit your product. Then make sure your salespeople use one of these proven objection-beaters to close the sale.

The common "your price is too high" argument may mean your salesperson hasn't given the prospect sufficient reason to buy. In effect, the customer is saying, "You haven't sold me yet, and if you don't try harder I have no interest in buying from you."

The best way to handle this is by having at least one new, additional sales benefit that can be shown to the customer. This added point may be just the reason the customer needs to close the sale.

Tell your salespeople to view an objection as a challenge that they should welcome. Objections help them identify areas that they did not cover as effectively as possible in their initial presentation. In effect, they are being given a second chance to win the sale. Eventually, however, through experience, your sales force should be able to plan a presentation that covers all commonly raised objections—including those dealing with price.

GET YOUR SALES FORCE TO RECOGNIZE—AND TAKE ADVANTAGE OF—THREE SALES-CLOSING OPPORTUNITIES

Hidden opportunities for selling more and earning more are available every sales day. In fact, the entire sales interview is a series of opportunities for closing. But there are certain times during the course of an interview when the chances of closing are better than at other times. Your salespeople should take the offensive as soon as they recognize these three closing opportunities.

Closing opportunity 1: agreement on minor points

When you've gotten prospects to agree with you on several consecutive points, try for the sale right then. You've got them already saying "Yes," so it's a perfect time to ask for the "Yes" you're really after—the agreement to buy.

For example, "This support fitting will add more strength to the eaves of your home—and safety is an important feature, don't you agree?" ..."Yes, that's true."... "This weather-resistant finish will add extra life to the house, and that's important, too, don't you think?"..."Yes, it is."

After putting three or four of these agreement-producing statements together—strung out a bit so it's not too obvious—go for the close.

Closing opportunity 2: agreement on a major point

One of the most overlooked—yet one of the most effective—opportunities for a sale is right after you've made a particularly strong point. Rather than continue your presentation, trying to pile up more points, you should seize the opportunity immediately.

For example, you're selling golf clubs and make the point to a prospect that the exclusive perimeter—weighted heads on the woods—will increase the distance of his drives by about 10%. The prospect wants very much to believe that this is true. He asks how he can be sure the clubs will be that effective.

At this point you present the statistical results of tests which actually prove these woods drive the ball farther. Then you ask for the order, while the prospect is ripe for closing.

Closing opportunity 3: after recapping your strong points

Another good opportunity to try for a close crops up right after you've made several strong selling points. You've gotten through most of your presentation and you pause to sum up the salient points made so far.

> *Sales rep:* "So, what we're saying here is that: (1) This electric saw's safety trigger is an exclusive feature that you will be able to offer; (2) Your customers could not buy it in any other local hardware store; and (3) This saw will be featured on national television, which will help bring customers into your store."

> *Dealer:* "Yes, you've got some pretty good points there...but I don't know..."

Mr. Dealer has already "bought" the summary of strong points. He comes up with a last-gasp objection. The sales rep answers—and leads into a close without the slightest hesitation.

> *Sales rep:* "What seems to concern you?"

> *Dealer:* "If this all adds up the way you say, every hardware dealer in town is going to want to tie in with you."

> *Sales rep:* "If they are, then you can beat your competition to the punch because we have only limited space for local dealer plugs on national TV and, frankly, it's first come, first served. I've seen in other towns what this TV exposure has done to increase sales traffic. Will you be a part of our exciting promotion? It starts just 30 days from tomorrow."

Keep selling until they buy. Top flight sales reps know from experience that they will have to make more than one closing attempt during the sales presentation. As soon as you sense a hidden closing opportunity, try for the close. If you get turned down, all you have to do is go back and bring out additional buyer benefits.

THIRTEEN TESTED WAYS TO GET THE SIGNED ORDER

Here are 13 tested techniques you and your sales force can use to close sales effectively. All of them can be of value to you at one time or another depending on the specific circumstances of your prospect.

The skilled sales "pros" master them all and have at their fingertips just the right one for each trial close. Or they may try the same technique several times in a row, then swing into another type when they think more power is needed.

You should have your sales reps initially master three or four of the closes that feel most "comfortable" to them. As they gain proficiency in them, incorporate others into their selling routine.

Assume the prospect is ready to buy (assumptive close)

You go into an assumptive close by making a statement that indicates that you assume the prospect is ready to buy. If the prospect "goes along" with this statement, the sale is safely closed; if the prospect balks, you resume selling until you are ready to make another trial close.

> A medical retailer works for a large pharmaceutical house. He has spent about 15 minutes explaining a new drug to his prospect. The prospect mentions that a gross lot costs ten dollars more than a type he has been ordering. But he also shows a preference for the new drug.

> The retailer realizes that the time has come to try to close the sale. He stops his sales talk and says, "I'm sure you'll be satisfied with it. Suppose I write up an order for one gross." Now he knows that his prospect may back away from this assumptive close by saying something like, "No, I haven't really decided yet." He also knows that if this occurs, he must go into a further sales talk until he reaches the proper place for a second trial close. Although most prospects will respond to an assumptive close by either expressing agreement or backing off, some will simply say and do nothing to indicate their response.

The assumptive close should never seem like a "closing maneuver" but rather like the sales rep's recognition of a decision already made by the *prospects themselves*. So, even if the prospects respond by backing off, they simply feel that the salesperson's own confidence in the value of the purchase has led to overestimating the prospects' own enthusiasm for it. Thus, no harm is done in any event.

Backing off simply means that the customers are definitely not ready to buy *yet*, and therefore need to be exposed to an additional presentation to provide the basis for another trial close.

When prospects meet an assumptive close with silence, the sales person must decide: (1) whether to take the chance of continuing to assume that the sale is closed, or (2) take the safer course of recognizing that the customers have actually not yet decided either way and are indicating by their silence that they are literally "on the fence." The first alternative is dangerously close to high pressure selling, which is normally not good selling. Furthermore, it tends to force an immediate decision, and since the silent response does indicate indecision, there is a relatively high chance of losing the sale.

While the salesperson would prefer a "Yes" response to an assumptive close, he or she is almost as well satisfied with silence at this point. The sales "pro" looks upon the silence as indicating two things: (1) indecision, and (2) enough interest on the part of the prospect to justify the expectation that a little more "selling" will very likely lead to the sale.

Act as if the prospect will buy (physical action close)

Closely related to the assumptive technique is another closing technique known as "physical action." Here the salesperson assumes the sale is closed, but expresses this assumption not primarily in words, but in some physical action.

Here are some ways to use the physical action technique:

- Begin to write out the order.
- Hand the order form and pen to the prospect for his signature.
- Pick up the telephone and say, "I'll phone the order in, to save time."
- Hand the item to the prospect and say, "I guess you want to take it with you."

The physical action close does not have the appearance of pressure—*provided* it is executed in a manner that leads prospects to think that the salesperson has merely overestimated the degree of the prospects' own enthusiasm or decision on the matter. If placed with some skill in the course of the interview, where the salesperson might logically seem to make such a "mistake," it is never offensive.

Get the prospect to decide on a minor point (choice close)

This closing technique is an attempt to get a decision from prospects on some detail of the sales offer by having them make a choice. A decision on the choice is obtained in such a way as to imply or involve a decision on the sale itself.

Salesperson: "Now that you've heard the facts, Mr. Prospect, do you think our Carbon Ribbon or Standard model would best suit your needs?"

The minor point technique can be applied mildly or forcefully, to suit individual circumstances.

Convince the prospect of immediate need (shock treatment close)

You're losing the "battle" with your prospects. The sale is quickly slipping away. Now is the time to reverse the direction of their thinking; to get them to see your product or service in a new light. If you don't move immediately, you'll lose the prospects for good. On the other hand, quick action can save the sale.

Use the "shock treatment" close. Convince the prospects of their immediate need for your product or service by hitting them with a bombshell.

> A booking salesman for a hotel chain was told by a prospect that he would rather hold off his decision for a while. He responded with this shock statement: "Now, let's be honest for a minute. You'd be in a fix if the accommodations you need and desire weren't available—not just with us—but with anyone. Right?"

> He opened the door to a sale with his shock statement. He got the sale.

Offer the prospect something for buying now (concession close)

In some types of selling, it's possible to get prospects to decide to place their orders immediately by offering them "something special" for an immediate favorable decision.

> A real estate agent has finished showing a prospect the premises he has expressed interested in. He has attempted several trial closes during the course of his presentation. Each time the prospect has argued for a lower price. His last close has

almost "worked," and he sees that the prospect needs only a little "nudge" to help him make a decision.

"If you'll close right now, I'll drop the price of the house $5000. Is it a deal?" he asks.

"Okay, I'll take it," says his prospect, induced by this price concession.

Induce the prospect to close (inducement close)

This technique involves offering something "extra" that is available to anyone who takes advantage of it. The offer of something "extra" tends to dissipate hesitation and delay and helps close the sale.

Salesperson: "We have a special introductory offer on this new product. The regular price is $12 a dozen, but we can take your order now at $9 per dozen."

Salesperson: "On any order you place with me now for fall merchandise, we will give you a 10% advertising allowance, to help you start the season with a good advertising campaign."

Give the prospect a reason to buy now
(last chance close)

When you can honestly state a condition that will or may arise in the near future that would make buying more favorable now than later, you are in a position to use the "last chance" close.

Salesperson: "We are closing out this model and have only 18 left to sell. They undoubtedly will all be sold within a week, and then you can buy only the new model at the regular price."

Salesperson: "There's a 7% increase in price on this item effective the first of next month. This is your last opportunity to stock up at present low prices."

This "last chance" close relies on an appeal to fear—fear that an offer that is available now will (or may) be lost if there is a delay in acceptance. Since fear of losing something of value is a strong buying motive, this closing technique has a lot of power. This technique can be used only when a factual situation exists or the possibility that such a situation will arise exists. On the other hand, the alert sales "pro" can often find such an opportunity where others see none.

Use the names of other buyers to persuade your prospect to buy (testimonial close)

The testimonial technique is based on the "follow the leader" instinct. If certain persons who are respected by your prospects—or great numbers of persons whose names they may not know—have decided it is advantageous to say "Yes" to a proposition, the prospects are inclined to "go along," too.

For example, a salesperson selling dresses to leading department stores might tell buyers of how successful the line has proved in an outstanding store or several such stores. The salesperson mentions names. These names should, of course, have some special meaning to those to whom they are mentioned.

Sometimes, the testimonial technique relies on sheer weight of numbers. For example, a salesperson may leaf through his order book, showing (on his copies) the name of buyer after buyer of his product.

Use the case history approach. Showing how someone else benefited from using your product is a tested and successful closing technique. But, to make this "case history" approach work, you have to key your story to what your prospects need. Many a good, solid success story has backfired on salespeople because the customer couldn't relate it to his or her own situation.

For example, a salesperson was trying to close a big sale. As part of his pitch, he cited another company's experience with the product. He showed how that company boosted production 50% by using the very line of equipment the prospect was being asked to buy. On the surface, this seemed to be an excellent pitch. But it resulted in no sale. Extra production capacity was the one thing the prospect didn't need. Because orders were far below normal, he was using only half his present capacity.

The salesperson hadn't acquainted himself with the prospect's business problems. As a result, he used an illustration that was practically guaranteed *not to work*.

When he told the sales manager how he had struck out with the "success" story, the manager did some investigating, and discovered the company's problem. Deciding that the proper angle was to play up cutting costs and turning out a better product, he called on the prospect and made this winning move. He showed the prospect the actual case of a company whose production was off and whose profits were down. By using his equipment, the company cut costs by 30% the first year, and was quickly able to increase profits.

The case history struck home in a big way. The customer bought the sales manager's complete line and was satisfied.

Summarize your strong points to convince the prospect to buy (summary close)

Many salespeople get excellent results in closing by summarizing all the reasons for buying their product.

> "Let's look at it this way, Mr. Tepper," says the stock salesman to a hesitant prospect. "This investment is abundantly sound—I'm sure you realize that. Second, it assures you a higher rate of return than most others of its class. Third, you recognize the unusual prospect of appreciation in value—you know the reasons why you may very likely realize substantially more than the amount of your initial investment when you do sell. And, finally, it is so readily marketable that you can sell at almost a moment's notice,...Now, Mr. Tepper, is there any reason to hesitate in view of these facts?"

The sales points gather impact as each one reinforces the others. Safety—high return—possibility of appreciation in value—liquidity—all these are brought up in the prospect's mind at the same time.

The salesperson's enthusiasm must be discernible as he quickly reviews the list of reasons to buy. When both logic and enthusiasm are joined in such a close, there is every likelihood that a sale will result.

Ask your prospect why he doesn't buy ("why not" close)

When they are unable to close by other means, many successful sales "pros" stop further "selling" and simply ask their prospects why they won't buy. For example: "Mr. Prospect, you must have a reason for hesitating, and I'm sure it's a good one. Would you mind telling me what it is?" This is one way to ask "Why not?" The experienced sales "pro" changes the wording to meet individual circumstances, but the "Why not?" question remains the bottom line.

Few prospects fail to respond to such a question. The question implies that the salesperson is at a loss to understand what is going on in the prospect's mind. Prospects know that under these circumstances, they must seem to be a bit slow, stubborn or even unreasonable. To justify their position in the salesperson's mind, they are likely to explain their reasoning.

This closing question is advantageous to the sales "pro" for these reasons:

- It puts prospects on the "defensive" since their reasons must have substance or their egos will suffer.

- It enables the sales "pro" to learn exactly what obstacles must be overcome to win the sale. If the obstacle can be overcome, it is most likely that the sale will be closed.

- In stating their reason or reasons, the prospects are acknowledging to some extent that they would buy if the reasons could be overcome.

- When the prospects give their reasons, the sales "pro" wins another opportunity to state his or her case in terms most important to the prospects.

Not every reply to this question is complete or accurate. A person who does not have authority to make the commitment may not give the true reason. Nor will prospects give the real reason if it is inability to pay, or anything else that they do not wish to reveal. It follows that the sale is not always automatically won even if the stated reason is blasted away.

How to close a "tough" prospect (the "hat trick" close)

This close is used by strong sales "pros" to handle tough selling assignments successfully. Use it when all other methods of closing have failed.

Ray Remington's job is to sign up companies to lease their company cars rather than buy them outright. He tells a strong story of the advantages of leasing. But since acceptance of his offer involves a change in the prospect's policy and practice, he often finds it difficult to close. "I want to think it over," is frequently the reply when he tries to close the sale.

When Ray feels that he has "stayed with" his prospect as long as he should, he picks up his briefcase, reaches for his hat and thanks the prospect for his time and courtesy. The prospect, seeing that the attempt to "sell him" is being terminated, relaxes.

Then Ray goes into his "hat trick" close. In what seems like an entirely casual afterthought, he asks, "Mr. Fulbright, do you mind if I ask one more question before I leave?"

Mr. Fulbright is glad to oblige. "Probably," he thinks to himself, "he's going to ask whether he can check back with me in a month, or something like that."

Then Ray gets in his "extra lick."

"Do you know, Mr. Fulbright, that if my figures are correct—and I'm sure they are—it costs your company at least $600 per week for every week you delay taking on our service?" Ray, of course, has chosen a point that hasn't been specifically stated before. Making such a point at this moment, when the prospect's guard is down, gives him one more excellent opportunity of winning the sale.

Most salespeople can use this device in one form or another. All that is required is that the salesperson, by action and words, indicate that he has "given up the fight." Then he does the unexpected by making one more strong appeal for the sale.

It's important to reserve a *strong* sales point to use in this close. If you use a weak point, or one that has already been mentioned in the interview, it might cause prospects to feel even more justified in their decision not to buy.

Ask the prospect for the order

Some orders are obtained by the simplest of all closes—by simply asking the prospect to buy. The other closing techniques already discussed are, in reality, different ways of asking for the order. But they "ask" in terms of logic, facts or some other appeal, rather than literally in terms of saying, "Will you give me the order?"

Many salespeople prefer not to use this close, feeling that it is an appeal to sympathy or a request for a favor. Some sales "pros," on the other hand, have great faith in it. They feel its frankness and sincerity get them business they might not otherwise obtain.

Whether this close should be used or not depends on the salesperson's temperament, the type of product sold and who the prospect is.

How to use the 'question close' on the questioning prospect

Answering a prospect's question with a question can be an effective sales closer. It can get you out of a tough spot. Here's the picture:

You're making your sales presentation and the buyer interrupts with a question. You sense that if you answer it completely, you could lose the interest you have built up. And if you fail to answer it, you can antagonize the buyer. Obviously you must do something. It's at this point that some salespeople stumble. But you can move forward.

Put your prospects on the defensive by answering their question with a question. In this way, you'll retain control—and be in a strong selling position.

The following two examples will show how the idea will work, and perhaps suggest other opportunities for using questions to answer questions:

> *Prospect:* "Which model do you think I should use?" (If the salesperson answers, "XYZ model," and the prospect has had a bad experience with a similar model, he'll lose all interest and the sale will be dead.) Instead—
>
> *Salesperson:* "For what purpose exactly will you use this equipment?"
>
> OR
>
> *Prospect:* "How soon can you deliver the paper if I decide to buy?" (If the salesperson says two weeks, and the prospect wants it in one week, the sale is lost.) But there is a way to handle this question.
>
> *Salesperson:* "How soon do you need it?"

The reverse-question technique puts you in a favorable closing position. Your prospects must spell out their needs—and if you can come through, the sale is yours.

Go into your close once the prospect gives you an answer. This is how it would work using Example 2.

If the prospect says he'll need the paper in 10 days and you can meet that deadline, follow through like this:

> "I can definitely meet your requirements, Mr. Smith. If you'll just OK this order right now, I can get my company working on it immediately. We will be able to meet and beat your deadline. But we have to start now."

SALES COMPENSATION METHODS THAT ENHANCE PROFITS

When you get right down to it, the number one motivator for most employees—and especially salespeople——is money. As the owner of a business that has to be run "lean and mean," one of your toughest challenges is to set up a sales compensation plan that not only rewards your top achievers but also fits into the company's bottom line.

The best sales compensation plans are responsive to differences in a company's product lines, market conditions and territories, as well as to the individual salesperson's contribution to the sales effort. However, one guiding principle shouldn't change: Compensation should always increase with the difficulty of the sales effort and the degree of skill required.

Regardless of the compensation setup you choose, members of your sales force should be able to easily calculate their earnings under it. The reason for incentive payments should be crystal clear. For example, you want sellers to understand that you pay more if they sell at list price than at a discount. And the term "sale" should be carefully defined. Sellers should know whether they earn their commissions or incentives when orders are written up, shipments made, accounts billed, or bills paid.

How to Set Up a Sales Compensation Strategy that Motivates Your Sales Force and Boosts Company Profits

The compensation setup for your company's sales force should be reviewed at least every three years. That's the advice of the President and Chief Executive Officer of a management consulting firm in New York.

According to him, the marketplace and a company's selling environment are constantly changing. It doesn't take long for a sales compensation plan to become obsolete. "What worked for a company when it was starting out in business may no longer be working," he says. "As a company becomes more established, its sales environment changes. Its approach to sales compensation must change with it if the company is going to continue to prosper."

Establish goals. The executive VP for the firm says the key to setting up a successful sales compensation strategy is to ask yourself: "What is my company trying to do? What are my company's sales objectives?" Always keep in mind that plotting compensation strategies is "a derivative process, not a lead process," he adds. "It isn't the engine, it's the caboose."

Three approaches to designing a sales compensation plan

There are three basic approaches to designing a compensation plan:

1. **The "cost of sales" approach.** The sales rep is usually paid a low base salary but can receive high incentive earnings, e.g., through

a fixed-rate commission. The ratio of base salary to incentive payments typically is 30/70.

This approach is appropriate when sales overhead must be minimized. You pay out commissions only as the sales reps generate sales. This approach is also appropriate when you have minimal information about product sales history and sales goals can't be accurately determined.

2. **The "cost of labor" approach.** You have to: (1) define the sales reps' performance goals in terms of sales volume, product mix, or both; (2) determine what your sales reps "are worth" in the competitive labor market; and (3) pay the sales reps what they're worth when they reach established sales goals.

This approach typically consists of a moderate-to-high base salary plus a bonus compensation plan. The ratio of base salary to bonus generally is 50/50 to 70/30.

This approach is useful when products, markets and sales jobs are well defined. The sales reps' roles should be clear relative to generating new business and servicing established accounts. Products should be established and recognized by potential customers, and sales goals should be accurately determined.

3. **The "combination" approach.** Here, you combine both approaches in one plan. Reps typically are paid a moderate-to-high base salary, and are offered a combination of commission/bonus incentive opportunities. For example, a fixed commission rate is applied to certain products that the company wants to push hard, and a bonus is paid when the sales reps reach a percentage of sales goals on the remaining products.

The ratio of base salary to incentive payments typically is 50/50 to 70/30. Incentives generally are split 50/50 between bonus and commission opportunity.

This approach is appropriate when a company's product line contains *both* established products and significant/important new products. It is especially useful where the new products are also targeted at new customers/markets.

Compensation setups in action

Here are some typical company sales compensation setups, and how companies must adapt their setup to changing business needs.

Situation 1: Company A needed to build its market share quickly. It installed a straight commission plan: The more the sales reps sold, the more they made. Sales volume climbed and Company A captured a larger market share.

Two years later, however, sales growth flattened out and Company A began to lose its market share. But its sales reps continued to earn $75,000 to $80,000 in commissions by doing significant repeat business with established customers (i.e., what essentially amounted to order taking).

The company felt that it was possible to expand the customer base in the market. But the sales reps were content with their $80,000 per year earnings. And under the company's straight commission set-up, there was little motivation for the sales reps to increase sales over current levels, open new accounts and create more work for themselves.

Solution: Company A should install a *cost of labor* approach where *specific sales goals* are set for its reps, and earning levels would be maintained only if these goals were achieved. Commissions would no longer be paid from the first dollar of sales the reps made.

Situation 2: Company B was an established company in certain markets, but was not as well established and had stiff competition in others. Its sales force was paid on a salary plus commission plan: 50% of expected earnings were through commission.

Sales rep Jones worked an established territory and consistently earned the target level of total compensation (i.e., base salary plus commission). Sales rep Smith worked a low volume territory with especially tough competition. After one year, Smith's commission earnings were next to nothing, and there was no relief in sight. He quit—just like the last four reps before him.

Solution: Company B would be better off using a *combination* approach. The cost of sales approach is working fine in the established territories. However, a cost of labor approach is required if Company B wants to develop the under-penetrated territories.

The company has to, in effect, temporarily subsidize its sales reps while they build up a sales base there. Management has to determine the value of a sales rep's job in this potential-growth territory and pay higher base compensation despite the low sales level—at least until the territory is better developed.

Situation 3: When Company C first went into business, it needed to establish market share quickly. So it elected to pay its sales force on a straight commission basis. After a few years, Company C built a large business base. However, two major problems began to crop up: (1) customers began to complain that the sales reps were not spending enough time with them on post-sales service and problem solving;

and (2) the sales reps spent little or no time selling *new* products that Company C was staking its future on.

Company C's commission arrangement didn't make it worthwhile for the sales reps to get involved with servicing customers or to spend the extra time needed to sell new products. They made more money by finding new accounts and selling established products.

Solution: Company C should adopt a *cost of labor* approach where sales reps earn compensation based on their ability to sell *both* new and old products. Also, a *combination* approach, where the company pays a bonus for established product sales and heavy commissions on new product sales would result in a greater focus on new products.

Change with the times. As companies and product lines mature, they should evolve from a cost of sales approach to a cost of labor or combination approach. However, the change in your compensation setup should be made gradually. This will ensure smooth implementation and minimize the potential negative effects on your sales force's morale. "Your company will be better equipped to determine and set appropriate goals, and your sales reps gradually will become accustomed to the idea of goals.

How gradual is gradual? A transition from say, a straight cost of sales approach to a cost of labor approach might take one or two years to complete.

HOW TO SET COMMISSION RATES

The appropriate commission rate depends to a large extent on the industry, the company, and the product. In practice, most companies pay what is customary in their industry. Paying more increases sales costs. Paying less will adversely affect the quality of the sales force. If no industry custom exists, you must estimate what average sales volume will be and set a rate that will result in competitive pay levels.

There are several basic types of commission rates:

- **Gross vs. net rate:** Gross rates include a provision for travel expenses. Net commission rates tell you what the sales rep actually receives in pay.
- **Uniform rates:** These don't change with sales volume.
- **Variable rates:** These change with sales volume. They can be progressive (a higher rate is paid as sales volume increases) or regressive (a lower rate is paid as sales volume decreases). Sales

reps generally consider regressive rates unfair and dis-criminatory. At the same time, your sales manager and other employees may consider progressive rates discriminatory if top sales reps out-earn them.

- **Multiple rates:** Multiple commission rates are used when various territories or products differ in sales resistance. The principle of multiple rates is generally accepted by salespeople, but the actual amounts are often a source of controversy. Multiple rates are most useful when distinct classes of accounts or servicing situations exist that aren't likely to change in the near future.

In a metropolitan versus a rural sales territory, the use of dif-ferent commission rates is necessary because of the typically greater sales volume done in the city. The country rep requires a higher rate per sales dollar than the city sales rep.

However, multiple commission rates should not be used to make up for differences that are not based on sales volume. For instance, the city rep's travel expenses may be greater than those of the country rep. But they do not vary with sales volume. So any adjustment should be made through a higher expense al-lowance—not through commission rates.

Company vs. individual incentives

Sales commissions are often based on dollar volume, units sold, achievement of departmental or company-wide sales targets, or some combination of these. Which works best to motivate your salespeople to bring in more—and bigger—sales?

One Florida battery manufacturer, in the process of merging its sales force with that of a newly acquired company, conducted a survey of its salespeople in order to answer that question. Previously, the company had based its incentive compensation on a mix of how well the company performed plus the individual salesperson's performance.

The study showed that the salespeople felt incentive pay should be based on how an individual—not the company—performs. Tying pay to individual performance was a key motivator. As a result, the firm modified its compensation setup so that salespeople are paid a base salary and have incentive compensation opportunities based on *in-dividual performance only*.

Also, the incentive compensation structure was changed so that incentives are now based, in part, on the *price* of items sold. This gives the sales force an opportunity to earn more and, in turn, helps the company recoup its rising costs for raw materials.

MATCHING SALES COMPENSATION TO SALES GOALS

A "gap" often exists between the goals business owners think salespeople are striving for and the reps' actual goals. The key to closing the gap is to realize that, in the long run, the sales force sets its goals in response to *how* you pay—not what you pay. Sales compensation should aim sellers right for your big-profit objectives.

Setting priorities among your sales goals is essential. It's okay to have two number ones, but no more than that. Your compensation incentives must drive sellers to achieve whichever of the following goals are your top objectives.

• **Maintenance selling:** This is the type of selling you need if profits depend on protecting your established business by retaining customers. Such an objective is found mainly in low-growth or slow-growth industries in which a company can't afford to lose customers.

• **Leverage selling:** You want maximum account penetration. That is, your company uses relationships with regular customers to sell an expanding array of new products.

• **Conversion selling:** Growth depends on aggressively taking business away from competitors.

• **Expansion selling:** The ability to expand your business depends on market growth. You need sales to new customers outside your usual markets.

Once you've decided on your sales objectives, you can set up a compensation plan that will produce the results you desire. For example:

– Your objective is high revenue growth. The sales environment is characterized by frequent product introductions, "boom" markets and a loose competitive structure. In this situation, you could adopt a commission approach combined with a modest $25,000 base salary. When a basic sales-volume target is met, salary plus commission equals $50,000. At twice the target level, the sales rep could realize an income of $125,000.

– Your aim is to protect earnings while achieving moderate revenue increases. The sales environment is characterized by slow growth, numerous competitors and relatively few new product introductions. Given this goal, a salary-plus-bonus approach may give you an edge in developing a knowledgeable, service-oriented sales force that will hold customers against the competition. Base salary is $35,000; bonus eligibility begins at 90% of quota. At quota, a rep gets a $5,000 bonus. At twice quota, the bonus jumps to $20,000, bringing the seller's total compensation to $60,000.

- Your objective is overall revenue growth from a balanced product mix. You deal with multiple customer markets, many product groups and high- and low-growth products. In this case, you could pay a commission and/or bonus above a base salary. With a commission based on sales volume, a sales rep can go from a base of $25,000 salary to $80,000 if sales are twice the expected volume. A rep who merely meets quota can receive a bonus of up to $12,000.

- Your objective is to convert customers from the competition. You could offer both a volume bonus and a new-accounts bonus. A sales rep who qualifies for the volume bonus could make up to $60,000 (as straight commission or some combination of commission and salary). The new-accounts bonus could add another $20,000. However, the rep must meet the goal on old accounts before becoming eligible for a new-accounts bonus.

If you want top producers to sell twice as much as average producers, you have to reward them with twice as much incentive. Thus, if average producers get 20%–30% of total pay in the form of incentives, top producers should get 40%–60%. Be careful. Imposing a cap on incentive earnings often encourages your top sellers to defer closing sales until the following year.

Key factors to consider in a compensation policy

The following are some factors compensation experts say you should consider when setting up or reviewing your sales compensation policy:

• What performance criteria should be used? Sales dollars, sales volume, sales dollars with numbers and kinds of units weighted to accommodate business goals, the number and types of customers sold to, or some combination of the above?

• What is the overall sales potential of a product? What is the sales potential of a product in specific territories?

• What should the commission rate be? Should it remain constant, increase as sales levels increase, or decrease after a certain level of sales? Also, should the commission rate be the same for all items sold? (This is a key consideration for companies that want their salespeople to "push" a particular item.)

- Should you set a ceiling on incentive compensation earnings? If so, how high? You need to weigh the disincentive effect a limit may have on your sales force's efforts versus the impact on sales managers when their subordinates end up earning much more than they do. Limits may be appropriate if a salesperson has little or no influence on making a sale (e.g., the product sells itself).
- Who gets credit for a sale? The answer may not always be clear cut, as in the following situations:

> **Example 1:** The actual purchase of a product is made in one territory, but the salesperson responsible for making the sale and the customer responsible for approving the order are located in another territory.

> **Example 2:** A sale is finalized after the rep who made the initial contact and influenced the sale is transferred out of the territory. Is the rep entitled to all, some or no credit for sales made up to, say, six months after the transfer?

> **Example 3:** Certain customers may be "house accounts." In these cases, either no commission may be paid or it may be negotiated or restricted.

How should payment of commissions be timed? Commissions may be paid monthly, quarterly, semiannually or annually. Payments generally are made subject either to a customer's acceptance of an order, a customer's actual payment, or some combination of the two.

CHAPTER FOUR

How Customer Service Can Put You– And Keep You– On Top

In most large corporations, "customer service" is handled by a separate department. In small companies, however, customer service is everyone's business—from the company owner on down.

In fact, top service companies that keep customers coming back because their service is superior are invariably run by management whose involvement with service is direct and personal. Indeed, delivering top-notch service is one of the best ways for small businesses to compete head to head with corporate giants.

Yet customer service in most companies is little more than a complaint department—and not a particularly effective one at that. Thus, for the small business owner, heads-up/hands-on customer service is a gold-mine of business opportunity. Consider the following facts:

- One customer in four is dissatisfied with the service in the typical commercial transaction.

- The dissatisfied customer, on average, will complain to 12 other people about the company that provided the poor service.

- Only 5% of dissatisfied customers complain to the company that offered the product or service. The vast "silent majority" would

105

rather switch than fight. They take their business elsewhere rather than risk an unpleasant confrontation.

These surprising statistics come from recent surveys conducted for the U.S. Office of Consumer Affairs. The survey reports found this surprising piece of good news, however:

Good service pays for itself:

Companies rated tops for service and quality charge an average of 8% to 15% more than their competitors, even in businesses where price competition is keen. For example, Maytag, the home appliance maker, whose "lonely serviceman" campaign supports a premium-priced product in a highly price-sensitive market.

In addition, according to several recent national surveys—

- The return on investment in service (i.e., successful complaint resolution) ranges from 15%–75% for packaged goods to 35%–400% in retailing.

- While only 9%–37% of dissatisfied customers who don't complain report a willingness to do business with the same company again, 50%–80% of those who complain *and* whose complaints are fully resolved will consider doing repeat business—even if their complaints were not resolved in their favor!

- A customer who has had a complaint that is satisfactorily resolved is *even more likely* to do repeat business than is a customer who had nothing to complain about in the first place.

When you also consider that it costs eight times as much to gain a new customer as it does to retain an old one, and that the average satisfied customer tells five other people of the experience, the importance of effective complaint-handling is clear. In short, customer service makes dollars and sense.

HOW TO CREATE A SERVICE STRATEGY TO BOOST YOUR MARKET SHARE

Service winners—those companies that succeed by providing unparalleled levels of service—have one thing in common. They have a clearly articulated *service strategy* that converts service intent into service action. Whether the company is a giant like Federal Express or a single shop like Stu Leonard's Dairy in Norwalk, Connecticut, service values influence company decisions at every level.

A service strategy is essentially a marketing and management approach that seeks to harness "service values" as a means of setting your company apart from the competition. Unlike such traditional alternatives as innovative design and manufacturing efficiency, a service strategy looks outward—at the customer—rather than inward—at the company.

When designing a service strategy, ask yourself the following three questions:

1. "What unique contribution can my company make in the service area that will distinguish it from its competitors?"
2. "Who are the primary recipients of our service package?"
3. "What values will inspire my frontline workers to serve customers enthusiastically and also be positively perceived by our customers?" (This can best be described as your "service mission.")

Say your business is a mid-sized hardware store in a large urban center. Your company, Professional Hardware, faces stiff competition in its major lines from price-cutting national chains. While revenues are strong, growth is flat and profit margins are razor thin. How can you survive without downsizing to mom and pop status or selling out to one of the chains?

Using a "service value" approach, you do the following:

- Look for patterns in customer complaints.
- Solicit complaints and suggestions more avidly from your customers and spend plenty of time on the sales floor.
- Check out your competitors, and listen to *their* customers' gripes and praises.

Here's what you find: While your "big ticket" trade customers seem fairly satisfied, the small individual customers are not. Among their main complaints are the following:

- The store is never open when it's needed most—nights and weekends
- Clerks are hard to find
- When the clerks are available, they know little about what products are in stock, less about how best to use them.

From these complaints, the elements of a service strategy emerge:

1. The unique service package that your company could offer is one that features a high degree of customer instruction and customer convenience.

2. The main service recipient is the urban do-it-yourselfer.

3. The service mission could be: "Professional Hardware guarantees that every customer will achieve professional results."

HOW TO IMPLEMENT YOUR SERVICE STRATEGY

Test your strategy with frontliners first. Your frontline people are critical to your strategy's success. So, you have to make sure that they are on board before you launch it on the world. Ask them what they think of the mission statement first. Do they agree that it's useful? Do they have any alternatives? Improvements? Refinements?

Next, ask a few customers how they react to it. If their response is less than enthusiastic, perhaps the idea needs some firming up.

Then, ask yourself the following questions:

• **Will the strategy help you hire and train?** One of the big pluses of having a strategy is that it focuses your hiring and training effort. The first part of the strategy calls for truly knowledgeable customer assistance. Thus, when you're hiring new frontline people, you should try to recruit people from the building and decorating trades, people with teaching/coaching skills, or even people who grew up on farms, where do-it-yourself experience is extensive.

• **Will the strategy help you manage your business?** The recipient of Professional Hardware's unique service package is the urban do-it-yourselfer. Accordingly, one of the big changes you would make is in your store hours. Since many of your customers will be unable to shop during the regular 9-to-5 slot, you can close up selectively during the regular weekday in order to stay open until 9 or 10 p.m., and all day Saturday and Sunday.

Another convenience-oriented approach you might try is a beefed-up delivery service. One to three minivans, stocked with routine painting and hardware supplies, would be cruising your sales territory at all times. Radio dispatched and staffed by seller/drivers, these vans will not only make shopping by phone a breeze for the customer, they provide both revenue and visibility for your service effort.

In fact, the whole concept of hardware shopping by phone is a sales-through-service notion that would flow directly from adoption of a service strategy.

- **Will the strategy help your business grow?** The acid test of any service strategy is whether it will help your business grow. Business people hesitate to invest because the existing market looks too small to be profitable. Service winners, however, have discovered that they can actually create markets where none had existed, and grow by dominating that market.

Case Example _____

> When Fred Smith created Federal Express, market research on overnight package delivery was impossible; the market existed entirely in his imagination. It was only when the service became available that customers discovered that this was a service that they couldn't live without.

A service strategy in itself costs you nothing to create. And you don't have to jump in with both feet before it works at all. You can put your service strategy into effect gradually, so you don't have to bet the farm on one throw of the dice. This way, while your risk is small, your payoff could be enormous.

HOW TO ASSESS YOUR COMPANY'S SERVICE RESPONSIVENESS

One of the key elements of top service delivery is *responsiveness*— that special extra effort that turns routine customer service into truly *customized* service.

Organizational responsiveness

Organizational issues to consider include your facility's physical layout, the telephone system you use for incoming calls, the location's accessibility to customers, and, perhaps most important, the policies and procedures that your employees must follow when working with customers.

To determine the extent to which these factors may be hampering top service delivery, ask yourself these questions:

- How easy is it for customers to do business with us?

- How many hoops do we make the customers jump through to get what they want?

- Are our policies and procedures designed for *our* benefit or for our *customers'* benefit?

- Is our layout set up for our convenience or for the customers' convenience?

- What recurring problems do our customers have in working with us?

Personal responsiveness

The people side of responsiveness refers to the way customers are handled as individuals. Consider the following questions.

- Do your frontline employees look for creative ways to help customers?

- Are they capable of gathering information and finding answers for customers instead of directing them from pillar to post?

- Do they work with customers to find solutions to their problems?

- Are they willing to juggle the system to satisfy a customer when they can do so without creating a liability for your company?

When assessing service from within, it is essential to involve your frontline personnel. They are the ones who know which policies and procedures hinder their ability to deliver quality service.

Go out on the floor with your employees to observe them in action. Be alert to situations where customers encounter difficulty, and see how they are handled. Is there some obstacle to service (an unclear procedure or obsolete policy) you can remove? Is there some kind of training you can offer that will prevent the same problem from recurring?

When assessing your outside sales reps' performances—through formal or informal customer surveys—it is essential to make the feedback as specific as possible. Consequently, you should—

Avoid "closed end" questions. Questions calling for a one-word response like "Yes" or "No" tell you little of practical value. Worse still, they tend to validate whatever it is you are already doing. Thus, you should stay clear of such questions as the following:

- "Did the representative give you the information you requested?"

- "Are our hours adequate?"

- "Is the product satisfactory?"

Ask open-ended questions that compel the customers to reveal their service needs with a reasonable degree of detail; for example, ask questions like the following:

- "How effective was the company representative in answering your questions or concerns?"
- "How would you rate the product?"
- "What are the most convenient business/service hours for you?"

HOW TO ASSESS YOUR COMPANY'S SERVICE RELIABILITY

Each time a customer deals with your business, he or she measures your company's product or service. A "high quality" product will lose points in the customer's mind in the wake of chronically depleted inventory, late delivery, or misinformation about the product's capabilities. All customers want and deserve the assurance that if the product does not perform as advertised, your company—and your personnel—will be there to help.

Every product offering raises three basic reliability issues: product performance, organizational performance and "people performance."

Product performance: The reliability of the product itself can be gauged in terms of:

- Whether it does what your promotional materials say it will do.
- Whether it does it for as long (and as well) as the customer thinks it will.
- Whether it meets the customer's needs consistently.

Organizational performance: A big part of the customer's perception of your company's service comes from the way your company is actually organized, in terms of both physical facilities and operating procedures. For example:

- Are the facilities designed for the use to which you are putting them?
- Can your company comfortably handle the volume of business you have without sacrificing quality?

- What are the chances that your systems (telephone, computer, shipping, etc.) will go down under pressure?

- Do your policies and procedures (for credit, returns, complaints, reorders, etc.) enhance or detract from the perception that the customer's business is eagerly sought?

People performance: This aspect of reliability is the human side of service. Examples of key elements here include—

- Follow through. Are calls returned promptly? Are appointments kept on time? Does delivery occur when expected? Are requests for information followed up with clear, concise answers?

- Product knowledge. Do customer-contact employees have a thorough understanding of product features, benefits, uses, warranties, etc.?

- "Company savvy." Are your reps skilled at using your company's systems to satisfy customer needs?

HOW TO MEASURE RELIABILITY

Once you know what you're looking for, it's easier to measure it. Regardless of the actual measuring method you use, you should set up separate categories for the different elements of service reliability outlined above.

Specific methods of gathering customer feedback

Many companies systematically send out written questionnaires to everyone who makes a purchase. While this is reasonably effective, keep the following limitations in mind:

- Mail-in surveys may have a response rate as low as 1%–2%.

- Most standard surveys feature multiple-choice questions that leave little room for customer comment.

Another way to gather feedback—increasingly favored by companies of all sizes—is installation of a toll-free 800 number for customer questions and complaints. The chief limitations here include:

- Cost. An in-house WATS line runs about $100,000 per year to rent and staff.

- As with all passive systems, the large majority of dissatisfied customers will not take the initiative to contact you.

The most effective methods for gathering feedback are telephone surveys and focus groups. Using these methods, you can control the interviewing process and probe for relevant detail. When gathering feedback in this manner, be sure to encourage customer comment. Don't force customers to answer a sequence of Yes/No questions.

HOW EFFECTIVE SERVICE MEASUREMENT CAN HELP SET YOUR COMPANY'S COMPETITIVE STRATEGY

Quality service is one of the most important factors in a customer's buying decision. That said, the question then arises: What aspects of service—and at what cost to your company—determine the buying decision? Only if you know the answer to this question can your company's service investment be seen as an integral part of a coherent competitive strategy.

A five phase process

Creating and implementing a service strategy can be seen as a five-phase process. In phase one, you examine the company's marketplace. In phase two, you audit your company's internal operations. In phase three, you determine the customer's service requirements, including customers' perceptions of both your efforts and those of your competitors. In phase four, you balance the costs and benefits to arrive at a strategy. Finally, in phase five, you set up a measurement system to monitor your performance.

Let's look here at Phase Three—establishing customers' service preferences. As long as you have reliable information on the aspects of service most important to your customers, any errors you make will likely be in the direction of *overserving*, rather than underserving, your customers' needs.

What do the customers want?

Before simply launching into some sort of off-the-shelf customer survey, it's essential to clarify your thinking about the sorts of information that will prove most useful. As a general matter, therefore, regardless of the measurement methods you employ, you'll want to know the following:

- What are your customer's specific service requirements?

- How do your customers rate your service performance relative to that of your competitors?
- What level of service will your company have to provide to become (or remain) the recognized service leader in the field?

Often it's helpful to put together some general service questions and present them to a small sample of customers in informal interviews. The responses can help you refine your questions so that they point to specific aspects of your service effort that your company can then fine tune.

Here's how to move from the general to the specific:

- Elements of service: Cycle times? Special order processing times? Delivery and warehousing needs? Information needs—who (at your company) meets them and how well? What's the systematic response to reported error? What's your company's concept of "As Soon As Possible (ASAP)"? What's your customer's idea of ASAP? What's your competitor's idea of ASAP?
- How do your customers rate these elements in terms of relative importance? (What's more important to customers: Fast delivery or full order? Availability of special services or low price?)
- How do your customers rate your service effort on each specific element—cycle times, inquiries, error correction, and so on. How do they rate your competitors on each element?
- How do these concerns translate into a purchase decision? If specific elements were improved, how much new business might be expected? If the service effort were eased in certain respects, would this translate into less business? How much less?

Let the customers know what you're doing

Before conducting any sort of in-depth customer survey—whether by phone, face-to-face interview, focus group or mail-in questionnaire—the importance of an introductory letter cannot be overemphasized. These letters should clearly express your reasons for soliciting this information—i.e., to better meet customer needs—and how much you would appreciate their cooperation.

Customers who receive such letters are much more likely to respond to interview requests or return mail-in surveys. Indeed, just sending out such letters can have the beneficial effect of raising the customers' consciousness of your commitment to service. *One word of caution*: Don't send out such letters unless you fully intend to follow through.

How to Survey Busy Retail Customers

Staying abreast of customer wants and needs takes more than just keeping track of what they buy and how often they complain. As leading customer service experts have long since established, customers must be surveyed directly—and the results acted upon swiftly—if customer service is to be more than lip service.

Soliciting customer feedback in the retail context can be inordinately difficult. Customers are in a hurry to get in and get out. What's more, few customers feel especially dependent on your product or service when there is so much competition out there. *Result:* Unless customers can see how they have some stake in the outcome, few will want to take the time to have their psyches probed for the information you need to judge service quality.

Take a lesson from a former food critic who now advises restaurants on marketing strategies. According to him, response cards don't work. You get too few responses, and the ones you get are either overwhelmingly negative or overwhelmingly positive. Then, too, it's not unknown for those with a vested interest in the results to fill out cards that will give you a distorted picture of reality.

Here's how his firm boosts customer responses in the restaurant field. You may want to adapt these methods to your own business situation.

1. The restaurant host or hostess hands customers a card before they sit down, asking them if they wish to participate in a survey. If they do, they fill in the cards—which ask only for their names and phone numbers. The incentive for filling out this card (which, after all, takes only a few seconds) is usually some sort of discount on their next meal at that establishment.

A tactic that worked particularly well was one restaurant's offer of home-made candies—from the restaurant's kitchens—in return for the agreement to be surveyed later. It was characterized as "The Chef's Dish of Gratitude."

2. Telephone interviewers then use these name-cards for follow-up calls. Interviews can therefore be much more detailed than would be possible with a point-of-sale approach.

3. Customers whose assessments are very negative—those who swear never to return, for instance—are then targeted for follow-up calls by restaurant managers. Not only does this give the manager a particularly vivid picture of what might have gone wrong, it allows for the possibility that negative customers can be turned around. Usually the incentive here is a "make-up meal" on the house.

He reports that almost half of the customers offered the free meal do in fact return. While this doesn't guarantee that they won't go away disappointed for a second time, converting even a small percentage of unhappy customers into happy ones—in an industry that depends so heavily on word-of-mouth—is well worth the extra effort.

This approach is not limited to the restaurant business. Just about any business with numerous retail customers—and the willingness to offer incentives for participation—can follow this three-step process.

Note, however, that surveys are frequently costly, and produce results that are tedious to tabulate and often difficult to interpret. Professional help may be necessary. To find such help, a good starting point is any big-city Yellow Pages that lists "Marketing Consultants." But be sure to screen for consultants experienced in telephone survey techniques. Expect to pay $5 to $10 per interviewee, plus data tabulation and interpretation fees of $2,000 to $5,000.

HOW TO TURN CUSTOMER COMPLAINTS INTO SOLID GOLD*

Nobody wants him. Everybody tries to avoid or ignore him. Yet he is one of your most valuable customers. Who is he? He's the dreaded complaining customer.

One question I ask people in my customer service workshops is "How many of you would like to get more complaints?" Rarely do more than one or two people out of 200 raise their hands.

You probably wouldn't raise yours either. Who wants to be yelled at? Who likes to be criticized? Who needs it? The answer is *you do!*

Let's ask the question another way. "If your customer has a problem, do you want to know about it?" Of course you do! And that's all a complaint is. It's a way of letting you know he or she has a problem.

The plain truth is that it's difficult to get an accurate measure of how many customers are dissatisfied with your company. Why? Because nobody wants to be a complainer. That's why most of us mumble an automatic "fine" in response to the waiter's obligatory "How is everything?"

This section was written by Bill Stevens, Director of the Center for Management Excellence, and a Milwaukee-based consultant, speaker, and trainer who has worked with a variety of Fortune 500 clients through his Value Added Customer Service seminar. (800) 234-8721.

I had a wonderful experience a few summers ago. I was driving through a small town on my way to a consulting appointment. I stopped for lunch at a small restaurant. I ordered a sausage sandwich. The sausage came cooked—but only on the outside.

I asked the waitress to have it cooked a little longer. She came back and the sandwich was just fine. If that's all that had happened, I would have eaten my now fully cooked sandwich, been on my way, and probably have tried another restaurant the next time I was in town.

But that's not all that happened. Right behind her was the restaurant manager, carrying a small sundae, covered with chocolate, and topped with whipped cream, nuts and a cherry. He set it down in front of me and sat down in the booth opposite me.

Then he said: "You know, we're pretty proud of our little restaurant. But sometimes we make mistakes. This sundae is our way of saying we care about you and sure hope you come back again."

He had me. I can assure you, any time I'm in that town I stop at that restaurant. It's the only place I would go for lunch. Not only that, but anybody who has heard me speak in Wisconsin knows about that place, and many have now become customers.

They turned my complaint into solid gold. That sundae probably cost the owner fifty cents, but his return on his investment was many times that.

Here is how *you* can turn complaints into gold:

1. Never argue, defend or explain. Instead, just listen.
2. Ask "Would you mind if I took notes?"
3. Summarize your understanding of the complaint in your own words.
4. Ask, "What would you like us (me) to do?"
5. Where possible and practical, do what the customer asks you to do, regardless of *short term* cost.
6. Follow up. Call a week later and ask if everything was done that was promised.

Being just good enough isn't good enough any more. Make sure the customer is fully satisfied—preferably, thrilled and delighted. Remember: It's not smiling at customers that will get them coming back; it's having them smile on the way out.

SERVICE SUGGESTIONS FOR YOUR FRONTLINE EMPLOYEES

HOW TO KEEP YOUR COOL WHEN CUSTOMERS CALL TO COMPLAIN

Coping with the verbally abusive customer on the telephone is surely one of the most trying aspects of your business. Helping your salespeople and other employees who deal with customers and callers on a daily basis learn to deal with anger—their own as well as the customers'—has to be one of your most important responsibilities. Verbal abuse can be so unnerving that productivity can come to a halt. Moreover, it is probably the main reason for high turnover.

Here's how to get a handle on this nasty aspect of customer relations.

You are not a door mat

Hold a meeting and ask your employees whether dealing with abusive customers has been a problem lately, and how each felt when it occurred.

With the subject suitably warmed up, take the opportunity to express what is—or ought to be—your company's policy toward abusive customers. A statement like the following is all you need:

Your job is to help customers receive value for their money. However, being a passive target for abuse is not a part of this job. You have the right to work in an atmosphere free from fear and intimidation. When a dissatisfied customer calls, it is your job to try to solve the problem. If the customer resorts to profane or degrading language, you have the right to terminate the call.

Establishing a "hang-up" policy

Depending on the nature of the exchange, it is sometimes appropriate to just hang up the phone. This is a *last resort*, however, because (a) It will usually make an angry customer even angrier, and (b) The customer is quite likely to call back and give another employee the works. Nevertheless, sometimes it's your only option.

It's up to you to decide where the line should be drawn. You may decide that it's never appropriate, and that abusive callers should always be offered the chance to speak with you first.

Business executives we consulted with, however, felt that there is definitely a line that callers should not be permitted to cross, and that it's important for your employees to know that they have the right to terminate the call when that line is crossed. In other words, there are certain words that can be said, or manners of expression, which are so intrinsically abusive and harassing that it ends the employees' obligation to say goodbye politely, and triggers the right to just hang up.

Instances where a hang-up is *not* appropriate, even if tempting, include exchanges where the customer is loud, sarcastic, critical, whining or "talkaholic." In other words, mere anger is not enough. Dissatisfied customers have a *right* to be angry, especially if they have already called to complain about some malfunction and been given the runaround.

Instances where a hang-up *is* appropriate, in the view of most customer service professionals, is when (a) a customer threatens physical violence, (b) a customer makes sexually provocative remarks, or (c) a customer uses four-letter words. Most abusive people act the way they do because they've found that harshness gets results. Consequently, rewarding this negative behavior by giving in to the abuser's wishes simply encourages more of the same.

TEN WAYS TO COPE WITH ANGRY CALLERS

Your employees may want specific how-to-help guidelines for dealing with angry callers—short of slamming the phone back in its cradle. Here are ten actions to take—or things to say—that will generally help steer the conversation onto a more productive course.

1. Say, "Sir, you're shouting."
Sometimes customers will get so carried away reliving the awful experience they've had with your company that they lapse into a rage response without realizing that they are doing so. Just pointing out to such customers that they are shouting often helps to bring them back into the present moment.

2. Try whispering.
An angry exchange can escalate out of control when the anger of one party reinforces the anger of the other. An angry customer speaks to an impatient employee, whose impatience inflames the customer, which makes the employee even more curt, which makes the customer even more furious, and so on. Deliberate whispering helps break this cycle of rage.

3. Say, "Why don't you start at the beginning and tell me exactly what happened?"

Even if the customer has been giving a ranting explanation for why he or she is so upset, it's never too late to start over. Often the reason for the rage is the perception that no one really cares about the problem or understands why the customer feels the way he or she actually does. Giving customers the chance to start over sometimes convinces them that someone is finally ready to hear their side of the story.

4. Do 6-3-6 Breathing.

Holding your breath is an involuntary response to attack—your body is preparing for combat. Consequently, forcing yourself to breathe tends to relax both your tensed-up body and your keyed-up emotions. A good breathing exercise is to inhale for six seconds, hold for a three-count, and exhale for six seconds. (Be sure to hold the mouthpiece away from your face when you do this exercise or the customers might think you're hissing at them.)

5. Say, "I need to check on some of this information. When can I call you back?"

The beauty of this response is that it's completely free of any kind of personal criticism on which they can key-in to validate their rage.

6. Keep asking questions, while minimizing your responses.

To the extent that an angry customer just wants to be understood, your questions cater to this need, and may very well help in the resolution of the problem. While the customer is talking, limit your verbalizations to: "uh-huh, yes...I see...then what?...oh?...uh-huh."

7. Say, "My supervisor can better deal with your problem, sir; please hold."

While this tactic won't calm the customer down very much, it gives you a graceful way to put the customer on hold while you regain your composure. You can then decide whether it's best to tackle the customer again (saying, "My supervisor's line was busy. Would you care to call back?") or actually pass the buck to your boss.

8. Build in a time-out.

If the exchange is just going around in circles, and you're not able to extract any more useful, problem-solving information, it could be time to call a "time-out." Tell the customer that you'll get to work on his or her problem right away, and that you'll call back in 30 minutes.

Give yourself a break, work on something else, then give yourself another few minutes to prepare what you're going to say.

9. Say, "That language is abusive, sir. We are instructed to report the names of people who use it. Would you please spell your last name again?"

This veiled threat is remarkably effective. It usually results in either an end to the offensive language or an end to the conversation—without the employee having to take the initiative to hang up!

10. Speak to the problem rather than the person.

Saying things like, "Why don't you call back when you calm down?" is telling the person something about himself—that he is not calm—which he won't want to hear. It's more effective to focus on the problem—avoiding judgmental use of the word "you"—by saying things like, "I'm going to need some help solving this problem. Can you tell me exactly X-Y-Z [some problem-specific piece of information]?"

HOW TO KEEP YOUR PEOPLE FROM COMMITTING FIVE COMMON "TELEPHONE FOULS"

Front-line employees often come in for more than their fair share of abuse over the telephone. When forced to listen to unending streams of customer complaints, it's easy to become callous and uncaring. With close supervision and patient training, however, you can turn things around *IF* you know what to look for.

Here are five "telephone fouls" often committed under pressure—with suggestions for appropriate remedies.

1. Muffing the customer's name: Calling a customer by the wrong name, or forgetting the name altogether, is one of the fastest ways to convince a caller that you either weren't listening or don't care. By the same token, getting the name right and using it frequently is one of the most effective ways to establish personal rapport.

Solution: Make sure your employees ask for and *write down* the customer's name *the very first thing*. Explain to your reps that it's more polite to ask the customer to repeat his or her name as often as necessary to get it right than it is to fake it now, and flub it later. Tell your employees that the call will not be considered answered unless they have the client's name in writing.

2. Arguing with customers: Winning arguments doesn't win customers. This is especially true if the dispute is over some technicality that has no real bearing on the resolution of the complaint.

Solution: Remind your employees of this variation on the old cliché that the customer is always right: *The customer is never wrong.* No matter how ill-founded the gripe, the customer is sure of—and entitled to—his or her opinion. And in 90% of the cases, no amount of arguing will change it.

Explain to the rep that the only thing that really matters to the customer—and, therefore, to you—is what actions the company is going to take to rectify the problem. Consequently, the only topic worth pursuing is a narrow one: whether or not the customer finds those solutions satisfactory.

3. Leaving customers on hold: Few things are more excruciating than having to listen to Muzak at long distance rates. Even if you're not paying for the call, time spent on hold feels like time stolen from your life.

The best solution—that followed by America's service winners—is to equip employees with comprehensive product knowledge, on-line access to the delivery system, and authority to resolve most complaints on the spot. Where these steps are not practicable, however, here's what to do.

- Have your employees find out right away if the call is local. If it's not, have the employee give the customer his or her name and offer to call the customer right back. Establish the procedure that no customer is to be put on hold for more than one minute. If it will take more than that to solve the problem, your employees should offer to call back. Make sure customers are told how long they will actually be placed on hold and are asked whether they would prefer to wait or be called back.

4. Soliciting off-point information with no explanation: When an unhappy customer calls in, all fired up to discuss the deficiencies of the new item your company just sent, it is usually a bad practice to answer the phone with marketing survey questions.

Most customers expect to give their names, and possibly account numbers, right off the bat. But that's it. Such further details as home or office address, phone numbers and purchasing information may be important to the ultimate resolution of the complaint, but are not foremost in the customer's mind.

Solution: Your employees should be reminded that common courtesy calls for the customer to speak first. Only after the reason for the call is thoroughly hashed out should the rep start asking for further information.

This is particularly true with regard to such personal information as a caller's home address. The relevance of such information may not be at all obvious to the customer. So the reason for asking this kind of question should be stated clearly up front. If the data has some bearing on complaint resolution, say so. If it is part of the overall marketing effort, this, too, should be explained. Be sure, also, that the information is *requested*, not *demanded* as the *quid pro quo* of service.

5. Laying blame: Blaming specific people in the company for foul-ups is bad policy on two counts. First, it makes resolving problems much harder, particularly when the person at fault must subsequently deal with the complaining customer. Second, by reducing the customer's faith in the company, it makes repeat business less likely.

Solution: Caution your employees to stick to the "whats" of what went wrong, avoiding the "whys." Even if the customer wants to know "why," make sure your people know how to answer a "why" with a "what we are going to do about it."

QUEUE-TIPS: HOW TO REDUCE FRUSTRATION FOR CUSTOMERS WAITING ON LINE

Almost all businesses are forced at times to make customers wait in line. All too often when this happens, a customer—who is already peeved with your product—now becomes *incensed* with your service.

Even when there's nothing you can do to make the lines shorter, there *are* simple actions you can take to make the wait more pleasant. Here are some methods used by other companies:

1. Contact the whole line. When people are lined up in front of a service desk, the tendency is for the service rep to pay attention exclusively to the customer he or she is currently serving. The result is that everyone else feels ignored. To counter this feeling, the rep should look up from time to time and scan the line as though counting heads.

As the line is scanned, the rep should make eye contact, nod and smile to as many customers as possible. While the gesture takes less than a second per person, this simple acknowledgment provides powerful psychological assurance that the customer has not been forgotten.

2. Keep them posted. Since lines tend to move at uniform rates, it's usually possible to project fairly accurately how long it will take to move from a given point to the front of the line. Consequently, it's a good idea to post signs along the line route to let people know how much of a wait they're in for.

When customers know what to expect, they're much less likely to become anxious about how slowly a line is moving. Knowing that it's going to take half an hour, for example, allows the customer to decide whether it's worth investing the time now or makes more sense to come back later.

3. Provide a diversion. Visitors to Disneyland frequently wait 45 minutes or more on lines for the most popular rides and exhibits. Yet visitors rarely recall standing in line so long. Why? Because Disney characters like Goofy and Mickey Mouse appear "as from nowhere" to divert and entertain them. This is no accident.

While few businesses can be expected to provide live entertainment on a par with Disney's, simpler measures may well be feasible. One possibility is strategically placed artwork, photographs or prints. Inexpensive and easy to find, such eye-pleasers provide a welcome break from bare wallboard and ceiling tiles.

Another option is to install one or more TV sets and VCRs to divert and entertain. For customers forced to wait in line, just about anything you show will help the time pass more agreeably. And with TV and VCR prices as low as they are today, the investment is a tiny fraction of what you would have to pay for even one more service person.

HOW TO GIVE SPECIAL HANDLING TO PROBLEM CUSTOMERS

Normally, kid glove treatment in the service area consists of having supervisors or managers perform (or at least orchestrate) the service process at every step. At a minimum, it means that supervisors will check the service given at each stage, making sure that orders, deliveries, paperwork, and the like are in order before being sent out.

In the case of telemarketing and helplines, special handling means that as soon as a problem account is identified, a supervisor then takes charge.

Provide a backup. Occasionally, a supervisor will be tied up with one problem account when another special case calls in. In these instances, it's a good idea to have a backup procedure in place.

One solution is to buck the problem up the line—to you. Another, and ultimately better, solution is to give your best one or two frontline people special training and authority to act as backups. These employees will usually feel honored to be singled out for special training and responsibility.

It's vital that *all* your frontliners are aware of and understand your system for flagging special accounts. The system should be thoroughly explained in your orientation period, as well as in any procedures manuals your company uses. Be alert to deviations from these procedures; one disagreeable receptionist could destroy in a minute what you have spent months trying to build.

HOW TO SAY 'NO' WITHOUT LOSING CUSTOMERS

It often falls to you to give customers the bad news that their request for help will not be granted. As distasteful as it is to administer such bitter pills, you also have to do it in a way that preserves as much goodwill as possible.

You may have to send a consumer a response to a letter indicating either that the merchandise is no longer under warranty, or that the service must originate from the dealer of purchase. At the same time you must preserve the reputation of the company and placate the customer. Here are some helpful guidelines.

Guidelines for breaking bad news to customers

You can't just say "No" to a customer's request and expect anything more than resentment and ill will from then on. Here are some guidelines for breaking the bad news gently.

1. Delay the bad news. Put the bad news at or near the end of a letter rather than at the beginning. If you lead off by saying, "We're not going to do a blessed thing for you, and here's why not," the chances are good that the customer won't even read the reasons, much less accept them.

While you're warming up to deliver the blow, it's a good idea to let the customer know that you know how he or she is feeling. You don't have to go overboard—a sentence or two is fine.

Don't forget to tell the customer about everything you tried to do to help. Thus, you could run down a list of people you spoke with, or steps you took, to find out what could be done before you found out that the answer was nothing.

If customers can be made to feel that someone really went to bat for them, the fact that you couldn't hit a homer this time should take some of the edge off the disappointment.

2. Thank the customer for writing. A good starting point is an expression of gratitude that the customer took the time to call or write—regardless of how angry or abrasive the communication actually was. You can take this opportunity to tell the customer— quite truthfully—that your company appreciates the opportunity to hear about problems from end users in order to do better in the future.

3. Explain but don't excuse. Explain why relief will not be forthcoming—as long as it is a real explanation of policy, not just a "because we say so" reason.

Some people make the mistake of outlining the gory details of a foul-up—as though the customer really cares. Others seek to cover up their responsibility by blaming quality problems on the delivery service or some other party. Still others simply state that relief will not be forthcoming because "company policy" forbids it, as if company policies were handed down by Moses at Mount Sinai.

4. Offer a compensatory token. Offer the customer *something*, if at all possible, even if it can't be what he or she really wants. Useful here are different kinds of sales premiums that are normally give-away items, or discount coupons for future purchases. Even if the customer is still unhappy—which unfortunately will be as often as not—the customer can still feel that at least it wasn't a waste of time to write.

5. Close with confidence. Make every effort to sound positive and upbeat at the end. Avoid tentative conclusions such as, "I hope you'll be able to see your way clear to doing business with us again."

Uncertainty merely invites the customer to complain all the more. Instead, consider a confident closing such as, "I'm sure you'll agree that we've done everything possible under the circumstances. We look forward to your continued patronage." Even if it does not in fact result in new business, it sends the message that the transaction is now over.

The sample letter in Figure 4.1 is an example of how you might respond to a customer who expects you to deliver on an expired or inapplicable warranty.

Figure 4.1 Sample Letter

Dear Customer:

Thank you so much for your letter of [Date]. Since we deal directly only with furniture retailers, hearing from the folks who actually use our products is always a big help. How else are we to know how to serve you better in the future?

We sincerely regret the trouble you've had with the [item in question]. It must have been very disappointing. We always hope that our products will last forever, even if this obviously can't be guaranteed.

As you can see from the enclosed warranty card (an exact copy of the one that came with your [item]), we guarantee our products to be free from manufacturing defects for a period of one year from the date of purchase.

A manufacturing defect is something that is wrong when the item leaves our factory. Our warranty is limited in this way because manufacturing is the only part of the process over which we have any control. A full year, we feel, is ample time for a reasonable purchaser to discover any such defect, and return the item to us for repair or replacement.

Now let me explain the '100% Guarantee of Satisfaction' to which you referred in your letter. This guarantee is offered by the store where you bought the [item], not by us. [Here's a token compensation:] Although we have no control over the store's operating policies, we contacted the store's manager and made a special request for service on your behalf. We want you to be satisfied!

Mr. [Store Manager] has offered to allow a partial store credit if you return the [item] promptly. We feel that this is a generous offer, and urge you to act on it promptly.

Again, thank you for taking the time to write. We look forward to serving you in the future.

HOW A SERVICE SUCCESS COMPANY TRAINS
FOR TOP PERFORMANCE

PC Connections, the nation's leading mail order supplier of desktop computer accessories, has survived and prospered in the face of cut-throat competition where dozens of others have failed. Why? Because the company puts a premium on providing first-rate service before, during and after the sale.

Where else, for example, can customers call for in-depth help running a balky piece of software that they didn't even buy from PCC? What other reseller refuses to subject customers to manufacturers' service programs unless the manufacturer can prove that its service is superior to PCC's? And what other mail-order operation of any description guarantees next day delivery for a flat $3 fee for Macintosh products and a $5 fee for other PC products?

For a company that lives or dies by telephone contact with customers it never meets, the key to success is a team of top-notch telephone sales and service reps. These people make sure that customers get what they want and help customers deal with the problems that invariably arise when using complex technology such as computer accessories.

Here's a look at how PC Connections trains its people to meet this challenge.

The founders of PCC started their now $120 million-in-sales company with $8,000 and a unique perspective: People buy computer products to solve immediate problems. Consequently, the company that can deliver solutions the fastest will have a competitive edge in a field where profit margins are minuscule.

As avid computer users themselves, the founders also recognized the importance of after-sale service for computer users. Computers and their peripheral devices either function perfectly or not at all, giving users either exactly what they paid for or expensive technotrash. As PCC's customer relations manager explains, "No one around here has an MBA. Most of our knowledge of business comes from being customers, so it's customer interests that spark all important management decisions."

• **The company established unusual career paths.** One example of the company's commitment to service values is that many employees start in sales and then move up to after-sale service. This career path moves sales reps into service positions called "technical support." All customer contacts after the sale are handled by the customer service department, with technical support staffers acting as the front line.

Only employees with truly extensive product knowledge will be able to quickly assess whether the problem is of a technical nature and, if so, how to fix it. Customer problems of a nontechnical nature are usually referred to general service reps who do not have a technical background.

• **There is a two-track service department.** The front line of customer service, staffed by the elite "techies," is backed up by half-a-dozen general service workers who handle things like order tracking and billing problems. Unlike the "techies," the regular service reps do not have to be college graduates, are not paid as much, and training is much less formal.

• **How reps are trained.** The general service reps are trained largely by working with and observing the team to which they are assigned. However, training for the technical support staff is a two- to three-month process, beginning with training in sales.

In effect, training begins with the hiring process. Only one in 30 applicants is hired for a sales position. Consequently, the company starts with employees whose technical knowledge, articulateness and enthusiasm are already of a high order.

Potential sales reps are then given extensive exposure to all phases of the operation. This includes a two-week stint in the warehouse where they can experience firsthand the consequences of mis-keyed orders.

Since telephone skills are a major part of the job, this area is not neglected either. In intensive phone-skill seminars, reps are barraged with both typical and atypical customer questions. Says the customer relations manager, "A customer might want part X and product Y, delivered C.O.D. to Alaska the next day. The rep has to know not only whether those two products are compatible, but also whether they're in stock, whether there's still time to ship to Alaska the next day, and whether the carrier going there will accept a C.O.D. order."

Phone-skills trainers even feign foreign accents to help trainees learn to cope with hard-to-understand customers. Although there is not yet a formal effort to make bilingual reps available, he pointed out that a sideline benefit of hiring highly educated reps is that calls can, in fact, be taken in Spanish, Russian, and Chinese.

DEALING WITH CUSTOMERS WHO ARE DISTRIBUTORS

HOW TO WALK THE TIGHTROPE BETWEEN THE CUSTOMER AND THE USER

When your customer—the one that writes you checks—is an independent distributor or dealer, you may have an exceptional service opportunity. Then again, you may also have a major service headache. The headache comes when the end-user—with whom you may never have had any prior dealings—brings you service or product problems that should be the dealer's responsibility.

On the one hand, if you just send the end-user back to the dealer, you're sending a loud message that the producer does not stand behind the product. The end-user is getting the brush, invariably finds the experience frustrating, and will rarely, if ever, reorder your product.

On the other hand, if you try to "get tough" with the dealer—demanding better service for the end-user—you risk alienating a customer. The dealer may drop you, throw more business to a competitor, order less in the future or find some other way to sabotage your marketing effort.

While the distributor acts as the "middleman" in the business sense, in this situation *you* should be the middleman.

Step 1. Contact the end-user directly as soon as you learn of the problem. This is your best (indeed, *only*) source of truly reliable information about the user's needs and expectations. Relying on the dealer-distributor for information on the user's problem simply invites a self-interested and garbled version of events.

Step 2. Once you understand the user's problem, contact the dealer/distributor to find out what can be done to resolve the problem. Instead of demanding solutions, find out how you can contribute to a solution. Think in terms of how you can make it easier for the distributor—as by rush-ordering replacement products, spare parts, and so on.

(Note, here, that you are not end-running the distributor—whose continued help you will need in the future—but are instead helping to improve the relationship between the wholesaler and the retail purchaser.)

Step 3. Follow up with a call to the end-user to find out how the dealer/distributor performed. This builds an incredible amount of good will, with many customers saying, "Wow, we've never gotten a call from the factory before. You guys must really *care* about your business."

FIVE STEPS FOR COOLING HOTHEADED CUSTOMERS

The successful company owner recognizes complaining customers for what they really are: a potential gold mine of new business. To tap that potential, however, your company must handle complainers skillfully; effective complaint-handling is a skill that is easily learned.

Once it's recognized that occasional errors are a natural part of doing business, handling customer complaints need not be an exercise in humiliation. Your company shouldn't view a customer grievance as an unwelcome surprise—or the need to correct your errors as an unpleasant intrusion. Instead, customer complaints must be seen as an opportunity to lay the groundwork for future sales by recapturing the customer's goodwill.

Here is a five-point plan for making the most of this opportunity:

Step One: Offer a sincere, personal apology. An impersonal, corporate "we're sorry" has nowhere near the psychological impact of a real person saying "I'm sorry" on behalf of the company. Why? Because personal acknowledgment of the mistake immediately suggests to the customer—on a subconscious level—that his or her human need for compassion is not being ignored.

Step Two: Provide "urgent reinstatement." "Urgent reinstatement" is the need to give the customer the impression that the perceived wrong is being righted as quickly as possible. It's critical here to foster the idea that the person providing the service has the customer's—rather than the company's—best interests at heart.

Step Three: Show empathy. The difference between empathy and sympathy is subtle but essential. Sympathy is an acknowledgment that the customer feels bad, and that the service agent shares that feeling. Empathy goes even further. It acknowledges the customer's feeling while also suggesting that corrective action is in the works.

For example, a sympathetic gas station attendant may say, "Yeah, it's a real nuisance to have a flat, especially when I'm closing up for the day." An empathetic response, by contrast, might begin, "I'd hate to be stranded myself," and continue, "Let me help you change that tire," or "Let me call around and find out who's still open and can come over and help."

Step Four: Offer symbolic atonement. The symbolic atonement—for example, the free drink the airline gives you when your flight is delayed—reinforces the idea that the service provider really wants to make amends. Other examples might include an extra-large portion if you've been kept waiting too long at a restaurant, or a free car wash from the service station that kept your car an extra day.

Remember, though, that this gesture is purely symbolic. It merely shows a willingness to make amends, and should not be confused with more substantial corrective actions that may be necessary. For example, while larger portions may be reasonable compensation for a five-minute wait in a restaurant, a free drink does not compensate for having to spend the night at the airport.

Step Five: Follow up. The follow-up step is the final nail in the coffin of the customer's resistance to repeat business. It's that extra step that convinces the customer that, while your remedial acts have made him "even on the night," he is now ahead of the game.

The follow-up need not be elaborate: A call, a letter, or another minor token are usually sufficient. However, to have the maximum effect, the follow-up gesture should occur when the customer thinks that the transaction is over. The idea should come as a pleasant surprise to the customer and make the customer think you're still concerned about him or her—long after the customer has gotten over his or her annoyance with you.

By following these basic steps, your company can often transform an apparent enemy into a lasting friend who will "goodmouth" your product or service.

HOW TO DEAL WITH WHINING AND SCREAMING CUSTOMERS

Let's face it, nobody enjoys being yelled at, insulted or verbally abused. The urge to argue with the complaining customer can be almost irresistible, especially when you and your customer reps know that the customer is really at fault. And even when you successfully resist the urge to give vent to your feelings, it's only natural to imagine how much you'll enjoy reading a complaining customer's obituary.

There are days when customer service is just plain tough. That's what makes good service an art. Have your customer reps follow the techniques that the pros use to deal with enraged and unreasonable customers.

• **Sidestep the customer's anger—don't swallow the bait.** Highly aggressive people who become verbally abusive are trying to get a hook into someone they can dump their anger on. So they may try to bait you or your employees with personal remarks, taunts and challenges. If you respond on the customer's emotional level or allow yourself to feel insulted, you're hooked.

Avoid starting a sentence with the word "I," except when delivering an apology. ("I'm very sorry that this foul-up occurred," is much more effective than an official-sounding, third-person apology such as "The company deeply regrets this error.") As soon as you say something like "I don't think that's fair," or "I'm not here to listen to stuff like that," *you* become the focus of the conversation and the target of the rage.

Remaining emotionally disengaged doesn't mean your employees shouldn't care. Far from it. They should care very much—about the customer—but not about his or her comments or personal criticisms. It may help in this regard for your employees to think of themselves as parents and to imagine that the customer is their two-year-old child, blowing off steam. They are concerned with the child, not the child's opinions. While the squalling arouses their concern, it shouldn't offend them personally.

• **Don't ignore the anger.** From early childhood we are taught to control our feelings. Consequently, when faced with customers who are clearly making no effort to control theirs, it's no wonder we find it upsetting. But as long as your employees remember that their task is to influence customers' purchasing decisions—not to control their emotions—they will be well on the way to mastering both.

When a customer is angry, it's tempting just to ignore the anger and try to focus on the problem at hand—a missed delivery, a defective product, or whatever. But ignoring the customer's emotions is a big mistake. (If you don't believe it, just try ignoring a child and see how well it behaves.) "Deal with the person before you deal with the problem" should be your motto.

Your first step should be to *acknowledge* the customer's feelings. This does *not* mean caving in to absurd demands. It just means lending a sympathetic ear and saying things like "That must really make you mad," or "I can see how that hit a nerve," or "No wonder you feel like no one is listening."

You'll be amazed how well it works. Just by acknowledging that someone is angry, you almost always make them less angry. Even more important: The customer, more often than not, now feels as if he or she has found an ally or protector. Having started out to abuse you, the customer—much like a child—comes to feel dependent on you. And when this happens, the dynamics of the situation shift to your advantage. As long as you don't abuse the trust, you will continue to hold the upper hand.

• **Don't sit on the steam valve—stay clear when the lid blows.** Say you have a real shrieker on your hands who won't even listen to your acknowledgment, much less let you begin a rational discussion of the problem. When someone really insists on bellowing, there's not much you can do about it. And that's the solution to your problem.

When customers scream at you over the phone and you remain silent except for the occasional "Uh-huh," they'll soon hear themselves shouting and usually will quiet down by themselves. If you try to interrupt them, you'll get into a shouting match. Even if you win the argument, you'll lose the customer. Thus, the best thing to do in these cases is just to listen and wait.

Of course, when the screamer is standing right in front of you, the experience can be quite intimidating. But it doesn't have to be anything other than routine if you and your employees follow these simple steps.

- First, remember that you're the only person you can directly control. By keeping control of yourself, you will wind up in control of the situation.

- Second, avoid the natural response to a threat—flight or fight. By controlling these natural urges, you're taking a giant step in the direction of controlling the situation.

- Third, send the right body language "cues." Stand easy, feet apart, shoulders squared. Keep your arms at your sides, or resting comfortably on the counter or desk in front of you. Don't cross your arms or put your hands in your pockets. (The first posture is "closed," the second rather weak.) Look the person in the eye from time to time to let him or her know you're listening, but don't stare. When you're not looking the customer in the eye, look over his or her head, possibly nodding slightly as though you're thinking about what the customer is saying.

- Fourth, try whispering. Crazy but true. Whispering to people who are shouting almost always causes them to lower their voices. The effect is virtually immediate, but it's also short-lived. Be prepared to seize the moment.

- Fifth, when your opening comes, lead with *empathetic* statements, followed up by gently phrased questions, such as "Gee, you must have really been *depending* on that shipment. You must have been very disappointed when it didn't arrive. Why don't you let me see when I can reschedule delivery?"

"BUZZ PHRASES" THAT HELP YOU DISARM IRATE CUSTOMERS

There are certain phrases you can use that will almost always smooth ruffled feathers, as if by magic. Others, however, are virtually guaranteed to ruffle the customer's feathers even more. Obvious examples are responses that begin with "Listen, Bub...." or "Look, dearie...."

Keep in mind that the irate customer is *expecting* to be frustrated, belittled and generally brushed off. This negative anticipation constantly fuels the customer's rage. The customer expects a fight and is prepared to do battle. Frustrate the customer's expectations. Give irate customers what they don't expect—warmth, support, and understanding.

An example of how this works can be seen in the muffler commercials in which an intimidating customer bursts into the shop proclaiming, "I'm not gonna pay a lot for this muffler, and it better be quality!" The person behind the counter simply smiles, shakes his head and *agrees*. The next shot shows the customer looking at the invoice, meek as a lamb, totally disarmed. The negative anticipation was frustrated.

If only life could be as easy as it is in commercials, you may be thinking. Well, it *can* be if you sprinkle your customer contacts with the customer-empowering "buzz phrases" that follow.

- **"Someone in your position...."** The suggestion here is that the customer holds an important job or social rank. Don't be afraid to pour it on. No one ever gets tired of being told how good they look or how important they are.
- **"I'd sure appreciate it if...."** This phrase implicitly asks the customer's permission, suggesting that the customer has the power to grant or refuse.
- **"You could really help me by...."** Suggests that the customer is not only taking a hand in the complaint-resolution process, but is also taking something of a guiding role.

- **"Because of your special knowledge...."** Suggests a high degree of skill or advanced study. People love to think that others view them as highly intelligent.
- **"As you, of course, know...."** This phrase is especially effective when you are telling customers something you know that they don't know. Most people don't like to admit that they are ignorant, even of things that they have no reason to know.
- **"You're absolutely right about that..."** A routine but effective "stroke." Use it to readily concede some minor point the customer makes. The customer will then be more willing to give ground on the major points of contention.
- **"Someone as busy as you are...."** Suggests that the problem will be resolved as quickly as possible.
- **"I'd sure be grateful if...."** Suggests an easy way to make someone happy.

Note that many of these phrases start with "I," a word you should normally avoid in *confrontations* with customers. You can use it safely here because you are using "I" in a totally nonchallenging way. If you are feeling more aggressive, however, and a more confrontational approach seems to be in order, just start your remarks with the word "You."

HOW TO ESTABLISH AN EFFECTIVE CREDIT AND COLLECTION POLICY

For many small businesses, aggressive sales efforts often lead to one key problem: "The customer wants to buy more of our product but doesn't have the cash flow to pay us right away. He'll be able to pay next month—after he fills his orders and gets paid by his customers. Can we sell to him on credit?"

Your credit and collection policy can provide the answer. Your policy can determine how and when to sell on credit, what kinds of terms to offer, the conditions that dictate when those terms should be changed, when to start collection efforts, and what form those efforts should take.

Selling on credit is the lifeblood of a successful company. But it can be the death knell when it's not handled properly. That's where a credit and collection policy comes in. A good policy—one that's clearly and concisely written—serves as a business owner's game plan for turning sales into paid-for sales—the only real measure of a company's ultimate success.

This chapter takes a look at the elements that make up a successful credit and collection policy. Taken together, they are the necessary ingredients for turning your company's credit and collection department into a profit center.

Keep in mind that credit and debt collection activities are subject to a variety of legal requirements, such as fair debt collection and truth in lending.

ADMINISTERING A CREDIT POLICY

To be effective, a credit and collection policy must reflect your company's individual goals, needs, operating structure and business environment. Some companies adopt elaborate policies spelling out how decisions on extending credit are to be made, who can make such decisions, how legal action is to be taken when the need arises, and so forth. In other companies, credit and collection decisions are made by the business owner alone or by a group of officers or executives on the basis of informal guidelines or individual judgments.

Figure 5.1 offers one example of a written credit policy. It encompasses all the key points regarding the duties and responsibilities of a credit and collection department that has its eye fixed on the bottom line:

Figure 5.1 SAMPLE CREDIT POLICY

- It shall be the policy of this company to extend credit to our customers in a manner consistent with the business practices and objectives of the company.

- The Credit Manager shall report to the General Manager and be on an equal level with the General Sales Manager.

- It is the Credit Manager's responsibility to approve all credit extensions, supervise timely collection of monies due, maintain accurate records, handle timely management reporting, and administer the functions with necessary firmness and tact so as to continue good business relations with our customers.

- The Credit Manager, or his or her designee, may represent our company in legal actions in concert with our attorney. The Credit Manager may settle account differences and disputes, place accounts in default with collection agencies and, after proper notification to management and the Sales Department, hold orders when the customer is over the credit limit or is extremely delinquent.

- The Credit Manager shall hire, train and supervise such assistants and administrative support personnel as may be approved by management and within budgeting guidelines.

- Credit, Sales and Management shall work together as a team. Credit shall be present at periodic meetings with Sales and Management, participate in the others' training programs, visit customers directly, assist in prospecting for new accounts, and maintain a professional customer relations program.

THE KEY OBJECTIVES OF A CREDIT POLICY

For a credit and collection policy to be effective it has to show good results in two critical areas: avoiding bad debts from the start, and pulling in a large share of payments from both consumer and commercial accounts. Here's how to use your credit and collection policy to meet these two aims:

Control bad debts. There's only one sure way to control bad debts—prevention. No company should be extended credit until it has been thoroughly investigated.

Stay up to date. Make sure a commercial credit customer's D&B report has been updated within the last two years. (Obviously, the more recent, the better.) Older information may now be inaccurate.

Check out the current owners. New ownership of an established company should be a red flag. The company's D&B report can read beautifully thanks to past ownership and past cash flow. But the new owners may have insufficient funds or excessive loan obligations.

Use caution with subsidiaries. Many times a parent company has no qualms about dumping a subsidiary when times get tough—and sticking you with a nonpaying account.

Get personal guarantees. Get personal guarantees from the principals and/or other financially secure backers when a commercial customer is a small firm. That way, you're secured to a greater degree if the outfit goes bankrupt.

Don't ship until you're sure. Don't allow deliveries to be made until someone with authority in the credit and collection department has initialed the delivery slip.

Obtain identification. When selling to a consumer account, ask for and verify the number of the person's driver's license, as well as his or her Social Security number. This can become very valuable information if the person later tries to "skip out" on the bill.

Use discount leverage. Offer attractive discounts for payment within 10 days of receipt of the goods. This keeps cash flowing and reduces your exposure to high losses.

Take the extra step. Always be willing to give a delinquent account more time to pay. Make it a point to go the last mile with every credit customer. Of course, after you collect, the customer's credit rating should be downgraded considerably, or the account closed out altogether.

Stay flexible. Offer to settle for two-thirds of the bill if a time payment can't be worked out. Point out to the customer that he or she can save court costs and legal problems by agreeing to this settlement. Of course, settling the matter is generally in your best interests as well. Taking a customer to court is always time-consuming and usually expensive.

WHY YOU SHOULD REVIEW YOUR CREDIT POLICY PERIODICALLY

When was the last time you reviewed your current credit policy on commercial accounts? A periodic three-stage review of your policy elements such as your requirements for credit, terms of payment and when and how you collect overdue amounts, can help you boost your company's profits.

Here are three key points to check and questions you should be asking yourself:

1. Customer requirements: "What do we require in order for the customer to be entitled to open-account credit?"

Your minimum standards as to a trade customer's financial solidity, past-payment record and business standing will depend, in part, on your company's marketing situation.

If you have heavy competition and a product that can be bought on any corner, you can't be as demanding as you might be in selling a unique line.

Reexamine your company's competitive position. If you have more competition now than you did when your credit policy was last revised, your policy may now cut out some customers who could help boost your profits.

2. Terms-of-sale problem: "Are the credit terms we offer as attractive as they should be to draw a maximum number of profitable accounts?"

How long you give commercial customers to pay their bills will depend on the same factors that influence your basic credit requirements: your company's position in its industry, availability of your product elsewhere and the customer's payment record with other creditors.

But it will also pay you to make a sales-terms check. Look at the most recent figures on pay patterns in your industry. The average "net" period may be longer than it was when your current policy was set, so the terms you're offering may no longer be so attractive to buyers.

If your "net" period is considerably shorter than the industry average, a high percentage of your accounts may be failing to pay before the deadline. One readily apparent result is the slow turnover of receivables. A less obvious effect is resentment among prompt-paying customers who learn via the grapevine what your slow-payers are getting away with.

3. Collection pressure: "How vigorously do we press customers for payment of overdue amounts?"

If you apply more zeal in going after payments from your commercial accounts, you should be able to reduce the amount of money you have tied up in receivables. Time factors are vital here, so look again at the following:

- The interval between the due date and the first collection letter.

- The interval between each collection appeal and the following one in the series.

- The period covered by the total collection effort from first message through your final writeoff of the account.

One factor to keep in mind here is the number of people now at your disposal for collection efforts. If you must handle a large number of accounts with a small staff, it may make more sense for you to drop your own collection appeals after a relatively short time and turn matters over to a collection agency.

A major virtue of this procedure is that it lets your people devote their time and energy to accounts where the payoff is apt to be most rewarding.

At the same time, there's sufficient "juice" left in accounts turned over to the agency so it can get a good percentage of payments.

HOW TO MAXIMIZE PAYMENTS FROM YOUR CREDIT ACCOUNTS

Here are some key tips that can help you collect payments—in full—from your credit customers:

Target key accounts to speed collections

Shortening the time between a sale and the receipt of payment is what an effective credit and collection policy is all about. Every business has its own approach to closing this gap. Here are two ideas that are part of an Illinois business owner's policy:

- Identify your largest customers. "Some people feel that 20% of their commercial credit customers account for 80% of their accounts receivable," this business owner notes. "While I think the figure might be closer to 50% or 60%, I do believe that a small portion of your customers are responsible for a large proportion of the money owed your company. It's vital, therefore, that you can identify these customers."

As these accounts go, so goes your cash flow. A trend toward slower payments on the part of your top 20% is a serious threat to profitability. It requires a quick, and intensive, collection effort.

- Put your top collectors on the top 20%. This goes against the policy of many companies. They prefer to divvy up big and small accounts on a roughly equal basis among collectors. This makes it easier to compare the performance of individual collectors. But what good is knowing who your best people are if they're not in a position to do you the most good?

Give your best collectors the biggest accounts. And tell them that reducing these customers' overdue balances is a top priority. Aim initially to get customers currently paying within, say, 90 days to pay within 60 days. Later, see if they can improve this to 45 days.

Coordinate sales and credit efforts

Your company's credit and collection policy is incomplete if it doesn't outline the ways your sales and credit departments should work together to garner more paid-for sales. Here are some tested methods for coordinating the efforts of these two departments to boost quality receivables.

- Communicate freely. "If the credit/sales 'marriage' is to work," says a Minnesota small business owner, "both sides need to know as much as they can about how each department functions regarding the selection of credit customers."

Have credit and sales department heads sit in on each other's meetings from time to time. They can use this opportunity to discuss shared concerns about the type of credit accounts you're aiming to land and the best ways to ensure that these customers pay on time.

"For example," the executive points out, "say your credit department is getting applications for credit that are incorrectly or partially filled out. Your credit manager can use this meeting to explain to the sales staff how important it is to let customers know that the faster an accurately-completed form is received, the sooner your company can okay credit and ship the goods."

- Require sharing of reading materials. The credit manager for a Syracuse, New York, firm says it's his company's policy to have the sales and credit departments share reading material. "Our aging reports—those documents that show how long a customer's account has been overdue—are required reading for both our sales and credit staffs," says the credit manager. "The idea of this policy is to have both departments keep in mind that a customer's signature on a *check* is more valuable than his signature on an *order form.*"

Collection problems can often be avoided when your managers take the time to look closely at the figures on the aging report, paying special attention to any significant changes in the financial status of credit customers. To ensure that they do this, send a memo to your sales and credit department heads asking them to call you to discuss the report's findings. Suggest the topics you'd like to cover, such as disputes over payment, changes in status, improving collection procedures, and so on. If they know they have to call you, your managers will take the time to carefully review the facts and figures on each customer.

Six Billing Rules for Bringing in Payments Quickly and Easily

Your company's *invoice* can be an important factor in securing prompt payment from customers. According to a leading expert in the credit and collections field, there are six critical rules business owners should follow in designing invoices:

1. Keep the invoice as simple and uncluttered as possible. Minimize data that have little or no meaning to the customer. Keep code numbers short. This will result in an easier bill to interpret. And this makes paying it much easier.

2. Be complete. Don't go so far in your attempt at simplification that you fail to include all the information the customer should have. Completeness is likely to cut down on questions that may delay payment.

For instance, here are the items that should be clearly spelled out:

- Who is the invoice from?
- How much is owed in total? When is payment due? Where should it be sent?
- What was bought? When? What does it cost? When was it delivered? Any sales tax?

- What will be charged if payment is late? What will be saved if it is early?
- What should be sent back with payment (e.g., invoice copies)? Who should be contacted if there's a problem?

3. Make the information clearly understandable. Avoid the following three common mistakes:

- *Vagueness:* For example, "Net 30 days." Do you mean 30 days from the date of shipment, receipt of merchandise, date of billing or receipt of bill?
- *Abbreviations:* You know what they mean, but will the customer? Be especially careful with product descriptions and information. If abbreviations can't be avoided, put an abbreviation glossary on the back of the invoice. This should clear up any mystery.
- *Trade jargon:* Most industries, and even companies, have their own special language, which may be confusing to the customer. Put your request for payment in layperson's terms.

4. Be courteous. This is a seemingly obvious point, but somehow one that is still missed by too many. For example, "Please pay this amount" is certainly preferable to "Pay this amount." Here are some other customer keepers:

- Put a "thank you" on your invoice.
- Get the customer's name right, especially when dealing with individuals.
- Include job titles to help avoid questions about who ordered what.
- Respond promptly to customers' requests regarding their bills. This is most important. For example, if a customer asks: "Please include our Purchase Order number on your invoice," failing to do so is not only poor public relations, but will probably also slow the customer's processing of your invoice.

5. Present a positive image. Make the invoice attractive and distinctive. If you have a logo, use it. Also use brightly colored paper, legible print and clearly defined columns.

6. Keep it easy to use. To minimize the amount of writing, calculating and reviewing the customer has to do, you should do the following:

- Provide enough copies.
- Make the bill fit smoothly, with the proper fold, into a standard window envelope.

- Include a self-addressed reply envelope (into which the bill and the customer's check will fit easily without excessive folding).
- Use preprinted remittance forms that convert into return envelopes.

HOW TO GET CREDIT INFORMATION AND WHAT TO DO WITH IT

Once you've set your policy for extending credit to customers, the next step is to decide who those customers will be. This is done by obtaining complete, up-to-date information on prospective accounts and using those facts to distinguish between financially solid businesses and potential bad debts.

Here are some time-tested ways of obtaining the kind of information that will help make your credit department a center of paid-for sales:

Key questions for commercial credit applicants

The starting point for landing profitable commercial credit accounts is your credit application. While the actual application you use will depend on the type of services or products your company provides, most if not all of the following categories should be included if you want to get the complete picture on a commercial credit applicant:

- full name and address of the customer;
- how long the company has been in business;
- the form of the business;
- name of the bank that handles the company's financial affairs;
- a list of the applicant's other suppliers (for the purpose of obtaining trade references);
- a list of current assets, including cash on hand, accounts receivable, inventory, notes and acceptances receivable, other current assets, and fixed assets such as land, buildings, fixtures and equipment;
- a list of current liabilities, including accounts or notes and acceptances payable for merchandise, accrued income taxes and other accrued taxes, rentals and payrolls accrued, an allowance

to cover unfunded vested pension liabilities, and long-term liabilities;

- total net worth;
- amounts for which the customer is liable either as an endorser or a guarantor;
- value of machinery or equipment the customer holds under lease;
- dates of the latest inventory count and most recent audit; and
- dollar totals of insurance carried, broken down by type, including fire, liability, key-person, etc.

Figure 5.2 is a sample credit application you can use or adapt to meet your needs.

Getting a business to fill out your credit application is only the first step in credit analysis. Your next move should be to follow up on the information the applicant has provided by contacting other sources, such as the customer's bank or other suppliers.

Getting key facts from bankers

"Regardless of how much credit is involved," says a Missouri business owner, "my approach to requesting information from an applicant's bank is always the same. I have specific points I want answered for each customer." The list of information he seeks to get from the bank includes the following:

- approximate average balance recently maintained by the customer;
- number of months or years the bank has had dealings with the customer;
- the amount and terms of any bank loans outstanding to the customer, including whether or not the loans are secured or guaranteed in any way (and if so, who is the guarantor?);
- customer's history in making payments on obligations to the bank;
- details on any special adjustment of payment terms the bank has made, and the customer's performance in meeting the new terms;
- date of the latest balance sheet that the bank has on file from the customer;
- the bank's observations on the current profitability of the customer's business.

Figure 5.2

APPLICATION FOR CREDIT

Date_____19_____

ISSUED TO _____
      [PLEASE ANSWER ALL QUESTIONS. WHEN NO FIGURES ARE INSERTED, WRITE WORD "NONE"]
NAME OF FIRM
Requesting Statement

FIRM NAME		TRADE STYLE		
STREET ADDRESS			PHONE	
CITY		STATE		ZIP CODE

FULL NAME OF OWNER OR OWNERS (OR AN AUTHORIZED OFFICER OF CORPORATION) LIST HOME ADDRESS & ZIP CODE FOR PARTNERSHIP OR INDIVIDUAL

PLEASE CHECK ONE	INDIVIDUAL	PARTNERSHIP	CORPORATION	FED. TAX NO. (FOR CORPORATION)	MARITAL STATUS

ADDITIONAL INFORMATION REQUIRED FOR CONDITIONAL SALES CONTRACTS UNDER THE UNIFORM COMMERCIAL CODE

DEBTOR (INDIVIDUAL SIGNING CONTRACT)_____ TITLE:_____

DEBTOR'S SOCIAL SECURITY NO. (FOR PARTNERSHIP OR INDIVIDUAL) _____

TYPE OF BUSINESS		DATE STARTED
ESTIMATED ANNUAL SALES		
FORMER BUSINESS	LOCATION	
OWN OR RENT BUILDING — IF RENT — FROM WHOM?		VALUE
REAL ESTATE MORTGAGE		

TRADE REFERENCES

NAME	ADDRESS

NAME OF BANK	
STREET ADDRESS	
CITY	STATE

APPLICANT'S SIGNATURE ATTESTS FINANCIAL RESPONSIBILITY, ABILITY AND WILLINGNESS TO PAY OUR INVOICES IN ACCORDANCE WITH FOLLOWING TERMS:

THE ABOVE INFORMATION AS WELL AS THAT GIVEN ON THE REVERSE SIDE IS FOR THE PURPOSE OF OBTAINING CREDIT AND IS WARRANTED TO BE TRUE. I/WE HEREBY AUTHORIZE THE FIRM TO WHOM THIS APPLICATION IS MADE TO INVESTIGATE THE REFERENCES LISTED PERTAINING TO MY/OUR CREDIT AND FINANCIAL RESPONSIBILITY.	FIRM NAME_____
	BY _____ TITLE
	BY _____ TITLE

Commercial Application for Credit (Front)

Reprinted with permission from the Handbook of Credit and Collection Management Forms and Procedures, by Jack Horn. Copyright 1980 by Prentice Hall, Inc., Englewood Cliffs, New Jersey.

Figure 5.2, continued

The following figures are present financial standing and business operation upon which you may rely for the purpose of establishing our credit:

CURRENT ASSETS:

Cash on hand and in banks	$ . . . .
Accounts Receivable	. . . .
Cost of merchandise on hand	. . . .
Other current assets	. . . .
TOTAL	$ . . . .

CURRENT LIABILITIES:

Bank loans payable within a year	. . . .
Tax obligations due	. . . .
Accounts Payable	. . . .
Other debts due within a year	. . . .
TOTAL	$ . . . .

FIXED ASSETS;

Business equipment	. . . .
Land used in business	. . . .
Buildings used in business	. . . .
*Other assets	. . . .
TOTAL	$ . . . .

INDEBTEDNESS NOT DUE WITHIN A YEAR

Chattel mortgages due on merchandise . . .	. . . .
Chattel mortgages due on other assets . . .	. . . .
Real estate mortgages	. . . .
*Other long term debt	. . . .
TOTAL	$ . . . .

NET WORTH	. . . .	. . . . $ . . . .

Average monthly sales	. . . .
% of sales made on credit	. . . .
% of sales at retail	. . . .
% of sales at wholesale	. . . .
% of sales on time-payment plan	. . . .
Peak season of year	
Date of last inventory	. . . .
Profit shown latest U.S. Income Tax Return	. . . .

Our firm is financially able to meet any commitments we have made and we will pay your invoices according to your terms.

*PLEASE SPECIFY:

Date _____

Title _____   Signature _____

Commercial Application for Credit (Reverse)

Personal visits to key customers

For an increasing number of businesses, the screening process for new and current accounts goes beyond a look at their latest financial statements or Dun & Bradstreet reports. These firms make personal visits to customers part of the process of gathering credit background information.

In Figure 5.3 we've reproduced a form used by an executive for a Pennsylvania manufacturer to gather information on prospective commercial credit accounts during visits to the applicants' plants or offices.

"Based on the facts and impressions I get from the visit, along with information from other sources," says the executive, "I can approve first orders from new accounts or revise credit limits for ongoing customers. What's more, I don't have to try and write a report about the visit from memory when I get back to the hotel or office. I already have the information on the form."

The form that follows is largely self-explanatory. However, to emphasize key points, we've included the exec's reasons for asking certain questions and the ways that he uses the answers to help him make decisions on whether or not to grant credit and for how much. (This material appears in italics.)

Figure 5.3
CREDIT CUSTOMER VISIT FORM
(Confidential)

[First and foremost, this form should contain the word "Confidential" on its title, and confidentiality should be adhered to at all times. Remember, your customer might be providing facts that could be misused by others. As a professional, you have an obligation to respect the information received.]

Customer Name :_____

Customer Address: _____

Date of Visit:_____

Name of Interviewee: _____

Title: _____

[Mark asterisk by names of principal sources of data for this form.]

I. Organization

A. _____Corporation
   _____Partnership
   _____Sole Proprietorship

B. Legal Name:_____

C. State of Incorporation or Registration:_____

D. Date of Incorporation or Registration:_____

E. Officers:

Name	Title
_____	_____
_____	_____
_____	_____
_____	_____

[Is this a corporation, partnership or sole proprietorship? What is the company's correct legal name? Upon returning to the office, verify the name with the Secretary of State.]

II. Ownership

Name(s)   Percentage

_____   _____
_____   _____
_____   _____
_____   _____

A. Describe inter-owner agreements, if any, regarding changes in ownership and related funding:

_____

B. Describe plans for succession:_____

III. Location

A. Headquarters:

_____   _____
Street & Mailing Address   City

_____   _____
State   County

B. Branches:

_____   _____
Street & Mailing Address   City

IV. Professional Assistance

A. Auditor(s)
Name: _____
Address: _____

B. Willing to provide financial statements (audited or unqualified opinion), balance sheet, income statement, statement of sources, and use of funds and notes?_____

[Who audits the books? Is it a large auditing firm or an independent? If they are unwilling to provide financial statements, what are they trying to hide?]

V. Nature and Scope of the Business

A. Customer's Product(s)_____
B. Customer's Service(s)_____

VI. Financial Information

A. Dun & Bradstreet Report Date_____
   1. Rating: _____
   2. Payments: _____
   3. Employs:_____
   4. Condition: _____
   5. Trend: _____
   6. Consistent with data developed during visit: _____

   7. Comments:_____

[Obtain a credit agency report before your visit, and compare this information with the data developed during your visit.]

B. Latest Financial Statement Date:_____
   1. Total Assets:_____
   2. Owners' Equity: _____
   3. Debit to Equity:_____
   4. Sales to Worth:_____
   5. Gross Sales:_____
   6. Gross Profit Margin: _____

[Review the latest Financial Statement with the customer, and get the answers to any pertinent or important facts.]

C. Terms of Sale _____
   1. Public:_____
   2. Government:_____
   3. Export:_____
   4. Days Sales Outstanding:_____

[What are the terms this customer uses to sell its products? This could give you an indication of the quality of its receivables portfolio.

For instance, are the payment terms your customer grants standard in the marketplace or abnormal, thereby causing poor cash flow? The point of reviewing your customer's receivables portfolio would be to see what amounts of money may be forthcoming into its hands, and what kind of aging problems, bad debts or potential writeoffs are shown.]

D. Aging Schedule:_____
   Current: _____
   1–29:_____
   30–59:_____
   60–89: _____
   90–119:_____

120–149:_____

150–Over:_____

Total:_____

1. Prior year's average days to pay:_____

Current year average days to pay: _____

2. Commitment:_____

3. Deductions taken: _____

[If a current customer, review any outstanding balances owed your company, and obtain a commitment to pay, or reasons for nonpayment. Also, review with the customer the average days they take to pay you. If within terms, congratulate the company for its fine efforts; if longer than terms, explain why your terms must be met.]

E. Bank Relationship

Name(s): _____

Credit Line Description:_____

Secured:_____

Interest Rate:_____

Describe any personal guarantees provided: _____

F. Credit References:

1. Bank

Name:_____

Address:_____

Contact:_____

Telephone:_____

2. Trade

Name:_____

Address:_____

Contact:_____

Telephone:_____

VII. Physical Facilities Description

A. Is the site suitably located for distribution of goods?

_____

B. Is the site surrounded by fencing to secure or protect its contents?

_____

C. Are the premises neat, orderly, and in line with safety standards?

_____

D. Is the decor reflective of professional styling or is it a combination of outlandish colors and designs?_____

_____

VIII. Local Economy Description

A. Is the area depressed with high unemployment and lack of industry, or very highly competitive?

B. Is the area suitable to distribute your product?

IX. Estimated Inventory Requirements

[While this is primarily a sales question, the response could alert you to the need for providing additional credit, or lowering the current amount.]

X. General Observations

A. What was your appraisal of the people you interviewed?

_____

B. Were questions answered in detail, or were responses couched in general or vague terms?_____

C. What are the company's prospects for success/failure?_____

_____

XI. Recommendations

[This section is primarily left for summarization and personal comments. For instance, should credit be extended, lowered or increased? Should further investigations be conducted, or are you satisfied with the results of this visit?]

TAP OTHER SUPPLIERS FOR ADDED INSIGHTS

To make sure your investigation of potential commercial credit customers is as thorough as possible, consider this key source. Obtain trade payment references from the applicant's other suppliers. These sources—particularly suppliers that have dealt with the customer for some time—may be able to tell you a lot about the ability of the customer's management team, the strength of its sales and marketing strategies, and the likelihood of future growth.

The application form or financial statement you receive from the applicant should list the names of other suppliers you can contact for more information. You have several options for getting in touch with these sources:

• **Use the direct approach.** The simplest way is to pick up a phone and call the suppliers direct. This is probably the fastest method. But it may also be the most expensive, particularly if you end up calling a large number of suppliers outside your local calling area.

- **Contact interchange bureaus.** The Credit Interchange Bureau of the National Association of Credit Management sponsors local credit interchange bureaus. Users can get information concerning suppliers' experiences with a particular account simply by making one trade payment request to the Bureau. The Bureau then provides a report on the customer based on the trade payment information it receives continually from participating suppliers.
- **Contact industry groups.** Companies that belong to the National Association of Credit Management can participate in industry credit groups. These meet to exchange current and accurate credit information on common customers for the purpose of assisting members in making credit decisions.
- **Contact credit reporting agencies.** You can also get trade reference reports on prospective customers from credit reporting agencies such as Dun & Bradstreet, TRW and others.
- **Rely on networking for credit news.** "I rely largely on the more common sources of credit data to supply basic credit background on potential customers," says a credit executive for an Alabama manufacturer. "But I don't stop there. Whenever possible, I take my investigation on applicants one step further and get bad risk protection."

"I make it a point," the executive says, "to attend as many industry and trade meetings as I can. These meetings give me a good opportunity to meet suppliers who extend credit to commercial customers such as ours." Thanks to this "networking," she's often able to dig up information about customers that's useful in deciding whether or not to extend credit.

"There have been times when other suppliers warned me of companies that were experiencing cash-flow problems that made them credit risks. As a result, I've either turned down the applicants or offered to sell to them on a cash-only basis. These meetings also make it easier for me to obtain a credit reference on a customer from another supplier because I've developed a personal—as well as a professional—relationship with the individual."

Another potential advantage of attending industry meetings is that you become aware of companies that have a need for your products or services. "When that happens," the executive says, "I get the name and phone number of a prospect and pass the information along to our sales staff. Many of our accounts have been established this way."

HOW TO SPOT UNRELIABLE FINANCIAL STATEMENTS

The smart business person tries to get the most complete picture of a prospect's credit-worthiness before extending credit. However, from time to time, your search may turn up information that is incomplete, misleading or even false. Knowing how to spot such problems—even though unintentional—can keep you from getting burned.

Each time your department receives a financial statement from a prospective credit customer, have your people take these preventive measures:

• **Check the signature**. The financial statement must be signed by the customer and, preferably, by a witness as well. If the customer submits more than one statement, make sure each is signed. If you receive an unsigned financial statement, mail it back to the customer for a signature. The signature is essential if you later end up in court over misleading data or misrepresentations in the statement.

• **Check the dates.** Don't accept a financial statement unless it shows both the date it was prepared *and* the dates of the period it covers. And make sure all key dates are consistent with one another.

Take extra care. If the dates are more than one month old, ask for the insertion of a declaration—signed and dated by the principals— that there has been no adverse development in the firm's financial situation since the statement was prepared. Specify that if a change occurs, it must be reported to you at once.

• **Check for completeness.** Return any statement that isn't filled out completely. If a legal dispute arises down the road, the customer may be able to escape liability for misrepresenting its financial picture if you don't challenge omissions on the financial statement immediately.

For example, a debtor had assigned all its receivables to a finance company. But the financial statement it submitted to its creditor suggested the receivables were free and clear. How? The debtor had left unanswered the question: "Are any of your assets pledged?" This would appear to be a material misrepresentation of the facts.

A court let the debtor off the hook, however. It said the applicant's failure to answer the question should have put the creditor *on notice* that the financial statement was defective. Simply because the customer left the question blank was no reason to assume the answer was "no," the court added.

HOW TO VERIFY YOUR CUSTOMER'S FINANCIAL STABILITY

It's only natural that a customer who submits financial figures to you should want them to present the best picture possible. The figures on current assets and liabilities are what you'll probably look at first. But if you have any doubts about the customer's financial stability, take this additional precaution. Verify that current assets shown on the statement are as large as indicated, and that current liabilities are no larger than stated. Here are helpful details to check.

- Cash reality: Contact the customer directly to make sure that: (1) No IOU's are included in the cash balance; (2) The balance has not been inflated by inclusion of amounts received after the "close-of-business" date shown on the financial statement; and (3) None of the cash in the total shown has been set aside for a specific use such as for a "sinking fund."

- Accounts receivable reality: What's the aging picture on the customer's accounts receivable? The relative value of various age groups will depend on the type of business plus the customer's collection experience and usual sales terms.

  For instance, in assigning values to the accounts of a customer with 30-day credit terms, a Miami business owner took at face value any account no more than 30 days old, 85% of face value for 31-to-60 day accounts, and 50% for accounts 61-to-90 days old. Older accounts were valued at zero.

- Notes receivable reality: If it's the usual practice in the customer's industry to receive notes at the time of sale, any note of this kind is an unusually good asset. It probably earns interest and can be discounted and turned into cash faster and at less cost than an account receivable.

  If the total of your customer's notes receivable includes any notes that have been discounted, assigned, or transferred, take this into account when you compute the notes' actual value.

EFFECTIVE COLLECTION STRATEGIES

Establishing a sensible credit policy and carefully screening new accounts will go a long way toward minimizing delinquent payers and bad debts. But no matter how diligent you are, some problem accounts are bound to turn up. That's when you'll need to put into action collection strategies that get you your money fast—and in full. Below are some proven methods used by executives from small businesses across the country.

• **Zero in on the person who can pay.** In collecting from commercial credit accounts, knowing the right person to contact is half the battle, says a San Francisco small business owner. "Having someone at each account that I can call—and keeping that relationship on good terms—is not only the best way for us to handle late payments, it also paves the way for future sales by keeping the relationship mutually profitable."

Establish a solid contact at each commercial credit account. This should be someone with the authority to see that you get paid on time.

• **Charge a fee for late payments.** "You can turn marginal commercial credit customers into prompt-paying accounts," says the head of a California supplier, "with a collection tool that I've found gets better results than the usual follow-up letters or phone calls."

The executive suggests imposing a service charge on accounts that are overdue more than a given number of days. "No collection tool could be more effective than hitting a late-paying customer in the pocketbook."

Have your credit application state that if payment is late, a service charge may be imposed. "Spell out when it will be imposed and specify the amount of the charge," the California exec says. "The customer's signature on such an application constitutes acceptance of these terms. By putting the service charge arrangement in writing from the start, the customer can't plead ignorance when you levy the charge."

FACE-TO-FACE MEETINGS CAN IMPROVE YOUR CHANCES OF GETTING PAID

How well a face-to-face meeting with a delinquent customer goes depends, to a great extent, on how well you do your homework.

You'll find that such meetings are more likely to turn up payments if you plan beforehand how you want to handle each account, depending upon the particular nonpayment situation. Write down your plan of action for each of the following considerations before calling on a debtor.

1. Evaluate the relationship. How badly does the customer need you? That's the key. If you know that you're a principal supplier, you'll carry a lot more weight than if you're just one of many who service this account.

2. Set up your countermoves. Sit down with the person responsible for handling the credit account and go over the payment history. Review the customer's no-pay reason and get the full facts about each one. The more you know about the account, the better equipped you'll be to puncture the credibility of any excuse. Once you've done that, you've begun to take away the customer's justification for holding up payment.

3. Establish concessions in reserve. Know before you enter the customer's office what adjustments you're willing to offer; that is, longer time to pay, reduced payment accounts, etc. Be sure to emphasize that any adjustment in the customer's payment terms must be met with a payment of the specific amount by a specific date.

Also, try to set up a solution that the customer can realistically handle given its cash resources. Otherwise, you stand little chance of ever seeing any of your money, and a good chance of winding up with a bankrupt customer.

4. Act professionally. A face-to-face meeting doesn't mean you have to get involved in a shouting match. Keep your discussion limited to the company's "temporary cash problem." Don't refer to any failure on the part of the person you're meeting with to make payment.

You'll leave the customer's self-respect intact, which will encourage him or her to be more cooperative. If it's a normally good-paying account, giving the customer a chance to save face will make it more likely that the customer will continue to do business with your company.

REMINDER CALLS HELP YOU OVERCOME EXCUSES

To get around customers' excuses that they haven't paid because of lost invoices or disputes over amounts owed, the owner of a Wisconsin trucking outfit uses a reminder call system. For example, they call the customer on the 15th of the month in which payment is due. They don't ask for payment at this time. Instead, they ask if the customer has received the statement and, if so, whether there are any questions or problems.

If the customer questions or objects to the bill, listen to the customer and try to resolve the situation at this point, the owner suggests. Once the problem has been taken care of, ask the customer if there are any further questions. If not, end the call by saying: "Since everything is in order, I will expect to receive your payment by (date)."

Thanks to the reminder call system, a customer's reason for not paying promptly is usually nipped in the bud—before it's had a chance to grow into a full-fledged accounts receivable headache.

HOW THE "RIGHT" COLLECTION LETTERS CAN SPEED UP PAYMENTS

Keeping a relaxed, cordial tone in an early collection letter—while you apply and keep up the "pay now" pressure—can be easier to talk about than to do.

Here are three letters that handle the problem well. The first letter takes a particularly offbeat approach.

```
Dear Customer:

It was once said by a letter-writing expert that
a good collection letter should be:
1. Friendly
2. Brief

In line with this, we want to remind you, in a
friendly way, that the amount now due on your
account with us is: $_____.

Sincerely,

P.S. The expert forgot to add that a collection
message is no good unless it gets results. We
hope you'll prove that our "brief and friendly"
letter works—by sending us your check today.
```

Here's a letter that gives the customer a clear reason to see the indebtedness from your point of view.

Dear Customer:

Have you ever stopped to think that when you pay a supplier promptly, you help the supplier stay in better shape to serve you in the future?

Only a firm that is kept "well-oiled" with cash to meet current operating expenses can continue to provide the products or services that you need.

To put it another way: We depend on you to keep the fast flow of shipments moving. Your payment for the amount below will be added lubrication. So please let us have your check for $_____ today.

Sincerely,

Our third letter draws on an elementary sports concept to find a spot of common ground with the customer.

Dear Customer:

The ball is in your court again.

You put the ball in our court when you sent us your order of last May 29. At that time, you asked for fast shipment and we shipped the items out within 24 hours. That put the ball back in your court.

Now it's time—more than time—for you to do your part. Our records show that your bill is 30 days overdue.

The enclosed duplicate invoice shows the amount that you owe us. Why not send us your check for this amount today? That way, you can send the ball back over to us for good.

Sincerely,

Appeal to the customer's reputation. If you can get a business to sit up and take notice of your collection efforts, you're that much closer to getting paid. One good attention-getter is the letter that points out what a business stands to lose in future sales if it jeopardizes its credit rating by paying its bills too slowly—or not at all. Here are two sample letters you can adapt to your own situation:

```
Dear Customer:


I'm still waiting for your check of $573.40
that's been overdue since June 1.

Given your company's generally fine payment
record, it would be a shame to jeopardize your
reputation over this delinquency.

Sincerely,
```

```
Dear Customer:


Your bill of $437.00 has been overdue since
March 15. We have received neither a check nor
an explanation for the delay.

I'm sure you understand the need for maintaining
good credit. However, should we be asked to
furnish a credit reference on your business, I
would have no choice but to disclose the
difficulty you have had in paying your bills
with us.

By sending a check for the amount due
immediately, you will be able to protect your
good credit standing within the business
community.

Sincerely,
```

HOW TO LOCATE AND COLLECT FROM MISSING DEBTORS

Locating and collecting from customers who have "skipped town" can be easier when you know how and where to look. When one of your credit accounts turns up "missing," follow these steps for locating and collecting from the skipped account:

• **Check with the current employer.** If allowed, call the debtor at work. If he or she is there and you make contact, your search is over.

• **Check with the previous employer.** Even though the skip has probably not returned to an earlier job, a previous employer may have gotten a request for a reference from the place where the debtor is now working.

• **Check bank references.** Contact the debtor's bank and ask what current address it has for the individual. If the bank is reluctant to give you the information, ask your own bank to make the inquiry.

• **Investigate references.** Be sure to check every single reference you have on the debtor. Conduct your inquiries here the same way you'd handle a routine credit check.

• **Check with relatives and friends.** These people may be willing to give you a current address for the skip. If so, a registered letter, with a return receipt requested, can verify the address for you. Few people can resist accepting such a letter, particularly if it's in a plain envelope and addressed by hand.

• **Avoid legal pitfalls.** In trying to locate a missing consumer debtor, make sure you're not in violation of the Fair Debt Collection Practices Act. This law restricts the methods you can use in trying to find out where debtors live or work. Among the principal practices the law prohibits are the following:

– Excessive persistence in digging up location information. Anyone being asked for information on a debtor's whereabouts can be called only once, unless he or she asks to be called back.

– Calling a debtor at home earlier than 8:00 a.m. or later than 9:00 p.m. local time, unless the debtor has consented or a court has authorized it.

– Calling a debtor at work if you know or should know that the employer has a rule prohibiting such calls.

– Any communication that could be considered "harassment" or "intimidation," or repeated telephone calls about the same debt.

Finally, if the debtor has an attorney—and you know who the attorney is—you must first ask the attorney to help you locate the debtor. If the attorney doesn't answer your request in a reasonable period of time, then you may pursue other sources.

MAKE SURE YOU GET YOUR MONEY'S WORTH FROM A COLLECTION AGENCY

With payments from customers getting harder to come by these days, more companies are turning to outside agencies to help them collect from long overdue accounts.

The following information can be used as a guide in choosing a collection agency that will pull in the most dollars for your company—at the least cost.

Question: When should a bad debt be placed with a collection agency?

Answer: Actually, the best time to employ an agency's collection services is whenever you feel you've exhausted all reasonable measures. Your "breaking point" will probably be different with each account. Ninety days has traditionally been considered the point at which further collection efforts on the part of the credit department become ineffective.

But in trying to decide when to make your move, keep in mind that time is money. The longer you wait, the more difficult it generally becomes for anyone to collect from that customer.

As time goes by, it becomes more likely that Mr. Jones has become a skip, or that ABC Company has gone under. If that's the case, it may take the agency longer—and cost your company more—to collect from that customer—if, in fact, the agency can manage to collect from the debtor at all.

Turn over credit accounts to a collection agency while the "trail is still warm." Don't wait until the customer has become a memory. For instance, if you're able to give the agency up-to-date information on the customer's whereabouts, you stand a much better chance of having your company's investment pay off.

Question: Does that mean I should only place accounts that appear to have a reasonable chance of paying?

Answer: No. Even if the situation looks hopeless to you, the agency may be able to bring enough pressure to bear upon the debtor, particularly a consumer credit customer, to shake out payment.

Even if the agency gets nothing out of a deadbeat, its collection efforts can provide the proof you need to confirm the account's bad debt status—a requirement if you are to take a tax writeoff.

Question: How are collection agency fees determined?

Answer: There are several ways collection agencies charge for their services. Most agencies work on a contingency basis. You pay an agreed-upon percentage of the amount received if a collection is made. In any case, make sure you settle this matter first before placing any accounts.

Contingency fees can vary, from 25% to 50% of the recovered amount. The lowest rate is not always the most profitable one, however. After all, the amount you realize from an agency's collection efforts depends not only on the fee but also on the agency's *recovery rate.*

This distinction is important because many times the collection agency with the lowest contingency fee is also the one that will make the least effort on your behalf, particularly if the account calls for a great deal of preliminary investigation.

For example, let's say ABC Company owes you $4,000. Collection Agency A offers to take the account on a 25% contingency basis. But it recovers only 25% of the bill, or $1,000, so your share comes to $750.

Collection Agency B, on the other hand, charges a 50% contingency fee, but has a 50% recovery rate. On the same $4,000 debt, it collects half. Your share, therefore, comes to $1,000, or $250 more than what Agency A recovered for you, even though you're paying a higher contingency fee.

Ask to see the collection agency's recovery records before you agree to use it. See what the agency's success rate is with the type and age of accounts you'll be turning over to it.

You'll have a better idea of how many dollars you can reasonably expect to be returned to you. That is the only real test of an agency's effectiveness.

Other types of collection fees

While a contingency fee is the most common type of charge for collection services, some agencies work on a *retainer* basis. Under this plan you usually pay a monthly fee.

There are two advantages with this setup. You can easily budget your collection expenses because you already know what your costs will be each month. Also, you receive the full amount, not a percentage, of whatever the agency collects from an account.

A third type of charge involves paying a separate fee for each service rendered. In other words, you pay a set price for skip-tracing, collection letters and so on, according to a written schedule of fees.

Whether you agree to a contingency fee, a monthly retainer or some other form of payment, be sure that the agency offers you this preliminary collection service. Most collection agencies provide their clients with what's known as a "free demand" service. This involves a letter, sent on the agency's letterhead, advising the debtor that the agency will begin collection activity unless a check for the amount due is received by a certain date.

If the customer pays by the date in question, you pay nothing for this service.

Question: What should we do if, after the bad debt is placed with the collection agency, the customer pays us instead of the agency?

Answer: Forward the payment to the agency. The agency will then make remittance to you. This helps the agency keep its books in order, and ensures that it doesn't continue collection efforts—that you may have to pay for—on an account that's already paid.

If the agency has initiated a lawsuit on your behalf, as is permitted in certain states, and you receive partial payment of the overdue amount, there is action you must take. Send the undeposited check to the agency at once. This allows the agency to continue court action for the remainder of the amount due.

When the agency sends you remittance, it should also include a statement that lists: (a) the names of delinquents from whom it has collected; (b) the date of collection; (c) the amount collected; and (d) the balance still due.

In addition, the agency should provide you with updated progress reports at your request.

Question: How can I investigate a collection agency's background and reputation?

Answer: Have the agency provide a financial statement as well as bank and trade references. If a license is required in your state, make sure that the agency has one, and that it remains in good standing.

Check the agency's credentials thoroughly. If you're interested in a commercial agency, look for one that holds a Certificate of Compliance from the Commercial Law League of America. If you're choosing a consumer agency, be sure it is a member of the American Collection Association or the American Commercial Collector's Association.

USING A TRACKING FORM TO STAY ON TOP OF THE COLLECTION AGENCY'S RESULTS

When you assign delinquent credit accounts to a collection agency, you're in effect hiring a new employee. And like a new hire whose work you review from time to time, it pays to keep an eye on how well your collection agency is doing.

Figure 5.4 is a chart you can use as is, or adapt to your particular needs. It lets you see—in black and white—your agency's effectiveness as a collector. For each time period listed, either monthly or yearly, mark down the amount of overdue payments you placed with the agency for collection. Then use the appropriate box to indicate when during the year these amounts were collected.

Your monthly and yearly totals will serve as a graphic illustration of just how quick and thorough your agency is in collecting. If you use more than one agency, the chart can help you compare results to see which one is providing you with the most cost-effective service.

Figure 5.4
ANNUAL EVALUATION OF COLLECTION AGENCY

Agency Name_____Address_____

L I N E			AMOUNTS PLACED THROUGH PERIOD ENDED _____ 19__														
			Prior Years	Last Year	Jan	Feb	Mar	Apr	May	Jun	Jul	Aug	Sep	Oct	Nov	Dec	Total
		PLACED															
	Collected by Month During Current Year	January															
		February															
		March															
		April															
		May															
		June															
		July															
		August															
		September															
		October															
		November															
		December															
		TOTAL															
		Balance Outstanding															

SECTION 2

How to Improve Employee Productivity and Lower Your Benefits and Compensation Costs

In today's competitive business climate, you need a team of highly skilled and dedicated employees behind you. All your efforts at building a winning business won't pay off if your people aren't willing to give 110%.

This section of *The Prentice Hall Small Business Survival Guide* covers the various types of management skills and strategies you'll need to ensure the growth of your business—growth not just in sales volume or revenues, but in *profits*. The chapters in this section provide the following:

- A detailed look at the techniques successful business owners use for finding, hiring and retaining winning employees.
- Tips on motivating your employees and executives to do better work at lower cost—even when you can't boost their salaries.

It's becoming more and more expensive to get the most out of those employees whose primary incentive is the paycheck. Good working relationships and a pleasant environment may not be enough to motivate employees who feel they're being paid less than they can get elsewhere.

With operational expenses, benefit costs and employment taxes rising every year, many small business owners can't sacrifice vital capital to cover meaningful wage increases. The answer for many is a shift in emphasis from traditional pay raises to packages that can include bonuses, incentive pay plans, "pay-for-knowledge" pay systems, benefits, tax savings, and employee perks.

CHAPTER SIX

HOW TO RECRUIT AND HIRE A QUALITY WORKFORCE

There is no one beginning point to building a quality workforce—just as there is no ending point. Part of building a top-notch workforce is making sure you hire the right people. But it certainly doesn't end there. Smart business owners know that training and motivating new workers so they perform at maximum efficiency is equally important as the hiring process.

And, of course, you can't forget about your current staff. A key part of building a quality workforce is improving and refining the skills of your current workers. Continuous training, promoting and motivating will result in your current employees giving you their best.

Finally, successful small business owners are looking in new directions to find workers—part-timers, seniors and "non-employees" such as independent contractors and leased employees. This "alternative" workforce offers businesses a way to get high quality producers at reduced costs.

SUCCESSFUL RECRUITING—KNOWING HOW AND WHERE TO LOOK

There are as many ways to find and recruit employees as there are available jobs. The key is to know what options are available and how each works so you can decide what's the best way to set up your recruitment drive. Let's take a closer look.

NINE TIPS FOR WRITING A HELP-WANTED AD

It used to be that you could just advertise your job requirements and wait for the résumés to pour in, says a senior account manager with a Massachusetts public relations and advertising firm. In today's tight job market, with so many people applying for each available job, you want to be sure to attract the best candidates. Your ad copy should sell your job.

Here are nine tips on how to make your help-wanted ads stand out, and get more mileage out of your advertising dollar:

1. **Make your ads attractive.** The classified section is often cluttered with similar-looking ads. So it's important to make your ad different. You have to try to attract the people who don't normally stop and read the ads, says the president of a Chicago outplacement consulting firm. The more visually attractive your ad is, the more likely you are to get the response you want, he adds.

2. **Don't sell your company short.** The longer the ad the better, he says. Longer ads give you more room to spell out your company's specific needs. Many employers just look at other companies' ads and copy them. As a result, you often see the same language over and over again. He suggests that you avoid generalities and spell out exactly what you want. A more detailed ad also helps screen out unqualified prospects.

   Watch biased language. Be extra careful in writing your ads to avoid using words or phrases that could be viewed as discriminatory on the basis of race, sex, age, national origin (for example: "Gal Friday," "recent graduate," and so on).

3. **Talk to the recruit.** Instead of using the traditional, bland classified ad language, try making your ad conversational and personal. Write the ad as if you're talking to the recruit. Example: Use the word "you."

4. **Highlight unique job features.** Another way to make your ad stand out is to spell out what makes your company or the job unique. If you offer something your competitors don't or can't, such as tuition reimbursement, extra vacation, a flexible workweek, travel opportunities or aerobics classes for employees, publicize it. Tell people what a great place your company is to work. Even if people aren't looking for a position now, they may remember your company when they are.

   Be careful not to oversell the job. On the other hand, make sure your ad isn't misleading. Sometimes employers are so eager to recruit people they stretch the truth, he says. This can turn people off and tarnish the company's image in the long run.

5. **Grab them with the headline:** With most readers, if you can't hook them right away, you've lost them altogether. Therefore, the headline is often the most important part of the ad. If you can get readers to notice your headline, they'll often read the whole ad.

   Make your headlines catchy and provocative. Instead of using just the job title—for example, "Salesperson Wanted,"—try something different, such as *"Triple Your Income."* For one client, Star Data Communications, the ad agency came up with the slogan: "Hitch your wagon to a Star."

6. **Omit salary figures.** Although listing a salary range can help weed out inappropriate prospects, the agency usually steers clients away from using it. "It limits you." While you might be willing to pay more than the advertised range for a person with the ideal qualifications, that person may not answer your ad if the salary quoted is lower than they're willing to take.

7. **Choose the right media for your audience**. Deciding where to advertise usually depends on the job. A large metro classified rate can be high, but you get circulation and results. So if it's a high-paying or specialized position, you may want to consider advertising in a large daily newspaper or national publication. If it's a lower-paying job, on the other hand, your local paper will probably bring in plenty of qualified applicants.

   And don't rely just on newspapers. You should try other outlets, such as trade journals that candidates you're looking for might read.

8. **Try the display route.** Because the classified section can be cluttered and crowded, you may want to try running a display ad. Display ads, while more expensive, tend to attract more attention and show job seekers that you're serious about the position.

9. **Make it easy to respond.** Once you've decided where to advertise, make sure the ad copy spells out clearly where and how prospects can reply. Make it as easy as possible for them to get in touch with the person doing the hiring. Use a toll-free number or let recruits leave a spoken résumé on an answering machine.

You shouldn't throw résumés away as soon as you've filled your immediate opening. Instead, keep them for three to five years. One agency recently hired someone it first interviewed three years ago.

HOW YOUR OWN EMPLOYEES CAN HELP YOUR RECRUITING EFFORTS

The best source for finding new talent may be right under your nose—your *current employees*. Employee referrals are an increasingly popular recruitment tool. A survey conducted by *Costello, Erdlen & Co.* (Wellesley, Massachusetts) found that referrals provided 27.8% of all new hires for experienced personnel. And they've been particularly effective in drawing higher-level executives and managers with salaries above $50,000.

Establish a company "bounty system" to reward successful recruiting efforts by your employees. The bounty encourages your employees to refer friends and relatives for your job openings. The amount of the award can vary with job type and salary.

For example, pay more for hard-to-fill positions (such as engineering or chemical specialists) and less for easy-to-fill and part-time placements. The reward may be paid to the employee recruiter immediately upon the candidate's hiring or after the recruit has worked for a probationary period.

Inform employees of the recruitment rewards by:

- Designing an eye-catching notice. One company designed an effective, old-fashioned *WANTED* poster that detailed the job openings and the recruitment bonus for each position.

- Posting notices, passing memos and using company publications to keep your employees aware of job openings.

- Using employee referral cards. These allow the employee recruiter to write down the job candidate's name, address, telephone number and the applicable job opening on a card and submit them to you.

Note that recruitment bonuses are considered wages and are subject to income and Social Security taxes. As a result, an employee's joy may turn to disappointment when he or she gets the bonus check and sees that Uncle Sam has taken his share. Consider increasing the bonus to make up for the tax bite. Employees will have more incentive to continue referring candidates if they know the company will be picking up the tax bill.

Let's take a look at some companies that have instituted successful bounty programs:

- Pitney Bowes (Stamford, Conn.) rewards its employees with a $1,000 no-strings-attached check when they refer a successful candidate for a professional, exempt-level position. The bounty is processed on the first day of the new hire's employment. And the company pays the tax on the bounty reward. An added bonus: Every employee who has referred a successful job candidate has a chance of winning a one-week travel package for two.

- Security Pacific Bank of Los Angeles has a "Superscout" bonus program. Employees who refer a successful applicant receive anywhere from $25–$500, depending on the new hire's job level. The bonus is given as soon as the applicant accepts the job.

- One East Coast company uses another approach: It pays a bonus after the new employee completes the company's three-month probation period. The amount of the reward is $300 for a full-time employee and $200 for a part-time employee.

Other companies offer employees merchandise or time off, rather than cash, as the bounty. These programs have also proven successful.

For example, Grumman Aerospace Corp. (Bethpage, New York) offers two bonus vacation days in recognition of successful applicant referrals. Job candidates must have three years' experience, be recruited for one of five critical skill areas and remain with Grumman for at least six months. Only full-time employees are eligible for the bonus vacation days.

While recruitment bonuses can be highly effective, they can pose problems in certain situations. For example, if your company has a policy that prohibits the hiring of employees' spouses or other relatives, make it clear that this rule applies to your recruitment bounty program. This way employees won't expect rewards for recruiting disqualified candidates—and you won't waste time interviewing them.

One danger of overreliance on employee referrals is that they may perpetuate past discriminatory hiring practices. For example, under federal job bias law, your recruitment methods may have to supply a pool of minority and women candidates that reflects these groups' representation in your local labor market. If your current workforce is made up predominantly of white males, chances are your employees will refer mostly white males. The point is that recruitment bonuses should be just *one* of the methods you use to find qualified applicants—not the only method.

HOW TO RECRUIT FROM WITHIN

Promoting employees already on the payroll to vacant positions is a good way to hold on to top-flight talent.

One way to do this is to let your people know when jobs open up. Use a job posting system to list all current openings in your company for which employees may apply.

Pick a heavily traveled area—in the employee lunchroom or near a time clock, for example—to place a bulletin board on which notices of job openings can be posted. The notice should include such information as title, job grade, qualifications, salary, department and name of person the applicant can contact to arrange an interview.

Along with notices of job vacancies, post your equal employment opportunity policy. Also include forms employees can use to apply for the posted jobs (see Figure 6.1).

Next, review each applicant's employment record with the supervisor of the department that posted the opening. Interviews may be appropriate. Once a decision is made, contact each applicant and explain the reasons for acceptance or rejection. Be sure to encourage rejected candidates to apply for other posted openings.

Change job notices every two weeks or so to encourage employees to check the board for the latest listings.

A job posting system can help your company:

- Fill vacancies with people who are already familiar with the way your company operates, thereby cutting down on training time and costs.

- Increase productivity and quality of work through the motivational value of a company-sponsored advancement program.

- Encourage employees to seek additional training by showing them the skills they need to acquire for higher-level jobs.

- Reduce turnover rates through internal promotion.

Figure 6.1

APPLICATION FOR POSTED JOB
Date _____

Name_____   Dept._____

Position_____   Supervisor_____

Years with Co._____   Years on Present Job_____

I hereby make application for the posted position of: _____

Reasons for wishing to transfer:_____

Qualifications for the position available:_____

I may be contacted at: (telephone number or extension)_____
Signed:_____

HOW TO GET TOP RESULTS IN CHOOSING AN EMPLOYMENT AGENCY

Another way to attract top candidates to fill a job vacancy is to work in partnership with a reputable employment agency. Here are some important steps you should follow when choosing an agency that you can work with effectively:

• **Visit the agency.** True, you can certainly get some helpful leads to good recruiters through general reputation, printed marketing brochures, newspaper advertisements, and the like. But these are only preliminary steps.

To be sure that you know what you're getting, you should contact the employment agency and arrange to make a personal visit to its offices. A top-flight service will welcome this.

Put yourself in the shoes of a potential job candidate entering that office. Does it strike you as being professionally and efficiently run? Are the employees who will greet the candidate courteous and professional in their demeanor?

In the case of the specialized recruiting service, are the people employed there knowledgeable about their field of specialization? Can they properly evaluate a job applicant's credentials and background in, let's say, a highly technical field? In short, are they as professional and as qualified as the specialists who will be coming to them and seeking new employment? If not, you'd better seek out another personnel recruiting service to fill your needs.

During this visit you should ask specific questions that will give you a good idea whether this particular agency is right for you.

Have the answers you're looking for clearly in your mind. If the agency doesn't respond in a manner you feel is appropriate, cut off the discussion. The questions:

- "How long have you been in business?"

- "What is your fee? Will you be charging us for your expenses? If so, how large do you anticipate they will be?"

- "What guarantees will you provide us with?"

- "We've been considering other personnel recruiting services. What strength does your organization possess that would be particularly helpful to us, and prompt us to choose you over the others?"

- "How many jobs of this type has your company filled?"

- "How long does it generally take you to fill a position such as this one, and how long do you anticipate it will take to fill this specific job?"

- "Are you able to seek out job candidates nationally? How many offices do you have, and what is their geographic scope?"

- "What is the background of the founders of your organization? What individual within your organization will be assigned to our account, and what are this person's credentials?"

- "How will you go about attracting candidates for this job?"

• **Ask to see a client list.** You should take into account the size of the clients and the agency's industry concentrations. Examine the firm's success record in matching candidates with companies, with an eye to how well attuned the agency is to intangibles such as corporate culture and work climate. Also, try to learn something about the agency's ethical standards.

Ethical recruiters won't raid client companies in search of job applicants for your available positions. After all, you wouldn't want them raiding your best employees for their other clients.

• **Get the names and numbers of several references**. Speak to recent clients to get their opinions about the agency's strengths and weaknesses. Find out how long they have used the agency. Ask the clients if they were satisfied with the caliber of the job candidates the agency sent them. Did the candidates have the proper qualifications or were they just bodies filling a quota?

- **Learn how assignments are handled.** You have a right to know who will be handling your company's account—a staff member, a junior- or senior-level recruiter, or a partner.

You also should ask about that person's background and success rate, how long he or she has been with the agency, and whether that individual has expertise in your particular line of business.

Keep peppering the agency with questions until you're satisfied it can do the job for you. The answers to these three questions could make your decision easier:

- Will you have an opportunity to review the résumés and interview notes—to see whether the recruiter's focus is too narrow, or whether it's emphasizing the wrong things?

- At what stage will *you* be asked to begin interviewing candidates? This is a very important point, and goes to the heart of the recruiter's special services to you.

- What is the service's philosophy concerning the number of candidates submitted to you for evaluation?

Some services will keep whittling down the field, until there are only one or two candidates left for submission to you. Others will initially accept a broader field. But either way, you'll want to find out what the service customarily does, and what you can expect.

What to do after you make your decision

Once you've made a decision to work with a particular agency, you should take these steps to protect your company:

- Confirm all details in writing. Either amend the standard agreement to suit your needs or provide your own agreement identifying the search, your expectations, rules for the search, the fee schedule and the length of guarantee.

- Agree in advance on who will be conducting the recruiting, screening, interviewing and reference checks, and on whether all candidates must be prequalified, or if on-the-job training is acceptable.

- Set the ground rules for updates on how the search is going— daily, weekly or biweekly reports.

- Insist that the agency not recruit from its other clients for your openings, and get assurances that the agency won't approach your employees for other clients' positions.

Even when you've decided on an agency, there are still some traps to avoid. Here are keys points to remember:

- Don't give too much work to an agency until you've tested it on a typical assignment. Quantity discounts should raise a flag of caution. When a recruiter has two searches going—one full fee and one discounted—guess which one gets top priority.

- Don't give search firms your files or the names of candidates *you've* found elsewhere. If you do, you're giving the recruiter an opening to disqualify a candidate you could have hired without the consultant's assistance or fee.

- Don't let the agency interview your other candidates as a service to you. People are never objective when their fees are involved. Not surprisingly, search firms invariably don't recommend candidates other than their own.

- Don't rely exclusively on the search firm's reference checking of its own candidates. Do some checking of your own if you are considering extending a job offer.

- Don't keep unsolicited résumés sent by recruiters you did not hire. Your use of such résumés could lead to fee disputes or equal employment opportunity problems. Immediately return unsolicited résumés with a written notice stating that this practice is unwelcome and must be discontinued.

- Agree on what expenses you'll pay for, how they should be documented, and the manner of reimbursement.

USING STATE EMPLOYMENT OFFICES—ANOTHER SOURCE

Local state employment offices are coordinated through state administration and through the United States Employment Service. They operate in all larger cities and in all counties. Here are some of the advantages of working with the government agencies:

- They have a large pool of job seekers, since they're associated with the unemployment insurance offices.

- They can refer applicants from other regions, since they're part of a nationwide system.

- They charge no fees.

The United States Employment Service operates specialized professional placement services in major cities throughout the country, where companies can recruit experienced technical, professional, and other highly trained personnel. Inventories of professional openings are maintained by a number of local and regional state employment offices.

State employment office staffers will want a complete job description and detailed information on hours of work, minimum experience, rate of pay, education and training, and working conditions. In addition, they'll want to know something about your company; for example, what employee benefits you offer, whether you're unionized, and whether you're working on government contracts.

HOW TO MAKE THE BEST HIRING DECISIONS

Some business owners make good hiring decisions almost intuitively. They can spot—as if by magic—dedicated, creative people who can make significant contributions with a minimum of supervision and hassle.

However, for most business owners, the hiring process is a hit-or-miss affair. And mistakes are costly. When you hire poor performers who turn out to be totally unqualified for the job, or even marginal employees who require more supervision and effort than they're worth, you pay the price in wasted time—and sometimes in lost business.

You can avoid many job hiring mistakes if you know how to pick up on the clues applicants drop in résumés and in the hiring interview. You also can get important information on job candidates by careful reference checking. And you need to carefully train and then closely monitor new employees during their first few months on the job to make sure they're living up to your expectations.

HOW TO READ A RÉSUMÉ: CHECK THESE THREE POINTS

Here's how experienced business people look at the three traditional areas of a résumé—education, experience and career objectives—to make these résumés reveal more than the applicant had intended.

1. Educational history. The business people we spoke to feel that a college degree in and of itself doesn't mean much. If the position requires that the applicant have a degree, they look for a good performance at a demanding college. They also look for a listing of major areas of study and how these areas relate to job requirements.

Supplemental education—such as attendance at conferences or special training programs—is a plus. But one business person offers this advice:

"I look for some rhyme or reason behind the education the applicant has taken. Do courses, for instance, follow a progression that shows interest in the area I have a job opening for? Or, does it look like the applicant has just been browsing; especially, has he done it on a former employer's educational expense reimbursement plan?"

2. Work experience. Watch for unexplained gaps and shifts in position that don't reflect substantial advancement. The manager of a California firm says, "I give high marks to a résumé that describes in clear, simple language, the applicant's past job duties."

He prefers to read "supervised four press operations in producing radial tires" to "had responsibility for implementation of management decisions/objectives in production area."

"The applicant has thought far enough to realize that what I—or anyone—will need are hard, precise facts on which to base a hiring decision."

A Minnesota business owner suggests that the facts in a résumé may not be as crucial as its presentation.

Look at the frills, too. "The grammar, punctuation, spelling—even the typing and layout—of a résumé say something about its author. So does its conciseness, or, at the other end of the scale, its comprehensiveness."

"If the job is such that a missed detail could be disproportionately costly, I don't want someone who paints in broad strokes," says the Minnesota business woman.

"On the other hand," she says, "if the job requires communicating with employees, customers or what have you, I'll interview someone who submits a 'bare bones' résumé. The applicant may be relying on his conversational skills during the interview to carry the day—and that's the skill I'm interested in."

3. Career objectives. Most business people look for statements of career goals that are realistic and relevant to the job that's open. But a Michigan manager offers this caution:

"In my experience, applicants' stated career goals are often *too much* on target. Everyone's goals are flexible enough to include *exactly the type of position* they're seeking. So, though I want the company's goals and an employee's to be compatible, I don't look for an exact match."

Look for long-range goals that seem over-ambitious for the size of your company. Provided the objective seems realistic for the individual, call the applicant in and try to sell him or her on the benefits of working for his firm.

Other areas to check

• **Look for profit-mindedness.** See if you can sense from the job description whether the candidate appreciates the fact that companies are in business to make money. "One of the things to look for," one owner says, "is how many times in the résumé a candidate mentions efficiency measures he or she had suggested that helped reduce company costs or streamlined office procedures."

• **Beware of qualifiers.** Many résumés are filled with phrases like, "knowledge of...," "assisted with...," "had exposure to...," Don't confuse these qualifying descriptions with *hands-on* experience.

• **Don't excuse sour grapes.** If you believe that the candidate is bitter about past jobs, don't grant the prospect an interview.

• **Be wary of the functional résumé.** A functional résumé is organized around descriptions of job skills and qualifications. Dates and places of employment may be difficult to determine. The candidate who writes such a résumé could well be fudging his qualifications.

Keep in mind that the functional résumé is an attractive format for candidates who have been excessive job-jumpers, or who may have other reasons for not revealing dates.

• **Don't gloss over the cover letter.** A good cover letter takes into account the fact that you will probably be very busy, have many similar letters to read, and need facts quickly. It should contain the applicant's name, address, and phone number distinctly set apart from the text. Plus, it should contain a reference to the specific ad being answered. If the actual ad is stapled to the letter, that's a big plus. It reveals that the person wants you to have the facts at your fingertips without having to guess what the letter is about.

Look for other details in the letter. For example, is the applicant overselling himself or herself? Is the information presented in an intelligent and easy-to-follow format?

HOW TO HANDLE UNSOLICITED RÉSUMÉS

Many companies receive a constant flow of unsolicited résumés and job inquiries, even when there are no openings and they're not hiring.

Aside from questions of time and storage that résumés pose, there's another problem with unsolicited résumés. There is a legal consideration. If you accept such résumés, the Equal Employment Opportunity Commission's (EEOC) recordkeeping rules require you to retain records on these "applicants" for a certain period of time. And you must include these individuals in your "applicant pool" for the purpose of job bias analyses.

Such considerations have led some companies to adopt a policy of not accepting unsolicited résumés—*period*. Other businesses have found unsolicited inquiries to be a valuable source of job applicants. Here's how these companies handle such inquiries—without wasting a lot of time and effort:

• **Acknowledge each letter.** Courteous responses to unsolicited inquiries create a positive image of your company. Explain briefly whether or not positions are currently available and whether the company routinely needs people with the applicant's qualifications. Be sure to thank the person for his or her interest in your company.

• **Follow up.** If your company keeps a follow-up file of résumés, inform the applicant that you'll retain his or her résumé and for how long. If not, and no jobs are available, suggest that the applicant resubmit the résumé at a future date.

One northern New Jersey corporation has successfully followed this approach. The company found that because of its desirable location and long presence in the community, local residents were always seeking employment. Rather than lose a valuable source of prospective job candidates, the company uses a follow-up file. It keeps applications on file for six months.

Of course, if an unsolicited résumé turns up an individual whose skills or abilities you need right away, have that person complete your formal application form and schedule an interview.

MAKE "OLD" RÉSUMÉS WORK FOR YOU

Do some comparison shopping before you sit down with an applicant.

Pull a few résumés of some of your successful employees to see how the applicant's experience stacks up. You'll have a clearer idea of what qualifications point to success in that particular job.

A St. Louis consumer electronics company struck pay dirt when it "profiled" its successful salespeople over the previous eight years. The company's owner explains:

"Some of our sales reps seemed to click from their first day on the job. But I had no idea why, until I looked over the résumés and job applications of these stars. The common 'success trait' practically jumped off the page. Education, experience, and knowledge of electronics differed, but our best sellers had all sold some kind of consumer product before."

The exec made consumer sales experience a requirement for future hires. And he attributes a good part of his company's sales gains in the past three years to this move.

Get a second opinion. Check with the supervisors for whom the successful job candidates will be working to see what their ideas are. They'll have a different perspective to add.

Send the applicant's résumé to a supervisor and ask if he or she would hire this person. And find out the reason the supervisor would or wouldn't hire the prospect. At the same time, don't indicate any preference or dissatisfaction. If you do, the supervisor will most likely just parrot your opinion.

HOW TO CONDUCT A WINNING JOB INTERVIEW

Make sure you start out on the right foot when you conduct a job interview with a prospective employee. By setting up the right mood and climate for the interview, you'll be better prepared to judge that person's future on-the-job performance. Here's how to set the right tone:

• **Go out to greet the person.** If you step out of your office to escort the candidate back to your office for the interview, you signal an unspoken concern and interest. The candidate is less likely to feel as though he or she is being summoned to your office for a judgment-type interview. At the greeting stage, you also may be able to get a pretty good idea of the applicant's personality.

Observe the applicant as he or she first meets you. For example:

• Is eye contact made?

• Does the applicant seem confident?

• Does he or she strike you as someone who would fit into your company without radical change on anyone's part? If so, chances are, you've already got a strong prospect.

• **Use small talk wisely.** Small talk that's relevant to the person being interviewed can contribute to a relaxed interview climate. For example, "I notice you grew up in the Midwest—so did I," is relevant.

• **Put the applicant at ease.** The setting in your office should be welcoming and informal. Avoid sitting behind your desk during the interview. Find two comfortable chairs and sit opposite, but near, the candidate. If your office is small, try to find an unused office or meeting room that will provide a more relaxed setting.

Interviewers who remain behind their desks establish a distance between themselves and the candidate. By sitting closer, the candidate feels more like an equal and is thus more likely to be responsive and at ease.

If you are comfortable working in your shirtsleeves, you might even hang up your jacket and offer to do the same for the candidate.

Treat the person being interviewed like a guest in your home, not like a salesperson or unwelcome visitor. This adds to the mood you're trying to establish.

How to probe

Once you've put the applicant at ease, you can try to obtain the information you must have to make a proper decision. The applicant's answers to the following questions should give you or the interviewer a good idea about the individual's work experience.

• What were the specific duties and responsibilities you performed in each of your previous jobs?
• What are the specific duties and responsibilities you now perform in your present job?
• What kind of career progression have you made?
• What did you most like about your previous jobs?
• What do you most like about your present job?
• What did you least like about your previous jobs?
• What do you least like about your present job?
• Why are you thinking of leaving your present job?
• What caused you to leave each of your previous jobs?
• Which of your previous jobs did you like best?

Among the questions that can be asked about the applicant's educational background are the following:

• Why did you select your college major (if appropriate)?
• What courses did you most enjoy in school?
• What courses did you least enjoy in school?
• What courses did you most excel in academically?
• What courses did you least excel in academically?

How to keep the interview moving

Now that the opening is out of the way, you should get the applicant to talk about his or her career. This not only gets the applicant to open up, but gives you a good idea of what the prospect considers important. Your initial question should be something like "Tell me about your job at the ABC Company." Give the applicant time to discuss this question. Don't interrupt. Once the prospect opens up, it will pave the way for you to ask further revealing questions like:

- Level and complexity of work. ("What did you find most challenging?")
- What are your strengths?
- What are your weaknesses?
- What decisions did you make? Who had to approve of them?
- What attracted you to that kind of job? What made you change?
- How did the job please you? Displease you? What do you consider an ideal position?

How to tailor an interview

With the information you have picked, you should now be ready to tailor the interview to the job. For example, if responsibility for supervising employees is one of the main characteristics of the position, you should zero in on how the applicant handled that aspect of the job in the past.

Prepare a series of questions that will make the prospect describe his or her techniques for handling responsibility. This isn't difficult for a skilled interviewer to do. A series of questions along these lines should give you a clearer picture of the applicant's approach to responsibility:

- When forced to discipline an employee how did you handle it? What were the results?
- Did you ever have to deal with a discrimination problem? Could you describe the circumstances? How was it handled? What were the results?
- If you had an employee who wasn't performing up to par, how would you get that individual to turn things around?
- What measures would you use—or did you use—to get more and better work from the staff?

- How do you encourage your employees to take on added responsibility?
- How do you determine which questions to ask when you conduct an employee interview?

You should now have a good idea of how this person deals with responsibility.

REFERENCE CHECKING—HOW TO OVERCOME RESISTANCE FROM RELUCTANT INFORMATION-GIVERS

"To put it bluntly," says an authority on reference checking, "it's important to get references to make quality hiring choices. Yet some employers are reluctant to give you the information you need."

No matter how adamant the person is about not giving out information regarding a former employee—other than name, position and how long employed—you stand a good chance of getting the information you need if you begin any conversation dealing with references with these *magic words*:

"Anything you tell me will be kept confidential." That usually loosens the tongue. There are times, of course, that even that declaration doesn't work. But you don't have to give up. Try a different approach—one that appeals to the former employer's sense of fair play. An administrative assistant for a Pennsylvania engineering firm advises this action after hearing that it's company policy not to release information. You could say:

"I respect your company's policy, and usually I don't press any further. I am, however, in a spot. If I can't get any information about (name) it will look quite bad for him. Under those circumstances couldn't you please give me some facts about the applicant?"

More often than not, the former employer comes through with an evaluation. "To show my appreciation," says the assistant, "I tell the former employer that if I can ever be a help to please call."

Once you get the go-ahead, restate that the information will be kept confidential and then approximate how long the interview will take. You can expedite the interview by having the questions you need to ask right in front of you.

Twenty questions you should ask

The Administrative Management Society of Willow Grove, Pennsylvania, in its guide *"How to Select and Retain Valuable Employees,"* suggests you should ask the following questions:*

1. How long was this individual employed by your organization?
2. What was the individual's job title?
3. What was the nature of the job duties performed?
4. What was the beginning salary? Final salary?
5. How many days was this individual absent during the last 12 months?
6. Did this individual receive any promotions while employed by your organization? If so, what were they?
7. Was this individual ever denied a promotion while employed by your organization?
8. How did this individual's work compare with others whose job title was similar or identical?
9. What criticisms did you have of the applicant's work?
10. What exceptional work-related strengths did this individual possess?
11. Did this individual get along well with superiors?
12. Did this individual get along well with co-workers?
13. Why did this individual leave your organization?
14. If given an opportunity to do so, would you rehire this individual? If not, why not?
15. What kind of job do you think is best suited to this individual's abilities?
16. How motivated was this individual?
17. Did this individual often do more than was reasonably expected?
18. Was the quality of work produced by this individual often higher than what might be reasonably expected?
19. Would you describe this individual as a team player?
20. Did any kinds of family or personal problems ever interfere with this individual's work performance?

*For information about the *AMS Guide* write to the organization at Willow Grove, Pennsylvania.

HOW THE ALTERNATIVE WORKFORCE OFFERS COMPANIES COST-SAVING STAFFING OPTIONS

With payroll costs for full-time employees notching ever upward, many small business owners are looking to various staffing alternatives to meet both short-term and permanent needs. Among the alternatives: part-timers, "temps," older workers, handicapped individuals and "leased" workers. Here's a look at these options.

HOW PART-TIME WORKERS CAN BE A FULL-TIME SOLUTION TO YOUR RECRUITING PROBLEMS

More and more companies are turning to part-time workers to supplement their dwindling workforce. Who are these workers? These employees range from entry level (young) to new mothers—and some fathers—to seniors to retirees. These retirees can even be your former employees.

Is it working? Yes. Survey after survey clearly shows that part-time workers are a plus to their employers. A recent Department of Labor study, for example, revealed that 62 percent of the companies who use part-timers reported higher production and only five percent reported decreased output. Production is just one of the advantages companies report. Other pluses include:

- Reduced absenteeism and lateness. A good example of how part-timers can be a force in these areas is to look at the experience of Control Data of Minneapolis. It opened a bindery in St. Paul and staffed it fully with part-timers. The company reported lower absenteeism and tardiness than full-time workers at similar worksites.

- Retention of valuable employees, especially older workers and women and men with children; more access to scarce talent.

- Greater flexibility in work schedules. When recruiting, this point should be stressed in your want ads. You might say: "Tell us what hours you can work and we will try to make the necessary adjustments."

There are disadvantages. These can include higher payroll taxes mandated by the government (unemployment insurance, workers' compensation and Social Security), higher costs for recordkeeping, more supervision and scheduling problems and greater turnover.

However, employers feel strongly that advantages far outweigh the disadvantages.

There is a key question that you must answer before you actively recruit part-timers: Do you need them?

Get a feel for the problem. Ask yourself a series of questions like the ones listed in Figure 6.2. The answers should give you a good clue on whether part-timers are for your company.

Figure 6.2
Part-Time Employee Need Evaluation Questionnaire

	Yes	No
1. Are there positions for which it is difficult to recruit good applicants?		
2. Have key staffers left our company because part-time work isn't a choice?		
3. Are some departments or job classifications experiencing above-average turnover or absenteeism?		
4. In order to process the day-to-day business, have you had to overstaff in some areas or use an excessive number of substitutes?		
5. Must your organization's schedules conform to work demand rather than having all tasks performed according to a standardized schedule?		
6. Is at least 50 percent of any department or job classification comprised of women of childbearing age?		
7. Is expanding coverage or extending your company's hours of operation an objective?		
8. If expanding coverage or extending hours of operation is an objective, would a part-time shift or the addition of some part-time personnel facilitate achieving this objective?		
9. Is burnout a problem for any of your company's employees?		
10. Would some senior employees prefer a part-time schedule?		

While there is a wealth of talent out there looking for part-time work, these workers are sometimes difficult to find. Employment agencies (Kelly Services is one of the national temporary firms making a special appeal to temporary workers through its Encore Program), state employment agencies, and some private agencies can help you locate part-time workers.

HOW TO RECRUIT AND RETAIN
OLDER WORKERS

Many companies have found older workers ideally suited for many jobs—full-time as well as part-time—because of their experience and reliability. Older workers will "be there when they say they'll be there," says an executive with the *American Association of Retired Persons* (AARP, Washington, D.C.).

The executive adds that older workers also tend to stay with jobs longer than younger workers, who tend to move more often from place to place and from job to job. Older workers, by contrast, would "rather stay on a job they know and like."

Attracting older people requires a slightly different approach, however. Here are some tips for recruiting older workers:

- Make sure your help-wanted ad says you're looking for experienced people. If you don't, older people may assume you want to hire someone younger.

- Run your ads in the local newspapers or "shoppers," but don't advertise in classified sections. The older person won't be looking there. Instead, place your ads in sections they're likely to see, such as the sports or living sections.

- Offer certain perks such as transportation, flextime or paid vacation. Often, what motivates older people isn't money but shorter hours. They're not looking for a major obligation but, rather, an opportunity to make a contribution.

- Make it as easy as possible for older workers to respond to your ad. Set up a hot line or run a coupon or application with your ad that they can fill out and send in. Older people often don't want to sit down and write a long résumé. Give them a specific person to contact so they can be taken care of quickly and not get lost in the shuffle.

- Use one of your older workers as a recruiter and have that person conduct the applicant interviews.

Your company can also collaborate with public sector senior employment programs to successfully recruit older employees. By working with these programs, your company stands to receive these benefits:

- Free recruitment services;
- Free training programs;
- Lower wage costs (available through participation in some on-the-job training programs); and
- Free publicity for your company (news organizations often cover community-oriented programs established by area employers).

There are federal grants available. The federal Job Training Partnership Act (JTPA) specifically recognizes the training needs of older workers and offers federal funds to assist companies in this endeavor. Check with your local employment office to find out if your training program qualifies for federal assistance.

Various private sector organizations also can help you in recruiting older employees. Among them are the following:

- SCORE (Senior Corps of Retired Executives), a nationwide network that operates in connection with the Small Business Administration;
- "Forty-plus," a membership club of older persons who are looking for work;
- Temps America, a temporaries agency that features a Mature Temps America division; and
- Local senior citizen centers.

Don't forget about your veteran employees. While you're busy trying to attract top-notch job applicants, don't forget about your older workers already on staff. Just because these employees have reached retirement age doesn't mean they're ready to retire. Many would like to stay on the job, but be able to work reduced hours or a flexible schedule.

Consider the following ideas for keeping your valuable, near-retirement workers on staff:

- **Offer training.** Retrain older workers to meet new challenges. Often, people will hold off retiring if they're retrained for new jobs.

- **Offer part-time retirement.** If you know an employee is thinking of retiring, find out if he or she would be interested in coming back as a consultant or a part-time worker. Since older employees know the company culture, they could fill in at a moment's notice during certain periods of the year, such as peak seasons or when regular employees go on vacations or medical or maternity leave.
- **Offer gradual retirement.** More and more people are taking the gradual retirement route by cutting down their work week—for example, working four days instead of five. This is great for people who want to keep their hand in at work, but like having the extra time for traveling, hobbies, etc.
- **Permit a rehearsal for retirement.** Often, older employees may think they want to retire but aren't sure if they'll like it. You can give them time away from work for an extended period of time (usually not longer than a year) so they can do community service work or travel and see how they like not working. After the trial time they come back to work. This gives them the chance to see if they can handle retirement without having to formally give up their jobs.
- **Offer job sharing.** Sometimes jobs can be redesigned so that two older people can work part time and share the work.
- **Offer flextime and flex place.** With flextime, employees don't have to work set hours. In many cases, they can arrange their own schedules, provided they work a "core" number of hours each day. With jobs that can be done at home, flex place allows the employee to work without having to worry about coming into the office every day.

If you're interested in finding out how other companies are handling part-time retirement or other such ideas, write on your company's letterhead to the *American Association of Retired Persons,* 1909 K St. NW, Washington, DC 20049. AARP will send you a profile of companies who have such programs and provide the name of someone at each company to contact for more information.

HOW TO RECRUIT AND RETAIN HANDICAPPED EMPLOYEES

In a survey by the National Council on the Handicapped and the President's Committee on the Employment of the Handicapped, managers and executives rated disabled workers as equal to or better than nondisabled workers in such areas as productivity, reliability and attendance, willingness to work, desire for promotion and leadership ability. Increasingly, owners of businesses of all sizes are recognizing that it pays to hire the handicapped.

Use all the resources at your disposal—federal, state, local and private organizations—to assist you in recruiting and training handicapped employees. It's important to match applicants' skills to job duties, and in some cases you may have to modify certain jobs or the work environment. You'll find the extra effort worth it.

With the passage of the ADA, successfully assimilating handicapped workers into your work place may involve making certain accommodations. These can range from installing brighter lights or providing magnifying glasses for employees with visual impairments to purchasing devices to help hearing-impaired employees "hear."

The Job Accommodation Network (JAN) offers assistance to employers in accommodating handicapped employees. JAN provides product information and can recommend appropriate job modifications and redesign, where necessary. (For more information about the organization's services, write: Job Accommodation Network, Box 468, Morgantown, WV 26505, or call, toll-free, 800-526-7234.)

There are scores of national organizations whose sole purpose is to further handicapped persons' rights and interests. These agencies are able and eager to help your company. Among their services:

- Placement: They can put you in touch with highly qualified handicapped job candidates.

- Job matching: They can tell you what job functions can and can't be performed by persons with specific disabilities.

- Counseling: They can advise you about physical accommodations your company would need to make for persons with particular disabilities.

For more help, contact the President's Committee on Employment of the Handicapped, 1111 20th Street NW, Washington, DC 20036 (202-653-5044). It publishes a directory that provides detailed information on organizations that assist employers in finding qualified handicapped job candidates.

Another source you can contact to fill job openings is your local state employment office. These offices have a large pool of job seekers, whom they will help to place, free of charge.

HOW YOUR COMPANY CAN USE SELF-EMPLOYED WORKERS TO CUT ITS PAYROLL TAX BILL

One of the best tax-saving strategies available today is the use of workers who are not employees. Under the payroll laws, you must pay and withhold tax only for workers defined as "employees." If your company's relationship with an employee meets certain conditions, that worker may technically be an "independent contractor"— and not your "employee" at all. Since independent contractors are self-employed, you don't withhold income tax, deduct and pay Social Security tax, or owe unemployment tax on their pay.

Another staffing option that frees you from payroll taxes and withholding is the use of *leased workers*. Such workers are actually employees of another company, which pays their salary, withholds the taxes, and provides their employee benefits. You pay a fee to the leasing agency or firm but aren't responsible for employment taxes because leased workers aren't your employees. (See section on employee leasing later in this chapter.)

If even one job paying, say, $30,000 per year could be assigned to an independent contractor or leased worker, you could save up to $3,000 in payroll taxes—FICA tax plus federal unemployment taxes. And that's not including the state unemployment costs. These savings can really add up when you factor in the cost of employee benefits, which for the typical employee can run 30%–40% of salary.

Using non-employees can also save on the cost of payroll administration and bookkeeping. Employers are required to file Form 1099-MISC for independent contractors paid $600 or more in a calendar year. And you're required to withhold from such a contractor at a flat 20% rate—known as backup withholding—if the contractor fails to give you a taxpayer identification number. Nevertheless, the withholding and reporting chores required for non-employees are far less cumbersome than those required for employees.

A burgeoning industry has grown up to match self-employed workers, leased employees, consultants, and a host of other "independents" with employers who want to save on tax and benefit costs, not to mention administrative expenses. But this trend hasn't escaped the notice of government regulators. The IRS estimated that 338,000 business taxpayers owe some $3.7 billion in back employment taxes, which it intends to collect.

The IRS is concentrating its collection efforts on businesses that *incorrectly* classify workers as independent contractors. It plans to double the number of agents performing payroll tax audits and has updated its procedures and computer systems to help with this crackdown.

As part of the crackdown the IRS is matching independent contractors' information returns with their tax returns. One red flag the IRS is looking for are cases where a worker received more than $10,000 from a single "employer." This crackdown would more systematically identify employers that are misclassifying employees as independent contractors to better target the IRS' audits.

This added IRS scrutiny shouldn't discourage you from using bona fide independents. However, you need to be extremely careful to make sure you're complying with the payroll laws. What you should do is take stock of any worker that you classify, or plan to classify, as independent. Ask the following four questions:

- Does the arrangement make sense? Or would it cost about the same to hire an employee for the job? The tax, benefit, and administrative costs assumed by the independent—whether a firm or an individual—don't disappear. Some or all of them are passed through to you in the form of higher fees, along with a margin of profit.

- Is there a solid legal basis for treating the worker as a non-employee? (You should check with your lawyer to find this out.)

- Is the worker being treated correctly under all the payroll laws that apply? A worker may be independent for income tax withholding purposes, but subject by law to Social Security tax. Similarly, a worker who is free from both these taxes may be covered under the Federal Wage-Hour Law. And state unemployment insurance laws apply tests of employee status that are different from those used under the Federal Unemployment Tax Act. The bottom line is that you can lose more through penalties imposed for violating one law than you save under all the others.

- Are there hidden traps in the arrangement? There are special dangers in some arrangements. We explain how to spot these traps and deal with them below.

Identifying who is an independent contractor

Generally, an individual may qualify as an independent contractor in one of two ways. The individual may pass the "reasonable basis" tests established by the Congress in 1978. (These tests are known as

Sec. 530 "safe harbors.") Or he or she may qualify as independent under the "common law" tests of employment status.

The reasonable basis tests rely on how the government, including the courts, has classified workers in your business or industry in the past. They are intended to provide a safe harbor from any IRS attempt to redefine who is and isn't an employee in the future. The common law tests deal with the substance of the particular job. The key question under the common law tests is: How independent is the worker of employer control?

- **The reasonable basis tests.** You have a reasonable basis for treating a worker as not subject to federal employment taxes if one or more of the following conditions exists:

  - A judicial precedent for treating workers in similar circumstances as non-employees.

  - A general statement by the Revenue Service that workers such as the ones in question are not employees subject to employment taxes. Most likely, this will be in the form of a Revenue Ruling.

  - A Technical Advice Memorandum or Private Letter Ruling to your specific company indicating that the worker(s) is not an employee.

  - A past IRS payroll audit that did *not* find individuals in the same positions to be employees.

  - A longstanding, recognized practice in your industry of treating workers such as the one in question as non-employees.

A federal appeals court recently expanded the safe harbor protection for workers treated as independent contractors by ruling that a new worker can qualify as an independent contractor, even if he or she performs a job *different* from the workers covered by the audit. In the case, a landscaper had hired and paid workers on a job-by-job basis and treated them as independent contractors. The IRS agreed when it audited the landscaper's return. When the business expanded into *janitorial* services, the janitors were again hired on a job-by-job basis and treated as independent contractors. The court said that an audit of one type of worker protects a company for a different type of worker as long as they both have the *same relationship* with the company.

Note that a safe harbor can be lost if the conditions of the worker's employment change. In other words, workers are not automatically independent contractors today because they were legally classified as such in the past.

The Tax Law has removed a large number of highly paid professionals from the protection of the last safe harbor category listed above. So-called "technical service workers," who are provided under an arrangement between a leasing company (usually a broker or agent) and a user company, are affected. A technical service worker is defined as "an engineer, designer, drafter, computer programmer, systems analyst, or other similarly skilled worker engaged in a similar line of work."

> **IMPORTANT:** Technical service workers who are not obtained through a broker, agent or lessor may continue to qualify as independent under the "reasonable basis test." The Tax Law crackdown applies only to three-party arrangements.

The employment status of a technical worker whose services you obtain through a third party is determined under the common law tests. The worker may be an independent contractor under the common law standards. This is especially likely if all the third party did was charge you a finder's or employment agency fee. On the other hand, the technical service worker may be the common law employee of the third-party, or your employee.

The IRS essentially relies on a 20-factor common law test to determine whether a technical service worker is the employee of a leasing company. In general, the factors are the same as the common law tests described below. Any differences are shown in italics.

• **The common law tests.** Even if you do not have a "reasonable basis," you may still be able to treat a worker as independent. Under the common law, if an employer does not have the right to control both what work will be done and how it will be done, there is no employer-employee relationship; the worker is an independent contractor. Note that what is crucial is the "right to control." Even a worker who is referred to as an "agent," and who is given substantial freedom of action, may be an employee. The employer has the legal right to control the "what" and "how" of the worker's job, even though it does not exercise that right.

In proving or disproving this element of control, many other factors are considered—from whether the worker can realize a profit or loss from the work to how the worker is paid.

Here are the 20 common law factors used by the IRS to determine whether workers are employees or independent contractors.

Workers are generally employees if they:

1. Must comply with employer's instructions about the work.
2. Receive training from or at the direction of the employer.
3. Provide services that are integrated into the business.
4. Provide services that must be rendered personally.
5. Hire, supervise, and pay assistants for the employer. (*If a technical service worker hires, pays, and supervises other assistants pursuant to a contract under which the technical worker agrees to provide materials and labor to obtain a result, it is a sign of independent status.*)
6. Have a continuing working relationship with the employer.
7. Must follow set hours of work.
8. Work full-time for an employer.
9. Do their work on the employer's premises. (*Technical service workers would be considered employees of the leasing company if the leasing company compels the workers to travel a given route or work at specific places.*)
10. Must do their work in a sequence set by the employer.
11. Must submit regular reports to the employer.
12. Receive payments of regular amounts at set intervals.
13. Receive payments for business and/or travel expenses.
14. Rely on the employer to furnish tools and materials.
15. Lack a major investment in facilities used to perform the service.
16. Cannot make a profit or suffer a loss from their services.
17. Work for one employer at a time.
18. Do not offer their services to the general public.
19. Can be fired by the employer.
20. May quit work at any time without incurring liability.

Identifying who is not an independent contractor

While certain types of jobs are more likely than others to be performed by contractors, the job title itself has no bearing whatsoever on whether the worker is an employee or non-employee. The common law tests are decisive (for a worker who is not in one of the safe harbor categories). For example, "siding applicators" working for a home improvement company were judged to be independent contractors.

They could work for the company's competitors and could reject work orders without affecting their future relationship with the company. The company exercised little or no control over the way the applicators did their jobs.

On the other hand, "siding applicators" who worked exclusively for one employer, and who didn't advertise their services, were employees of another home improvement company. The company exercised control over the way the applicators did their jobs.

There are other misleading "signposts" of independent contractor status that have led employers down the road to penalties. For example, a worker is a "casual laborer" hired on a day-to-day basis to perform assignments that are infrequent or outside the regular course of business. Even if he is employed a single day, the worker is an employee if he meets the common law test of an employee.

The same rule applies to a "temporary" who subs for a vacationing worker. The temp is someone's employee—an agency's or yours. If the temp is not engaged through a third party who is the employer, the brief duration of the employment does not relieve you from treating the temp as on your payroll.

The same can be said for "moonlighting" employees. A worker can have more than one employer. A person who works for you at night *after* a regular daytime job is your employee if he or she meets the common law tests of an employee.

There's no magic in the title "consultant." Many consultants are independent contractors. But take the case of an ex-employee who was an expert on postal regulations. She is recalled as a consultant to iron out a problem with the post office; basically her old job. If the consultant meets the common law tests of an employee, she *is* one and must be paid through payroll, not through accounts payable.

Having a contract may help. A contract that designates a worker as independent will help only if it gives the worker the rights of independence (for example, control over the work product, substantial notice before termination, ability to hire assistants, etc.) and the worker exercises these rights in practice. You cannot change what is, in truth, an employer-employee relationship by calling the worker an independent contractor on paper. However, as explained on the following page, a special rule applies to real estate brokers and direct sellers. They must work under a written contract to be considered independent.

WHEN EMPLOYMENT STATUS IS SET BY LAW

Some workers who do not meet the tests of an independent contractor listed previously may, nevertheless, be treated as self-employed workers—provided you meet some preliminary conditions. On the other hand, some workers who do meet the tests are considered employees by law, unless special circumstances are present.

• **Statutory non-employees.** Federal law classifies the following categories of workers as non-employees, subject to the conditions noted:

Real estate agents: Licensed real estate agents are treated as independent contractors for federal income tax, Social Security tax and unemployment tax purposes provided you meet two conditions:

- They work under a written contract that says they will not be treated as employees for federal tax purposes, and

- Substantially all their earnings come from real estate sales or related output.

Direct sellers: A direct seller either sells consumer products in private homes (or anywhere other than a retail store) or sells products for resale to people who sell door-to-door. They are exempt from federal payroll taxes provided the same conditions listed above for real estate agents are met. Their earnings must be based on sales made, not number of hours worked.

• **Statutory employees.** The following categories are, by law, employees:

Life insurance salespeople: The earnings of full-time life insurance salespeople are subject to Social Security tax unless they have a substantial investment in the facilities of the business *or* the services performed are single transactions, not part of a continuing business relationship. (Full-time life insurance sellers' earnings are *not* subject to federal unemployment tax if the earnings consist entirely of commissions. If the salespeople receive any salary, however, *all* of their earnings are subject to FUTA tax.)

Traveling and city salespeople: Commissions paid these salespeople are subject to Social Security (and federal unemployment tax) if *all* of the following circumstances apply:

- They work full-time for their employers (though they may make some sideline sales);

- Their work consists of sending orders to their employers from wholesalers, retailers, contractors, hotel or restaurant operators, or the like who buy the merchandise for resale or as supplies;

- They have agreed to perform the work personally;
- They have no substantial investment in business equipment or facilities (other than for transportation); and
- Their employment is part of a continuing relationship.

A fine line may divide a tax-exempt seller from one whose earnings are subject to tax. For instance, a salesperson may sell trucks to trucking firms that use them in fulfilling hauling contracts. The buyer is a "contractor." But the seller is *not* a statutory employee. Trucks are capital equipment, not "merchandise bought for resale" or as "supplies."

Commission drivers: Even though they may otherwise qualify as independent contractors, commission drivers are subject to Social Security tax (and federal unemployment tax) if they meet *all* of the following tests:

- They distribute meat, vegetables, fruits, baked goods, beverages (other than milk), laundry or dry cleaning;
- They perform the work personally;
- They have no substantial investment in equipment or facilities (other than a truck or van); and
- The business relationship is continuing.

You can save Social Security taxes by subtracting the fair rental value of the truck or van owned by the employee from the employee's taxable receipts before figuring the tax due.

Industrial homeworkers who receive at least $100 a year: Homeworkers are subject to Social Security tax unless they have a substantial investment in equipment or the services are performed as a single, occasional transaction.

How the IRS views "control"

The factor of "control" is the government's basic test for determining who is and who is not an independent contractor. The Revenue Service considers other factors, such as the furnishing of equipment, the continuity of the relationship between the employer and worker, whether the worker risks making a profit or loss and whether or not the worker's services are an integral part of the employer's business. But one factor takes precedence over all others: Who controls the "what" and "how" of the job—the employer or the worker?

Here are several IRS rulings that demonstrate how the government zeros in first and foremost on the factor of control. The following cases were judged in the company's favor:

• Commission sales reps were engaged by a company to sell clothing to retailers. They were required to perform the services personally. But they furnished their own transportation, paid their own selling expenses, and were not controlled or directed as to selling activity. The IRS ruled they weren't employees.

• Guest speakers and lecturers for a family relations institute were not its employees. They received no salaries, and only a percentage of fees paid by the institute's clients. They were not eligible for bonuses, vacation pay, or pension benefits.

• A commercial artist was hired by a film company. He worked in his own studio, provided his own materials, and delegated work to others who were hired by him. He also worked for other firms and was paid on a time or job basis. The IRS ruled that the artist wasn't the company's employee.

• A person who operated and managed an auto body repair shop in a space provided by an auto sales agency wasn't an employee. He furnished his own tools and supplies, hired and fired helpers, set his own prices, and assumed losses on debts.

• A person doing bookkeeping and related services for several clients wasn't the employee of any of them. He set his own hours, had his own office, was paid on the basis of work done, and did not have an exclusive relationship with any one client.

The following cases were judged against the company:

• Commission sales reps sold a cable TV system at prescribed prices and terms within assigned territories. They had to follow up on leads furnished by the company, appear at the company's premises, and submit daily reports that could be the basis for termination. The IRS ruled that they were employees of the cable company and employment taxes were owed.

> Payment of a guaranteed salary, or at a fixed hourly rate, usually indicates that a worker is an employee. So does treatment of the worker as an employee for payroll tax purposes and/or the providing of "employee" benefits.

• A securities salesperson who was paid by commission, but guaranteed a minimum salary, was an employee. He had his office on the firm's premises, was required to follow regular office routine and working hours, and the firm paid for his license and included him in employees' insurance plans.

Your right to terminate a worker at will, to require that he or she work on your premises, and to insist that the work be done personally are signs of an employer-employee relationship.

• A carpentry contractor supervised and controlled its workers' activities, supplied major tools and had hiring and firing power over the workers. The IRS ruled that the workers were employees of the carpentry contractor.

The larger a worker's capital investment in the job, and the greater the expenses he or she incurs without reimbursement, the more likely the worker is to be considered an independent contractor. The fact that a worker stands to lose—as well as to make—money is a strong argument in favor of the worker's being considered self-employed.

• An architect was hired to perform architectural services on a project-by-project basis for the employer's premises. She was given office space, secretarial and telephone service, and material and equipment necessary to complete each particular job. The IRS ruled that she was the firm's employee.

If you restrict a worker's ability to work for other employers, this is strong evidence that he or she is your employee. On the other hand, if the worker is free to offer his or her services to other businesses or to the public, this is evidence that the worker is truly independent. It's especially strong if the person actually does work for other parties.

• Models working for a modeling agency were free to accept or reject assignments and had to furnish their own transportation and cosmetics. However, they could be fired by the agency and were prohibited (by oral agreement) from doing freelance modeling. The IRS ruled that they were employees of the agency.

IMPORTANT: You can learn from the experience of these employers—but you can't use these rulings to back up your own practices. That's because a private letter ruling *is* private—intended only for the use of the parties involved in the case. At most, the employer who receives such a letter can use it only for the worker(s) in question, and other workers employed under substantially similar circumstances.

In fact, receiving the letter ruling isn't always the end of the story. Recently, the IRS revoked two different letter rulings that held that couriers and messengers were not employees. Originally, the IRS cited such factors as the workers' providing their own transportation, having the right to accept or refuse assignments, and incurring a loss if packages in their care were damaged as indicative of their independent contractor status. In revoking the favorable rulings, the IRS explained that it is currently studying the status of such workers.

HOW TO DETERMINE IF EMPLOYEE LEASING IS RIGHT FOR YOUR COMPANY

Much has been made of the advantages of employee leasing. Leasing arrangements free employers from payroll taxes and hassles, and the responsibility for administering personnel programs and benefits.

On the other hand, while leasing is a valuable staffing option for many companies, even its supporters concede it's "no panacea." Here's a look at some of the factors—both positive and negative—of which you should be aware.

When leasing works best

There's some disagreement as to which types of companies can benefit most from using leased workers. Some experts claim that employee leasing is best suited to young, struggling companies that can't predict how many employees they'll need and don't want long-term commitments. This is not so; while leasing can work well for companies of any size, struggling start-ups generally are not good candidates because they usually lack the stability necessary to accommodate the kinds of arrangements offered by leasing companies.

Employee leasing is in fact a commitment to people small employers want to have on a long-term basis by providing them with benefits and other opportunities normally available only from larger firms. Leasing is intended to give the small and medium-size company a measure of competitiveness in getting and keeping good people.

In the right settings, leasing allows the owners of small companies to do what they do best—focus their energies on building their businesses and making a profit—while the leasing company handles all personnel decisions, administrative chores and legal compliance matters. Thus the company can avoid costly legal mistakes.

One of the key benefits of leasing is that the client company gains the leasing company's expertise in recruiting, hiring, personnel management and the proper methods of firing and disciplining problem workers. These are areas in which many new business owners can easily get themselves into legal trouble unknowingly, because they don't have the expertise.

It has been suggested that leasing is most effective for companies with 10-400 employees where the entire workforce, except the owners, is on the leasing company's payroll.

Potential pitfalls of leasing

In spite of the advertised advantages, management experts advise employers who are considering leasing to be aware of the following legal requirements and possible drawbacks:

* Pension obligations: Recent tax laws have made it more difficult for companies to exclude leased workers from their retirement plans. The current rule is that leased workers must be provided the same retirement coverage as the client company's other employees unless the leasing company contributes 10% of each worker's compensation to its own money-purchase pension plan. And if more than 20% of a client company's non-highly-compensated workers are leased, the leased employees must be covered by the client's retirement plan—if it has one—regardless of whether the leasing company maintains one as well.

* Loyalty: On the day your employees become employees of a leasing company—but continue to work on your premises—more changes than simply who signs their paychecks and provides their benefits. Your company's relationship with the workers also changes and their attitude toward your company may change as well. You may find a different commitment level from employees and, consequently, some increased turnover.

  On the other hand, a Small Business Administration study found "higher employee morale over time" among leased workers.

* Loss of control: Among the biggest concerns for many employers is the limit leasing imposes on their ability to manage the workforce. When you lease employees, you're no longer their "employer." It's the leasing company that must direct the work, control employee scheduling, mete out punishments and rewards, and so on. If you continue to exercise these employer prerogatives, the tax and other legal benefits you enjoy under

the relationship could be jeopardized. Thus, leasing may make it harder for you to make needed changes in the way the work is done, and even to get rid of undesirable workers and retain good ones.

Before you make any change, explain to your employees what is going to happen. Reassure them that the leasing arrangement will benefit them as well as your company. And emphasize that they are still valued employees of your company.

What to look for in a leasing company

Deciding whether employee leasing is right for a company is only the first step in many cases. If your company concludes that leasing is the way to go, the next decision—a very important one—is which leasing company to use. Here are some tips on what you should be looking for from National Staff Network, one of the nation's largest employee-leasing companies:

- Check the leasing company's track record. Ask the company for names of its clients in your industry. And then make some phone calls. What you're looking for is demonstrated experience in serving employers in your industry and a record of financial stability.

- Make sure the company will bill you for the payroll after it pays your employees, rather than using your money to cover the payroll.

- Billing should be based on a standard fee schedule rather than a cost-plus basis. With cost-plus, your costs increase every time you raise salaries. With a fee schedule, the leasing company charges one fee for each employee earning, say, between $300 and $350; a slightly larger fee for employees earning $350 to $400.

- Make sure the leasing company certifies at least quarterly that all taxes, health insurance premiums, etc., have been paid.

Many leasing experts suggest that you check to see whether the leasing company you're considering is a member of the NSLA. This industry trade association sets ethical standards for its members and requires quarterly independent verifications that member firms handle their tax and other legal responsibilities in a timely and proper fashion. Such verification is extremely important because of the substantial fiduciary responsibilities borne by the leasing company.

HOW TO AVOID HIDDEN TRAPS WHEN USING NON-EMPLOYEES

Here are some of the common pitfalls businesses have encountered when using leased or independent workers and how you can avoid them.

• **The prior status trap.** The IRS may reclassify an independent contractor as an employee if at any time in the past you (or your predecessor within the company) treated the worker as an employee. This assumes, of course, that the worker is still performing the same job, under the same terms and conditions.

Make sure that no W-4 or other employee information return has been filed on behalf of a worker whom you intend to treat as an independent contractor.

• **The workers' compensation trap.** Employees are generally barred from suing their employers for injuries caused on the job. They collect workers' compensation instead. Workers' compensation usually provides much less than what a worker might win as a personal injury award from a court. So workers' compensation offers valuable protection for employers that may be lost if the worker is a non-employee.

Check with your insurer to see if independent contractors who will work on your premises or with your employees can be covered by your workers' compensation policy. If not, see if the contractor will agree to *indemnify* you in the event that you must pay damages. Alternatively, you can agree to reimburse the contractors for the cost of their own workers' compensation insurance if they waive their right to sue.

On the other side of the coin, you should be wary of indemnification clauses in contracts you sign with employee leasing companies. Such a clause may, in effect, shift the leasing company's liability to you.

• **The unlawful hire trap.** The Immigration Reform and Control Act (IRCA) makes it unlawful to knowingly hire an alien who is not authorized to work in the United States. It also makes it unlawful to "contract for the labor of" an illegal alien. This language was put in the law because Congress was well aware that employers might try to circumvent its effect by using independent contractors.

You'll probably have little difficulty with this where you contract for services that are outside the ordinary course of business—for example, repair services, landscaping, janitorial work. Here, you have little or no say-so in choosing the workers who do the work. But when the work is done in the ordinary course of your business, it's a different story.

For example, XYZ contracts for production services to be performed on its premises. It pays the subcontractor (not the employee) directly. The subcontracted worker uses equipment provided by XYZ. If a particular worker performs unsatisfactorily, XYZ can have him replaced. The salary level for each worker is negotiated on a case-by-case basis by XYZ and the subcontractor. Therefore, both the subcontractor and XYZ may be liable for the unlawful hiring of unauthorized aliens.

In a deal for contract or leased labor, insist on seeing the I-9 Forms (Employment Eligibility Verification) of workers who are referred to you. Make copies of them and retain them with the I-9 Forms you keep for regular employees. These forms are proof that, at the time they were referred to you, the contract workers were apparently eligible to work.

CHAPTER SEVEN

HOW TO TRAIN, MOTIVATE AND KEEP YOUR QUALITY WORKFORCE

Let's assume you've gone through the résumé reading, interviewing and reference checking process and have hired the best and the brightest job candidates. The next challenge facing you is: How do you keep them that way?

Most small business owners agree that two things go into building a top-notch workforce: training and motivation.

In this section, we'll take a look at some successful orientation and training techniques that every company owner—large or small—can use to turn those attractive applicants you just hired into profit-producing employees.

HOW TO SET UP AN EFFECTIVE ORIENTATION PROGRAM

An effective orientation setup can eliminate many of the anxieties and questions that new employees are likely to have—and get them off to a positive, productive start.

However, "orientation often misfires because companies don't plan their goals," says a management consultant at *TPF&C*, a Towers Perrin Company (New York City). A typical program consists of a dry recital of company benefits and a pep talk. New employees are then left to do anything they want with the information (usually nothing).

What should be your orientation program's aim? Here are some sample goals suggested by TPF&C. Your orientation program should:

- Give new employees a clear picture of what your company offers and what it expects from them;
- Introduce them to the experts on various aspects of the company;
- Familiarize them with the work they'll do and introduce them to co-workers doing similar work; and
- Tell them whom to see if a problem comes up.

When deciding on a structure for your orientation program, keep in mind there is no one formula. Your orientation program should be structured around the makeup of your company, its size and the nature of the job.

Decide what to cover by listing priorities. Give newcomers only the information that's essential for their next few hours or days and give the rest when it's needed. For example:

- Mention benefits at orientation; give details when eligibility starts.
- Tell new employees the timing and basis for performance appraisals; give details a week or two prior to the first appraisal session.
- Talk about production standards; deal with specific quality and quantity factors when the employee is on the job.

Keep in mind that entry-level employees, with little or no knowledge of how the business world operates, may need a specially tailored introduction.

One New York company uses a "new-style" orientation program to develop a group of workers who previously would have gone untapped and unused. The case history listed below is of a large department store, but the basic approach can be used by other employers.

Case Example _____

"The thinking behind our orientation program," says the vice president of community relations, "is that these new employees are missing the basic skills: work ethic, proper way to communicate and how to dress for business."

The program gets underway with an explanation of why the company has established rules. They are told that rules are to ensure that all employees are able to work as a constructive group. Rules for a company deal with guidelines on lateness and absence, proper dress for the work area and unsafe practices (i.e., fighting or the use of drugs at work).

In the next phase of the orientation the employees are asked to remember the word *"DEEP."* That's an acronym for Dependable, Enthusiastic, Expressive, Persistent. It's explained that remembering that will help them to have a meaningful experience on the job. The workers are then given some working tips which could be used by any company indoctrinating employees into the workplace.

- Arrive on time to work—no one is interested in *"The train was late."*
- Observe how your co-workers dress. (However, don't follow those who appear to *disregard* rules.)
- Don't hide your mistakes; *ask questions if you don't understand.*
- Employers expect a full day's work for a day's pay. If you finish an assignment early and your boss is not available, *go on to another job or assist someone else.*

The program gives the workers a definition of how to proceed. It's the ability to:

- See a task to its completion;
- Work with others;
- Listen and follow directions;
- Understand and follow company policies;
- Stay with a problem and solve it;
- Work rapidly and accurately with enthusiasm, and a positive outlook.

When a worker masters those skills and shows an ability to produce at a consistently high level, the employee is told that he or she is on the promotion track.

THE SUPERVISOR'S ROLE IN THE ORIENTATION PROGRAM

Ultimately, your hands-on supervisors are an important part of an orientation program. For that reason, supervisors need training in how to work with new employees. Here are some tips you can pass on to supervisors to help them get new workers off to a good start.

A warm welcome should be each new employee's first experience in the department. As a supervisor, you should know new employees' names and pronounce them correctly. Also, you should introduce yourself (with your title) and tell new employees what to call you (by your first name, for example).

These are the critical areas you should discuss with the new employee:

- Pay, including salary, incentive plans and bonuses, overtime rates and conditions, deductions, when pay can be docked, paydates, and facilities for check cashing.

- Attendance, including whom to notify (and when) in cases of absence and lateness, penalties for excessive absence or lateness, rewards for good attendance, vacation allowances and planning, sick time, and holiday schedules.

- Probation, including length, conditions, how benefits and other entitlements are affected, and what supervisors will look for (like punctuality, attendance, aptitude and attitude).

- Problems, including whom to see and what grievance machinery exists.

- Policies, including general company rules that cover the department as well as rules that apply only to the particular department.

Don't try to cover everything at once or you may intimidate new workers. As a result you will have to go over the missed ground again.

The following ideas can help you carry out your orientation responsibilities.

- Show new people around the department; introduce them to department members and other employees they'll be in contact with.

- See that new employees' desks or work areas are neat and properly supplied and show them how to order supplies.

- Review workplace rules and give the employee time during the first few days to read the employee handbook and/or department rules or safety manuals. (Have employees sign for any information they're given.)

- Tell new employees the names of company officers and personnel staff members they may need to contact.

- Join the new employees for lunch the first day (arrange to eat with their co-workers, if possible) or ask a co-worker to look after the new worker.

- Start job training or introduce the new workers to their trainer.

HOW TO ASSESS YOUR COMPANY'S TRAINING NEEDS

A properly organized training program anticipates need. The following checklist sets up the steps you'll need to follow to organize a program:

1. Evaluate your training needs. What kinds of training do your employees lack? What new skills will your company be needing in the future? Decide which of these needs is the most immediate, and concentrate on this one first.

2. Figure out what material must be covered in your training course. Supervisors will probably be the best source for this information.

3. Determine the most effective method of instruction for the particular employees and subject matter involved. Develop or find appropriate training materials, and decide on the proper length for the training period.

4. Decide how to select employees to be trained. Then select instructors for the program and instruct them in how to train the employees.

5. Schedule and hold the training program.

6. Set up a system to record training results and evaluate the success of the training program.

7. Communicate. Whether the program is voluntary or mandatory, you'll need to sell it to employees.

8. Go back to Step 1. A successful training program is one that is continually re-evaluated and changed in response to changing needs.

FINDING OUT WHAT TRAINING IS NEEDED

To discover what kinds of training are needed, you'll have to do some legwork. Here's how:

• **Forecast.** Anticipate your staffing needs, both short-range and long-range, so you can project your training needs. For example, observation may do the job.

You may be able to pinpoint areas where training is needed by watching how jobs are done in various departments. Be sure to talk to other employees—they're likely to know better than anyone else what would help them do their jobs better.

• **Keep up with technology.** Stay informed of changes in your industry that may create new jobs or a need for new types of training. This should be part of supervisors' planning duties. Check the trade journals for your industry. This is one way to keep current. Also attend trade meetings and keep in touch with business groups in your area.

• **Ask employment interviewers.** Are they having trouble filling particular types of jobs because of a scarcity of applicants with a certain skill? Perhaps on-the-job training or a remedial course can remedy the situation. If employment tests are administered, is there a particular area in which many employees do poorly? If so, you have a ready-made training target.

• **Check job evaluations and merit ratings.** Job descriptions can tell you precisely what skills are required for each job in your organization. Review your job descriptions. Are they current? Do they reflect the job as it's done today? You may find that the job description must be revised.

• **Look at personnel records.** Evidence of dissatisfaction among employees (absenteeism, tardiness, high turnover, many grievances) may point to training needs. Employees may feel inadequate in their jobs, or they may feel that they are not in line for promotion or upgrading.

Check trainee turnover. Do new employees leave during their training periods? Do they tend to stay through training, but quit soon after they make the transition to the actual work? If either of these conditions is present in your company, you have a problem in your present training program. Begin here!

• **Check production and cost records.** Low productivity, wasted time or materials, or both, may mean that cost-control or skills training is needed.

• **Review accident and safety reports.** Are there problem areas—certain departments or certain types of jobs—where safety training is needed?

• **Check customer complaints.** Do the same problems—either with quality control or with customer service—keep cropping up? If so, perhaps you need to give a refresher course for employees handling these jobs.

HOW EMPLOYERS DEAL WITH THE LACK OF BASIC SKILLS AMONG WORKERS

Your company should be in the "education business" if it wants to stay competitive. That's the message many business owners of large and small companies alike are getting.

Companies who have veteran employees without basic skills (such as reading and writing) have to set up some form of educational program or these workers will fall by the wayside. They have found that technology goes up and ability goes down.

"If we don't train our workers to at least read instructions, we're heading for disaster," says the secretary-treasurer of a metal manufacturer in Illinois. That company had a $7,000 part ruined by a worker who improvised rather than followed instructions.

Here are thumb-nail sketches of what two companies have done to upgrade workers. These programs could give you an idea of how to deal with this lack-of-basic-skills problem.

Case Example _____

One company hired a faculty member from the local community college to instruct its workers in English. (Quite a few of the employees were Hispanic and had difficulty with English.) On top of that, some of these workers had been employed by the company for some time.

Why did these workers suddenly have problems? The problems began when the company added complex machinery. To operate it, workers had to follow instructions. It was necessary, for example, to read blueprints. Before the new machinery, the workers could handle assembly-line type jobs.

Here's how the program works. Two one-and-a-half-hour courses are given twice a week after work. Attendance is not mandatory, but the workers know that if they don't learn to read, they will not advance.

The employees pay for the instructional material. The company feels the program has more meaning that way. The company pays the instructor.

The program is working very well; so far, two members of the class have been promoted. They are now supervisors.

Not all the workers take part in the program, but when nonparticipants see the success of their friends, they are more inclined to sign up.

Case Example

Another company looked at the way it was doing business and realized that if it was going to remain competitive, its employees would have to change along with the new technology. That company came to the conclusion that it would have to help its employees to upgrade their skills.

The company determined it had a problem when it started a quality improvement program. Some employees had difficulty with their reading assignments which were to help upgrade their skills. The company realized that something had to be done to help them cope with technological change.

Employees were asked to conduct an evaluation of their current skills as well as what "coping" training they thought they needed. Employees could then volunteer to take a test to determine their level of understanding so training could be designed especially for their needs.

For example, if someone had trouble with math and not with reading, naturally that person would be excused from the reading class.

The company provides instructors, workbooks and an on-site training room. Employees, in turn, attend these voluntary classes for two hours a week, either before or after work depending on their shifts.

If a worker doesn't want to attend these voluntary classes, it's all right, but the worker is told that if his or her work isn't up to par, the employee could be terminated.

The program has been extremely successful. Most of the workers have become problem-solvers. Their self-esteem has never been higher. There has also been a big reduction of scrap, meaning that the workers are getting the job done right the first time.

For the longest time American industry has told its workers "to bring your body to the plant and leave your brains home. Our company tells them to bring their brains."

Take a page from the companies cited above. Make any educational undertaking voluntary. However, explain that you're initiating these programs to upgrade employees' abilities. Emphasize that those who do not attend face the risk of eventual dismissal if they can't reach and maintain the new standards.

SET UP A PROBATION AND EVALUATION SYSTEM

Most employers hire rank-and-file workers on a probationary basis. This period—usually three months from the date of hire—gives the company time to evaluate each employee's suitability. During the probation period, the company generally can dismiss an unqualified or otherwise undesirable employee without advance notice. If, at the end of the probation period, the employer decides not to offer regular employment status to the new employee, that worker is released.

To get the most out of the probation period, you need a set of goals for employees to meet and a thorough system for evaluating the new hire's performance in pursuing those goals. This evaluation should ideally be conducted twice: the first time about midway through the probation period, the second at its conclusion.

The early evaluation can be an effective *unemployment tax-saving tool*. The longer unqualified workers are retained on the payroll, the more unemployment benefits your company will have to shell out when they are finally discharged. Nearly every state charges unemployment benefits to employers in some proportion to an employee's length of service

GET NEW WORKERS OFF TO A FAST START

The sooner you get your new employees out of the blocks and working hard, the sooner they will have a profitable impact on your company's bottom line.

Here are some ways your managers can use to get new workers off to a fast start:

- **Have a timetable.** Know beforehand what you want your new workers to accomplish, and by when. To do that, ask yourself this question: "The employee should be able to do what job and do it how well by what date?"

- **Break down the job.** You probably have an outline in your mind of how every job in your company should be done. Share this information with the new hire. Before he or she begins, write up a brief memo that outlines the key points in every operation the person will be handling. This eliminates a lot of unnecessary guesswork that can take time away from the real task at hand.

- **Have everything ready.** Have your secretary make sure that all the necessary office equipment, training manuals and other tools are on hand and properly arranged—before the worker arrives. Have the new employee's work station prepared the way you expect it to be kept. When you have everything set up right, the worker is more likely to follow the same pattern.

- **Get the individual interested in learning the job.** Explain how the job or operation is related to the final product, so that the employee knows the work is important.

- **Test performance.** After a week on the job, sit down with the new employee and have him tell and show you how it's done. Have him explain the crucial parts of his job and ask if there are any ways the job could be done differently.

- **Loosen the reins.** Give the worker a chance to grow. The employee has to "get the feel" of the job by doing it. Provide the names of other employees he can go to if he has any questions.

HELP YOUR SUPERVISORS EVALUATE EMPLOYEES

An employee's immediate supervisor should handle the evaluation. You may find, however, that your supervisors are reluctant to take the lead in discharging a new worker. After all, they need all hands on deck, and firing an employee is never a pleasant task.

To counter this reluctance, a Wisconsin manufacturing company has developed what it calls a "negative option" evaluation policy. Under this approach, probationary employees are not retained, nor current employees promoted, unless the appropriate supervisor actively recommends that the employee advance.

On the third biweekly pay date after a new employee is hired, payroll sends a new employee evaluation form to the supervisor. Unless this form is completed satisfactorily and returned to the personnel department within 10 days, the new employee is automatically taken off the books. Personnel forwards the completed forms to payroll. A sample of the form is shown in Figure 7.1.

Figure 7.1
Probationary Employee Evaluation Form

Name _____

Hire date_____

Job title_____

Pay rate_____

Supervisor_____

Important: Unless this form is completed and returned to personnel by (date_____) the employee named above will be subject to automatic dismissal.

1. Has the employee required more training from you than is normally needed for this job? _____

2. Has the employee shown an ability to handle the job with little training?_____

3. Is the employee performing at, above or below (circle one) the standard for this job?

4. If below, when do you expect the employee to reach the standard? _____

5. Is this employee developing satisfactory working relationships with the other employees within your area and throughout the company? _____

6. Has the employee maintained a good attendance record and exhibited the type of attitude that you want in this job? _____

7. Has the employee expressed any dissatisfaction with the job?

_____

8. Do you recommend that the employee be taken off probation and retained permanently?

Yes_____ No_____

Supervisor's signature_____

Date_____

Unless a supervisor goes on record in favor of keeping a new employee after the review period is up, the employee is discharged.

In enforcing the probationary policy, the company owner tells harried supervisors to "look beyond this week's or this month's production quota. If a new employee doesn't measure up we're better off in the long run letting him or her go." But the company advertises for, interviews and lines up a replacement for a faltering worker before he or she is discharged. This cuts the amount of time a department is short-handed. The supervisor still has to train the replacement. But if the replacement employee is good, this may actually take less time than correcting the previous employee's continual mistakes would have taken.

"What I want to avoid," says the company owner, "is a department that's in the habit of *emergency hiring*. This practice adds more and more below-average employees to the payroll. The department gets the work out, but over the long haul, productivity drops and payroll costs escalate."

How to Avoid Performance Appraisal Pitfalls

Performance evaluations are commonly used to set the size of employee raises. Properly prepared evaluations also can save your company big dollars should disgruntled employees or ex-employees decide to sue. This could happen if an employee:

- Feels that he or she was being judged unfairly.
- Wasn't told that dismissal was a possibility if work didn't improve—and then was subsequently fired.

Offer company supervisors—particularly newer ones—guidelines on conducting employee reviews that are fair and complete. When dealing with supervisors, you should:

- Stress that they should not judge an individual's performance on the basis of one trait to which the supervisor may be particularly sensitive.
- Emphasize the need to base the review on facts—rather than opinions or impressions—as much as possible. Supervisors should consider what an employee has done—not what the person's capable of.

- Have your supervisors substantiate why the employee's performance is not satisfactory (for example, an employee's behavior was improper, the employee failed to respond properly to criticism, or anything else that provides good cause for a poor review).
- Make it clear that ratings should be based on an employee's job performance during a specified period of time. They should not be influenced by previous reviews.
- Help supervisors identify their own rating tendencies— whether they tend to average out ratings, rate too high or too low, or whether they tend to be overly lenient or strict. (If some supervisors consistently mark on a curve and other supervisors do not, employees in certain departments may systematically be at a disadvantage.)

Workers should be given a chance to respond if they feel their reviews don't accurately reflect their work for the past year. Your company could set up a grievance procedure to hear these complaints or you could leave a space on the review itself for employee comments. Then be sure to respond as soon as possible.

MOTIVATING EMPLOYEES TO GREATER PRODUCTIVITY

Successful companies learned long ago that the way to get greater productivity is by letting employees know what you expect, inspecting what is done and—most important—showing appreciation for jobs done well.

That's the idea behind the following proven-in-action methods of getting greater production from workers.

HOW TO SET UP JOBS TO GET GREATER PRODUCTIVITY FROM YOUR EMPLOYEES

The opportunity to accomplish attainable, self-set and largely self-monitored goals is what motivates top-notch workers. Have every employee develop a personal job *plan*. This is not just a job description. It is a *plan for growth*, where employees list changes that may be expected, or that can be introduced to improve the job.

With this plan as a guide to what is expected, the employee can keep track of changes, or *exceptions* that crop up in day-to-day work.

Here are the key ingredients that employees should include in their job plans—to ensure greater personal and professional satisfaction for them, as well as increasing success for your company.

• **Jobs should have a learning function.** To fight "burnout," a job should be structured so that it requires continual learning. Have employees include *learning objectives* in their job plans. This includes training sessions, seminars, etc., that help employees do better jobs and prepare them to move up to more challenging positions.

• **Every job should have a "client" relationship.** Employees should be encouraged to recognize that they have *customers* to serve rather than just bosses, supervisors or procedures. The "customer" can be an area, department or actual customer. Have employees specifically define their "customers" within their job plans. They should list the key influence on the customer's decision to "buy" (accept) their products (reports, for example) and/or services (such as recommendations).

• **Employees should have the right to schedule their own work as much as possible.** Experienced workers usually know how to do the job, and how to schedule it better than anyone else. You should give them the opportunity to do so. Have employees prepare an *Operational Schedule* of primary work objectives and supporting projects—in order of priorities.

HOW TO TURN YOUR CRITICISM OF AN EMPLOYEE'S WORK INTO A BLUEPRINT FOR HIGHER PRODUCTIVITY

Nobody likes to be criticized, no matter how constructive the comments may be. But there are times when you or your managers have to point out an employee's mistakes—before productivity takes a tumble. But there is a right way—and a wrong way—to criticize an employee. Pass along to your managers these five steps for providing helpful—and profitable—criticism.

• **Don't wait for the "right moment."** Engaging in small talk before you level your criticism only postpones the inevitable. Let the employee know immediately what the problem is. It may sound harsh—but you're better off getting straight to the heart of the matter.

• **Spell out the problem.** Telling the employee "Your work is sloppy," is not nearly as effective as saying, "Mistakes in your work cost us $500 in lost sales last month." Putting the problem in dollars-and-cents terms helps the employee appreciate the seriousness of your criticism.

• **Encourage feedback.** The meeting shouldn't become a one-sided conversation—with you being the one doing all the talking. Invite the employee's comments on how the problem can be solved. By seeking the person's ideas, you dull the sting of your remarks and avoid lowering the worker's morale any further.

• **Seek agreement.** It's important that the employee you criticize agrees with you that there is a problem. Otherwise, it's doubtful you'll be able to find a solution. Once agreement is reached, work with the employee to locate the source of the difficulty and possible solutions. Perhaps the employee is unfamiliar with all the responsibilities of the job. Then consider a training session. Or maybe there's friction between the employee and a supervisor. A transfer to another department may be the answer.

• **Tie up loose ends.** Don't let the employee leave the meeting without clearly understanding what's been discussed and the steps to be taken. Set a date for a follow-up discussion. And let the person know you're available should he or she have any further problems.

KEEP EMPLOYEES FROM BECOMING BURNOUT VICTIMS

"Job burnout" isn't just another employee relations buzzword. It's a serious problem—one that could have an adverse impact on your company's productivity.

Job burnout happens when workers feel trapped in their jobs and lose all enthusiasm and interest in their work. The result in many cases is someone who's content to do just enough work to get by. In the critical stages, the burnout victim stops contributing anything at all to the company and is eventually let go.

The reasons for job burnout vary, but most cases result from a combination of inner stress and on-the-job pressure. You can help your people avoid this problem. Pass along these tips for coping with job stress. Make sure the suggestions are circulated among employees on all levels.

- Leave your work station or desk for lunch. Eating where you work doesn't give you a chance to take a break from your job.

- Where possible, change the way you do your job. Look for new and different ways to apply your skills and talents.

- Share your problems with other employees. Get their ideas on how you can solve on-the-job difficulties.

- Learn to manage your time better so you don't take your work home with you. For instance, get in the habit of doing your paperwork immediately, rather than letting it pile up on your desk.

GIVE WORKERS TIME OFF—AND GET MORE WORK DONE

A number of companies have found that their employees actually get more work done when they're forced to take a 15-minute break each hour. These companies claim that this 25% cut in work time actually increases output per person by 10% or more. Here's how it might work for you.

- **Tight time limits raise performance pressure.** Most people work harder as deadlines loom, and cutting the work hour to 45 minutes forces workers to be more efficient.

- **Breaks improve accuracy.** Staring at a VDT screen for hours on end is as mind-numbing as any other kind of repetitive labor. As boredom and fatigue take their toll, accuracy inevitably declines. The visual and mental rest frequent breaks provide almost always lowers the incidence of preventable errors, which your workers must spend additional time correcting.

- **Use "rotating" breaks.** Naturally, if all your people took quarter hour breaks at the same time, your staff would be effectively "off-line" 25% of the time. Be sure to stagger staffers' breaks so that overlap is minimized.

HOW TO BOOST THE SATISFACTION LEVEL AT YOUR COMPANY

If you think your workers are among the ranks of the unhappy, you may want to change some of your management policies.

Here are some suggestions for boosting the satisfaction level at your company from Robert Half, founder of Robert Half International, Inc.:

- **Encourage good performance by acknowledging it**. When employees perform exceptionally well, reward them: upgrade their functions, give them incentives, perks, bonuses and titles, Half suggests. The most effective way of recognizing a job well done is with praise. "Never lose sight of the fact that it is tough to find well-motivated, hard-working employees," Half says.
- **Keep lines of communication open.** All employee complaints—justified or not—deserve your prompt attention and a prompt reply. When you do report back to the employees, be sure to tell them what action, if any, you took or are about to take.
- **Titles do count.** While promotions aren't substitutes for raises, they do boost a deserving employee's self-esteem.
- **Don't forget little things.** Common courtesy is important, but easy to overlook. Don't berate or make malicious comments about an employee in front of others. Smile, say "good morning" and "thank you" and give a note of appreciation when the situation calls for it.
- **Be fair.** Most employees don't mind a reasonably tight ship, as long as the discipline is tempered with compassion and is administered even-handedly.
- **Get rid of "bad apples."** You can't afford to tolerate employees who are disruptive, regardless of how skilled they are. Consider transferring them to a more isolated area. If that's not possible, you're better off letting them go. Bad employees set bad examples. By keeping them on your payroll, you are undermining overall employee morale.
- **Promote from within.** Many companies make it a practice to look at their present employees before they seek outsiders. Passing over employees in order to bring in an outsider almost invariably erodes morale. People often have their résumés ready at all times, Half says, not necessarily to look elsewhere but to prepare for a better job in their own companies.

CHAPTER EIGHT

How to Get the Most Out of Your Employee Benefit Dollar

The paycheck may be most people's prime motivator, but it's by no means the only factor that attracts and keeps good workers at a company. Employee benefits—ranging from traditional medical and life insurance to innovative savings and investment plans—are now a significant part of the compensation packages offered by businesses of all sizes and types. Small business owners today can choose from a large array of benefits, many of which can be tailored to meet the specific needs of their employees.

Employee benefits also have become a significant—and growing—part of the cost of doing business. Recent studies estimate that approximately 40% of payroll is spent on employee benefit costs and that this percentage is expected to increase.

Most employees probably don't realize that the benefits you provide actually represent another "paycheck" to them. That's why it's imperative that you stress the strong points of the benefits package you offer. When hiring new workers or explaining a new benefit to current employees, emphasize the protection they get, or the interest that will build up. By dwelling on the *limits or restrictions* of a par-

227

ticular benefit, you run the risk of souring employees on a perk that's meant to build enthusiasm and morale.

One sure way to sell employees on the value of your package is to show them what it would cost them if they had to purchase the benefits on their own. This way, employees will realize how much the company is giving them above and beyond their paychecks.

BASIC BENEFITS: EMPLOYEE INSURANCE

Whether you're choosing benefits for the first time or revamping an existing plan because of costs or changing needs, you'll want to include certain basic kinds of insurance to protect your employees. They get the peace of mind that comes from knowing that, even though they may not have accumulated a large reserve fund on their own, they can still survive a costly illness or an injury that keeps them from working. Employee insurance is important to the small business, too. Secure employees are likely to be more productive. And when the workforce is small, every member is more valuable to the company's bottom line. Here's a look at some basic forms of group insurance:

MEDICAL BENEFITS

Because of the high and continuously climbing cost of medical care, this is the benefit most needed by your employees. Your package should include a medical plan that can be expanded over time from minimum coverage to full coverage. If you can't afford to provide a liberal plan, consider a plan with a high front-end deductible and 100% coverage after some defined cost has been paid by the employee.

Such a plan might impose a $250 annual deductible per person, 80% coverage of the first $5,000 of covered expenses, and 100% coverage of all additional covered expenses for the rest of the year. It might also cap coverage at a certain level, say $1 million, over each covered individual's lifetime. If this plan proves too costly for your company, you can investigate sharing premium costs with employees.

Many employers are adding dental benefits to their medical plans— but it's a costly addition. To help contain costs, choose a plan that encourages preventive care and cleaning by paying 100% of these relatively small expenses. Your dental insurance provider also should give you the option of excluding "cosmetic" procedures from coverage and limiting coverage of orthodontia to, say, 50% of the procedure's cost. Lifetime coverage caps are prevalent among dental plans.

Once you've settled on a plan, you'll find the key to ongoing control over medical expenses lies in reducing the number and size of claims. And this is where you'll need your employees' help. Any changes you make that end up costing your employees more money won't sit well with them initially. However, if you can show them that ever-increasing costs are making changes necessary—and that your company is picking up a fair share of this increased burden—you will soften the blow. In addition, you may be able to make changes in your plan to cut claims—and promote employee cooperation—by showing your employees how they will benefit from the changes.

The cost of providing health care insurance to employees is skyrocketing. Here are several ways your company can cut plan costs and still keep employee goodwill.

• **Share premium costs with employees.** More and more companies are requiring their employees to take greater financial responsibility for health care benefits.

For example, over half of the plans surveyed by benefits consultants, *Hewitt Associates* (Lincolnshire, Ill.) require premium contributions from employees for individual coverage, and over three-quarters require premium contributions for family coverage.

When premium contributions are required, the employees generally end up paying less than one-third of the full costs of coverage. And nearly two-thirds of the surveyed companies require employees to pay a "front-end deductible" before insurance coverage kicks in. The front-end deductible generally ranges between $100-$200 for individual coverage and $200-$400 for family coverage.

Nearly three-quarters of the plans surveyed by Hewitt reimburse 80% of covered medical charges. So employees are responsible for picking up the remaining 20% of medical costs. However, this liability generally isn't open-ended.

Over 90% of the plans have a so-called "stop-loss" feature that limits an employee's out-of-pocket expenses. Once this limit is reached, the plan picks up 100% of the covered expenses instead of 80%. For example, the stop-loss limit for individual employees may be pegged at $1,500 or less (including the deductible). The per-family stop-loss limit may be between $1,000 to $2,000.

• **Require second opinions.** Some companies require employees to obtain a second opinion before they undergo non-emergency surgery. This may reduce the likelihood of unnecessary surgery being performed. And employees, of course, benefit from not undergoing unnecessary surgical procedures. However, the Hewitt survey found that the second opinion requirement recently has come under scrutiny. In fact, several companies have dropped this provision—generally because they found that it didn't produce cost savings.

• **Make sure hospital stays are really necessary.** Over two-thirds of the companies surveyed by Hewitt require mandatory hospital *precertification* prior to admission. Under a hospital precertification procedure, if an employee obtains approval for a treatment prior to hospital admission, the plan will pay a greater percentage of the employee's medical expenses—generally 80%—than if the employee doesn't. Typically, plans will pay only 50% of the medical expenses if admission is not reviewed or approved.

Hospital stays are extremely expensive. This is, of course, separate and apart from the cost of actual medical procedures for which the patient is admitted. Therefore, any measures that reduce the number of admissions or duration of stays can significantly cut costs. The next three items give some ideas for accomplishing this.

• **Advise employees to request preadmission testing on an *outpatient* basis.** Hospital stays are uncomfortable to the patient, regardless of who is paying. Employees who were not aware of this alternative may welcome this cost-cutting advice.

• **Discourage weekend admissions.** Hospital stays also can generally be shortened if employees are not admitted to the hospital on weekends. Most hospitals function on a five-day workweek. So if an employee is admitted on a weekend, he or she may end up waiting until Monday for the intended procedure to be performed.

• **Encourage employees to look to alternatives to hospital care.** These include birthing centers, hospices and home care (which may follow an early discharge from a hospital). Employees may prefer the more personalized service they can get outside of the institutionalized setting of a hospital.

• **Watch for billing errors.** A company can get employees to help tighten the administration of claims by offering a cash reward to employees who discover billing errors. At the same time, if your company has any questions about a medical treatment, talk to the hospital or doctor involved. The Hewitt survey found that nearly one-quarter of employers reported that they (or their claims administrators) have approached hospitals or doctors to question high charges or billing errors.

• **Find out what other coverage the employee has.** For example, in a two-wage-earner family, a worker could have coverage through his spouse's employer as well as your company's plan. The spouse's coverage may help defray the costs to your plan.

• **Educate employees about wellness and ways to achieve it.** A growing number of companies sponsor so-called "employee wellness" programs. The most common programs are smoking cessation, weight control and stress management. Companies with such programs indicate that the most cost-effective wellness programs are hypertension screening, cholesterol screening, smoking cessation and on-site exercise facilities. A benefits package can provide some sort of coverage for the cost of programs to reduce smoking, drug dependence and obesity. In addition, if your company has a cafeteria, its menus should be reviewed to determine whether nutritionally sound meals are being served.

LIFE INSURANCE

At a minimum, your life insurance plan should allow for a decent burial and some extra cash to help the deceased employee's family through the first few months of adjustment. Generally, plans offer benefits ranging from a fixed dollar amount of, say, $3,000 to $10,000, to the more generous benefits of one or two times salary. Again, if the costs of life insurance coverage are putting a strain on your budget, you may want to check out the possibility of *sharing premium costs* with your employees rather than reducing their minimum coverage.

One of the most popular forms of life insurance is employer-provided *group-term* life insurance. And with good reason—the premiums are generally deductible by the employer and completely tax-free to employees for up to $50,000 of coverage. Also, employees usually don't have to take a physical examination to qualify for it.

Group-term life insurance has no paid-up or cash surrender value. The policy generally runs on a renewable year-to-year basis. The premiums on employees who stay with the company will increase annually because the premiums are based on age. But since the workforce is constantly changing, with some employees retiring and younger workers taking their place, age-based premium cost increases generally even out.

One disadvantage to employees is that they lose the benefit of group-term coverage when they leave the company through retirement or other termination. Group-term insurance generally ceases at retirement and is prohibitively expensive for retirees to retain on their own. Employees who leave the company before retirement may discover that, while they have a right to convert their coverage to individual policies, this also may be quite costly. In addition, employees may be left unprotected if you discontinue the plan or your carrier refuses to renew it.

SHORT-TERM DISABILITY PLANS

Most employers protect workers against income loss through paid sick-leave plans, sickness and accident insurance, or both. These are paid-leave plans that continue employees' income when they're absent because of *nonoccupational* accidents or illnesses. *Occupational* illnesses and accidents are covered by state workers' compensation insurance, which provides income protection and pays medical and rehabilitation expenses for employees.

Generally, a sick-leave pay plan provides for full pay from the employee's first day of absence, but your plan can limit the number of sick days and the level of benefits allowed. Sickness-and-accident insurance plans usually provide 50% to 70% of pay for employees (after a wait of several days) for up to 26 weeks. You can require new hires to wait, say, three months to be eligible for paid sick leave or sickness-and-accident insurance.

When employees are absent due to short-term disability, they retain their seniority rights with regard to promotions, layoffs and retirement benefits. Employers generally continue their employees' health and life insurance benefits during such absences. Many group-term life plans will waive premiums for both the employer and the employee for the term of the absence. However, this benefit continuation is usually spelled out in each individual benefit plan, not in the short-term disability plan itself.

If you can't afford a generous paid-leave plan, you might consider providing 100% of pay for the first two weeks of a short-term disability, and half pay for any additional time. If you opt for a noncumulative plan (one in which allotted sick days expire at the end of each calendar year and can't be carried over or "banked"), you can vary the days of leave at full pay and partial pay according to employees' years of service. That way you can reward long-term employees, who are likely to need more time off than younger workers.

LONG-TERM DISABILITY PLANS

Coverage for long-term disabilities comes from a number of sources, including Social Security, workers' compensation (in the case of work-related disabilities) and private employer disability insurance. Private employer long-term disability (LTD) insurance is usually designed to be supplemented in part by Social Security disability benefits.

Employees also can contribute toward the employer plan. Benefits attributable to those contributions are tax-free to the recipient.

Generally, employees who have worked at least five years during the 10-year period immediately preceding disability are eligible to receive Social Security disability benefits. (Young workers may qualify for these benefits after shorter periods of employment.)

When choosing a long-term disability plan, you should take these Social Security disability benefits into account. But keep in mind that there are several legal requirements employees must meet to receive these payments. For example, to qualify as disabled under the Social Security law, an employee must have a "medically determinable physical or mental impairment which can be expected to result in death or to last at least 12 months." In addition, the person must be unable to engage in any substantial gainful activity (employment) by reason of that impairment.

State vocational rehabilitation agencies generally make the medical determination of disability according to regulations issued by the federal Department of Health and Human Services. A disabled worker also must complete a five-month waiting period before Social Security disability payments begin.

Your LTD plan should have two basic goals: to protect dependents if the employee dies, and to protect the family against loss of income while the employee is totally disabled. The second goal is particularly important, since permanent disability is more likely than death. Your plan should also have a strong rehabilitation component.

Worker eligibility is a key concept to consider in designing an LTD plan. Many LTD insurance plans require longer employee service for benefits than do sick-leave or health insurance plans, which may start immediately or within a month of employment. A year's wait for LTD insurance eligibility is not unusual.

You also can limit your exposure through your plan's definition of disability. For example, typical LTD plans require that, for the first two or three years, the person can't work in the occupation he or she previously held. In the case of professional employees, this period may be extended to five years. After this initial period, the definition becomes inability to work in any occupation for which the employee is suited by education, training or experience. Your plan can require periodic monitoring of disabled employees to determine any changes in their conditions.

Your LTD insurance plan also can exclude several conditions from coverage. Common exclusions are for self-inflicted injuries, pre-existing conditions, alcoholism, disabilities that arise while a worker is abroad and mental illness. Some plans do not pay benefits for periods when the disabled person isn't under a doctor's care.

> **IMPORTANT:** The Pregnancy Discrimination Act says employers can't discriminate on the basis of pregnancy-related disabilities, which have to be treated the same as other disabilities.

The LTD insurance plan should replace about 50% to 60% of predisability earnings. With offsets for Social Security, worker's compensation, employers' pension plans and state nonoccupational disability insurance (available in several states), the total level of benefits from all sources may not exceed 75% of predisability earnings.

To contain benefit costs, consider establishing a cap on the benefit that can be received, regardless of the employee's predisability earnings. On the other hand, to ensure that all disabled workers, regardless of salary or other benefits, get at least some LTD protection, you can set a minimum level of benefits at, say, $50 a month.

When figuring your total benefits ceiling and the level of protection in your plan, consider factors that will affect disabled workers' financial status, like mortgage payments or children's education. On the other hand, keep in mind that a disabled worker will pay less in income taxes, which are payable only on a maximum of 50% of Social Security benefits (and then only in the case of high-income recipients). And remember: If your plan is funded with employee contributions, all LTD benefits that can be attributed to those contributions are tax-free to the employee.

HOW FLEXIBLE HEALTH BENEFIT PLANS GIVE EMPLOYEES MORE CHOICE—AND SAVE COMPANIES MONEY

As noted earlier in the chapter, the days of providing employees with first-dollar health coverage for free are over for almost all companies. Year after year of 15%–20% jumps in the costs of health coverage have made the price tag too high. On the other hand, many employers are reluctant to shift all the rising costs onto the shoulders of employees. However, according to a benefits consultant with *Hewitt Associates* (Lincolnshire, Illinois), there are steps businesses have been taking to bring health care costs under control.

These steps fall into two primary areas: (1) Sharing costs with employees by charging higher premiums or raising the deductible; and (2) Using so-called managed care arrangements or health care "networks" (e.g., HMOs, PPOs) to control health care access, price and quality.

The cost sharing and managed care arrangements can be implemented separately or together. According to Hewitt, however, a company's cost control effort will be most successful if it combines the two arrangements.

Implementing these steps is no guarantee that your company will *cut* its health care costs from current levels. But it may well do just that. In any event, by sharing costs with employees, educating them against making unnecessary expenditures and directing them to more cost-effective doctors and hospitals, your company can at least slow the rate of cost increase or freeze costs at their current level.

Cost sharing

Cost sharing, or "flex," arrangements allow companies to put a brake on "first dollar" expenses by giving employees a choice—absorb higher deductibles or pay higher premiums. Employees get to select the amount of deductible expenses they must incur before insurance coverage kicks in. The higher the deductible they select, the more out-of-pocket medical expenses employees have to absorb. The tradeoff, however, is that an employee selecting a higher deductible pays a lower insurance premium. Here's an example of how this might work for an employee selecting "single employee" coverage under a simple flex arrangement:

Option A	Deductible	Coinsurance	Premium/Year
A	$1,000	80%/20%	$ 250
B	500	80%/20%	500
C	200	80%/20%	1,000

There would be several more levels of premiums if, for example, your company offers family coverage, or different types of family coverage (e.g., employee plus one dependent, employee plus two or more, etc.).

Managed care

The managed care arrangement helps control the bigger portion of medical expenses (i.e., everything over the deductible amount). One part of such a program is a tight "utilization" review of high-cost claims, or high-volume claim areas (e.g., mental health expenses). This is to make sure treatment is necessary, appropriate and cost-effective.

The other part of managed care is price control. Discount prices or some other type of cost-saving arrangement usually is negotiated with a "network" of health care providers, either by an individual employer or, more likely, your insurance company. Employees are given strong *incentives* to use these network providers.

What kind of incentives? Money. It costs employees less to use network providers than non-network providers. Here's how one company has combined "flex" with managed care:

Option	In-Network Benefits Copayment	Deductible	Coinsurance	Out-of-Network Benefits Deductible	Coinsurance
A	$5	$400	90%/10%	$400	80%/20%
B	5	300	90%/10%	300	80%/20%
C	5	200	90%/10%	200	80%/20%

If an employee goes to an out-of-network physician for an office visit, he must first meet the deductible before insurance coverage kicks in. And once it does, insurance covers 80% of his expenses; the employee is responsible for the remaining 20%.

If, on the other hand, the employee uses an in-network physician, he or she is out-of-pocket for the doctor's services for only a $5 copayment; insurance picks up the rest of the bill. The deductible and coinsurance payment features generally apply to all other medical charges (e.g., tests and other services performed in a doctor's office, hospital charges for room and board, outpatient services, etc.) After meeting the deductible, 90% of the employee's other expenses would be covered by insurance.

The big question is: Will these steps save my company money? They can—and they have. One Hewitt client's health insurance premiums were scheduled to jump nearly 40%. However, after switching from its traditional "indemnity" health insurance plan to a managed care plan with flex options, the company was able to hold its health care costs to current levels.

OTHER BENEFIT OPTIONS

Companies can offer a full-service "cafeteria" of benefits to employees, without having to pay extra for them. For example, some of your employees may want vision, dental or long-term care coverage in addition to their regular health coverage. Or your company may also want to offer employees non-health care benefits, such as child care, life insurance, etc. Employers can provide a "pool" of funds that the employees can use to "purchase" a benefits package tailored to fit their own needs.

The company says to its employees: "Here is a 'credit allocation' of XXX dollars to spend on total benefits. You each have to figure out what combination is best for you and/or your family. If you want coverage that exceeds your credit allocation, you have to pay for it." (Some companies allow employes to pay for these extra benefits on a pre-tax basis under a salary reduction plan.)

The company in our example breaks down each of its options (A, B and C) into "Employee-Only," "Employee with One Dependent," and "Employee with Two or More Dependents." Here's what the employee premium structure looks like:

Employee premiums per year for:			
	Employee-only	Employee w/1 dependent	Employee w/2 or more dependents
$400 deductible	$500	$600	$800
$300 deductible	725	875	1160
$200 deductible	1135	1320	1715

The company also provides each employee with a $966 credit allocation. The employee can use these credits to "purchase" health insurance coverage, as well as other benefit options, such as dental, life or disability insurance. So, for example, if an employee elects the "Employee Plus One Dependent" option with a $400 deductible, he or she can use $600 of the credit to pay her basic premium and use the remaining $366 to buy other health benefits. (The company also allows employees to use the credit for non-health care purposes, such as contributing to their 401(k) accounts.)

Communications a key

It's important to keep in mind that no matter how you slice or sugarcoat flex and managed care programs, employees who have been getting 100% medical coverage at no cost are going to be worse off than before. The simple fact is, they were getting something for nothing, and now they have to pay for it.

Show employees why *it's necessary* for your company to make changes. Employees have responded best to managed health care programs when employers have them know what's been happening with health care costs. Employees will better accept the changes if they are made to understand that your company has a serious cost problem and that they have to be part of the solution. A well-thought out and well-executed communications plan can significantly reduce employees' negative reaction.

Allowing a transition period is a good public relations move. During this period, employees under treatment for a particular condition (e.g., pregnancy) may continue to use their current physician with full coverage—even if the physician isn't part of the network. This option generally can be negotiated with the insurance company.

In addition, representatives from your insurance company should be brought in to explain to employees how the new health programs work, and what—in dollars and cents terms—it will mean to them. Another good idea is to set up a program that assists employees in finding new physicians who are part of the network.

HOW A SIMPLE COMPANY HEALTH PROGRAM CAN REDUCE ABSENTEEISM AND CUT COSTS

What can you do to help your company improve productivity, cut costs and reduce the frequency and duration of absenteeism—all at nominal cost?

Have your company set up a "blood pressure control" program. This type of program isn't just for the detection of high blood pressure. It also can be used as a substitute for regular follow-up visits to the doctor by employees who are receiving blood pressure-related treatment. It's this latter function that can save your company money.

Fifteen to twenty percent of the adult population has blood pressure high enough to require regular visits to a physician for checkups. Employees have to take time off from work to make office visits that are usually paid for through your company's insurance fund. The cost to a company with 200 employees can be as much as $25,000 a year.

Your company may not fall into that category, but it's not immune from the costs of the disease.

"A good program can be started very easily and cost as little as $3 per person per year," says the benefits manager of a Florida company. "All you need is a blood pressure cuff, a stethoscope and a nurse who knows how to take blood pressure readings and interpret the results," she adds. "You don't even need an in-house nurse. A public health nurse or physician may be willing to do the actual screening for you."

Designate one day a month as "Blood Pressure Day" at your company. Put up a notice announcing that an open clinic for voluntary blood pressure testing will be held during the lunch hour. Emphasize that the screenings only take a few minutes.

If you think that a blood pressure control program sounds right for your company, or if you would like more information, you might want to check with the American Heart Association. You can call your local chapter or contact its national headquarters located at 7320 Greenville Avenue, Dallas, Texas 75231 (214) 373-6300. It will advise you on how to start up an employee health program at your company.

CHAPTER NINE

TAX-SMART WAYS TO COMPENSATE YOUR EMPLOYEES

Bonuses and pay incentives are a great way to motivate your people to produce more and better work. But, as with any increase in current income, your employees actually will receive less than what you're giving them because of the income tax bite.

That's why more small business owners are turning to profit-sharing plans and other types of tax-deferred compensation arrangements. Such plans provide a triple benefit: current tax deductions for your company, added compensation for employees, plus tax-free growth of their money.

Keep in mind that company owners also can participate in these plans. Indeed, such plans should be an integral part of your personal financial and retirement planning.

> **IMPORTANT:** The law and regulations that govern tax-favored pension, profit-sharing and other retirement plans are undergoing constant revision by Congress and the IRS. Major changes have been made within the past year, and it's almost certain that additional changes will be made this year. The rules are complex, and noncompliance could

be costly for both the company and its employees. Be sure to consult with your attorney or benefits adviser when implementing or amending your company's retirement plans.

Here's a look at some of the most popular tax-favored compensation strategies for employees and executives.

HOW TO MAKE THE MOST OF THE MAGIC OF PROFIT-SHARING

Profit-sharing plans are the tax law's biggest and best wealth builders for many employees (especially younger ones). Why? Simply because of the special treatment the tax law grants profit-sharing plans.

Here's how a profit-sharing plan works. The plan calls for the employer to contribute a percentage of before-tax profits. The amount contributed to each employee's account varies because the contribution is tied into the employee's compensation for the year. The tax law puts a ceiling on how much can be contributed to an employee's account each year. Contributions and other additions (such as voluntary contributions and forfeitures) can't exceed the lesser of $30,000 or 25% of compensation.

The corporation's maximum annual deduction is usually 15% of the employee's compensation, but carryover contributions can raise the maximum to 25%. The contributions are not only deductible by the corporation, but are also tax-free to the employee. The employee's account grows tax-free until he or she later withdraws the funds.

Case Example

Robert Jones is 40. His top dollars are taxed at 28%. Let's compare the results if Jones' employer sets up a profit-sharing plan for him, contributing $7,500 per year, to results we'd get if Jones' employer gives him a $7,500 bonus each year and Jones invests the net-after-tax bonus himself. We assume no forfeitures.

	Without Plan	With Plan
1. Gross annual bonus...............................	$7,500	$7,500
2. Less tax at 28%	2,100	—
3. Net annual amount available for investment.......................................	5,400	7,500

4. Gross annual earnings on investment 8%   8%
5. Less tax at 28% .... 2.24%   —
6. Net annual earnings on investment 5.76%   8%
7. Gross amount accumulated at

Mr. Jones' age 50	$74,333	$117,341
60	$204,744	$370,672
65	$302,945	$592,158

Obviously taxes have been paid on the self-invested accumulation but not on the plan's funds. But in this respect, too, the plan wins out. Assuming Jones retires at age 65 and takes out his entire account in one year, he'll wind up with this big net after-tax advantage. Mr. Jones comes out way ahead. The payout could be taxed at a top rate of 33% ($195,412 tax bite). Jones still pockets $396,746 with a plan—$89,352 more than without a plan.

Your company can provide still more financial security—without laying out any more cash. It simply amends the retirement plan to let you (and other employees) build a kind of personal tax shelter.

The plan amendment allows employees to make *nondeductible voluntary contributions* to their profit-sharing accounts. The investment return on your contributions accumulates tax-free, just like earnings on company contributions. But unlike the company's contributions, your voluntary contributions can be a source of ready cash. You can withdraw voluntary contributions any time you want without paying tax (withdrawal of accrued interest is, of course, taxable).

HOW A CASH-OR-DEFERRED PROFIT-SHARING PLAN CAN PROVIDE AN EXTRA TAX SHELTER

Many people are no longer making contributions to Individual Retirement Accounts. But that doesn't mean they can no longer make contributions to a tax-deductible savings plan. Their company can help them sidestep the IRA crackdown with a cash-or-deferred profit-sharing plan (also known as a 401(k) plan).

Employees elect to have the company contribute an amount to a profit-sharing plan instead of paying them that amount in cash. The contributions may be in lieu of part of the employees' current pay, annual cash bonuses or salary increases.

The money set aside is not taxable to the employees and is deductible by the company. The contribution and its earnings grow tax-free until they are withdrawn.

The net effect is that the plan operates as a tax-deductible savings account for participating employees. Instead of the employees saving *after-tax* income (and paying current tax on what their savings earn), they can direct their employer to set aside *before-tax* income. No dollars go to the tax collector until the savings are withdrawn.

A cash-or-deferred plan allows employees to defer up to 25% of their compensation to a profit-sharing plan. There is also a dollar limit on deferred contributions. The ceiling is adjusted for inflation annually.

> **IMPORTANT:** Your company can continue making large contributions for your retirement by using other types of retirement plan setups. The 401(k) annual dollar limit applies only to elective deferrals. The 25% ($30,000 maximum) limit continues to apply to total retirement contributions made by you or on your behalf.

If your elective deferrals for the year exceed the annual limit, the excess amount is treated as taxable income in the year of the deferral. But if that excess is not distributed to you by the plan before April 15 of the following year, you are hit with a big tax bill.

To begin with, the excess deferrals are taxed to you in the year to which the deferrals relate—the same as if they were distributed. But they also are treated as deferred compensation when they are later withdrawn. So the funds are taxed a second time. And if the withdrawals occur before you reach age 59½, they are hit by the 10% penalty on early withdrawals.

A cash-or-deferred plan must benefit rank-and-file employees. While it can benefit you more than the rank-and-file, there are limits that must be satisfied.

- The actual percentage of salary deferred by highly paid employees cannot be disproportionately higher than the percentage of salary deferred by lower-paid, or so-called non-highly compensated employees (NHCEs). The rules in this area are extremely complex. But for simplicity, we will boil them down into these two general tests:

- The percentage of salary deferred by highly paid employees must not be more than 125% times the percentage of salary deferred by NHCEs; or

- The percentage of salary deferred by highly paid employees cannot exceed the lesser of (a) two times the percentage of salary deferred by NHCEs or (b) the percentage of salary deferred by NHCEs *plus* 2 percentage points.

Employees can withdraw their elective deferrals (but not employer contributions or income on any contributions) upon the occurrence of certain "hardships" prior to death, disability, separation from service, retirement or reaching age 59½. The tax law provides that an employee must meet two conditions in order to qualify for a hardship withdrawal:

(1) an "immediate and heavy financial need" and

(2) a "lack of other means" to meet this financial need.

The regulations recently set out a list of "safe harbors"—circumstances in which an employer can permit a hardship withdrawal without causing compliance problems for the plan.

Financial need test: The IRS regs list the following situations in which hardship withdrawals are justified based on financial need:

- Medical expenses of an employee, the employee's spouse and dependents;

- Purchase of an employee's principal residence;

- Expenses necessary to prevent the eviction from, or foreclosure on, the employee's principal residence;

- Tuition for post-secondary education for the employee, the employee's spouse and children.

Lack-of-means test: The IRS says that in addition to meeting the financial needs test, a company must establish that the hardship distribution is "necessary to meet such need." The company can meet this test either by using a "facts and circumstances" test or by using the safe-harbor procedure set out in the regulations. The safe-harbor procedure requires that:

- The distribution is not in excess of the amount needed;

- The employee must first take all available distributions and loans (other than hardship distributions) from all plans maintained by the company;

- The employee's contributions (both pre- and post-tax) to all company plans be suspended for at least 12 months after receipt of the hardship distribution; and

- The 401(k) dollar maximum in the calendar year following the year the hardship withdrawal was received must be reduced by the amount of the 401(k) contribution the employee made in the year the hardship withdrawal was received.

According to the regs, a company must meet *all* of the safe-harbor requirements to ensure its plan's qualified status. In addition, even though an employee may be allowed to withdraw the elective deferrals under the cash-or-deferred plan rules, the withdrawals may still be subject to the 10% penalty for early withdrawals (those made before age 59½, death or disability).

Other considerations

A cash-or-deferred plan can be a good idea, but there are certain other factors to consider.

- The company's deductible contribution to a profit-sharing plan cannot exceed 15% of covered payroll. And what is deferred is lumped in with regular contributions. So if a company is already contributing 15% of payroll to a regular profit-sharing plan, it would not be able to deduct the deferred amounts.

- There is a limit on the yearly contribution to a profit-sharing plan on behalf of any one employee (25% of the employee's total annual pay, but not more than $30,000). This includes an employee's salary reduction contributions. So any money an employee defers may reduce the dollar amount the company can contribute to an employee's profit-sharing account.

- If company profit-sharing contributions are used to help the cash-or-deferred plan pass the tax law's nondiscrimination tests, special rules come into play. For example, the contributions must be *nonforfeitable* at all times. In other words, the profit-sharing contribution must vest totally and immediately in the employee—something not normally required of profit-sharing contributions.

- Amounts deferred under a cash-or-deferred plan are counted as compensation for purposes of the Social Security tax. That means deferred amounts also count toward figuring Social Security benefits. In addition, the government has said that deferred salary can also be treated as compensation for pension purposes. So deferred amounts can be treated as salary and boost pension benefits.

- Deferred amounts are not entirely income tax-free. Several states and cities have decided to tax amounts deferred under a Sec. 401(k) plan.

HOW LONG-TERM INCENTIVE ARRANGEMENTS CAN HELP YOU KEEP YOUR KEY EMPLOYEES

It's not easy to keep your most valuable workers with you over the long term. According to benefits experts, one of the best ways to achieve this goal is through the use of long-term incentive compensation plans, such as stock options and other plans that let employees reap the benefits of the company's growth. Such plans, when carefully designed, will not only help you retain your best employees, but will also motivate them to work toward better meeting the company's current and long-term objectives.

HOW TO KEEP YOUR STAR PLAYERS PLAYING ON YOUR TEAM

Your company has a problem: One of your key employees is thinking about jumping ship. You've got to come up with a compensation package that will convince the employee to stay on board.

The solution to the problem might seem to be to pay the exec more money. And that may work in many cases. But sometimes more money won't do the trick.

There are many reasons an executive leaves a company. Sometimes just providing additional money isn't the answer. He may be leaving for more responsibility, a career shift, increased responsibility in a different area, etc. Or the employee simply may want to go to a greener, or at least a different, pasture.

Find out what the employee wants and then determine if you are willing and able to satisfy these requirements. In most cases, you'll have to come up with a combination of compensation and other job-related improvements.

Compensation experts note that if a company is serious about retaining a valued employee, it tends to take three primary steps: Number one, the company may match salary offers or adjust a key exec's salary to be more responsive to the competition's offer. Number two, the company may redefine the scope and responsibilities of the employee's job. And, number three, the company may also issue restricted stock or give other long-term incentives to the employee.

Compensation packages for holding on to key employees

Long-term incentives and capital accumulation programs serve as the most significant retention tool available to companies today. These programs involve the use of stock options, stock appreciation rights (SARs) and restricted stock awards. In smaller, privately owned companies, they often involve the use of performance shares and phantom stock plans. And companies that are already using one or more of these compensation techniques to hold on to key players may want to think about upgrading their packages.

• **Stock options:** Stock option programs are the most widely used plans today. A stock option grant can encourage key employees to remain with the company because it gives them the right to buy a stake in the company's future. If the company does well, they share in its success.

Companies and their shareholders favor stock option programs as well. It requires the employees to put some of their own money at risk in return for the stock. And the execs' gain theoretically is tied to the performance of the company through the increase in stock value. Executives will only receive appreciation and value in their stock holdings if there is subsequent appreciation in the value of the underlying stock.

• **Restricted stock:** Restricted stock plans are both the fastest growing and most powerful retention tool around. These plans provide for outright grants of stock to valued employees. However, the stock is "restricted" for a certain period of time, for example, five years. The executive can vote the shares and receive dividends on the shares, but cannot use the stock as collateral during the restriction period. Once the restrictions lapse, the property then becomes transferable. However, if the exec leaves during the restriction period, the shares are forfeited.

The most often-heard complaint about restricted stock is that it isn't connected to the company's or the individual's performance. Once the stock is granted, the exec gets it simply by staying with the company.

Some companies try to minimize this problem by granting restricted stock together with stock options. The ratio is often three stock options per share of restricted stock. This way the more significant portion of an exec's long-term wealth appreciation is tied to long-term performance of the company.

• **Phantom stock and performance units:** Private or closely held companies tend to use phantom stock and performance unit plans more often than equity plans (i.e., plans where actual stock is used). In many cases, owners of smaller companies don't want to dilute their ownership by giving away shares or granting stock options to employees.

These plans help encourage key employees to remain by tying their gains to the success of the company. Phantom stock and performance unit plans generally are implemented with a fixed time frame (i.e., appreciation over a base measure during a 5-year period; the base measure may be the fair market or book value of stock, or a formula based on return on equity, earnings per share, etc.).

• **Employment contracts:** Another way to hold on to employees who are thinking about leaving is through the use of employment contracts. These contracts may range from straight employment guarantees to incentive arrangements to golden parachute agreements.

According to a senior executive compensation consultant with the *Wyatt Company* (Wellesley Hills, Massachusetts), "the critical thing from the employee's standpoint is that these arrangements guarantee continued employment under conditions favorable to the employee. It represents a commitment on the part of the company to the employee." And "if the employee is terminated during the contract period, he or she usually will receive a significant severance payoff."

There are benefits for the company as well. For example, during stressful business situations, such as takeover bids or LBOs, it's to the company's advantage to have the continued employment of these key employees. The employment contracts give the employees a financial incentive to stay on board.

• **Miscellaneous perks:** A company can increase its chances of retaining key players by offering status fringe benefits. For example, giving perks like cars, country club or luncheon club memberships provide psychic income for restless execs. Although these perks tend to run only about 5% of execs' income, they feel good when they get them.

Companies can also try to accommodate top performers by giving them time off ("burn out prevention") or flexible schedules.

Preventive action

The best way to deal with the problem of key performers who want to leave is to make sure they don't become unhappy in the first place. Of course, providing competitive salaries and benefits is a must. But there are other steps a company can take to prevent this situation from cropping up.

- *Don't ask for trouble.* Companies that operate so-called "discretionary" bonus plans may end up with key employees missing in action. These are bonus plans where management says to its key employees, "If we have a good year, you'll earn a bonus"— but no one knows what a "good year" is. One sure way to lose a key employee is to have the exec think he's walking on water and doing a good job in a given year, and then have the CEO say there are no bonuses.

  Senior management should identify and communicate the specific internal performance measures and levels required to pay or earn bonuses. Everyone benefits because there are no surprises.

- *Emphasize performance appraisals and future goals.* The further up you go in an organization, the less emphasis is placed on performance appraisals. But the executive level is as anxious to know how they're doing in the eyes of their superiors as any other level.

- *Career development and succession planning.* This is an often overlooked activity that should be done on an annual basis. Companies should give key players the opportunity to talk about their future aspirations. Management should learn what their top employees are expecting in terms of career advancement and any potential problems they foresee along the way. Then management can make informed decisions on what steps to take, if any, to satisfy these expectations.

Keep your programs in perspective

Whether you're designing compensation packages aimed at keeping your top employees, or setting up compensation programs for employees generally, the experts agree that it's vital to keep your priorities in order. "Incentive compensation packages must be designed to support the business's goals and objectives, not vice versa," says an executive compensation consultant with *Hewitt Associates* (Lincolnshire, Ill.). "Companies can end up going in the wrong direction by focusing on their compensation package without looking at the business's needs."

Think strategically. The senior manager of compensation and consulting with *Deloitte & Touche* (Western region), says, "You've got to focus on business and strategic objectives rather than compensation objectives." For example, does your company plan to launch any new business ventures that might leave it cash-poor; or does the company anticipate having a strong cash flow? The answers will influence the type of incentive plan that's appropriate for your company.

CONSIDER EMPLOYEE STOCK OWNERSHIP PLANS (ESOPS): THEY'RE NOT JUST FOR BIG COMPANIES

Employee stock ownership plans, or ESOPs, have received a lot of attention lately. And big companies aren't the only ones using them. Companies large and small are using ESOPs set up with borrowed money to generate cash for company owners or to help pay for other benefits the company provides. Some ESOPs have even been set up to help companies fend off hostile takeover attempts.

In their simplest form, ESOPs are trusts that companies set up to distribute shares of stock to employees. The company contributes stock to the trust, which apportions the shares among the employees based on years of service or other conditions upon retirement or separation from service.

There are tax benefits. The company can deduct the value of its contributions to the trust—up to 25% of its total payroll outlay. And employees pay no tax on their growing stock ownership until they actually receive their shares. What's more, dividends paid to ESOP shareholders are deductible in many cases, unlike other types of dividend payments.

Once received, the employees can hold on to the stock, or turn around and sell it to the company, the trust or to the public, if the stock is publicly traded. Generally, however, they must first offer to sell the stock back to the company or trust before they can sell it publicly. This is one of the ways ESOPs help companies retain control of their shares.

The leveraged ESOP, a variation on the basic ESOP (described above), is a way for company owners to take cash out of the business or raise capital for expansion while also rewarding and motivating employees. These so-called leveraged ESOPs, or LESOPs, use borrowed money to buy the stock contributed to the trust. The following illustration shows how a company can put a LESOP in place with the help of a third-party lender, usually a bank or insurance company:

- Step one: The company sets up an employee stock ownership plan and employee stock ownership trust. Under the ESOP plan, the company agrees to sell a certain amount of stock to the trust.

- Step two: The trust takes out a loan from a bank to purchase the stock from the company. The trust turns over the loan proceeds to the company in return for the stock, and the bank holds onto the stock as collateral for the loan.

- Step three: The company, as part of the ESOP agreement, makes payments to the trust equal to the amount the trust owes the bank for repayment of the loan. The trust turns these payments over to the bank. The bank, in return, releases stock to the trust. As the loan gets paid back over time, the bank turns all of the stock over to the trust.

- Step four: The trust apportions the stock among company employees according to the terms of the ESOP.

The tax law provides incentives for lenders to make such loans to ESOPs. Subject to the conditions spelled out below, 50% of the interest the lender receives from ESOP loans is tax-free. As a result, banks can make ESOP loans at favorable rates—typically about 80% of the prime rate. And the company can deduct the interest portion of its payments to the trust, in addition to the *principal* repayments of up to 25% of its payroll costs.

The lender gets the 50% exclusion *only if*, right after the ESOP acquires the employer securities, the ESOP owns more than 50% of (1) each class of the issuing corporation's outstanding stock, or (2) the total value of the corporation's outstanding stock. Failure to meet this 50% threshold results in an increase in the cost of the ESOP loan (since the lender doesn't get the 50% exclusion break).

This change was made by Congress to make sure that tax benefits only go to ESOPs that are set up primarily to distribute company ownership to the employees, and not to raise cash for the companies themselves.

How Companies Come Out Ahead

Perhaps of greatest interest to small business owners is how ESOPs can be used to pay for or expand the other benefits a company provides. According to consultants Hewitt Associates, "The driving motivation for leveraged ESOPs today is as a low-cost source of financing. In most of the large company situations to date, the ESOP has been used as a vehicle through which to finance all or a portion of an existing [employee] benefit on a more cost-effective basis."

For example, some companies use ESOP loan proceeds to finance the company matching portion of a 401(k) savings plan. Other companies use ESOPs as a substitute for another type of employee benefit.

For example, a spokesperson for Boise Cascade Corp., which established a $300 million ESOP, indicated that the company intends to reduce medical benefits for workers who retire in the future. The ESOP payouts will help future retirees offset the planned cuts in their medical coverage.

Keep in mind, however, that the tax law crackdown on a lender's income exclusion may put a limit on what a company can do with ESOP loan proceeds.

Several recent studies have found that ESOPs enhance employee morale and result in higher productivity. Employees tend to identify more with the company's interests when they own part of the company.

Charles Hughes, co-founder of the *Center for Values Research, Inc.* (Dallas, Texas), notes that companies with ESOP-type arrangements have been found to "outperform" those without ESOPs in a number of studies. "These types of plans are consistent with the move toward more employee involvement in the business. They open the door to greater employee involvement and profitability for both the company and the employees," Hughes explains.

> **IMPORTANT:** ESOPs are subject to strict requirements under both the tax code and the Employee Retirement Income Security Act (ERISA). So be sure to get your company's professional advisers involved early in the planning stages should your company decide to look into the possibility of setting up an ESOP for your employees.

CHAPTER TEN

INNOVATIVE BENEFITS, COMPENSATION, FRINGE BENEFITS, AND PERKS

HOW TO CUT COSTS WITH INNOVATIONS IN PAY AND BENEFITS

Good help is hard to find—and in today's economy, even harder to keep. There's always someone willing to pay capable, responsible workers just a little bit more. You invest a lot in recruiting, training and employment taxes, and you must protect your investment like any other valuable asset. In the pages that follow, you'll discover a variety of compensation strategies that let you give maximum rewards to valuable workers while you keep costs low and efficiency high.

WHAT SMALL COMPANIES CAN OFFER EMPLOYEES THAT BIGGER FIRMS CAN'T MATCH

Big companies pay bigger salaries. There's no getting around the fact that, in general, large companies have financial resources that smaller

255

companies can't match. So if you're competing with the big boys for top-level employees strictly on a salary basis, more often than not you'll lose. But that doesn't mean you have to stop going after these employees!

While you may not be able to compete for the best people on the basis of salary alone, you can offer certain benefits and perks that larger firms often can't or won't match. Small companies have greater flexibility to provide both "visible" and "nonvisible" perks that can be used to attract and retain talented people. Among them are the following:

• **Equity.** One visible benefit offered by many small companies, particularly start-ups, is equity in the business. A capital accumulation plan, such as a 401(k) plan, is another draw that many companies offer.

• **Health benefits and perks.** In spite of steep health insurance costs, most small companies do offer medical coverage. While small company health plans tend to be less comprehensive than the benefits offered by large corporations, and small company employees may be required to contribute more toward the cost, experts say that there are ways to help close this gap. (Strategies that can help keep health benefits affordable were discussed in Chapter 8.)

Experts note that small companies can also offer memberships in country clubs or health clubs, financial and legal counseling, and estate planning help.

• **Family leave and benefits.** Some small companies are offering expanded maternity and paternity leave and creative dependent care assistance programs to help with recruitment and retention of employees. A few small employers also are trying out programs that allow employees to fund the costs of long-term care for elderly family members on an after-tax basis.

• **Flexible hours and special recognition.** On the "nonvisible" side are flexible work hours, spontaneous bonuses and raises, and special recognition for promotions and hiring. In addition, a smaller firm might supplement wages by allowing employees to use an office computer or telephone for personal purposes during off-hours or by giving them use of a company car or extra time off.

• **Entrepreneurial style.** Many times the difference in management style between large and small companies can be a key factor in an individual's choice of where to work. Large firms tend to recruit and retain "classical conformists," while smaller companies tend to look for more "entrepreneurial" employees and try to make the workplace more fun.

Employees who gravitate toward smaller companies are attracted by the challenge, career development and training opportunities. There's also a better chance of attaining a corner office. Big companies have more management levels and bureaucracy, which might not appeal to individuals who want to be more involved in decision-making processes and have more control over their work.

You should make sure that the people who conduct your job interviews are aware of any special perks or benefits your company offers, both under written plans and under unwritten policies. The special small-company touches mentioned above can help your company get—and retain—the people it wants even when you can't match big-company salary offers dollar for dollar.

USE MULTIPLE PAY STRATEGIES TO REACH MULTIPLE GOALS

Keeping pay practices uniform throughout your company can simplify a variety of payroll and personnel tasks. However, the easiest system to administer may hurt your company in the long run. In order to attract and retain competent workers at the lowest price, you should take a serious look at maintaining multiple pay plans. Analyze the needs of the various segments of your company. If there are differences among them, then a company-wide compensation system can be the wrong way to go. This is particularly true if your company operates more than one line of business.

For example, XYZ Company's main division operates in a mature industry. Its prime concern is maintaining market share and increasing profits from a fairly stable group of customers. XYZ also has entered into a new venture in an emerging growth industry. This venture has high startup costs and isn't expected to turn a profit for a number of years.

It would be unfair—and counterproductive in the long run—to compute bonuses using the same standard measure (e.g., company earnings) for both segments of XYZ.

Division-wide measures should be used. And they should be tied to an aspect of the business that's important to the company's success in each—and that's within the control of those being compensated. For example, profits could be the test for the mature line of business and sales for the new one.

Job titles and a numerical job grade ranking system can help but shouldn't be followed blindly. For example, two employees may both be called sales representatives. However, one is more of an order-taker while the other really has to hustle to sell the product. An hourly wage would be more appropriate for the order-taker, while a commission would be more appropriate for the rep responsible for actually bringing in new orders. (For more tips on pay plans for motivating your sales force, see Chapter Three, *"How to Turn Your Sales Force into a Profit Force."*)

HOW BONUSES CAN BOOST MORALE AND CUT PAYROLL COSTS

As a small business owner, you know that sharing company profits with employees is a sure-fire productivity booster. If you're like the average employer, you probably think of the annual pay raise as the simplest way to share the wealth. But did you know that giving a raise today essentially commits you to making larger wage payments, year in and year out, regardless of profits?

That's the problem with raises. A generous raise given in a good year becomes part of the employee's base pay in future years—locking in higher payroll costs for the long term. What's more, some fringe benefits—including retirement plan contributions and disability insurance —are based on the employee's actual earnings for the year. So the true additional cost of the compounding of traditional raises is even larger.

This is why a growing number of companies are switching from pay raises to bonuses for rank-and-file employees and management alike. Each year's bonus can be tied to the particular year's profits or an employee's individual performance. The cost savings result from the fact that a bonus is a pay increase that lasts for only one year. So, if an employee has been receiving raises of 5% per year, you can switch to giving bonuses equal to 5% multiplied by the number of years since the base year.

Suppose in Year One, an employee's base salary is $25,000. With the traditional wage setup, the next increase would be $1,250. However, the following year's increase would be based on a $26,250 salary. Five percent of that is $1312.50. Result: In year three, the company pays out $27,562 and in year five, the salary is $30,388.

Now let's suppose the company substitutes a bonus system for the raises. If it gives a 5% bonus the first year, it would be in the same position as with the raise setup. But in subsequent years, the dollar difference would appear—and grow. For example, it could give a 15%

bonus in Year Three and pay out a total of only $28,750 to that employee in Year Four. The $190 savings multiplied by dozens of employees would be substantial. Those savings come from the fact that the bonus levels would not be compounding.

Keep in mind that the switch from raise to bonus is a radical step and is bound to cause some employee resistance. You may wish to use a combination of the two approaches. You could set caps on salary increases—such as no more than the rate of inflation—and pay the difference in lump-sum bonuses. Thus, bonuses would be given only for above-average performance for the year.

Your company would pay more only when it or a particular employee performs especially well. And an employee who performs exceptionally well in one year—but then slacks off later on—would not continue to reap financial rewards for that extra effort made years before. What's more, a supervisor's incorrect performance appraisal in one year would not skew the employee's wage history for the long term.

In years of low inflation, wage increases tend to be small. Spread out over 26 or 52 paychecks, the dollar change may appear minuscule to the employees. On the other hand, the same amount of money paid as a lump-sum bonus could have a greater psychological impact.

Here's a look at some types of bonus plans and the pluses and minuses of each approach.

• **Performance bonuses.** A natural way to distribute bonuses for outstanding performance is to set up an annual pool from which managers draw to reward deserving employees. The bonuses supplement annual salary increases.

For example, an insurance company sets aside an annual fund of 2% of eligible salaries. Managers draw on their pro rata shares of this fund to reward particular excellence on the part of an individual or group. On average, one-half of eligible employees get a performance bonus. The average award is $1,000, with a range of about $300 to $1,300.

A bonus is included in the paycheck following the short-term result it recognizes. This increases its motivational impact, gives the manager an opportunity to commend the worker and decreases the chance that the bonus will be perceived as unjustified by other employees.

On the plus side, since the bonus pool is fixed, the company has tight financial control over how much it pays for "performance." On the other hand, managers still choose who gets a bonus, how much, and for what. So the plan can be exposed to charges of favoritism toward individuals and inconsistency between departments. In one company, its survey showed that 75% of its supervisors thought the bonus program worked well, but only 30% of the rank-and-file workers agreed.

• **Targeted bonuses.** One way to diffuse criticism of bonuses paid to individuals or small groups is to lay down *objective* ground rules that aren't subject to a supervisor's personal judgments. In other words, employees earn bonuses by shooting for targets you set up in advance.

Targeted bonuses can generate tremendous productivity from individual employees without stirring up resentment from the group. On the other hand, you have limited control over costs. You can quickly find the company paying out more in bonuses than it budgets—in a good year—for raises.

The following steps can help make sure that targeted bonuses pay off on the bottom line:

• Look for a close link to revenue. The added work generated by targeted bonuses should quickly convert into more income or lower costs. In other words, the plan should pay for itself.

• Select targets carefully. The targets can be numerous. One Florida company has 32 different types of bonuses—for 312 employees. Be careful. Some targets can trigger a negative reaction. For example, a New England company discovered it took customers three times as long to get a customer service rep on the phone after the company offered the reps a bonus for processing more written correspondence.

• Leave time to tinker. It took one company's president several years of trial and error to arrive at the firm's current bonus setup. The difficulty of administering the payroll forced him to simplify the plan several times.

No one can hand you an off-the-shelf, ready-to-run targeted bonus plan. And, in general, employees understand this situation. Studies indicate that employees are tolerant of necessary changes, provided the rules aren't changed in the middle of the game.

• **Lump-sum salary increases.** Lump-sum salary increases have something in common with bonuses, but the key difference between the two should not be overlooked. Like bonuses, they can consolidate an annual increase into a single paycheck. On the other hand, while the bonus setup can be a cost-saver, lump-sum raises can be *more costly* than a regular raise arrangement.

In a typical lump-sum wage plan, employees receive (or have the option of receiving) a full year's worth of salary increases in one payment—right after the raise is awarded. Thus the employee gets his or her hands on the cash sooner, which makes this arrangement popular with employees. On the flip side, though, the company has a cash drain that much earlier in the year.

In addition to losing the use of the money sooner, a company that pays upfront lump-sum raises bears the risk that the employee will leave before the year is up. The company can, of course, seek to recover the unearned portion of the lump sum. But this may be easier said than done. Also, as a matter of personnel relations, your company may be hesitant to seek recovery of the "unearned" portion of the salary increase when an employee has died, suffers from long-term disability or has been subject to job abolishment.

• **Pay-at-risk.** This looks like a deal that's easy to refuse: The company guarantees a worker 80% of the market rate of pay for his job and puts the other 20% at risk. But surprisingly, a joint venture/startup company that offers this pay package generally has no trouble attracting high-caliber employees. The reason is that there is great upside potential for employees.

In two to three years, when the prospects for the venture are clearer, employees will begin receiving quarterly and annual incentive bonuses. Depending on the venture's success, employees will end up being paid at, above or below market. But there's no cap on the incentives. Spectacular success would mean employees get many times the 20% of compensation they put at risk.

These so-called entrepreneurial pay plans were pioneered by small, young companies—for obvious cash flow as well as personnel reasons. But they've caught on at large companies as well.

One Fortune 500 company has implemented an incentive-pay plan that links employees' pay raises to the company's profits. The incentive plan covers approximately 20,000 employees in one of the company's divisions—from hourly workers to vice presidents, union and nonunion alike.

Unlike most profit-sharing setups, the plan doesn't require employees to take a pay cut or freeze employees' wages. Instead, the employees in the covered division get smaller guaranteed pay raises than their counterparts in other company divisions. In return for putting part of their annual increase "at risk," the employees can end up with a significantly bigger payoff down the road.

Each year, the company sets a profit goal. The employees can get back some or all of what they give up by hitting 80% or more of that target—and even more if the division produces exceptional profits. Here's how this would work:

- If the division's profits fall below 80% of the profit goal, the employees get nothing back.
- If the division's profits reach 80% of the profit goal, the employees get a 3% bonus.
- If the division meets the profit goal (100% of the target), they get back the full 6% they gave up.
- If the division's profits are 150% of the profit goal, the employees get a bonus that puts their pay 12% above that of their counterparts.

The profit goal you set has to be realistic and reachable if you expect the plan to motivate employees to work harder and smarter. If the employees feel that the target you've set will be unreachable no matter how hard they work, the plan will provide little incentive for extra productivity.

- **Gainsharing.** Another way to share profits can also help foster team spirit among your employees. With gainsharing, the employees in an especially productive or innovative area of the business receive a share of the profit that their department directly helped to create. Since all members of the team—rank-and-file as well as management—have a shot at personal rewards, they cooperate more closely to achieve the goals you set.

Gainsharing is a great way to achieve specific, concrete goals, like increasing sales or boosting production. But it can also be used as a reward for improvements that don't have such a direct impact on the bottom line—for example, better attendance or improved quality control.

Gainsharing is particularly effective when you spread out the potential for reward among several departments. For instance, during the first quarter, you can offer a gainsharing bonus to the department with the most improved attendance record. In this way, you let clerical workers know their efforts are just as important to the company's success as increased output on the production line.

HOW TO MAKE PAY-FOR-PERFORMANCE REALLY WORK FOR YOU

More companies are looking into incentive plans, pay-for-performance systems and one-time cash awards for key contributors. However, one of the key stumbling blocks to implementing these new compensation systems is clearly identifying measurable factors for performance. Unless you can identify job factors and objectively quantify performance, it's difficult for companies to identify key contributors.

Most companies want to jump in and set up an incentive pay or pay-for-performance system, without really knowing what they're rewarding employees for or how to allocate their incentive pay.

To have a successful pay-for-performance system, you have to figure out what the job parts and performance standards are. Most companies haven't established the performance standards for each job. Or they simply try to have the same performance standards for each job. And that doesn't work.

Of course, "quantifying" performance is easier to do with some jobs than with others. For example, a salesperson's performance can, by and large, be measured by the amount of sales dollars generated or volume of goods sold. Likewise, the performance of an assembly-line employee can basically be measured by the quantity and/or quality of units produced. But it is more difficult to measure or quantify the performance of someone in, say, a customer service or clerical/secretarial position.

For example, a multi-hospital organization is in the process of implementing a pay-for-performance system. Part of this process includes formulating criteria-based performance standards for all employees.

According to the director of human resources, this means developing standards for jobs that aren't always easily quantifiable. For example, how do you objectively measure a nurse's performance in areas of communication, patient contact, professionalism, team work and other behavioral standards? The same situation arises when you try to measure a receptionist's performance. Part of the receptionist's job includes greeting visitors, and his or her performance is judged on such criteria as making eye contact, greeting visitors in a specified manner (e.g., with a smile) and making sure questions are answered within a reasonable period of time. These things may not be 100% measurable, but they are observable.

Hospital employees, together with their supervisors, work to break down job parts by filling out a job description questionnaire. They also work together to set standards for job performance. Management and employees don't always agree on what the job standards should be. However, even when there isn't total agreement about job standards, at least the employees know where management is coming from.

The hospitals place a lot of stock in both formal and informal feedback sessions. The hospital, like most companies, has an annual performance appraisal/salary review with employees. In addition, at least once during the year, the supervisor will sit down and discuss performance standards with employees, and make observations about their performance. But perhaps the most important feedback comes on a *daily* basis. Part of a supervisor's duties is to give feedback—positive or negative—when he or she observes an employee doing something.

Simply installing a performance appraisal system will not cure whatever ails your company. Nor is there one ultimate performance appraisal system your company should adopt. Regardless of the type of program a company adopts, the key is that it be well-managed and continuous. Companies are always searching for the perfect performance appraisal system. But what usually ends up happening is that individual managers fail the system, not the other way around.

Objectivity in the appraisal system by supervisors is crucial. And top management has to oversee the system and make sure it is being used consistently throughout all levels of the company.

HOW LINKING BENEFITS TO PERFORMANCE CAN CUT COSTS AND BOOST PRODUCTIVITY

Earlier in this chapter we discussed so-called pay-for-performance compensation systems—awarding pay raises or bonuses only when employees meet individual performance goals or the company or department meets specific targets. One company—a Houston, Texas-based engineering, architecture and construction management company—has taken the concept of pay for performance one step further. It makes health insurance and other benefit contributions only for employees who perform to the company's satisfaction.

"We believe that health and other employee benefits are not automatic employee entitlements," says the company's manager of employee benefits. "We feel very strongly that benefits should be treated the same as wages—employees have to earn them." She adds that employers should "stop looking at benefits as a separate area and recognize that it's simply a part of compensation."

In keeping with this philosophy, the company has put its novel performance-based benefit program in place for its approximately 3,000 workers. The company's workforce is made up primarily of architects, engineers and construction managers. While the system was designed in part to offset rising benefit costs, it's really just one part of an overall system of tying all forms of compensation—including a company-wide bonus plan—to job performance.

Here's a closer look at how the benefit program works:

• Newly hired employees are responsible initially for paying the full cost of their health benefits. The cost ranges from approximately $40 to $90 per month. The company offers a flexible benefits plan, so employees can choose from a number of options, including several levels of medical deductible, dental and life insurance coverage.

• After six months on the job, employees can begin to receive employer contributions to their health plan costs *if* they achieve a high rating on their employee performance reviews. Employees who get lower performance ratings must continue paying the full cost of their health coverage until subsequent reviews show improvement in their performance.

• Job performance is also taken into account in awarding other types of employee compensation and benefits, including sick time, vacation time, merit pay increases and bonuses. For example, the employee bonus plan takes a percentage of the net operating income and distributes it to 90% of the employees. Employees can qualify for cash bonuses ranging from 1.5% to 10% of annual pay.

Of course, whether or not there will be a bonus depends on whether the company performs well. And then, depending on his or her performance rating under the company's appraisal system, an employee can multiply his or her base performance share by up to six times.

The company's benefits manager says, "We intend to show that we are a performance-oriented group and want to spread this message to our employees. We want to spread the idea of quality performance and results."

• Since the company's benefits and compensation system are tied so closely to employee performance ratings, the company takes extra pains to make sure its appraisal system is equitable, effective and understood by all employees.

Each new employee's performance is reviewed by his or her immediate supervisor twice a year. Supervisors rate employees on how well they have met project goals. Employees are involved both in setting the goals and in determining how progress toward those goals will be measured.

The company recognizes the potential problems that can arise when so much is riding on performance appraisals. "I've never seen an appraisal system that was perfect," says the benefits manager. "When there is less than optimal objectivity in the rating process, then some people may end up being compensated inequitably." Thus, in an attempt to keep subjective factors and supervisor biases from skewing the performance ratings, "We are constantly fine-tuning our system, training our supervisory personnel and changing with the times in setting goals and measuring progress," she adds. "This rigorous performance-oriented setup obviously won't work for all types of organizations. Our workforce is composed of innovators and creative people. Companies like ours have a higher than average turnover rate. At the same time, we're not particularly interested in longevity."

This system may not be as well suited to industries like manufacturing, where repetitive processes are used.

PAY FOR SKILLS CAN HELP EMPLOYEES WORK SMARTER

Skills-based pay systems are an innovative way to compensate rank-and-file employees. Unlike the incentive plans discussed above, skills-based pay increases the employee's regular raises; it doesn't award bonuses. But the raises bring an extra benefit to the company— they are awarded not simply in exchange for years of service or cost-of-living increases, but in return for employees' acquisition of certain knowledge and skills.

For example, a company recently implemented an innovative pay-for-knowledge program in one of its manufacturing plants. The plant, located in Michigan, employs about 500 workers in manufacturing automobile and truck components. The plan encourages employees to learn new job skills by basing their pay on what they know and can do—not on what they're actually doing at any one time.

The benefit of this approach, says the plant's personnel manager, is that as employees acquire a broader range of skills, the company has "much greater flexibility" in assigning work among employees.

The plant produces three different components—a locking differential, a power steering mechanism and a clutch. There are four or five separate job skills involved in producing each component. When an employee masters *all* of the job skills needed in his product line, he gets a significant salary increase.

Compensation experts note that this all-or-nothing approach is a departure from the typical pay-for-knowledge setup, in which a worker gets a salary increase each time he masters a new job skill.

The early results of this plan are quite encouraging. Skilled employees are earning more (which helps with employee retention), while the plant's overall labor costs have dropped substantially in the first two years: by a whopping 25% in the clutch unit, and by 6%-10% in the locking differential unit (with an additional 15% reduction expected in that unit in the future).

You may end up with higher labor costs per employee once they learn the new job skills, but the higher costs will be offset by increased efficiency and productivity. Since your employees can do more, you can do the same job with fewer employees. However, pay-for-knowledge plans should not be coupled with layoffs—for example, introducing such a plan as a way to make layoffs more palatable for the employees who remain. If you do, the plan's not going to work.

HOW FLEXTIME CAN MOTIVATE WORKERS WHEN YOU CAN'T RAISE THEIR PAY

Every small business owner gets caught up in a vicious cycle at some point in the company's development. Whether you're in a startup mode or just facing lean times, you need top effort from employees at the very time you can least afford to pay them what they're worth to you. When the capital just isn't there, you need a creative, noncash approach to rewarding your workforce.

Flextime rewards employees at zero dollar cost. You may not be able to give employees more money. But you can improve their working conditions and boost their morale with another precious commodity—time.

Today, two-earner couples, where both parents work full time, are common. For these employees, work and home make competing demands on their time. They need time during the day to get children to and from day care or school, for example. This makes working 9-to-5 nearly impossible.

What's more, many companies have occasional attendance problems with otherwise hard-working employees. Besides parents with young children, some employees like to avoid rush-hour traffic, get home before dark in the winter or work on their suntans during the summer. Still other employees can't seem to function on Monday morning after a weekend at the beach. With more working parents, unmarried people and seniors in (or returning to) the workforce, you're more and more likely to encounter such problems.

If your company wants to retain these workers—but also get a full day's work from them—flextime may be the right approach. A flex-time program allows employees to choose their arrival and departure times. However, as we see later, you don't have to give employees completely free rein in setting their schedules for the program to work effectively.

In addition to helping attract and retain key workers, flextime also offers your company the following advantages:

- Decreases in paid absences (personal business, sick leave) and idle time on the job.

- Better organization of work. That's because meetings, telephone calls, and visits are concentrated into so-called "core" hours, thus key work is handled when there are fewer distractions.

- More efficient production because employees are able to schedule work according to their own "biological clocks."

There are some potential disadvantages with flextime. The problem areas include the following:

- the added need for managers and supervisors to plan and schedule the work flow and ensure the coverage of critical functions;

- the possible lack of supervision during some hours;

- added timekeeping needs;

- nonlabor costs associated with more hours of operation (for example, heating and air conditioning)

How flextime works

Under flextime, employees can vary the times their workdays begin and end. The arrangements vary among establishments, and even among units within an establishment. The particular arrangement a company settles on generally depends on such factors as production, customers' needs and other coverage requirements; public laws and collective bargaining agreements; and the attitudes of individual managers and supervisors.

In establishing flexible hours, most companies require that all employees work a certain set of "core hours"—for example, 9 A.M. to

3 P.M.—and that they stick to a fairly fixed schedule. Employees should not come in at a different time every day, but they can change the time periodically.

Keep an open mind when you get a request from a group of employees asking for a change in their workweek. With any such request—flextime included—you should find out why the workers want the change. You then have to view the request from these two angles:

- *Impact on the company.* Will production schedules be hard to meet? Will supervisors be able to manage in an orderly fashion without having all the workers present at the same time?

- *Impact on employees.* Will it solve their personal problems? Will they remain productive employees?

Sit down with your employees after you have answered those questions. You should be able to work something out that answers the needs of the company and its employees.

To determine what's best for both the company and its workers, several issues dealing with procedures must be resolved, according to Barney Olmstead and Suzanne Smith in their book, *Creating a Flexible Work Place* (New York, Amacom, 1989). Here are some of the key issues:

• *State and federal labor laws:* What effect will existing legislation have on the proposed flextime program?

• *Length of company workday and workweek:* What are the organization's operating hours? What are its normal workdays?

• *Allowable starting and quitting times:* What is the earliest time that an employee can start the workday, and how late can a regular, albeit flexible, schedule go? The most common span extends from 7:00 A.M. to 6:00 P.M. (In a 24-hour, continuously operating plant, these questions may have to be answered in terms of flexible "shift schedules" rather than in terms of flexibility within a specified range of day-shift hours.)

• *Lunch hour:* Is a lunch hour required each day? Of what duration?

• *Personal time off:* How will flextime affect existing provisions for personal time off?

• *Carryover hours:* If your state does not have legislation prohibiting workdays longer than eight hours and workweeks longer than 40 hours, will employees be allowed to bank hours? Within what time limits (a week, a pay period, other)?

• *Degree of individual flexibility:* Within the established parameters, how much choice will employees have? Can they vary their hours day to day? Week to week? How much notice must they give their supervisor? If schedules are expected to remain constant for an extended period, how long a commitment must employees make to a particular schedule? What process is there for changing the schedule if it proves inappropriate?

• *Eligibility:* Who will be eligible for flextime? Will it be a company-wide option, a pilot project, or a departmental option? If one of the reasons for flextime is to enhance employee morale and commitment, then eligibility should be as broad as possible.

If your company is considering setting up a flextime program, here are some tips you can use at the planning stage to help avoid some of the problems that may crop up once the plan is adopted.

• Allow enough time for adequate planning—a month or more.

• Include your key personnel in the planning stage.

• Try to sample a cross section of employee opinion before switching. While most employees might welcome a change in work hours, some will be reluctant to accept it.

• Prepare for difficulties that may come up. For example, what will employees do if a problem arises and there is no supervisor present?

• Make sure departments coordinate with each other. If one department will be working late, but repair tools are locked up in another department that isn't staffed at that hour, problems and tie-ups will result.

• Consider safety precautions. For instance, no employee should be allowed to run dangerous equipment without a fellow worker present.

• Coordinate your plans with all managers and be sure that they communicate the plans to their employees, especially on-line supervisors.

• Make any additional skills training that may be needed for operating under a flextime program available to employees as well as supervisors. Ongoing training will help workers acquire new skills while maintaining their present ones.

• Consider personnel problems, such as employee theft. If your company has had such problems in the past, flextime may aggravate them unless you take special precautions.

• Have managers set clear guidelines in every department. Set strong controls at first. You can always remove unnecessary controls more easily than if you try to add them after the program is in place.

- Give employees plenty of advance notice of any intended changes.
- Plan on monitoring and evaluating so you'll be able to assess and fine-tune the program. This will help you nip minor abuses before they develop into big problems.

When you implement flextime, announce that the new schedule will be used on a "trial" basis until the company—and employees—see how it works out in practice. Recognize that there will be some complaints no matter what. But the number you receive will help you gauge whether or not the program is working.

Also, when instituting your program, remind your managers and employees that making use of flextime is a privilege and that anyone who abuses it will be removed from the program.

USE LOW-COST, TAX-FREE FRINGES TO BOOST EMPLOYEE MORALE

At many companies, it's the "little things" that keep employees happy and loyal for years on end. They want to work in an atmosphere where every member of the team is important, and where you, the boss, know them by sight or even name. And they enjoy the small touches and personal perks that just aren't available at larger firms.

- **De minimis fringes.** The tax law says your company can write off the cost of many of these small perks (in tax parlance, "de minimis fringe benefits") without having to go through the bother of reporting them as income to your employees. By definition, the value of a de minimis fringe is any property or service with a value so small as to make accounting for it unreasonable or administratively impractical.

In evaluating whether a benefit qualifies for this tax break, you must take into account the frequency with which your company provides similar fringes to employees. In other words, certain benefits that would be taxable if given out on a regular basis would be tax-free if furnished only on rare occasions.

For example, an employee is generally taxed on his or her personal use of a company car. Suppose, though, that you let your secretary commute in a company car on the day that her own vehicle is in the repair shop. Her use of the company vehicle should qualify as a tax-free de minimis fringe benefit.

A number of de minimis fringes are spelled out in the tax regulations:

- Occasional typing of personal letters by a company secretary;
- Occasional personal use of the company photostat machine (provided sufficient control is exercised over the machine's use to ensure that at least 85% of its use is for business purposes);
- Occasional cab fare, meals or supper money *if* provided to enable employees to work overtime;
- Occasional cocktail parties or picnics for employees and their guests;
- Free or low-cost parking provided employees at or near their job;
- Traditional holiday gifts of tangible property (not cash) with a low fair market value—such as a turkey on Thanksgiving;
- Use of employer-owned athletic facilities;
- Monthly public transit passes sold to employees at a discount of no more than $15 per month, and tokens, fare cards or vouchers if their value isn't more than $15 per month;
- Occasional theater or sporting events tickets.
- Bargain-priced meals in a company eating facility if the facility's annual revenues equal or exceed its direct operating costs.

Except for employer-operated eating facilities, de minimis fringes aren't subject to nondiscrimination rules. That is, these benefits qualify as tax-free even if they're provided exclusively to company officers or other key or highly-paid employees.

In addition to de minimis fringes, you can offer the following tax-free perks:

- **No-additional-cost services:** Such a service is one you offer customers and that, when offered as a fringe benefit to employees, does not substantially increase your costs. The benefit must be available to each member of a group of employees on roughly the same terms, so you can't discriminate by providing it just to officers or high-salaried employees. You also can offer this kind of fringe to retired and disabled former employees.

- **Qualified employee discounts:** These include any discount you offer employees on goods or services offered for sale to customers in the same line of business in which the employee works. To qualify as tax-free benefits, the discounts must conform to the following limits:

An employee discount on *goods* can't exceed the gross-profit percentage of the price at which the goods are offered to customers.

An employee discount on *services* can't exceed 20% of the price at which the service is offered to customers.

As with no-additional-cost services, qualified employee discounts must be available to each member of a group on substantially the same terms; you can't discriminate by offering a discount only to key employees.

• **Working-condition fringes:** Employees can also exclude from taxable income the fair market value of any property or service you provide if the employees would have been able to deduct the benefit as a business expense had they paid for it themselves. (The tax law says that the 2%-of-adjusted-gross-income floor on miscellaneous itemized deductions is disregarded for purposes of determining whether the fringe benefit may be deducted.)

HOW COMPANY-SPONSORED CHILD CARE CAN HELP YOU RECRUIT AND RETAIN VALUABLE EMPLOYEES

Recent studies show that child care is a key concern of many U.S. workers—and an increasingly popular company benefit. According to the U.S. Census Bureau, more than half of new mothers stayed on the job after their babies were born. And 40% of all married couples of childbearing age are two-income families.

Many companies already provide some type of child care aid to their employees, and many more will take the child care plunge in coming years to help attract and retain qualified workers. At the same time, however, a number of recent tax law changes make it harder for some workers to take advantage of child care. In fact, some companies that offer child care assistance may find fewer workers using their programs.

The benefits from child care arrangements are a two-way street. The payoff for employees is clear: lower after-tax child care costs and fewer worries about children during business hours in many cases. And in a recent survey of companies that offer child care programs, almost all said that employers benefit as well. The benefits are easier recruiting, higher productivity, lower absenteeism, more positive employee attitudes and lower turnover.

The interest in child care programs extends beyond the Fortune 500 companies, although the majority of firms that now offer this benefit are larger companies. Child care management companies report that an increasing number of small companies are seeking help in setting up child care programs.

Child care assistance doesn't have to take the form of expensive on-site day care facilities such as those offered by some of the larger companies. It can be as simple as a referral service to match working parents with suitable child care providers in the community. Some of the most common arrangements are:

- an on-site sponsored facility
- a referral service
- a subsidized off-site facility
- employer reimbursement of employee (or facility) for child care costs (i.e., voucher system)
- an off-site consortium (i.e., where a group of employers jointly finance one or more child care centers)
- a vendor system (i.e., employer contracts for guaranteed slots in an outside facility)

If your company is thinking about offering some form of child care assistance program, benefits experts suggest that you start by surveying your employees to determine how many workers currently use child care, what type of arrangements they use (e.g., a center, an individual, etc.), and how many may need it in, say, three to five years.

In addition, you may want to start keeping track of how many days employees are absent or have to leave early because of child care problems (child is sick, babysitter is sick, etc.). This information will give you a basis for the cost data you'll need to make decisions on child care programs and to justify your expenditures.

CHILD CARE PROGRAMS AND TAX LAW CHANGES

An increasingly popular child care benefit is the so-called "flexible spending account," which allows employees to set aside *pre-tax* dollars from their salary—up to $5,000—that can be used to pay child care expenses. In other words, up to $5,000 of an employee's salary can be spent on child care and be entirely exempt from income tax.

However, the tax law has made several important changes that are bad news to working parents who've been getting tax benefits from child care expenses. These changes may discourage some employees from using flexible spending accounts.

- **There is a limit on double dipping.** Working parents can no longer make full use of both a flexible spending account and the child care tax credit (which can provide a dollar-for-dollar tax reduction equal to as much as 30% of $4,800 in child care expenses for two or more children).

Before 1989, an employee with two children could set aside $5,000 in tax-free dollars for child care and claim the tax credit on an *additional* $4,800 in child care costs. But thanks to the Family Support Act of 1988, now the extent to which an employee uses either tax break reduces the amount of child care expenses available for the other break.

- **There are age restrictions.** Working parents can no longer get tax breaks for child care expenses incurred for their 13- and 14-year-old children (either through the child care credit or under a flexible spending account). As of 1989, only those expenses incurred for children *under age 13* (or for older dependents who are incapable of caring for themselves) qualify for the tax breaks. The old law provided tax breaks for children under age 15.

- **There is a reporting requirement.** Working parents must report the Social Security numbers or taxpayer identification numbers of their baby-sitters or child care providers in order to claim either tax break for child care expenses. This rule generally poses little problem for parents who use institutional child care providers, such as day care centers or on-site facilities sponsored by their employers.

But this rule creates a big problem for working parents who've been using "off the books" child care arrangements—for example, relatives, neighbors or other unlicensed providers, including, in some cases, household help that may lack immigration authorization.

As a practical matter, many "off the books" providers may be unwilling or unable to furnish Social Security numbers. Some employees simply will give up their tax breaks rather than pay their babysitters taxable wages. Such employees certainly won't want to put aside money in a company plan if they can't get a tax benefit out of it.

Employees in this situation have several basic options for dealing with their predicament. An employee can offer to increase a babysitter's wages by, say, one third in return for reporting the sitter's Social Security number (and subjecting the sitter to tax liability). The added payments are designed to offset the income and FICA taxes.

However, the employee should first figure out whether the tax breaks are worth the added cost.

If the sitter adamantly refuses to furnish an ID number, the employee may try to negotiate a lower child care rate to make up for the lost tax break. Unfortunately, this appears to be occurring to some extent. When it does, the employee is likely to drop out of the company plan.

Communicate with employees. Explain clearly and simply what the child care rules are: the need to report the provider's Social Security number, the age limitations, etc.

Companies can help meet their employees' child care needs in other ways. For one thing, companies can help recruit and train individuals who are already providing child care services and help them operate as legitimate businesses.

The company can help defray such providers' costs—thus lowering the costs for employees using them—by providing accounting, legal and other support services.

Companies may also consider establishing on-site or off-site child care centers. This is a big project and, generally speaking, is a viable option only for larger companies. However, several companies in a community may be able to get together and *jointly* fund such a project.

Start-up costs of day care centers vary greatly, depending on the size of the facility, whether space is available or must be built, equipment and furnishings, etc. Start-up costs range from a minimum of $20,000-$50,000 up to as much as $1 million or more. The average, however, is in the $200,000 range.

The average annual costs of operating a facility range from $5,000-$7,000 per child. The bulk of these costs is for staff. Generally, it's more costly to provide care for infants because they require closer attention than do older children.

Of course, few companies are willing to contribute this much for the care of employees' children. Employers typically subsidize no more than 20% of worker child care costs. The other 80% is paid by the employees.

In certain cases, city or state governments may be willing to help subsidize an employer's child care program. You should contact appropriate government officials in the early stages of developing any child care program for your company's employees.

SECTION 3

How to Reduce Operating Costs in Production and Office Management

With the tightening economy and intensifying competition for sales and customers, the marching orders of the day in companies large and small call for cutting costs to the bone. Almost no business is exempt. Everyone—from yesterday's high-flying financial services and high-tech companies to retailers, transportation firms and basic industry—is feeling the pinch.

The problem is that indiscriminate cost-cutting can cripple your operation. Sure, you can take shortcuts. But if you squeeze costs too much, sales and quality may suffer.

To make matters worse, the conventional wisdom on how businesses can become more efficient and competitive seems to change from year to year, sometimes from month to month. One day it's Japanese management methods and "just-in-time delivery" of materials. The next it's automation and robotics. Sometimes it seems as if a little old-fashioned penny-pinching would get you as far as all the "innovative solutions" that come out of the business schools and think tanks.

The chapters in this section provide the following:

- An overview of strategies for controlling inventory, production and other costs.
- Guidelines for how your company can take profit-advantage of the breakthroughs in office technology.
- Practical advice on how you can be a more effective executive.

CHAPTER ELEVEN

HOW TO REDUCE OPERATING COSTS IN PRODUCTION, PURCHASING, AND SHIPPING

This chapter gives you a look at cost-control techniques that have already worked for other companies. While some are based on the experts' theories or on Japanese methods, it took the hard work and perseverance of business owners and managers to put them into practice. Keep in mind that no matter what new system you may try for controlling production costs, there's no substitute for constant hands-on management and good old common sense.

To get you started, we'll show you a five-point cost-cutting program that will make sure you don't miss cost-saving opportunities—and that the cuts you make are lasting. Then we'll take a closer look at successful strategies for holding the line on specific kinds of costs: production costs, purchasing and equipment costs, shipping costs and the like.

While you read this chapter, keep the following in mind: The key to making any cost-control program work can be summed up in three words—no sacred cows.

Your cost-cutting plan has to be comprehensive enough to provoke an exhaustive search for reductions across the board.

Don't let any part of your operation escape review or be exempt from examination because someone thinks there isn't fat to be trimmed. For example, top management for one company purposely proposed a 10% cut in all departmental budgets, when in fact the company was willing to settle for 5%. To its surprise, most departments were actually able to reduce their budgets closer to the 10% mark.

FIVE KEYS TO CUTTING COSTS

Here are five basic strategies for cutting the fat out of your company's costs—without sacrificing efficiency:

1. Concentrate on one or two top priorities. You may be wasting your resources and energy by trying to do too much. Trying to launch a new product line, overhaul your production system and institute new accounting methods are all worthy goals. But in trying to do them all at once, you end up doing them all poorly—and wasting a lot of time and money in the process.

In tight times, focus on the one or two priorities that will give your bottom line the biggest boost and put the rest on hold until you have time to give them the attention they deserve. Be sure, however, that the projects you mothball aren't vital to your company's success over the long haul.

2. Review your use of space and facilities. Do your sales reps who are in the office only two days a week really need 150-square-foot offices? Could two or three reps share an office, phone and personal computer? Is it essential to keep nine months worth of materials on hand, taking up valuable space in a warehouse or in your production area?

Go over your facilities layout to pinpoint excess or unused space, and to see where productivity could be enhanced by moving people, equipment or materials. Take a walking tour and talk with employees to see how the space is actually being used—and how it could be used better.

Maybe your people could get just as much done—and more efficiently—in three-quarters of your current space. You could sublet, sell or abandon the excess space—for a big reduction in your overhead budget.

3. Wait a while before replacing staffers who leave. Key people must be replaced, of course. But some positions can easily go unfilled without hurting your company's productivity. One of the best ways to find this out is to wait a month or two after an employee leaves before trying to fill the slot. If other employees can take up the slack without pulling them away from critical assignments, the unfilled position was probably unnecessary.

Even if it turns out that you do need to hire a replacement, you at least will have saved a few months' worth of salary, payroll and benefit costs. And if your budget crunch becomes acute, keep in mind that downsizing by attrition is always preferable to layoffs.

The danger comes when one of your top performers leaves. Even if that person wasn't in an essential job that absolutely has to be filled, he or she may have been providing vital backup and support to other employees—in other words, doing the work of two or three people.

That's why it's important to keep a close watch on the work produced by that person's co-workers in the weeks immediately after the person leaves. If important profit work begins to suffer, you'll want to replace the employee—whatever the cost.

If your budget problems require you to hold the line on salary increases, the crackdown shouldn't fall on your top performers and key profit-makers. Salary freezes must be applied carefully and selectively. Remember: Money you spend to retain good people is an investment—and, in fact, a cost-cutter—over the long haul.

4. Postpone nonessential big-ticket purchases. Your secretary has been grumbling for months that your office copier can make only 50 copies at a time and always jams on big jobs. So you've finally decided to buy a bigger, state-of-the-art model that makes four-color copies, collates and staples up to 100 copies at a time.

That's great when you're not feeling any budget pressures. But is it the best way to use your money when you're under the gun to trim costs—especially if it means freezing salaries or not filling vacant slots? How often do those big copying jobs come up? Do you really need to make color copies, or is the top-of-the-line copier just serving someone's ego? Maybe a local print shop can handle those special jobs when they come up—for a fraction of the cost of the new machine.

Don't put off needed maintenance. Big-ticket items are one thing. Routine maintenance and upkeep are another matter entirely. Never put off needed service of key pieces of equipment or make jerry-rigged repairs to avoid paying for a service call. Such penny-pinching can jeopardize a much bigger investment and invalidate product warranties.

In addition, how often are expensive supplies or materials thrown away because they're ruined by a machine that jams? A maintenance call could pay for itself many times over.

5. Eliminate wasteful use of supplies and equipment. Management efforts to save money on "nickel and dime" items such as office supplies, postage, phone and fax use often fail because they're viewed as Mickey Mouse measures by employees. In many cases, the reason for such failures lies in the way these cost-cutting efforts are communicated to the staff. Typically, the message is communicated in orders or directives that are impersonal, overly general, long on negatives and fail to explain the need for the savings and how employees will benefit from cooperating.

Example #1 (wrong approach)
Effective immediately, all personnel must reduce their use of the copying machine, fax machine and telephones by no less than 20% to meet new budget restrictions. Failure to cooperate will result in the imposition of tight restrictions on who may use these facilities, and for what purposes.

Example #2 (better approach)
Due to a recent rise in costs, we need to reduce our outlays for copier paper, telephone and fax use immediately. You can help by: (1) using the mail instead of the fax machine to send documents that aren't time-sensitive, (2) putting copier paper that jams back in the paper tray instead of discarding it, and (3) keeping your personal use of the office copiers and phones to a reasonable minimum. While these may seem like minor items, the costs do add up. Last month alone, our copying and telephone outlays (which include the cost of fax transmissions) came to more than $600—a 25% increase over a year ago. Your cooperation in bringing these costs down will help us avoid more drastic cost-cutting steps.

HOW TO CONTROL PRODUCTION COSTS

HOW TO BOOST PRODUCTION WHILE SLASHING COSTS

You can slash your costs without using fancy frills and work gimmicks. How? Adapt some of the following ideas that work effectively for other companies:

- "Let a winner lead the way." That's the advice of a Fort Worth manufacturer. He says, "First, set challenging work standards. If the work standards aren't challenging, you won't derive any benefits from them. When the first employees meet these goals, pass the word along to your other workers."

According to this business owner, your other workers will see that the goals are obtainable and will redouble their efforts to attain the standards the leaders have set.

- "Go to the grass roots." Says a Toronto manufacturer, "Give your employees a chance to sound off on anything that's bothering them." The manufacturer finds that his people will talk freely if he visits them at their workbenches.

"This will enable you to uncover profit-eating problems that might never come to light if you relied solely on memos from your supervisors. We have found that workers will cooperate once you show them you're interested in them."

- "We pick—and the employees work." So says a Salt Lake City manufacturer. This setup keeps profit work rolling without letting other work get in the way of priority orders. The manufacturer came up with the idea because he was faced with this problem:

"Some supervisors, trying to 'score' in the production race, kept a 'busywork' backlog near their workers' machines. It became a grab-bag affair. Seeking to keep up volume, the supervisors let workers pick the easiest—but not necessarily the most profitable—work. That was a profit disaster as far as I was concerned. Something had to be done—and done fast."

The manufacturer now controls the work flow. His supervisors can only feed enough orders to operators to meet daily requirements. Top priority is now given to work that will prove most profitable.

- Use a supervisor incentive plan as an anchor against rising production costs. The beauty of this plan is that it involves the individual who has the *most* control over these items.

One company judges its supervisors in the following areas:

- *Labor costs:* Decide which ones you can reasonably expect supervisors to reduce, and set a "labor reduction goal" for each.

- *Primary materials:* Figure out just how many processed and semiprocessed parts should be consumed in producing a unit of a finished product. Once you've arrived at your figures, hold your supervisors to them.

- *Quality control:* Make an estimate of how much reworking should be necessary before producing an acceptable finished unit.

- *Maintenance:* Compute each section's average monthly maintenance cost and use it as a "maintenance cost ceiling." Tell your supervisors they must stay below this ceiling. Then give the supervisor who scores perfectly on the target a bonus. Fifteen percent of base salary is a common figure.

Get your supervisors solidly behind the program by giving them a say in setting up the targets. Most likely, they will come up with figures you had in mind—but now the supervisors will look at them as "their figures" and will work just a bit harder to be on target.

HOW TO CUT COSTS WITHOUT CUTTING QUALITY

Here are some ideas that companies use to slash costs—without sacrificing on quality.

• **Get more for less.** "To determine if we were overstaffed, we evaluated the cost-effectiveness of every position in the company," explains the owner of a small chemical manufacturing outfit. "From prior experience, we knew just how many dollars of sales should be produced per salaried employee (sales, clerical, etc.). Based on our evaluation, we set new, lower staffing levels that we felt could be achieved. We told our managers to figure out a way to make the new staffing levels work."

The company eliminated one customer service clerk position and distributed the balance of work between the two remaining clerks.

As important as a cost analysis is when it comes to eliminating jobs, your "gut reactions" have to come into play also, according to this business owner. He notes that "We eliminated every 'Assistant to ...' position in the company. We felt that in a company of our size, nobody needed an assistant. If the assistant was a valuable employee, then he or she was reassigned."

As a result, "Payroll dollars were redistributed, so that we were able to hire people for jobs that the company really needed." We now have a full-time industrial nurse. This is an important position for us, because we manufacture chemical products.

A vital factor in getting the job redistribution plan to work, the executive says, was sharing the savings with employees. "Let's go back to the three customer service clerks. One clerk was eliminated, saving $250 a week pay. Two remaining clerks do that job and each gets paid an extra $75 a week. We saved $100 a week—plus benefits. The company saved well over $8,000 a year in salary and benefits in this case. The work still got done and the morale of the two remaining clerks stayed high."

• **Decrease costs and improve safety.** "One indirect benefit of cutting costs at our company," the chemical manufacturer says, "was the creation of a more efficient and safer workplace." Here are some examples:

  — *Space efficiency:* "Bad housekeeping frequently caused managers to ask for more space. For example, we were thinking about building a $200,000 storage warehouse. A group of us made a tour of the existing warehouse and sprayed a dab of fluorescent orange paint on the machines or materials that had dust on them." The business owner then gave this order "If it looks like it hasn't produced money for a while, get rid of it. All of a sudden we had enough space, and $200,000 did not have to be spent. The total cost: one can of spray paint."

  — *Safety savings:* "Safety problems generate needless expenses, primarily in the area of workers' compensation. We took full advantage of our insurance company. Many small companies don't know that 5% of their premium is allocated to engineering services that the insurance company will provide. We now have our insurance carrier come in twice a year to conduct foremen training programs and plant inspections."

  — *Two benefits:* "First, we saved on premium costs because our experience rating improved. Second, employee morale has improved. Employees see that we're doing something to make the plant a better place to work."

• **Slash materials costs and improve products.** "In many cases, you can cut the cost and improve the quality of a product at the same time," this savvy executive continues. Value analysis can help do this. We reviewed major products for cost reduction and quality improvement opportunities. Here are two examples:

Example 1: Paint-mixing machine.
This machine was made with gray iron castings in its structure. We redesigned the machine to eliminate the castings and substituted a structural molded foam housing.

We improved the quality of the machine. And part of the savings gain from the change in the structural housing construction was *reinvested* in upgrading certain parts within each mixer unit (using higher quality components).

Example 2: Repackaging program.
A great proliferation of package sizes for our products had evolved over the years. So we set up a *size consolidation program.* We pared 36 sizes down to eight standard package sizes.

We reduced our inventories and were able to give our suppliers longer runs that lowered the purchase cost. Then we took part of those savings and plowed them back into a higher quality package.

• **Cut costs with aggressive buying.** The company buys coiled steel as raw material. This coiled steel takes up a lot of space. The owner explains, "We looked at all the different sizes that we were buying. Engineering then did a size consolidation program for steel material."

"We went to our suppliers and said, 'We are going to buy fewer sizes but in higher volumes. We expect a better price. Then we added, 'Mr. Supplier, in return for our buying from you, we expect you to stock the master coil and cut it to our specifications.' The suppliers went along with us. Their sales volume still looked attractive because there would be frequent orders, and there were now fewer sizes for them to stock.

"We reduced inventory carrying costs by $62,500 a year."

HOW ONE COMPANY FOUND A RECIPE FOR PROFITS IN STATISTICAL QUALITY CONTROL

Despite an increase in the number of American manufacturers experimenting with quality control methods used by the Japanese, a nagging question remains unanswered: Can management successfully graft another culture's industrial methods onto our own? Results, so far, are mixed. But among the big winners is Campbell Soup's processing plant in Camden, New Jersey.

A few years ago, the Camden plant made a revolutionary change from its traditional production system to what it calls a "total systems approach." The new approach combines elements of just-in-time purchasing and production methods with Dr. W. Edwards Deming's pioneering work in statistical process control. This esoteric-sounding combination has had a clear impact on production costs.

During the first two years the new system was put into effect, the Camden plant realized a 28% drop in finished product inventory, a 57% drop in packaging inventories, large decreases in products that were not "made right the first time" and in consumer complaints, and a significant reduction in worker absenteeism. The total systems approach has been so successful that it has been extended to the company's other production facilities.

According to the Camden plant manager, these new techniques of quality control sound more daunting in theory than they were in practice. But he adds, "Don't even think about attempting to implement this kind of turnaround unless you are willing to commit time, money, never-ending patience and total top management support to the effort."

• **Statistical process control in action.** Quality control begins with the premise that the quality of a product can't be any better than the process or system that is being used to make the product. Improving that process means finding out where, when and why problems occur—and then fixing them.

Employees at Campbell's Camden plant (and now throughout all Campbell plants) are trained in "extremely simple techniques" that help them do just this. Quality is now monitored in appropriate areas by sorters using check sheets or making control charts in production areas of the plant, as well as by those in maintenance and administration. The charts monitor daily the critical control points throughout the manufacturing system at the plant.

The plant's production process is monitored statistically from top to bottom.

• **Let's look at the system in action.** Starting in the receiving area, dock loaders themselves inspect the vegetables that come in. When the ingredients reach the sorting area, other checksheets show the proper start-up and clear-up procedures for vegetable sorting. Conversion charts and tables help employees plot control charts that monitor the ingredients going into the plant's soups and sauces.

In the blending area, where chopping, weighing and mixing are coordinated, other operators monitor each aspect of the cooking operation. The goal is to see that the job gets done right the first time.

Taking over from the blending area employees, filler operators keep detailed downtime sheets that document any problems in the container-filling process. Operators in the critical sterilization process follow yet another "preflight checklist" and plot any downtime before their product gets labeled, packaged and sent to the pallet operators.

The information documented on daily control charts is the basis for weekly quality control meetings within each department. Hourly workers, supervisors and managers work to find the root causes of poor performance and identify possible remedies. But the idea of communicating problems and working for solutions extends beyond department barriers.

Each area of the plant—from receiving to shipping—is looked upon as the "customer" for the product of the preceding operation. In other words, each operation is held accountable to the next. Regular brainstorming sessions are held to allow the "customers" and "vendors" of each operation to work together to improve the final product before it goes to the real outside customer.

Indirect labor and outside vendors are held to the same problem-solving approach. Quality circles in the maintenance department concentrate their efforts on maintaining equipment and machinery in the condition needed for both quality and productivity throughout the plant. Suppliers who can't supply quality goods and materials are eliminated. But the emphasis is on brainstorming ways to improve quality first.

• **Selling quality control.** Campbell's decision to adopt the total systems approach came as a shock to both managers and employees at the plant.

When you tell an employee who's been around 30 years, "We're going to change everything," the news probably is not going to be well received. So, you have to introduce the ideas first, without any expectations. By the same token, managers—including those who understand the theoretical underpinnings of statistical quality control—find the reality hard to deal with. Often, it's not easy for a manager to accept the idea that a worker who's been doing the same job for 30 years may know more about it than anyone else. And many managers are skeptical that employees with "high absentee and low productivity rates" can become more productive under a different system.

Here are some of the steps that were taken to introduce Campbell employees to what was to become the total systems approach:

- Plantwide meetings, starting with managers and supervisors, were held to explain the company's new operating philosophy.

- A new systems department was formed, staffed by managers who first received specialized training in both statistics and "people" skills. They acted as in-house consultants to the entire plant.

- Outside consultants were hired to come to the plant and talk to small groups of employees about the Deming philosophy. A cross-section of people from all departments attended these meetings.

- Managers, supervisors and rank-and-file workers were sent to courses and seminars throughout the country, wherever appropriate training was available. Campbell also contracted with the University of Tennessee to provide courses of varying lengths geared to the company's managers, operators and even outside vendors.

Patience is absolutely essential to a changeover of this kind. Reinforce everything by action.

To drive home the point that problems *had* to be solved by talking about them, the plant manager began what he calls "unfocused gripe sessions" for hourly employees. At first, the air at these meetings was thick with individual, and often self-serving, complaints. But the manager returned again and again with regular updates on action taken in response to what he was told. When they realized they were being taken seriously, the workers began voicing general work concerns. This was the start of effective quality circles.

HOW EMPLOYEE SUGGESTIONS CAN HELP COMPANIES CUT WASTE-DISPOSAL COSTS

More and more companies today are taking environmental concerns seriously for a simple economic reason: Waste-disposal and treatment costs are soaring, particularly for hazardous substances and industrial wastes that can pollute the environment.

Within the last few years, a growing number of companies in environmentally sensitive industries such as chemicals have tapped their employees' concern about the environment to help cut their waste-disposal and pollution-control costs. How? By adopting employee-suggestion programs and giving awards and bonuses to employees who come up with effective waste-control and pollution-prevention ideas.

Whether your company's operations produce toxic byproducts, or merely plain old everyday garbage, your employees probably have some ideas that could help make your operation more efficient and reduce the volume of garbage or waste material that must be disposed of—at an ever-increasing cost. Here are some examples of low-cost programs that other companies have adopted to harness their human resources for the purpose of conserving natural resources:

- Employees at a Monsanto Chemical Co. plant in Bridgeport, N.J., can earn $100 savings bonds and favored parking spaces in the company parking lot by putting winning pollution-control ideas in a special suggestion box. And if the plant meets quarterly and annual emissions-reduction and workplace-safety goals, *every employee* gets a day off with pay or a $200 savings bond. So if all four quarterly goals and the annual goal are met, plant workers can get an extra week of paid vacation for the year.

  Employee suggestions have already contributed to more efficient use of raw materials and a reduction in wastes that must undergo expensive on-site treatment—for a savings of several hundred thousand dollars.

- Pollution-prevention suggestions can earn employees two types of awards at an American Cyanamid plant in Linden, N.J. Employees who win departmental awards get to choose merchandise such as patio furniture and sporting goods from a gift catalog, while those who win a plant manager's award receive a $50 check good for dinner for two. The names of all award winners are posted on a special honor roll at the plant gate.

  Plant managers estimate that award-winning suggestions have cut raw-material wastes at the 200-worker chemical facility by more than 2 million pounds over the past three years.

To ensure fairness and build employee enthusiasm for any incentive awards system, involve employees in the program's design and administration—from top to bottom. And it's especially important that employees play a role in reviewing the suggestions and picking the winners.

Award winners at the American Cyanamid plant, for example, are selected by a special waste-watching team made up of supervisors, professionals and rank-and-file production workers. The team holds regular meetings and is responsible for actually following through on suggestions.

At the Monsanto plant, "The incentive program itself was designed by a task group of a dozen employees," notes the plant manager. Employees set "both the criteria for the rewards as well as the reward system itself," she says.

> **IMPORTANT:** Employee-suggestion programs can backfire if top management isn't committed to putting good ideas into practice. When worthwhile suggestions *aren't* implemented, employees often conclude that manage-

ment doesn't take their ideas seriously and is merely paying lip service to the concept of employee involvement. Keep in mind that some waste-reduction and pollution-control measures can be prohibitively costly to put in place. So having employees involved in reviewing and trying to implement suggestions can yield a big public relations benefit when a seemingly excellent suggestion proves on closer examination to be unworkable.

CUTTING PURCHASING AND INVENTORY COSTS

SIX SMART-MONEY WAYS TO TRIM PURCHASING COSTS

Business owners are always looking for ways to slice operating expenses. Here are six ideas that may help you cut your company's purchasing costs:

1. Set a reorder deadline. "RUSH" is a four-letter word that should be eliminated from purchase requisitions. Reason: If your production employees wait until the last minute to place orders, you run the risk of losing both on-time delivery and favorable prices.

Insist that production people adhere to set deadlines for reordering each item they use. See to it that they let you—or the person designated to be in charge of ordering—know as soon as inventory is reduced to a predetermined level. In this way, you have time to shop around and work out the best price.

2. Let suppliers reorder for you. Many owners and managers battle hard to keep suppliers off their backs about reorders. But a Connecticut chief executive suggests you may win the war by losing this battle.

"Give clearance to your regular suppliers to check your stock on the items they sell you," this business owner says. "Have them tell you when it's time to reorder—when the items you have drop to a level you both agree to in advance." You will thus be free of the annoyance and cost of periodically checking supplies.

3. Check to see if minimum stock figures are still OK. These figures may be out-of-date and bear little relation to your current lead time or consumption rate. A Dallas, Texas, company owner recently had the minimum stock figure checked for his company's inventory items. The results were surprising.

"Our minimum figures were way too high. We were reordering and getting delivery as much as a month too early. Now we've set new minimum stock figures." As a result, the company saves a great deal in inventory costs.

4. Let delivery dates cut cash needs. A Scranton, Pennsylvania, executive observes: "We find that some suppliers need to be instructed in the matter of deliveries. They claim they need lots of advance notice for orders, so we shoot the purchase orders to them early. Lately, we've found that they're plunking the material on our loading dock weeks before we need it."

This business owner took command of the delivery schedule. He now specifies a delivery period on all company purchase orders, calling for delivery "after...(date), but before...(date)."

"If we specify the earliest date we'll accept the merchandise, we not only (a) get delivery when we need it, we also (b) avoid paying invoices too early and (c) don't needlessly tie up extra cash in inventory."

5. Keep shopping around. Just because one supplier offered the best deal some years ago is no guarantee that it's not taking your business for granted, or that its price and delivery terms are better than what someone else can offer. Many companies fall prey to this "let's-stick-to-old-reliable" attitude.

Shop around regularly. When contacted by potential suppliers, hear them out and evaluate their offers. And don't forget suppliers you've turned down in the past. You may find that some of these companies may now be able to give you a lower price or handle your job faster than "old reliable."

6. Figure out your turnover times. "Use your next slow period to go through past purchase orders for each item," suggests an Arizona businesswoman. "A year's worth should give you a fair idea of an item's average turnover period. Jot down the turnover periods and keep your record handy. Now all you have to do when a shipment arrives is to check the contents and prices against the purchase order, and mark a conservative reorder date on the calendar. The turnover period for that item gives a good idea of when it will be running low.

"A close look at turnover times also helped me pinpoint items that had been over-ordered in the past," she adds. "I cut excess purchasing on these items and reduced the amount of space we needed for storage."

THREE EFFECTIVE TECHNIQUES FOR BUYING AT A BETTER PRICE

An experienced company owner may think he or she knows all the angles when it comes to getting the most favorable price quotes from a supplier. But in many cases, the price that looked so right when the order was put through turns out, when the items have finally hit your receiving dock and the invoice must be paid, to be not as good as it might have been. It's wise, therefore, to stay alert to these three problems:

• **The first price not always final.** In looking for new sources of supply, you may be tempted to use marginal or unfamiliar vendors. These may be located in out-of-the-way places, involving unexpected transportation delays or other added costs. Goods may arrive inadequately packed and damaged, further holding up completion of the purchase.

When buying from an unfamiliar vendor, be even more careful than usual to check in advance on all details that could affect the final actual cost of the merchandise.

• **The "price on shipment" pitfall.** In some purchase contracts, you may not be able to pin down the vendor to a firm price for all anticipated deliveries. Perhaps the vendor is using raw materials whose prices fluctuate so he can't predict his own costs. Or his outlays for wages and materials may be rising at a rate he can't predict. But in leaving the shipment price open, how can you make sure the price will be fair?

State in the purchase order that the price will be based on published indexes of raw materials. Or state that the price to be paid will be the manufacturer's current published price at the time of shipment.

In addition, make every effort to speed up delivery on the order. The sooner shipment can be secured, the less chance there is that the supplier's costs will get out of bounds.

• **Ignored quantity-price possibility.** On items ordered often, the total your company buys over a year's time might well add up to a quantity that merits a lower price if the year's purchases are taken as a whole. With foresight, an excessive cost need not be tolerated.

Look ahead and anticipate the total purchases on an item over a period of months. Try to get the most favorable price based on all shipments in that period. At the end of the period, price can be adjusted on the basis of the amounts actually ordered.

"BOILER ROOM" SUPPLY SCAMS: HOW TO MAKE SURE YOUR COMPANY DOESN'T GET RIPPED OFF

Boiler room supply scams rip off thousands of companies every year. Boiler rooms, otherwise known as "paper pirates" or "toner phoners," are high-pressure telephone sales operations. They make their living by selling inferior office products at exorbitant prices to unsuspecting office employees—*very possibly yours.*

To avoid getting taken, it helps to know the difference between the "good guys" and the "bad guys." Supply scammers shouldn't be confused with legitimate companies that also choose to sell their products via telemarketing.

Most telemarketers are honest. They offer good customer service and high-quality products, and can claim many satisfied customers. They're in business for the long term. If they don't keep you happy, you won't buy from them again.

Then, there are the so-called paper pirates. What paper pirates attempt to do is *blend in* with the legitimate telemarketing crowd. These supply scammers put little or no emphasis on repeat business. For them, each sale is a one-time event. That's not to say they won't rip you off repeatedly if you let them. They will. And they're successful—the Better Business Bureau estimates that boiler room scams extort about $1 billion annually in the United States.

How boiler room scams operate

The typical "toner phoner" uses deception and coercion to paint a rosy picture of low prices and high quality for their victims. In reality, they're often selling inferior quality products because those are the very items that assure them the maximum markups. And the deception works because they know that the average employee is unaware of the exact selling price of the thousands of office products available today.

Here are two examples of how deceptive vendors offer their merchandise:

Example 1—Inflated price
Ball point pens that normally retail for $4.20 per dozen (35 cents a pen) are offered to an office employee at an inflated price of, say, $10.68 per dozen or 89 cents a pen. The supply scammer then offers the inflated-price pens for a "fantastic 40% discount" price

of $6.40 per dozen. The scammer's cost for the pens? Probably less than 80 cents per dozen.

The scammer winds up with an 800% markup. And because buyers were told they were receiving a 40% discount from list price, they think they got a great deal for their company and suspect nothing.

Example 2—Brand-name switch.

Another trick scammers use is to incorporate brand name products into their sales pitch. At best, however, the brand name products the scammer is offering are manufacturer's seconds or rejects. At worst, the pirate is lying about the brand name altogether. The buyer may find out about the lie (assuming he or she is alert enough to catch on to the difference) only after the unbranded, or falsely labeled merchandise arrives and has been put to use.

Your company gets ripped off and nobody may realize it—least of all the person who placed the order in the first place.

Some other problems office employees come up against when dealing with boiler room supply scams include the following:

• **You have no recourse.** Paper pirates often operate from a post office box, unlisted phone number or telephone answering service. When something goes wrong, there isn't much you can do about it.

• **There is a limited selection.** Compared to conventional office products vendors who offer thousands of items for sale, supply scammers market very few items and usually only those that permit huge potential markups such as toner, pens, markers and ribbons.

• **You get shoddy goods.** Unlabeled, inferior-quality products are the paper pirate's stock-in-trade.

• **You are charged high freight costs.** Boiler rooms often add on freight charges that are 10 times the actual cost.

Be alert. To catch you off guard, paper pirates create elaborate sales scenarios. You may have already heard some of the more popular ones. For example:

• *The "you've just won a CONTEST!" pitch*: As the "winner" you're entitled to a "prize." The "winner" is then asked where the "prize" should be delivered. Toward the end of the conversation, the subject of special prices on supplies comes up and the high-pressure sales pitch begins.

- *The "cut out the middleman" pitch:* "Mr. Jones, I'm the supplier to your current vendor. Buy direct from me and you can save yourself a lot of money." This approach is simple—but effective—with naive buyers who may not know any better.

- *The "now or never" pitch:* "Ms. Smith, I have a customer in your area who just canceled an order. I can sell you this merchandise at rock-bottom prices, but I must have your immediate okay. Our delivery truck will be in your area in the next hour or so. Shall I have the order delivered at 1 P.M. or 3 P.M.?" The truth is, there is no canceled order. This is just a ploy to catch you off guard long enough to make a "now" sale.

- *The "survey" call:* The solicitor calls in with "survey" questions about the equipment in your office: copiers, computers, printers, faxes, etc. He or she may also ask for model numbers, supply stock numbers, etc. In addition, the solicitor may inquire as to who's in charge of ordering supplies for those machines. After getting this information, the caller hangs up. Later, the same (or another) solicitor calls and asks for the buyer by name and presents a very appealing sales pitch based on the critical information he or she gathered during the first call.

Other shady sales tricks may involve the following:

- A delivery arriving with the claim that it was ordered by a previous employee or that the delivery is the balance of an earlier (back) order.

- Doubling or tripling the merchandise quantity ordered.

- Billing a customer—fraudulently—for the same order twice.

Six ways to protect your company

You and your employees can take steps to avoid being stung by boiler room scams. Here are six of the most effective safeguards:

1. Order only from approved vendors. Establish and maintain a list of approved vendors. This way, even if a toner phoner ships in an order, your accounts payable department will question it because the supplier is not on the approved list.

2. Allow only one authorized buyer. Designate one person to order all office products and supplies. This sounds basic, but surveys show that many companies allow more than one person to order office and machine supplies. This can be a BIG mistake.

3. Avoid deals that sound too good to be true. To avoid verbal misunderstandings with a vendor, request that all purchasing deals be put *in writing*.

4. Ask for references. Request that all new suppliers provide several local references from satisfied customers.

Check to see if the caller's company appears in the phone book—both in the yellow and white pages. If you have any doubts about a vendor, ask to call the solicitor back. Illegitimate vendors generally won't cooperate.

5. Don't accept credit card or C.O.D. orders. Order only on an open-account basis.

6. Return unordered merchandise. Request a return receipt. If a shipment does get accepted by an unsuspecting employee anyway, don't pay for it. Instead, write to the company and request that they pick it up.

If you think you've been ripped off by a paper pirate, contact your state Attorney General's office with all the particulars. Also, notify your local postmaster about what has occurred.

LEASING VS. PURCHASING: HOW TO EVALUATE EQUIPMENT FINANCING OPTIONS

When it comes time to buy new equipment, one of the more important factors you must weigh is whether to lease or buy.

Leasing is the financing method of choice in most companies today. The reason has to do with how most firms approach the purchasing process. Their first concern is the "affordability" factor—not just the total cost the company ends up paying. At first glance, leasing may seem more favorable because:

- Leases usually require only a modest up-front cash outlay often limited to the first and last month's lease payment.

- Lease obligations do not appear as a major liability on your company's balance sheet—as does an installment loan.

- Tax considerations often favor a lease over a purchase.

Nevertheless, there is a downside to leasing. A lease usually costs more than an installment loan—sometimes substantially more. And vendors anxious to sell their product often dwell on the benefits of leasing—the low monthly payments, for example—and leave out other important factors that should be considered in the actual cost of the equipment.

To be sure you're getting a good deal when buying new equipment, shop equipment first, financing second. Your job is to find the equipment that's best for your company. Of course, you'll want easy financing terms, but you'll want performance too. You shouldn't pass up a machine that does everything you want it to do simply because of financing concerns. For example, business owner Mary Johnson is negotiating for an office full of furniture. The retail list price is $20,000. She can lease the furniture for an affordable monthly payment, but the lease (finance) charges will be added to the $20,000 price. The equipment cost gets "bundled" into the financing equation.

If Mary purchases the furniture for cash, she can more than likely obtain a meaningful discount (say 20% off) from an office furniture dealer—a savings of $4,000. Under this scenario, her net cost (and the amount she needs to finance) would be $16,000—not $20,000.

"Unbundle" the financing costs from the price of the equipment itself. Shop for the equipment separately (as if you're going to pay cash for it). Negotiate with one or more vendors for their best price first, then bring up the subject of financing. By divorcing the cost of money from the cost of equipment, you'll stand a good chance of obtaining a better deal on both.

Inquire about interest rates. It's often difficult to find out what interest rate is built into equipment leases. Sometimes the salespeople don't know. But more often, they will be hesitant to quote the rate because they know it's not competitive with what you can obtain elsewhere—say from a bank or an independent leasing company.

Tell the sales rep that you must know what the built-in interest rate is in order to make a final decision. Once the vendor supplies you with the interest percentage, you can go ahead and figure out how much the equipment will actually cost under a lease arrangement. For example, let's use a 60-month lease on a $6,000 purchase. The lease payment equals $163 per month. The first and last month's lease payments equal an initial $326 cash outlay. Multiply the monthly payment by the total number of months under the terms of the agreement (58 remaining months × $163 per month = $9,454.)

Now you must determine how much money will still be due at the end of the lease if your firm wants to actually own the equipment outright. This is known as a *residual* payment. A six-month residual (approximately 10%) equals an additional $978.

IMPORTANT: If your company doesn't make the residual payment, the leasing company can take possession of the equipment and you'll lose any equity you've built up during the term of the lease.

Now, total the costs ($9,454 plus $978). In this example, the grand total of all payments for a 60-month lease is $10,758.

The final step is to take the original selling price of the equipment ($6,000) and deduct it from the grand total ($10,758). The actual "cost of money" in this case is $4,758.

Repeat the same cost evaluation with your bank (on an installment loan or lease) and an independent equipment leasing company to find the best "cost of money" value. Then obtain your best price on the equipment via bids from several vendors. After securing your best deal on both financing and equipment, "bundle" the two together.

HOW TO DECIDE WHICH INVENTORY CONTROL METHOD WILL WORK BEST FOR YOUR COMPANY

Smart inventory control can provide more profit at less cost. It can be especially effective in helping you fight inflation. But the control method that's best for you depends on conditions in your company and the type of business you're in.

Let's look at the two most basic approaches to inventory control—minimum method and maximum method.

The owner of a Midwest plant uses the minimum method. He says, "Cutting inventory to the bone is better than buying at bargain prices. If we don't need supplies right now, we don't buy."

The reason is that carrying costs on inventory not currently needed can erode profits. And in his company, another situation applies: The company is in an industry where some parts grow obsolete almost overnight. "We just can't afford to be stuck holding a quantity of some item we won't be able to use again."

On the other hand, a toy manufacturer has tried the minimum inventory route and been burned by it more than once. The problem usually starts when a supplier falls down on delivery promises. If the manufacturer then runs out of stock on a key item, production comes to a halt and a disaster results. He prefers the maximum method.

"To get around this risk, we keep more than ample supplies on hand," the head of the company says. "That way, we always have what we want when we need it."

Picking the best method for your company

Weigh the advantages of each approach in terms of your specific situation. A **minimum inventory** setup may be better when—

- Cash and space are limited;
- Demand for your finished product stays fairly constant;
- Supplier delivery is reliable;
- Your suppliers stock an adequate inventory of their own;
- Carrying costs outweigh any benefits from buying in large quantities or before expected price hikes.

The **maximum method** may be justified when more attractive quantity prices can be secured for big orders. Or longer delivery times may compel you to stock more—despite higher cost—so you'll have *essential* items on hand when you need them.

The **middle-ground approach,** a third method of inventory control, helps you spot items over which you might want to exercise strict control, while you simplify accounting for certain other items.

Concentrate control on high-value items. To determine items where strict control will best pay off, take five steps:

1. Compute your company's total inventory control costs. Include everything from carrying costs to paperwork, but not cost of the inventory itself.

2. Divide this figure by the number of items in inventory to determine the unit control cost.

3. Ascertain the cost to purchase or make each inventory item.

4. Arrange prices of all inventory items in descending order of value. You'll see at a glance the relative values of all items.

5. Analyze this list to determine the value distribution of inventory items. About each item, ask: "Does this item warrant the cost of controlling inventory on it?"

Don't be misled by the low price of some strategic parts. The production of an important assembly might be held up for lack of an inexpensive part. So be sure to single out these *critical* items for special treatment.

BUYING NEW TECHNOLOGY—WITHOUT BUSTING YOUR BUDGET

Today, even the smallest companies need to keep pace with the latest information-processing and communications technologies if they hope to survive. (For more on how your company can use computers and other new office technologies, see Chapter 12.) Problem is, the technology is changing so rapidly that you can spend a small fortune on the newest, most-powerful systems—and still fall behind in the information technology race.

But buying the right computer or telecommunications system for your business doesn't have to bust your company's budget. The keys are shopping carefully and knowing what you're looking for. As many small business owners have found, it's easy to have the wool pulled over your eyes by computer vendors' claims and your employees' demands for the most up-to-date high-tech wizardry. That's why the biggest computer cost-saver may be this simple step:

TO SAVE UNNECESSARY OFFICE AUTOMATION COSTS—JUST SAY NO!*

Never lose sight of the fact that some jobs are performed better and more economically *without* the aid of a computer. Also keep in mind that many tasks can be handled perfectly well by systems that are a decade or more old. The trouble lies in convincing your managers, supervisors and employees that new computer equipment isn't a magic solution to missed quotas and sagging morale.

Take a cold-hearted, dollars-and-cents approach to any "computerization" request that comes across your desk. Don't approve the purchase of any new hardware or software without first analyzing the situation. If the projected benefits don't justify the cost, deny the request. For example, a manager wants several new personal computers to replace the old PCs currently used by his department. His rationale is that the current systems are yesterday's technology and the faster machines will boost productivity. But the department's only application is word processing. Since few employees type fast enough to outpace the processing power of the old machine, the request should be denied.

This section was written by John Edwards, who writes extensively on computers and office automation. He is based in Mt. Laurel, New Jersey.

The problem is that, in many companies, fancy computer equipment has replaced the key to the executive washroom as a sign of status and power. As a result, turning down a system request is often a thorny political decision fraught with the possibility of bruised egos and endless in-house feuds.

If someone persists in his or her demand for new computer gear, try turning the tables. Ask the person making the request to justify the purchase in black and white. Don't accept vague promises of "a better turnaround" or fractional benefits such as where one worker will save 5 minutes per day and another 20 minutes per week. Demand a detailed study that shows how the new gear will benefit the company's bottom line. Chances are, your decision will stand unchallenged.

HOW TO GET TOP-OF-THE-LINE PERSONAL COMPUTERS AT ROCK-BOTTOM COST

You shouldn't have to pay top dollar when you're planning to buy new personal computers for your business. If you shop wisely, there are ways to get around the high prices and still get quality products. Here are five cost-saving tips from a computer consulting firm in New York City:

1. Buy IBM clone computers whenever possible. Popular name-brand computers are a lot more expensive, and the IBM-compatible models can do the same things these products offer.

2. Look for discounts at department stores rather than shopping at full-service computer stores. The discounters typically charge a third or a fourth of what you'd pay at a computer store. They usually have a large volume of a couple of low-end computers. Since they don't want to risk having a lot of returns, the computers are usually good-quality machines.

The full-service vendors have higher markups in part because their salespeople work on commission. What's more, the reps will try to sell you a whole computer package, which may include training, installation and other services. While these extras *may* be worthwhile, they sometimes can be merely an added expense that you don't need.

3. Be careful when buying software: There are software packages available for virtually every imaginable business application. But they can be expensive. Check computer and trade magazines to find out what the best package is for your needs. Think seriously before spending more than $600 for software. If you spend more than that, you can probably get a more efficient package made specifically for your business.

Also, beware of vendors who try to sell you a complete system, including software. The markup may be so great that it's not cost-effective. Generally, you can get a better price if you purchase the computer and the software separately.

4. Don't be fooled by a high price tag. Just because a computer is expensive doesn't necessarily mean it's better. Many top-of-the-line products cost less than lower-quality brands.

5. Do your homework. If no one on your staff is knowledgeable about computers, it might be well worth the money to retain an independent consultant to help you purchase and install the equipment. The consultant's fee (typically $50–$150 per hour) should be less than the markups many vendors will charge you for a complete package system. And it can save you from getting talked into buying far more equipment and options than you need.

Be careful not to hire a consultant who's affiliated with a vendor. The *independent* consultant may really be a computer salesperson. Such consultants' opinions may be biased toward a specific product. Make it a point to ask about any such relationships up front.

WHEN IT PAYS TO RENT COMPUTERS

Personal computers may seem out of reach for your company even when you find the best possible deals. Here's a look at cases in which it may make more sense to rent a PC system than to buy:

- Renting can be cheaper than buying, but only if you need the computers for a short time. Six to eight months is usually the dividing line. If you need PCs for only a month or two, it's clearly cheaper to rent. After nine months, it becomes cheaper to buy.

- Renting can be convenient if you're in the market for a computer and want to try out a system for a few months before locking into a deal. Renting can also be useful for short-term projects.

If you do decide to rent there are a few things you should keep in mind:

- Be sure the price you're quoted is the *complete installed price*. Ask if the rental company will tack on additional delivery fees or other costs.

- Be sure the rental company is capable of delivering the computer on time. This can be critical if you need it at a specific time. The company might tell you it has the equipment when you're shopping around, but it may not be in stock when delivery day arrives. Although this problem is sometimes unavoidable, you should make it clear that the computer must be delivered on time when you're negotiating the deal.

- Make sure service policies are spelled out when you commit to a rental. Find out exactly what kind of service the company offers if something goes wrong.

HOW TO SAVE BIG BUCKS ON COMPUTER SUPPLIES*

Business owners spend many sleepless nights fretting over the big-ticket items: buying new equipment and software. Few, however, lose a wink of shut-eye over the computer *supplies* their companies consume.

While computer supplies may account for only a small part of your budget, dollars wasted on overpriced, inappropriate and poor-quality materials can still have a significant impact on your bottom line. Here are some techniques you can use to get the most for your money:

1. Buy in bulk. Supplies purchased in volume quantities are always cheaper than products purchased in small lots. Many items used by one department—like floppy disks and printer ribbons—are also needed by other departments. Remind the person in charge of purchasing that your company may be able to save money by combining computer supply requests from various company departments.

Hardware products manufactured by competing companies often use identical supplies. An ABC printer may use the same ribbon cartridge as an XYZ printer, even though the manufacturers list different parts numbers. Give your dealer a description of your company's hardware devices and ask him to check which units can use identical supply products.

This section was written by John Edwards, who writes extensively on computers and office automation. He is based in Mt. Laurel, New Jersey.

2. Use only one or two dealers. Don't be tempted by "once in a lifetime" sales or "unbelievable" offers. A long-term relationship with an established dealer can pay big dividends when supplies are tight or when you need to locate a discontinued product.

3. Don't order at the last minute. Most dealers charge extra for "rush" orders. Track your use of supplies closely and order heavily used items before you run low. On the other hand, don't order items too far in advance. Some products, like printer ribbons, have a limited shelf life.

4. Stay abreast of the marketplace. Your company's purchasing or supply officer should regularly browse through supply catalogs. If your dealer is charging higher prices than most of the competitors, ask why. He may be selling you a higher-quality product. On the other hand, he may be gouging you.

5. Keep a close watch on your inventory. Employee theft is a major problem for many companies. But even if your firm's workers are completely trustworthy, supplies can still be lost through careless handling. Store your products in a central, locked closet or room.

Establish a sign-out procedure for all workers who request supplies. This will help you keep track of how many products each employee is using. It also subtly reminds workers that they may be asked to explain excessive supply use.

HOW PAYING YOUR BILLS BY COMPUTER MAKES YOUR MONEY GO FARTHER—FASTER

A paperless society may still be a ways off. But at some companies, the future is now—at least when it comes to writing checks. An increasing number of businesses are paying their bills by electronically transferring money via computer from their accounts to the accounts of their suppliers.

The National Automated Clearing House estimates that this year more than 110 million business payments will be made by computer. While this is just a fraction of the 10 billion business checks written each year, the trend toward electronic payment appears to be growing. Here's why:

- Big savings: Significant savings seems to be the chief reason companies are throwing away their corporate checkbooks. For example, at Sears, where electronic payment accounts for 40% of all payments made to other businesses, the company has found it saves almost half a dollar—thanks to lower processing and postage costs—for every electronic payment it makes.

- Accuracy: Accuracy is another benefit of the new bill-paying mode. General Electric estimates that the accuracy rate for its electronic payments is almost 95%, versus 60% for written checks.

- Efficiency: Companies are also discovering that electronic bill-paying helps streamline the entire manufacturing process. It enables companies to order and pay for goods immediately and helps to reduce inventories. General Motors, for instance, orders almost all of its parts by computer and pays one-quarter of its suppliers the same way.

HOW TO SAVE 30%–60% WHEN BUYING PHONE EQUIPMENT

If you're in the market for phones but you don't want to spend a lot of money, you may want to consider buying used equipment.

A consultant with *TELEOS Resources,* a market research company in New Jersey, says you often can get used phones for 30%–60% of what new phones would cost. And the used phones are just as functional as new ones, he adds. You get "equal performance for a lot less cost."

However, even though the used equipment can be just as good as new, you have to make sure the vendor you're buying from is reputable. The secondary or used market is still relatively new and it hasn't been "cleansed of unethical companies out there."

One thing you can do is look for a label from the *National Association of Telecommunications Dealers,* a Washington, D.C.-based association of used equipment dealers. While the label won't guarantee good service, it should at least give a strong indication that the vendor is reputable and stands behind its products.

The president of *Rhyne Communications Inc.* (Parsippany, N.J.), which refurbishes and sells used phones, suggests checking the credentials of the vendor and the original manufacturer. Also, find out what warranties are offered and ask for references. If the company is reputable it should be willing to give references and be flexible on trial periods and warranties.

Before purchasing used equipment you should also find out what kind of service and maintenance the vendor offers. Some used-equipment companies don't offer maintenance and you would have to hire a company to provide the service. Be sure to ask before you buy so you don't end up with a phone system that no one will repair and maintain.

The standard warranty for used phone equipment is generally 90 days. However, since most used phone equipment is refurbished, it's often better than new equipment on the market because the bugs have been taken out.

FOUR WAYS TO GET THE MOST OUT OF YOUR CELLULAR TELEPHONE—AT THE LOWEST COST*

Whether the equipment is used to keep in contact with the home office while on the road or to transfer data from a remote site, many busy executives now view the cellular phone as a powerful—if not indispensable—communications tool. But before you sign a contract with a cellular phone vendor, here are four critical points you should first consider:

1. Purchasing vs. leasing. In the early days of the cellular phone industry, most systems were leased. Since those times, prices of basic cellular units have fallen from over $2,000 to less than $700. Unless you're buying phones for an army of vehicles and users, purchasing the unit outright is probably the most cost-effective way to go.

2. Phone functions. Many vendors adorn their products with a variety of impressive-sounding, but ultimately useless, functions. Which features you'll consider vital depends primarily on your personal preferences. Popular options include call waiting, call forwarding, hands-off dialing, route selection and accounting management. To minimize confusion, all of your company's cellular phones should have the same features.

3. Signal strength. A cellular phone operated from a car will usually have no difficulty in making and holding cell connections. Using a unit at a remote construction site or inside a plant, however, poses special problems. Before acquiring a cellular phone, make sure it has the power and battery capacity to meet your needs.

4. Service rates. Cellular service providers offer various rate structures. Some plans are geared toward heavy daytime users and others for off-peak-hours callers. Plans are also available for individuals who make lots of brief calls and those who make relatively few, but lengthy, transmissions.

It pays to shop around and to analyze your probable usage habits before signing a contract.

This section was written by John Edwards, who writes extensively on computers and office automation. He is based in Mount Laurel, New Jersey.

Holding the Line on Shipping and Mailing Costs

Use These Sure-Fire Ways to Slash Your Shipping Costs

Your company can hold the line on shipping costs, avoid unnecessary expenses—and get better, faster service, too. Here are some of the best ways to do it:

• **Get the proper freight classification:** Make sure you use the right classification for whatever product you're shipping. This is what really matters in determining freight costs—more than *where* you ship, or *how*. Names, if you use the wrong ones, can hurt you.

For example, let's say you're shipping a 500-pound order of sponges, impregnated with glycerin to keep them soft, from New Jersey to Chicago. You describe them merely as "sponges."

If you had described them, correctly, as "wet sponges," they could have been shipped for less than half the amount.

Suppose you're paying for a shipment you've described simply as "metal sinks," instead of using the correct designation, "metal sinks with legs attached." Your shipping costs will be about double what they should be.

How can you make sure you're using the description that will get the lowest freight classification? Use the "National Motor Freight Classification," published by the National Motor Freight Traffic Association, 2200 Mill Road, Alexandria, VA, 22314. Phone: (703) 838-1810.

If you're paying freight on incoming shipments, make sure these, too, are properly described. Specify the product description in your purchase order.

• **Get the best freight rate from the carrier.** Contrary to a widely held view, the Interstate Commerce Commission does *not* establish freight rates. Each carrier establishes its own rates, charges and services. The law only requires carriers to print and file their charges, and to make them available to the public.

This, of course, means a carrier might charge you—legally—three times what a rival outfit would charge for the identical shipment. And you might not even get better service for it. So don't hesitate to pick and choose. Besides comparing prices, find out whether there are "stop off" privileges, with only a nominal charge for partial unloading. Also, find out about pickup and delivery times—so you can hold down costly idle time for your own people.

• **Check bills of lading with special care.** When you write a bill of lading, remember that you are, in effect, writing a check. If it's filled in completely and accurately, the carrier will charge you the lowest applicable rate for the item being shipped. But if anything is left unclear—especially in the description of the goods—you'll probably pay too much.

The reason for this is if the carrier is given a choice between rates, it's entitled to charge the *higher* one.

Make it clear to your shipping people that every bill of lading represents money—money saved if it's made out completely and accurately, or money wasted if it isn't.

Get this message across to your suppliers, too. This is particularly important when they ship to you collect, and the cost is immaterial to them.

• **Don't pay for clerical and computer errors.** The number of mistakes that can be made in freight bills might surprise you. They may be clerical errors, or they may be "computer errors" (which are really clerical errors, too). But they do happen, and they can easily result in overcharges or duplicate billings. Let's review the following examples:

• A New York company was billed for $952 on a shipment of plumbing chemicals—not an unreasonable amount. But a double-check of the "pro number" (the number on the freight bill) revealed that the charge already had been paid a couple of months earlier.

• Another company received a carrier's bill with a misplaced decimal. The bill should have been for $2,600—but instead was for $26,000. The company didn't check the arithmetic and didn't notice the error.

Check freight bills with care before paying them. Make sure the amounts billed are the amounts due. And don't stop there. Have paid bills checked, too. Let outside experts audit your freight bills. Have this done regularly. Reason: There's a three-year time limit for filing a claim for a refund.

• **Get expert help in controlling costs.** One of the best ways to cut the cost of shipping is to get help from a specialist. This kind of help can allow you to head off many problems in advance and save money in ways you might not have considered.

For example, a carrier offered a New Jersey chemical manufacturer a 25% discount on a shipment—which seemed like a great deal. But following the advice of a shipping specialist, the company asked whether the discounted rate was *published*—i.e., filed with the ICC. It was not, as it turned out, so the company did not accept it.

The carrier could have come back later on and billed the New Jersey firm for the difference between the discounted rate and the published tariff. It could have done this as long as *three years* afterward—and longer if the carrier went bankrupt.

This means that if you get a discount that's *not published*, you risk getting billed for more—no matter what your contract says. One carrier gave discounts over a period of years, but did not have them published. About a thousand of its customers, who had not realized the discounts were unpublished, were later hit with "balance due" bills.

Whenever a carrier offers you a discount, ask to see the published rate. If it's not published, ask the carrier to get it published—which takes about 10 days.

This is just one example of the kind of money-saving guidance a shipping specialist can give. There are a number of others. But here's the biggest dollar-saver. Probably the most valuable service a shipping specialist can provide is *auditing freight bills*—picking up duplicate payments, spotting wrong classifications and even finding extension errors.

Despite a shipper's best efforts, such errors do slip by from time to time. These can really add up if they're not caught. But a shipping specialist can catch them and help you save thousands of dollars.

HOW TO MAKE SURE YOUR SHIPMENTS ARE HANDLED WITH CARE

When your company ships products, the last thing you want is for them to be damaged before they get to your customers. Not only is it expensive to replace damaged merchandise and a headache to file insurance claims, but shipping mishaps can also jeopardize the loyalty of your customers. Some transportation analysts estimate that $1 billion is lost each year in the United States because of shipping damages.

Some products damaged in shipping may look fine on the outside but have problems internally. Now, however, there are devices you can use to detect when a shipment has been handled roughly—even if the goods show no visible signs of damage. These devices cost anywhere from about $1 for a disposable sensor to thousands of dollars for sophisticated computerized mechanisms.

One inexpensive device is called the *Shockwatch*. Marketed by *Media Recovery, Inc.* (Dallas), the device is a sticker with a small glass tube containing a liquid held in place by surface tension. Normal handling or vibrations will not activate it, but when excessive impact or vibrations occur, the red liquid drains into the visible portion of the tube. There are different types of labels available to measure different sensitivities.

The labels cost $1 or less when bought in large quantities and up to $3 each for a small order. A companion product called *Tiltwatch* turns red if a package is tilted or turned on its side.

The Shockwatch helps control the handling environment for your shipments from your door to your customers' by putting handlers and carriers on notice that the packages require special handling. One company that ships sensitive avionics equipment used to have six to eight damaged shipments returned each month, at a cost of $1,500 per repair. After putting Shockwatch labels on the shipments, returns were cut to two in six months, saving the company a bundle.

WHAT YOU CAN DO TO KEEP MAILING COSTS DOWN WHEN RATES GO UP

Postal rates have increased and continue to increase. The rate hikes will pinch profits for companies that mail a heavy volume of customer correspondence, billings, marketing materials, etc. But there are a few steps you can take today to help hold the line on your company's mailing costs.

Here's what one postal consultant suggests for keeping your business mailing costs to a minimum:

• **Keep your addresses "clean."** Double-check the addresses in your mailing lists to make sure they're correct. A lot of mail is improperly addressed and never reaches its destination. And you still pay for it even though your client or customer never sees it. Losses include not only your costs to print and mail improperly addressed correspondence, but also the sales or collections you could have made—but didn't—because your mailings went to the wrong place.

• **Less may be best.** Keep records on customers with the best mail response rates. You may be able to get the same results—at lower cost—by being more selective with your mailings and avoiding the scattershot approach. For example, mail sales and marketing literature only to those who seem able to afford your services. And if your records show that certain customers place orders only after your salespeople call them on the phone, stop sending them sales promotions and have your sales force contact them directly.

• **Be sure your postage scale is accurate.** Check it regularly. Keep the scale on a level surface and in a location where workers won't damage it by "temporarily" piling all types of material on top of it.

Five U.S. quarters weigh about one ounce. You can also purchase brass weights from your local hardware store in one-ounce and two-ounce sizes. Use them often to check the accuracy of your scales. In addition, your post office offers an on-site meter service at reasonable rates. This could save you and your staff valuable time.

- **Post a rate chart near your meter.** A postal chart with current rates and rules should be posted in a prominent place near your meter so staff members can easily determine the proper postage for the weight of the material to be mailed.
- **Assign a trustworthy employee to control postage.** Whether you use a postage meter or stamps, be sure that proper security procedures are observed—and regularly checked. Lock your postage meter at night and on weekends. Have the employee keep a log so you can spot-check it if your meter's been tampered with or improperly used.
- **Redeem "spoiled" meter mail.** Ninety percent of the face value of meter imprint errors can be recovered. For example, if an envelope is imprinted $1.80—instead of $0.18—save the envelope and prepare a new one.

Submit all meter errors with a special claim form to the post office servicing your meter. Be sure all employees who use the meter know about this service and use it.

- **Investigate lower-class rates.** Mail should not automatically go first class. Ask your postmaster whether some of your mailing materials can qualify for a lower second- or third-class rate. If mail is properly prepared, you can realize solid savings and still get acceptable delivery. If your company does large mailings, a lower-class rate can represent substantial savings.

Be sure to keep up-to-date on the best mailing methods. Two key sources for such information are both free from the U.S. Postal Service. The booklet, *Mailer's Guide,* covers basic services and procedures, while the monthly bulletin, *Memo to Mailers,* keeps you current with continual postal changes.

- **Consider using a commercial mailing service.** If it's vital to your operation that incoming mail be delivered early in the day, consider retaining a commercial service to pick up your mail at the local post office. This will enable you to get a good jump on delivery. These services will also pick up mail at the end of the day and take it directly to the main post office. The service can help you avoid hassles and speed your mail by as much as a day.
- **Keep in touch with your local postmaster.** Request a visit by a customer service official—either from the local post office or within your postal region—so that all your mailing procedures and facilities can be informally reviewed by postal experts. Ask about various discounts available to customers who prepare their mail for speedy processing by the postal service's new optical scanning equipment. The new rate proposals include new and expanded discounts that the postal service hopes will encourage more customers to use barcoding and presorting.

CHAPTER TWELVE

HOW TO HARNESS THE POWER OF COMPUTERS, AND OTHER OFFICE AUTOMATION TECHNOLOGIES

The companies most likely to succeed in the 1990s are those that make fullest use of new office automation and information-processing technologies. Automated systems such as computers and new communications technologies are no longer high-tech luxuries. They're essential tools for every company that needs to keep track of a large volume of information and move its products faster and farther than ever before—while keeping labor costs to a minimum.

However, many small businesses have been slow to take advantage of new technology to boost productivity and improve their delivery of information, services and goods. For some, the cost of buying a computer system or network of personal computers (PCs) is the biggest hurdle. For other small business owners, the main impediment may be simply fear of the unknown—and lack of time and expertise to figure out what your company needs, how to train your people to use the new equipment, and how to maintain a complex data processing system once you get it.

While automated systems can help you cut costs and unlock big productivity gains, computers can also drain precious time and resources if you don't do your homework. As with any piece of complex machinery, your people must be trained to use computers properly. You or someone in your company must understand the technology well enough to monitor how it's being used and establish procedures to protect your investment.

That's where this chapter comes in. We've ferreted out key information from several computer experts—people known for their experience in working with small businesses—on the best and most cost-effective ways to get your company "on line." You'll also find tips on how to handle some of the difficult technological and people problems that inevitably crop up. For example, in the following pages you'll discover:

- How to cure your employees of "computer phobia."

- How to train your people to use a new system—without spending a small fortune on training costs.

- How you can arrange your workplace to make it safer and more efficient for your employees who spend the better part of their days sitting in front of a computer terminal.

- Important safeguards you need to establish to keep your computerized business records and data safe from "hackers" and "viruses."

- Tips on low-cost ways to transmit computerized data via "fax boards"—the computer that doubles as a fax machine—as well as advice on how to keep your fax transmissions from dragging you into court.

But, first, let's look at some of the practical benefits computers can offer your company and give you some ideas of how business owners are using new data-processing technologies to gain a competitive edge.

FIVE WAYS TELECOMMUTING CAN BOOST YOUR COMPANY'S PRODUCTIVITY*

For many business owners, executives and employees, one of the biggest attractions of high technology is its potential for freeing them from their desks and offices. By linking computers to increasingly sophisticated telecommunications devices, you and your staff can now get important work done at home, on the road, in your car—you name it. Your sales reps and service people can communicate with the home office from customers' offices, remote job sites and the shop floor.

Some small companies are already exploring the possibilities of "telecommuting"—the practice of having employees work from home. The concept simultaneously intrigues and frightens most business owners and managers. On the one hand, telecommuting offers the potential for lower overhead, fewer lost workdays and happier employees. On the other, it raises fears about loss of management control, poorly focused work and administrative chaos.

It is possible, however, to realize the benefits of telecommuting while sidestepping its perils. Here are five advantages successful business owners are gaining from the concept:

1. Reduced turnover. Studies show that telecommuters are less likely to jump ship than in-office employees. Since home workers have complete control over their working environment, and thus tend to be more satisfied with their working conditions, they're less likely to seek greener pastures. The fact that work-at-home jobs are still relatively scarce also adds to the overall stability of the telecommuting work force.

2. Larger labor pool. Since telecommuters don't have to live within daily driving distance of work, employers have a potentially vast pool of job candidates to select from. With many skilled technical specialists in chronically short supply, this is an important consideration.

Managers who have been successful with home workers realize that they can't hire people on the other side of the country. It's important for managers and employees to be able to meet in person when the need arises. Also, many telecommuters need the occasional psychological lift and stimulation of seeing other workers face to face and exchanging ideas with their colleagues. Meetings, conferences, planning sessions and other get-togethers may also require the physical presence of telecommuters from time to time.

This section was written by John Edwards, who writes extensively on computers and office automation. He is based in Mount Laurel, New Jersey.

3. Lower absenteeism. Telecommuters are more likely to continue working through minor illnesses and other at-home pressures than in-house employees. This extra productivity can reflect positively on your company's bottom line.

To maintain control over telecommuters, managers should be sure to establish regular work quotas. Workloads should be based on the output expected of on-site employees. If a telecommuter fails to perform up to these standards, he or she should be disciplined in the same way as a conventional worker.

4. Better retention of top performers. Telecommuting is a great way to hold onto valuable employees you might otherwise lose. For example, incapacitated workers, parents who need to take care of young children and employees who care for aging parents or other disabled family members in the home are ideal candidates for telecommuting positions.

5. Cost savings: Since home workers don't need office space, furniture or a parking spot, telecommuting can save your company a bundle.

Some employers are also tempted to shave payroll expenses by hiring telecommuters as independent contractors. But since the Internal Revenue Service is cracking down on companies that misclassify employees as independent contractors purely to escape their payroll tax obligations, you should check with your company's accountant or legal adviser before embarking on this practice.

HOW AN ELECTRONIC BULLETIN BOARD CAN KEEP YOU IN TOUCH WITH CUSTOMERS AND EMPLOYEES*

Computer bulletin board systems are best known for the services they provide to PC hobbyists. But while bulletin boards are widely used for fun and games, they can also serve as valuable communication tools for many businesses.

A bulletin board system (BBS) can function as an extension of a company's electronic mail system, allowing managers and co-workers to keep in touch with traveling, vacationing and sick employees. A BBS can also be used to distribute news and product information electronically to customers and suppliers.

This section was written by John Edwards, who writes extensively on computers and office automation. He is based in Mount Laurel, New Jersey.

For example, a Boston electrical supply house encourages its customers to submit orders directly to its BBS. The system provides convenient 24-hour access and allows products to be shipped the same day. A San Jose, California, software publisher uses its BBS to answer users' technical questions.

Since system access isn't restricted to account holders of a particular electronic mail service, a BBS can be made available to any PC user with a modem. System maintenance usually requires nothing more than checking the BBS once a day for pending messages. What's more, a BBS is one of the computer world's great bargains, typically costing only a few hundred dollars per year to operate. Many companies dedicate an older, outdated PC to BBS use. An 8086- or 8088-based system with a 10MB hard disk and a 1200-bits-per-second modem is suitable for most BBS applications.

BBS software is widely available and generally inexpensive. A good way to test BBS software is to dial up a system using the program. Ask the software publisher for several telephone numbers. If possible, discuss the program with several system operators before installing it on your machine.

Security is an important BBS concern. But hacker-induced problems can be kept under control by isolating the BBS from other systems. A BBS should never be used as a "gateway" to a local area network. To prevent virus contamination, don't allow floppy disks or files downloaded from the BBS to be used on your employees' workstations.

HOW TO RETAIN A TOP COMPUTER CONSULTANT—WITHOUT GETTING TAKEN

Since few small business owners have the time or patience to become computer experts, many small companies hire technology consultants to help them select and install their computer systems and troubleshoot problems that arise later on.

Finding a computer consultant is easy. Finding a *knowledgeable* consultant who won't take you for every available cent is the challenge. Here are some techniques savvy business owners use to find the right person for the job:

• **Open your ears.** Listen for names dropped by your peers. No one is going to brag about a consultant who's doing a poor job. Even if your colleagues aren't the world's greatest judges of talent, the names they provide can give you a solid starting point for conducting your own search.

• **Interview carefully.** Your initial meeting with a consultant should follow the same rules as a job interview. Talk to the consultant about his or her qualifications and references. Ask the individual to define the work at hand and to explain how he or she expects to perform the task.

The interview is a good time to judge a consultant's communications and interpersonal skills. Introduce the consultant to several of your key people and observe the interaction. Remember: A top-flight expert won't do you much good if he or she can't communicate and work closely with key members of your staff.

• **Know to whom you're talking.** Make sure that the expert you interview is the person who's going to do the work. This is particularly important when dealing with a large consulting company, where "junior consultants" are often assigned to handle what they perceive as low-priority clients.

• **Study the proposal.** Shortly after the interview, the consultant will send you a written proposal. Study this document carefully. Look for a clear understanding of the work to be performed. Also check for clearly defined services and costs. Be wary of any consultant who attempts to enlarge a project. An individual who claims you need a 50-terminal network—not the 10-terminal system you requested—may be trying to sell you a bill of goods.

• **Beware of extravagant claims.** A consultant who makes sweeping statements about cutting costs and boosting productivity should be viewed with extreme caution. Ask the consultant for a list of some of his former and present clients. Then ask several of these clients to provide "before and after" comparisons. Check with your colleagues to see if they believe the consultant can deliver on his claims.

• **Get everything in writing.** The final contract should specify all of the deal's critical components, including costs and completion dates. Leave nothing to chance. Keep in mind that if a service or product isn't included in the contract, the consultant isn't required to deliver it.

HOW TO CONQUER COMPUTER PHOBIA

Computers are designed to cut costs and improve productivity. But employee resistance to computers can create the opposite effect, turning your "workplace of tomorrow" into an old-fashioned nightmare.

Here are five tips that can help cure employees' "computer phobia":

1. Eliminate the mystery. Fear develops out of ignorance. So, to ease workers' fear of the unknown, let them examine and use new equipment before they actually go "on-line." By letting your employees gradually become accustomed to the new technology, they'll find out there's really nothing to be afraid of.

Ask your vendor for brochures describing the new gear and distribute these to your employees when you announce that the new equipment is coming. Some manufacturers provide materials designed especially for computer-phobic workers. NEC and Fuji Film, for example, offer a 22-minute VHS videocassette entitled, "Computers to the Rescue: An Easy Introduction to Personal Computing." Call (800) 367-3854 for details.

2. Introduce new equipment gradually. Don't install a complex array of computer gear in one swoop. Give your workers a chance to become accustomed to the new way of doing things before throwing yet more changes their way. Asking employees to deal with several new pieces of equipment right off the bat is unfair and unreasonable. And you'll likely see the damage reflected in your bottom line.

Offer a transition period during which workers can switch back and forth between the old and new methods. If your gear is any good, they'll quickly discover that the new routine really is the better, easier way.

3. Train, train, train. Training is the best way to reduce employees' fears and build confidence. A complete training program, whether conducted on-site or at an outside center, is an absolute necessity. Make sure employees receive training manuals that include step-by-step instructions on how to use the new equipment.

Follow up. Once training is completed, make certain someone is available at all times to answer users' questions. Many vendors provide toll-free telephone support lines. Other firms offer support at a nominal fee. In either case, make sure your employees have access to these services, particularly if you don't plan to provide on-site aid.

4. Explain the equipment's benefits. Many workers view a new piece of computer equipment as an alien intruder. Remind your employees that the unit is there to help—not replace—them. Explain its function fully and show your workers exactly how it will fit into the office environment. Ask an employee who's currently using the equipment to explain how the device simplified his or her job. If such an individual isn't available, your vendor or consultant may be able to "borrow" someone from another customer to help you out.

5. Sell yourself first. If you're not sold on a new technology's overall value, you'll never convince your employees to accept it. Before committing to any new piece of computer equipment, determine its specific role and how it will fit into your business. If a device's value isn't readily apparent but you still suspect it could prove beneficial, ask an automation consultant (one without a stake in selling new equipment) to help you evaluate the pluses and minuses.

HOW TO KEEP YOUR COMPUTER USERS' HEALTH COMPLAINTS TO A MINIMUM

As many business owners have learned the hard way, plopping a fancy new computer down on an employee's old-fashioned desk is merely asking for trouble. Reason: People forced to spend long hours working on computer keyboards and staring at video display terminals (VDTs) often complain of vision problems and so-called repetitive-motion injuries—ailments of the hand, wrist and back.

Experts suggest that computer users' work areas be redesigned so they can do their jobs more comfortably—and productively. It doesn't have to cost a fortune. Here's a look at some simple, cost-effective solutions to computer-related health problems:

Viewing problems

Poorly positioned and badly lit VDTs can cause burning eyes, fatigue and a loss of productivity. They can also lead to blurred vision and potentially serious eye problems. Here are five techniques professional lighting consultants suggest for enhancing display screen readability:

1. Use an adjustable VDT base. Moving a VDT's angle can reduce or eliminate reflections caused by sunlight, jewelry reflection, office lighting and other factors. Many VDTs are now equipped with a built-in adjustable base. Such devices can also be ordered from most computer and office supply stores. When shopping for VDTs, look for units with "matte-finish" screens. VDTs with highly polished glass screen surfaces invite glare and reflection. Many inexpensive VDTs still use such reflective screens.

2. Provide indirect lighting. Most offices already use indirect lighting systems. Many workers, however, augment office lighting with desktop lamps. Such lights can cause annoying reflections, even on adjacent users' display screens. If a worker requires additional illumination, extra indirect lighting should be provided.

Note: A small mirror held over the VDT's screen will help you locate the direct or indirect source of an annoying reflection. (Example: Sunlight hitting a bright wall.)

3. Use matte-finish work surfaces. VDT work areas should be decorated only with "nonglare" wall coverings and substances. Such material will reduce the amount of light that bounces from the walls and other surfaces onto the user's screen—and eyes.

To detect an office illumination problem, stand at the end of the room. Shade your eyes from the lighting fixtures with your hand, then drop your hand. If you notice a significant difference in brightness, you've got a glare problem.

4. Consider the user. Different users have different VDT lighting needs. Older persons generally need more light to see. They may also experience difficulty in adjusting their vision from the display screen to written copy. Be patient with such individuals and help them design their work environments to allow for maximum productivity. For example, small "tasklights" can be focused on the written copy to make it easier for the eyes to adjust when moving back and forth between written copy and the VDT screen.

> **IMPORTANT:** Despite what you may have heard or read, *don't* use attachable nonglare screens. Such devices attack only the symptoms of the VDT glare and do little in the way of actually reducing reflections. They can, however, cut screen contrast and make characters fuzzier and more difficult to read.

5. Employ variable lighting. Light for the task, not for the whole office. Office areas with large numbers of VDT users should have less powerful lighting than other work locations.

Detailed information on resolving VDT lighting problems is available in the publication, "Solving the Puzzle of VDT Viewing Problems." The $5 booklet is published by the National Lighting Bureau, 2101 L St. NW, Suite 300, Washington, DC 20037.

Hand and wrist ailments

Here's a brief checklist of expert recommendations for preventing repetitive-motion injuries of the hand and wrist among computer users:

- Users should be able to adjust the height of their chairs or the surface on which the keyboard rests so that they can reach the keyboard comfortably with arms hanging at their sides and forearms extended at approximately a 90% angle from the body.

- The surface on which the keyboard rests should afford support for the wrists or hands.

- Users who must work at their keyboards for prolonged periods should take breaks (at least a few minutes every hour or so) to get up, stretch and walk around.

Studies have found that properly designed workstations can boost computer workers' output by up to 25%, while also helping to reduce health-related complaints and insurance costs.

HOW TO SAFEGUARD YOUR COMPANY'S COMPUTER INVESTMENT*

If you decide to computerize some or all of your company, you're probably looking at an investment of at least several thousand dollars. So it's crucial that you train your employees in how to protect your company's tremendous financial investment in computers. Here are some important safeguards that everyone can use to keep your PC terminals, modems and other hardware in good working order:

- Don't overload electrical circuits. All your computers should be on isolated or dedicated electrical lines. Connecting a computer to the same electrical line as typewriters, copiers, air conditioners or other office equipment will not give the computer the constant level of power it needs to function reliably.

- Computer components should be on a surge protector circuit. These cost $15–$45 and are usually on a power strip plugged into the dedicated outlet. The surge protector will help protect your computer from power dips and surges that occur on many electrical lines.

- Do not put too much stress on the cables that connect the computer's components to each other. There are extended cables available ($3–$25) if the distance between your components is more than the cables supplied allow. Too much tension on a connector cable may result in the cable disconnecting itself.

This section was written by Steven Sweet, who is a personal computer expert with Strothman Associates, Chappaqua, New York.

How far your printers are located from your systems unit will determine whether you should use parallel or serial cables.

For instance, parallel cables will work best when distances are under 30 feet. If you are placing your printers more than 30 feet from the computers, use serial cables for better data transfer reliability. All cables should be placed so that they are not crimped or at risk of damage.

- Don't use extension cords for the power connections of your computer. Computers should be plugged into the nearest wall outlet using the power-surge protected power strip. Also, check to make sure that all cables are out of the way of someone walking or tripping on them. Check to make sure all connections are strong and secure.

  Consider installing an Uninterrupted Power Supply (UPS) (price: $250–$1,000) for your computer system. This can help you deal with regular power brownouts or actual outages during summer heat waves or severe weather conditions.

  A UPS will automatically provide enough power to allow your computer to operate normally if a brownout occurs. It will also allow you to shut down normally and back up the system in the event of a power outage.

- Connect your modem to an isolated phone line. This should be a line dedicated to communications. A party line, jumper line, call-waiting, conference calling, or other telephone accessory service will cause interference or disconnection of the modem and data transfer. A phone line surge protector ($20–$40) will protect your computer from phone line power surges.

- Follow safe procedures for turning your components on and off. This can save the computer strain on its circuits. Your computer peripherals, printer, monitor and modem should be turned on before the computer is turned on. At the end of the day, your computer is the first thing that should be turned off after you bring it back to the DOS prompt. This procedure helps control any power surge your computer components may produce to your computer.

Computer software protection

Here are a few safeguards you can use to protect your computer's software:

- Leave floppy disk drives open when the computer is turned on or off. A floppy disk should be placed into a drive only when the computer is warmed up, and taken out before the computer is switched off. This will avoid damage to data on the floppy disk and to the read/write heads in your floppy drive.

- There is one safe way to handle a floppy disk: Hold it by the label and insert it into the drive. The label should be facing upward and at the edge closest to you. Don't force a floppy disk into the drive, and don't bend it. Never touch the open areas that expose the disk. The oil on your fingers can damage the data so the computer can't read it.

- When disks aren't being used, keep them in the jackets they came in. Store them in a closed container that protects them from dust.

- Place disks away from phones or other magnetic products. Magnetic fields can destroy the valuable data on your disks. Periodic use of a floppy disk drive cleaning kit ($15–$40) will add to the life and accuracy of the drive's read/write heads.

- Back up all your work. This is the *best* safeguard for your programs and data. Make copies of all programs and data in case something happens to the originals. Once you have created your copy, you should check it against the original to verify the exactness of your copy. After you have made your copies, place your originals in a safe place and use your copies to do your work.

HOW TO KEEP YOUR COMPUTER DATA SAFE FROM VIRUSES, VANDALS AND OTHER INTRUDERS*

Computer systems raise a host of high-tech security problems undreamed of in the days of typewriters and carbon paper. And we're not talking about the obvious risk of theft or vandalism to the machines themselves. Among the biggest worries in the computer age are so-called computer viruses and hackers.

"Viruses" are programs that alter or erase data or even disable expensive hardware or software. *The Computer Virus Industry Association* (Santa Clara, California) estimates that over 90,000 computers suffered a virus attack in 1988. That figure has undoubtedly risen in the last few years and is certain to rise even more in the future.

This section was written by John Edwards, who writes extensively on computers and office automation. He is based in Mount Laurel, New Jersey.

"Hacker" is the term coined to describe the human intruders who plant viruses, steal or alter data, and commit other forms of mischief. Some are merely teenage "whiz kids" who use personal computers and modems to break into government or commercial computer systems for fun. Others may be real computer criminals or even disgruntled employees who have malicious motives. In either case, almost no system is immune to these pesky intruders.

You need to keep in mind that power interruptions, equipment breakdowns and acts of nature pose far greater threats to your system than hackers and viruses do. Still, you should always consider the possibility of a virus attack after other likely causes of failure have been eliminated. And it's a good idea to take a few simple precautions to make it harder for viruses to infect your system.

Common virus symptoms

Keep an eye peeled for these warning signs:

- An unexplained slowdown in response time or processing speed
- An unexplainable decline in available address space
- Invalid calculations
- Blank screens, confused displays and taunting screen messages (obvious example: "The hacker has struck!")
- Unexplainable system errors
- Total system collapse

The best way to confirm the existence of a virus is to use a virus detection program. Several publishers offer such software, and some are even free. Programs that cure as well as detect most viruses include *Virus Guard* (IP Technologies, 714-549-4284) and *Anti-Virus* (International Computer Products Inc., 602-870-0233).

How to prevent virus attacks

Keeping destructive codes away from your system is the best way to avoid virus-related headaches. Following these three simple steps will all but eliminate the chance of a virus outbreak on your system:

1. Use only sealed disks from known software publishers. Avoid using free programs given to you by acquaintances. Never download public-domain software from bulletin boards.

2. Control access. Keep both systems and software locked and away from all unauthorized individuals. Don't allow users to bring in disks from outside. If a user must use a disk from home or elsewhere, screen it with a virus-detection program on a noncritical stand-alone system before allowing it into your multiuser environment.

3. Isolate and contain suspect software. Never move a possibly infected program to another computer or another part of your system to see if it will run there. You may unwittingly spread the contagion. Always examine malfunctioning programs in their current location only.

Always make backups. Regular and thorough backups can't prevent a virus attack, but they can help to minimize the damage. Remember, however, that recent backups may be contaminated by the same virus that brought your system down. That's why it's important to keep several generations of backups plus all original program disks.

Keeping hackers at bay

As any "hacker" will tell you, your company's computerized business information, sensitive financial data and customer lists can easily be damaged or stolen by a disgruntled employee—or even an outsider—with a computer, a modem and a little know-how. In fact, you may be the victim of a computer attack and not even know it.

Unlike ordinary robberies and break-ins, the consequences of a computer crime can go undetected for days, weeks—even months. The artful and cautious hacker will use time-delayed programs to cripple your system. Often, by the time you discover your computer has been victimized, it's too late to do anything but repair the damage.

Protect yourself. Train your employees to recognize the warning signs that can show your system is under attack. The key here is to beat the hacker at his own game. Think like a computer vandal. Analyze your system for security violations on at least a weekly basis. Detect and delete destructive files before they can detonate. Encourage your employees to report instances of curious activities.

Hackers leave *electronic fingerprints*. Recognizing and acting on a computer attack's warning signs can mean the difference between a smoothly operating system and disaster.

Here are five security moves you can make today to help minimize the chances that your vital business data will be tampered with:

1. Examine accounts for excessive usage. Hackers need time to operate. Beware when a system user's connect-time suddenly doubles or triples. Also check for frequency of log-ons. A sudden spurt in the number of daily, weekly or monthly system accesses should be investigated. Repeatedly rejected accesses typically identify the work of a password cracker.

Put a reasonable *connect-time* ceiling on all users if your software can't alert you to changes. Have the system automatically disconnect after three failed password attempts. Encourage users to change their passwords frequently. Also check for unusual log-on times—day workers logging-on after midnight, for example.

2. Look for moved, deleted or altered system files. Since system files control all aspects of your computer's operation, they are a prime target for destructive hackers. Most hackers prefer to go after source files—text files that can be easily read and modified—leaving your computer's operating programs unmolested. If a hacker is unable to compile a source file on your system, he can do the job on his home computer.

Lock system files and restrict access to those files only to employees who absolutely need them. Investigate all new source files and executable programs that appear in the system directory. Check user directories for unauthorized source files and programs.

3. Beware of new directories. Hackers often like to hide their files in a subdirectory within a user's main directory. Often these subdirectories are labeled with a nonprinting character, rendering them invisible to the authorized account owner.

Investigate immediately if a system audit shows invisible files that weren't installed by you or the system vendor. To cut confusion, don't let authorized users create invisible subdirectories.

4. Audit "help file" use. Although help files exist to aid legitimate account holders, hackers use them to learn about your system. Hackers don't want to spend thousands of dollars for a copy of your system's complete documentation library, even when it's readily available. Most hackers prefer to download and print out a computer's help file set.

Establish decoy files with names like "SECRET" or "HACKER." Have the system flag the accounts that read these files. Veteran authorized users, with printed documentation, rarely access help files. In any event, someone who spends four hours perusing your help areas and reads files with curious names isn't likely to be a legitimate user.

5. Watch for strangers in a strange directory. Users typically access either their own files or files within the directory of an allied department. For instance, an accounting staffer may need to check an employee's payroll record or some human resource file. But this person shouldn't be wandering through, for example, the company's engineering files. Question the account holder about suspicious activities. If he or she can't provide a plausible explanation, investigate.

WHAT TO LOOK FOR IN COMPUTER-FAX DEVICES

When is a fax machine not a fax machine? When it's a personal computer equipped with a fax board, a device that lets your PC send and receive transmissions like a fax machine—for about half the price.

A fax board slips into one of your computer's expansion slots and plugs into a telephone line like a modem. The board logs all transmissions, giving you a record of all faxes sent and received. The more sophisticated boards let you work on a program at the same time you're transmitting. (This is called "running in the background.") Fax boards cost from $295 to $1,000 and capabilities vary.

Here are some factors you should be aware of if you're considering buying a fax board for your office or home computer:

- Your actual savings with a fax board will vary, depending upon the kind of documents you send and receive. For example, if you plan to send documents with signatures and letterheads, you'll need a scanner. This is a machine that converts the paper document into a computer file before it can be transmitted. (Scanners begin at about $800.) If you have to buy a scanner and a fax board, invariably this equipment will cost more than a stand-alone fax.

- If your documents are in PC form already, it's probably more efficient to send them via fax board than to print them out and send them via stand-alone fax. If they're not in PC form, you need to find out if the fax board will transfer fonts, type styles, formatting commands, graphics, etc. This is particularly important if you transmit desktop publishing documents. With a stand-alone fax, what you send is what the receiver gets. But that might not be so with a fax board.

- Another point to consider is whether or not the fax board operates in the background. If not, you'll have to stop working every time a fax transmission is in progress. If that's the case, your best bet is a stand-alone fax machine.

- Finally, is the board compatible with your word processing or spreadsheet software? Some boards make you create a conversion file, which takes time. Others do the conversion automatically. Sending a fax should be as easy as printing.

Some older fax boards won't communicate with the newer, faster boards now available. You'll want to buy a board with the new capability that will still connect with the older boards, which many businesses still use.

HOW TO ENSURE THAT YOUR FAX TRANSACTIONS ARE WORTH THE PAPER THEY'RE PRINTED ON

A big order for your product comes in over the fax machine. Your sales people uncork the champagne and your production department works overtime to deliver the goods.

The customer, however, refuses the shipment, claiming it never placed the order. You go to court to collect, but the customer attacks your evidence, saying your copy of the faxed order was doctored and that it lacks a valid signature. It comes down to a case of your word against his. The judge finds no reason to doubt the customer's credibility and no proof that the customer actually sent the fax in question.

Sound far-fetched? Maybe. But with fax transmissions rapidly replacing the mail and even overnight delivery services as the fastest way to send business documents, it may not be long before cases similar to this find their way into court.

The legal enforceability of faxed documents is "a legitimate concern," an attorney and consultant in law office automation advises. "Even if business people haven't been thinking about this, they ought to be," he cautions.

Here are some ways for making that faxed piece of paper more reliable as evidence in court should a dispute arise over its validity.

1. Make sure your machine receives the sender's "signature." You probably don't pay much attention to it, but at the top of every page a fax machine prints out is an electronic code. This "transmit terminal identification" code (as it's called in the technical literature) is what is called the machine's "signature." Machines can be programmed to print out either the sender's or receiver's code.

Make sure your fax is programmed to print the sender's code—not yours—on all incoming documents. This provides a record of where the document originated that can help establish its authenticity.

2. Keep copies of everything. Always preserve complete copies of important documents that come in over your fax—including the cover sheet (showing the number of total pages, sender, date sent, etc.) and a copy of each and every page received. Don't just keep the page or paragraph you need and throw the rest away. And be sure the copies you retain for your files include the electronic "signature" of the sender's machine.

These records will make it harder for the sender to argue later that he or she didn't send a document, or that the document you have is incomplete or altered.

3. Ask for follow-up verification. Last and most obvious is to verify every order, request, or other fax transmission that could be considered to create a legal obligation before you act upon it. At a minimum, call the sender to acknowledge that you've received the document and ask for written confirmation by mail.

For any transaction involving a great deal of risk (such as an order for custom goods that you couldn't easily sell to another buyer), you should be very careful to get written confirmation.

You might want to include a statement of your policy on doing business by fax in your standard purchase agreements and other contracts.

For example, your customer contracts might state that you will accept fax orders for off-the-shelf items but not for custom goods, or that your people will start filling fax orders as soon as they're received but won't actually ship the goods until you receive written verification bearing an original signature.

CHAPTER THIRTEEN

HOW YOU CAN BE A MORE EFFECTIVE EXECUTIVE

"There's never enough time in the day!" That's a chronic complaint among most owners of small businesses. Sometimes, it seems almost impossible for you to do all the things that need to be done.

There's no magic solution. Running a small business takes hard work and time—lots of time. But there are ways for you to find the time to do more work. How? By mastering the art of being a better executive. Some business owners have already learned from hard experience how to delegate, how to set priorities, and how to challenge their subordinates to take on more responsibilities.

By doing so, they've freed themselves from routine chores and countless minor headaches. They leave themselves with more time to focus on the important things a business owner needs to concentrate on—for example, long-range planning and developing new markets and opportunities.

This chapter lets you in on some of their secrets.

MANAGING YOUR TIME

Your most precious asset is your time. It's your responsibility to see that this vital business resource isn't wasted on minor details that could be handled by others.

HOW TO USE A TIME-SAVING CHECKLIST TO MAKE EVERY MINUTE COUNT

The following 11-point checklist can determine whether you're making every minute count. "Yes" answers reveal time-saving, efficiency-boosting work habits. "No" answers highlight areas for improvement.

1. Do I insist that my people think through suggested solutions to problems *before* bringing them to me?

2. Do I insist on hearing proposed actions *first* and explanations which I may need later?

3. Do I let subordinates and supervisors know when I can't spare time for interruptions? (One area where you should try to make time is for your rank-and-file workers. After all, they keep the company's wheels turning. If you have time for them, they'll have time for you when you need them most.)

4. Do I consider delegating certain tasks—including ones I enjoy—before tackling every one on my own?

5. Do I perform all "easy" tasks as quickly as possible?

6. Do I rate all "difficult" tasks in order of importance—then immediately get to work on them, beginning with the most urgent?

7. As soon as my work is done on a problem, do I delegate responsibility for follow-up?

8. If a course of action didn't work, do I attempt to learn from the error and gain from its correction?

9. Do I avoid walking into meetings where my presence isn't needed?

10. Do I avoid letter-writing when a phone call can settle the matter quickly and finally?

11. Do I avoid memo-writing when a personal visit would be as effective and faster?

Your answers will reveal areas where a small change in style can lead to a big gain: More time each day to devote to serious activities.

HOW TO CHART YOUR WAY TO MORE PRODUCTIVE TIME

Here's an easy-to-use system that lets you find more time for key work. That "extra" time can help you increase your efficiency.

Create a time saving card

It helps you keep tabs on how your time is being spent—and where it's being wasted.

To give you an idea of just how valuable the card can be, here is what one Chicago business owner has to say: "You'll get time working for you—not against you."

For example, the card clearly points out if you are—

- Being forced to spend too much time on routine tasks.

- Losing valuable hours in unprofitable conferences and meetings.

- Keeping associates waiting excessively long—or worse yet, letting them keep you waiting.

- Letting people constantly interrupt you. The interruptions can do a number on your day.

How to set up a time-saving card

There's nothing difficult about this. You can make it as simple as you like. Here's how:

- Divide your day into 15-minute segments. That's not too insignificant—and not too broad.

- Across the top of the chart, divide the sheet into two headings: *major responsibilities* and *minor tasks*. As the Chicago business owner notes: "My office is the control center of the company. We can't get bogged down in nickel-and-dime work. If an activity doesn't contribute to that goal, it's a minor activity."

- Under "Major Responsibilities," list whatever descriptions are appropriate to your job. For example, you may include drumming up new business, fine-tuning production processes, keeping tabs on inventory, scheduling future office work, hiring new employees and preparing budgets and salary reviews.

- Next, divide the "Minor Tasks" into broad categories. Your first category heading, for example, might be *Routine Office Activities*, to cover the time spent on correspondence, supervision, routine reports, and the like. For your second heading, try something like *Outside Activities*—to cover time spent on association meetings, charity drives, conferences, civic affairs, as well as on family affairs.

Finally, you should include a *Miscellaneous* heading which covers all other time that doesn't contribute directly or indirectly to the smooth working of the office.

How to keep score

As you go through each day, it isn't necessary to write down what you did. Simply check under the appropriate heading how each fifteen-minute portion of the day is used. However, you may want to jot down a general description of what you did during that time period under the "Explanation" column.

Add the check marks at the end of the day to get the amount of time you spend on each activity. For weekly totals, all you have to do is add together the hours for each day. Try this for at least one week. This should give you a pretty good idea of just how the hours each day are being spent.

Adding up where your time is spent is just half of the job. There is another big step. Be ruthless in cutting the minor activities from your day—jobs you like doing, people you like helping, phone calls you'd like to return yourself, even outside activities to which you're committed must take a back seat to profit activities. Here are some ways to do it:

- Schedule for profit. Schedule the most profitable parts of big projects first. Often you won't have to do the rest; your subordinates can take over.

- Do your problem-solving on paper. A problem well written is half solved. Besides, good ideas that aren't preserved can be quickly forgotten.

- Use your peak times to the hilt. Work alone creatively at the time of day you usually feel most energetic. Use the other time for less productive duties.

- Manage by exception. Stop listening to reports that everything is going as planned. Give subordinates the leeway you consider acceptable or normal on a project. Then tell them to report to you only when something unusual or unacceptable develops.

HOW TO TRAIN YOUR MANAGERS TO THINK FOR THEMSELVES

How can you get your managers to ease up on their requests for your time—and take over more of the workload themselves? Here's what other business owners we talked to recently had to say:

- Keep it brief. "Brevity and decisive action are the key words when I'm discussing problems at a meeting with executives," says the president of a Los Angeles garment distributing company.

"In the past, there were too many times when I found myself listening to an avalanche of different ideas on how to solve a particular problem. No one could agree on *anything* during meetings.

"I told my people that I make *decisions*, I don't solve problems. I want them to thrash out the problem *before* the meeting and to present only the best possible solution. Naturally, if someone has a strong minority opinion, he or she is still entitled to report it.

"Now, a great deal of time is saved, and meetings are more productive. At most, I have to listen to just two carefully-thought-out ideas, rather than four or five hasty opinions."

- Ask for packages, not strings. "Bring me the complete package—not just bits and pieces—when you come to me for a decision," is the advice a North Carolina business owner gave her managers.

"I found myself being interrupted far too often for decisions on *parts* of a problem. I realized how much of my time this was wasting when the same person interrupted me three times in a single hour to ask about the schedule for computerizing our new filing system.

"I passed the word along to managers. Wrap the package up nice and neat for me. Check with me only after you're ready to make a complete presentation."

Now we get quicker decisions, fewer interruptions, and more time to handle management-level problems of greater importance.

Ask for warnings, not disasters. One exec has a caveat. "The only time the 'don't bother me with minor details rule' *doesn't* apply in my company," says a New Orleans manufacturer, "is when there's a crisis. Then, of course, I want to know about it immediately.

"Everyone tried to follow the rule and protect my time by keeping *all* problems away from me. One day, they just couldn't handle a crisis situation that cropped up unexpectedly. But I was told too late and it took me weeks to get things sorted out.

"I put my people on notice to alert me the minute they see anything building that could become an emergency. That doesn't mean I don't want them to find a solution. I do. But I also don't want them to bring me into the picture *after* the crisis has hit."

Now, major problems are averted before they happen, and that saves time, manpower, and profits.

• Take time out for problem-solving. An Oregon president told us: "When a significant problem crops up, I take 10 minutes right away to find a positive solution. Later I devote a little more time to finding a way to prevent the problem—or a similar one—from happening again." The Oregon president asks himself:

- Why did things get fouled up?
- Who was responsible?
- Did I contribute to the problem?
- What's the best way for us to handle this situation the next time it starts to occur?

"With this solve-it-now method," he explains, "I get the problem out of the way quickly. But I also take steps that will prevent me from having to troubleshoot the same problem again in the future."

• Discourage interruptions. The president of a human resources management firm in Illinois reports: "Supervisors used to feel free to walk into my office at any stage of a project because they knew it would eventually require my approval. A lot of these interruptions involved questions that supervisors could have answered themselves.

"But I finally put an end to those interruptions," says the Illinois top exec, by installing a time-conservation plan. "Now I have my assistants hold their routine questions, and we discuss them in the first half-hour of each day. This leaves much more of my time clear for the tasks at which I can achieve top-profit results."

There is also a double benefit. "Not being able to just rush in with questions forces supervisors to confront the problems themselves—and they often manage to solve them. Quite often my 'half-hour' morning sessions last only 10 minutes, and the topic is a solution, not a problem."

• Attack your problems one-on-one. If you're a typical small business owner, you're probably trying to juggle 20 or more problems at one time. But if they're all on your mind at the same time, none of them gets more than a little piece of your attention—and only some of them get solved.

As one top exec puts it: "Any job that's not worth your full attention is a job you shouldn't be doing." Those jobs go to other management people.

Isolate the problem you want to handle. Put everything else on the back burner. Give the particular problem all your attention until you come up with an answer.

To make the "one thing at a time" idea work best, give first attention to the important or urgent problems. Many business owners pinpoint these by making lists of all the jobs waiting to be done. The jobs are broken down into two categories—those that only they can do, and those that can be handled by others. The jobs are put in the order of their importance.

Keep an item on the list only after you consider the answer to this question: If I don't handle this item myself, *today*, what's the worst that can happen to the company?

Then tackle—one at a time—the items on the "do today" list. At the same time, have key subordinates pitch in to tackle the "do today" jobs they're responsible for. But keep in mind that too many items on the "do today" list can ruin the list's whole purpose.

Don't get bogged down in details. On the day you make the list, ignore the items that don't require immediate attention. Take a look at them the following day. Some of the items may have to be put at the top of the list; perhaps others can be crossed off altogether because they're no longer important.

- Live with the problem for a week. This was the order a Chicago business owner gave to one of his managers. The manager was told to concentrate on a particular problem for one full week, and then come up with a workable solution that would be put into effect immediately.

The president got the answer—a good one—and it was put into effect, because the manager knew that the president was counting on him. "Other times," the manager said, "the president would have thrown me both the problem and *his* idea for solving it, and said, 'I think this will do the trick, don't you?' "

Here are some other successful approaches to delegating you can use:

- **"I'm going out of town, and when I get back, I want you to let me know how you handled it."** This will quickly drive home the point that you're staying out of the problem.

- **"From now on, you take care of this."** Here's a direct way of letting a manager, supervisor or assistant know that he or she is responsible for a particular job, and that you're not going to be involved with it any more.

- **"How would you handle this?"** This question encourages people to come up with suggestions on their own. They know you're in the market for a winning idea. To get your point across, you don't have to walk around with a sign on your back announcing that you are delegating more work. Your workers will get the message as soon as they detect a change in your attitude.

- **"See what the trouble is and straighten it out."** This is another way you can show an assistant that he or she should take control of a problem. But it's hard for that person to step in when the people concerned expect you to referee personally. Make it official. Send out a memo letting everyone involved know that "from now on any and all problems concerning (the particular subject) will be handled by John Smith." Make it very clear just what work you have relinquished and what areas still remain firmly under your control.

You can easily select areas of responsibility to delegate if you ask yourself:

- Am I the only person in the office who knows how to make a decision?
- Am I the only person in the place who ever has a new idea?
- Is my way of doing things the only way that works?

If you've answered "yes" to any of these questions, it may be time to invite your subordinates to exercise their skills and abilities.

HOW TO SAVE VALUABLE TIME AT STAFF MEETINGS

You can make sure your staff meetings mean business by avoiding these three time-traps:

1. The "spur-of-the-moment" meeting. This one is called to order because a manager or supervisor (perhaps even yourself) comes up with an idea that looks like a winner. That's reason enough to call the staff together to discuss the idea's prospects. Usually, little, if anything, is accomplished. Because no one has any prior knowledge of what is going to be discussed, the person who called the meeting does all the talking. No one else is sufficiently prepared to evaluate the idea.

Make sure that the people who should attend the meeting are given advance notice of its purpose. It's the only way those who attend will be able to contribute ideas and make the meeting at all productive.

2. The "why-am-I-here?" meeting. Here the meeting is important—but the wrong people are asked to attend it. Managers or supervisors who have nothing to do with the issue quietly doze, while those who are directly concerned with the issue are not invited. Every few minutes a call goes out to secure information from the one person who should have been there—and isn't.

Make sure you invite those persons—and those persons only—who'll have something definite to contribute to the discussion. Again, give them time to get their facts together. If someone with essential information can't attend, put the meeting off to another time.

If someone is needed to give information on just one or two topics, try to take up these matters consecutively—preferably early in the session. This way, the right person is there when needed, and his or her time away from regular work is held to a minimum.

3. The "sorry-about-the-interruption" meeting. This gathering grinds to a halt time after time as people leave "momentarily"—one to answer a phone call, another to answer a secretary's question, a third to check on a pet project, and so forth. And they usually add: "Don't do a thing until I get back." The predictable result is a meeting that's long on waiting and short on results.

Put your meetings on a "do-not-disturb" basis. In most cases, telephone calls for meeting participants can be handled by subordinates. Give instructions to your managers that interruptions are to be permitted only in *emergencies*—and see that this rule is followed.

Make sure the meeting will achieve results by not ending it before everyone has the answer to: "Who will do what, and when?"

MANAGING YOUR PEOPLE

Your key people are another vital resource. As your company's top executive, it's up to you to get the most out of them.

You've got to learn when to give them more responsibility, and when to step in and exert control. And you've got to do it in ways that make them want to do more and better work for you.

HOW TO MAKE DELEGATION WORK FOR YOU

You can ease your workload—and make yourself an even more effective executive—by mastering the art of delegation.

Grade your management abilities against the following checklist. You'll see whether your methods of delegating are up to par and you'll find out in what areas you can improve the way you assign work.

- Do you know your employees' skills? Selecting the right person for the task is a key element in effective delegation. As the chief executive, you will be judged on how well you develop your staff's skills. First, describe the job being delegated, and then train people to take over the reins.

- Do you communicate clearly? Your workers should be told precisely what kind of results you expect, the time frame for the assignment, the extent of authority being delegated, and the style and timing of any progress reports you want.

- Do you show confidence? Effective delegation requires a high level of mutual trust and confidence that can only be developed over time. Show your people that you're willing to stand by their results or suggestions. By taking that key step, your employees will be willing to assume more difficult work and greater responsibility.

- Do you delegate consistently? Results will suffer if a job is only occasionally delegated. Once you assign a job and are happy with the results, make it a permanent part of the employee's responsibilities. Make sure to tell employees that the more responsibility they assume, the faster they will get ahead.

  Also, keep in mind that if only unpleasant or difficult tasks are delegated, you may not get the quality of work you expect.

  How do you choose which tasks to delegate? A Minnesota exec uses this procedure: "I prepare a list of all the basic types of assignments I usually handle. Then I try to arrange to delegate between one-quarter and one-third of them to members of my staff on a regular basis. As a result, I have more time for my 'must' work and a more versatile staff," she says.

- Do you allow for worker input? Encourage commitment on the part of your workers by letting them have a hand in deciding which tasks will be delegated.

- Do you delegate wisely? Delegating to one subordinate exclusively can create resentment among his or her peers. It also prevents you from developing the talent of the rest of your staff.

  Keep a record of what work you have assigned and to whom. Then make sure that no one employee gets disproportionately more to do than any other employee.

- Do you delegate whole tasks? This enhances the skill development of workers more effectively than handing out bits and pieces of a job. It also keeps you from being drawn back into the operational details of the job.

  A Philadelphia executive accomplishes that by doing the following:

  "I call in an assistant and inform him or her that I am going to be busy for the next week and I want that person to handle the assignment. The job usually gets done on time and I have developed another key person."

- Do you provide the required authority? Be sure you invest the worker with the clout needed to get the job done properly.

  Introduce the worker to the people he or she will have to deal with in getting supplies, facts and cooperation. Let these people know the employee is doing important work for you.

- Do you mix criticism with praise? Naturally, you must prevent poor work, and you must teach workers how to avoid producing it. But if you only comment about *errors*, delegated work will grow unpleasant for your staff.

  And if the result is that they won't want to take on extra duties in the future, you're back to square one—doing the work yourself.

  To avoid this, praise what is correctly done. When you praise your employees for their good work, it also makes it easier for them to accept your criticism when it's justified. Also, encourage workers so they appreciate how their performance benefits them, the company and, ultimately you. In this way, your people will increase their knowledge, skills, and confidence, and you'll gain valuable time to work on the assignment or projects that only you can and should handle.

HOW THREE KEY WORDS CAN MAKE YOU A MORE EFFECTIVE EXECUTIVE

You can improve your own management skills and, at the same time, get more and better work from your key people by skillfully using three executive techniques.

These management winners are based on three key words: "respond," "anticipate," and "inspire." Here's how to put these words into action:

• **Respond.** You want your key people to keep coming up with new ideas. However, "Just giving signals that you want ideas isn't enough," says a Pittsburgh exec. "You must make sure that your execs know that no initiative goes unrecognized." That's why she does the following:

"I make it a rule to respond to an idea submitted to me within seven days—even if just to say that I need to look into it further. And if I do need the extra time, then I tell the exec when he or she can expect an answer."

• **Anticipate.** You and your execs have to know today what the trend in your industry, or demand for a product or service, will be tomorrow.

"Knowing what tomorrow will bring could be the most important job of an executive. Misreading a broad trend that's important to your business can mean disaster," says a Boston manufacturer.

How you get these key facts can improve the overall performance of your top people.

"Go directly to people in the know," adds the Boston exec. "For example, in my business I consult frequently with my company's engineers and technicians. I find that this is the best way for me to keep current. I also make sure to look beyond the company to the competition and to general economic conditions. In short, I do my homework."

This combination of managerial skills and technical know-how means that the company is seldom the victim of a last-minute surprise move by the competition.

The Boston exec identifies an added benefit: "My top people keep on their toes. They know they must have the answer to my question: How do these trends affect us?"

• **Inspire.** Encouraging your key people to give you their best—all the time—is a key part of a business owner's job. Here's how the president of a California computer software company inspires his sales department:

"I made success a little more difficult to attain by changing the definition of what it meant. I altered the focus from watching sales climb to *increasing our share* of certain markets. This created a whole new set of goals. It took the emphasis off strategies like cutting costs and turning over inventory, and put it on new product development, more efficient advertising, improved customer service, and so on."

As a result, "Sales shot up. Most of the execs in the sales department—and the salesforce itself—rose to the challenge and met the new goals I established."

HOW YOU CAN FIRE UP YOUR EMPLOYEES TO GET THEIR TOP EFFORT

How you motivate your workers is one of the keys to boosting production and performance. Here are some motivation techniques used by some successful business owners:

• **Create a crisis within a group.** Your strategy is to constantly create small crises in your company to maintain a "sense of emergency." Nothing hurts more than the apathy routine brings.

Shake things up a little (and only a little) from time to time to keep employees alert. You could, for example, make minor cuts in a budget, speed up a customer order date slightly, even go to shorter hours or periods.

These slight changes help maintain a "tempo" in the company, making the corporate body stronger simply because of the "extra exercise."

Until you try these variations, you can never be certain of your workers' maximum capabilities. Also, these fabricated crises test the company's ability to deal with possible real crises. For example:

- Making small budget cuts will test the validity of the present budget, and your employees' ability to do without certain items temporarily.

- Speeding up a customer order will test your employees' ability to deal with such a future necessity.

- Cutting back to shorter hours will test if you're getting maximum production in your normal hours.

Judiciously create minor crises in your company. You are sure to receive some surprises, both positive and negative ones. But above all, you'll know more about your organization from such crises tests.

• **Create a crisis one-on-one.** Your objective here is to show an employee that he or she can rise to the occasion.

For example, a business owner regularly picked employees to "help him out of a jam." In such cases he would present one employee with a problem that he had already solved in his mind, but would pretend that a solution had escaped him. He tested various employees' capacities to solve problems.

He thus gained insight into who were the most promising for future promotion. There are many ways you can use a crisis to learn more about your workers. One owner, for example, was very pleased with a young assistant. He considered the man to have great capacity for heavy responsibility in spite of his age. He wanted to test him under "game conditions."

He contrived to have a series of "emergencies" in his personal life that gave him excuses for suddenly leaving the office for one or two days at a time. These were always sudden departures that forced the young assistant to take over a variety of different problems in his absence. In a few years the young man was ready to take over the job full time.

• **Ask for help.** Say you discover a credit manager who has stretched two days of work into five. You can approach this employee directly by saying: "Do me a favor. Give me a note at the end of each day telling me roughly how much time you spent on what." When you discover a pattern of free time available, or time wasted on the wrong functions, it's easy to correct the situation in the guise of "helping."

Now you can get specific. In the case of the credit manager, you might say, "Only make your credit telephone calls between 10:00 and 11:00 and keep the last three hours for doing..." or, "Keep all your paperwork in the first two hours of the day." Find an excuse for making the request that seems to help the employee, such as: "I heard 10:00 or 11:00 are the best times to get through to customers," or "The last three hours of every day are best for reports. I want to have a chance to sit down with you as you go over them, and this matches my schedule best."

• **Encourage exploration.** Your objective here is to help sharp, inquisitive employees satisfy their curiosity by allowing them to explore as much as possible. If a person in one department of your company is always asking questions about other departments, don't turn him or her off by saying, "That's not your area." Instead, find ways to give the employee access to new experiences.

Be selective. This won't work for all your employees. Most are probably content to "leave well enough alone." Choose the inquisitive employees who already have the genuine desire to learn more. Satisfy their curiosity as much as possible by exposing them to new information.

For example, the president of a food processing firm reports that his secretary, while typing a memo on a new production package, asked him to tell her more about the proposed container. He took the time to fill her in on this area unrelated to her normal responsibilities. The next morning she came in with her arguments against the new package. "She saved us $1,000 per month," says the exec.

HOW AN ACTION MEMO CAN GET WORKERS TO PRODUCE THEIR BEST WORK

"Setting things straight from the first day a worker is on the job can often keep bad habits from developing," according to the owner of a Chicago company. He starts his employees off by giving each of them the following action memo their first day on the job:

> In this company, time is crucial. Time-wasting isn't tolerated. If we're late with an order, it means trouble for our company and our customers. That's why we have the following rules. And that's why they must be strictly obeyed by *all* employees.
>
> **1. Absences:** If you won't be in, let your supervisor know by starting time. Don't call someone else in the office. Your supervisor will have to make the necessary adjustments, and he or she will want to make them right away.
>
> **2. Lateness:** The same rule applies. Nobody should walk in more than 30 minutes late without having called first.
>
> **3. Working:** You must be at your desk—and working—by 9 A.M. It's your responsibility to see to it that you have an assignment for the next day before you go home each evening. Ask your supervisor for a new assignment when you are nearly finished with your present one.
>
> **4. Assignments:** If you don't think you're going to be able to meet a deadline for an assignment, let your supervisor know. That way, the work can be divided up so that it gets done on time. This is a must. If we can't meet a deadline, we lose business. It's as simple as that.

INJECT NEW LIFE INTO FLAGGING PERFORMERS

To keep efficiency in your company from dropping, get your people back on the ball with these performance boosters:

• **Shake up coasting workers.** Even good workers can fall prey to "pay hike hypnosis" and take salary, benefit increases, bonuses—even promotions—for granted. They coast along on average output they consider "good enough for another raise."

Use money to snap workers back into line. Tell them tomorrow's raise—despite what they may think—is not automatic but depends on solid performance *today*. Then spell out the criteria raises are based on: superior output, above-average attendance, willingness to assume added duties, etc.

Firing up even one worker this way can improve the output of many employees.

• **An unlikely candidate may be the most likely choice.** Build a stronger work force by not assigning routine duties to the first employee who comes to mind. The reason is that the person you think of first may, in fact, be overqualified. Assign the task to someone who barely meets requirements.

You avoid dumping routine work on your best people, leaving them free to handle jobs only *they* are capable of dealing with. Also, less qualified workers get on-the-job training, upgrade their skills, and increase their potential.

• **Make the P.M. worker more productive in the A.M..** Some workers don't hit high gear until afternoon. This pattern can cut into morning output, especially when the worker must be a "self-starter" or work with little or no supervision. To effect this, assign the "afternoon" worker a specific task for the first hour of the day by putting the worker on it the last hour of the day before. Starting when energy is high is easy for the worker. Next morning when energy is "low," the job is already underway—and easier to do.

WHAT TO DO IF A 'STAR' EMPLOYEE BEGINS TO FALL

A star employee can be worth his or her weight in gold. But what can you do when a top performer begins to falter? Here are the five basic steps many business owners follow:

1. Try to pinpoint the problem. Has the employee been assigned a different task? If so, he or she may lack the skills needed to handle the new job. A top-notch draftsman, for instance, may turn out to be a mediocre project supervisor.

Talk to the individual. If a "knowledge gap" exists, arrange for additional training. It's also possible that the worker may need some time to adjust to the new environment. If performance doesn't pick up within a few weeks, think about diplomatically reassigning the person back to the old job or another slot where the employee can make the most of his or her skills.

2. Check for burn-out. A high-flying performer can crash to the ground if he or she works too hard for too long. Encourage star employees to undertake less demanding assignments occasionally. This gives them a chance to recharge their batteries.

Explain the move. Never move a top-performer to the sidelines without first discussing the move with the individual concerned. The employee may view the sudden work change as a demotion or evidence that you're displeased with his or her performance. You've got to make it clear that you're merely giving the person a breather before the next big challenge.

3. Be sensitive to personal problems. It could be that the employee is experiencing personal difficulties, such as a death in the family or marital strife. Many employees try to hide personal problems, preferring to keep such matters private. But if an employee's personal difficulties are affecting his or her work, you have a duty to inquire into the matter. Keep the focus on the employee's work, not on his or her personal life. Tell the person you're concerned about his or her job performance, and ask if there's anything you can do to help the individual get back on track.

If the employee then confides in you about a personal problem, be understanding. Assign the person to a less rigorous task. If the individual continues to slump for a prolonged period, suggest counseling and other channels of assistance.

4. Be alert to possible drug or alcohol abuse. Telltale signs of substance abuse include unexplained absences, missed deadlines and sudden drop-off in productivity. Unfortunately, these are also symptoms of many other problems. Don't try to handle the problem yourself.

> **IMPORTANT:** Never accuse an employee of drug or alcohol abuse on a hunch—you'll be opening up yourself and your company to possible legal action.

5. Consider your management style. An employee who excelled in his or her previous job only to falter under your supervision may be reacting to a change in management style or philosophy. Talk with the employee's previous boss to determine the type of management style the star performer prefers. Then adjust as best you can—without compromising on your standards and expectations.

If the employee can achieve key job goals with more or less supervisory direction, fine. But it also may be a case where a promising employee was simply misassigned and doesn't belong in the particular job.

TWO MANAGEMENT MOVES THAT CAN PREVENT SUPERVISION 'SAG'

You can nip a slump by your company supervisors with these two management moves:

1. Give them clout. One reason supervisors sometimes sag is that they are unsure of their authority. You can put a quick end to that problem by establishing clear policies and rules. This way supervisors can act with confidence when disciplining an employee. For example, a supervisor must be able to determine if an employee's infraction of the rules is minor or serious.

Give supervisors specific guidelines for dealing with the most common problems that come up. The guidelines should cover offenses that justify immediate dismissal of an employee, and offenses that justify progressively stronger discipline.

Tell the supervisors the extent of their authority. They can't operate in the dark. For example, some members of Johnson's crew were hit by sickness, and production began to fall behind. When this had happened in the past, Johnson usually went to his boss to get a temp or two to fill in. But this time, his boss was at a convention, so Johnson failed to get the temp he needed. As a result, Johnson's group missed its quota, and Johnson was called to explain. He discovered that he could have called a temporary agency himself—something he didn't know he had the authority to do.

Don't assume supervisors know what they can or can't do. Set up specific guidelines. Then explain to supervisors the situations in which they can take "management" action without your official okay.

2. Let supervisors lead. Here's what you can do to bring out supervisors' leadership skills. Keep them current. This simply means that supervisors should know what's happening in the company; supervisors will know exactly how the company handles things.

Make your supervisors insiders. Impress upon them the importance of their contributions to maintaining high production standards. Explain to them why certain changes have been announced—for example, changes that affect their work schedules. Better still, get input from your supervisors before the changes are made. They may have some objections or constructive suggestions.

As one business owner says:

> Because supervisors are actually administering company policies out in the work areas, they see the effects on productivity and morale. They know which policies are workable and which pose problems. And, most important, they know which changes pose the worst problems because *they* must take the flak if things go wrong.

Also, if you don't keep supervisors abreast of changes, you could face this leadership letdown: Supervisors might just give lip service to new plans. Instead of being leaders, they could fall in with the troops and adopt this poor attitude: "We don't understand the change any more than the employees we supervise do." That way, everyone loses because supervisors' enthusiasm fades.

Give your supervisors one more push: Announce to the staff that (name) will be in charge of implementing the new program. This move accomplishes two things. First, it removes any doubt from the employees about who's in charge, and second, you can be pretty sure that the supervisor will see that the program is followed. Your announcement has put the supervisor on the management team.

HOW TO MOTIVATE YOUR CREATIVE PEOPLE

Getting the most out of the creative people in your company can test your people skills to the limit. It requires a somewhat different management approach from the one you use with people who do more routine work.

Genuinely creative people are self-driven. You can't motivate employees who do creative work just by throwing money at them. It's the least remembered, least effective thing you can do. Give each person something to 'own'—some job, project or activity for which he or she alone is ultimately responsible.

Set up an environment in which creative people can do their best work and feel that their contributions are appreciated.

Here are five keys to producing such an environment in your company:

1. Give people the right to fail. It's vital to let your creative people know it's all right to fail—and even that you expect them to fail occasionally. This encourages them to reach for bigger things.

2. Review everyone's work periodically. Give formal performance reviews at least once a year. You should also give "informal" reviews more often. Everyone who works for you wants to know how he or she is doing. Some think they're doing okay if they just show up every day. You owe it to them to show them how they can improve.

3. Cut out the dead wood. Firing is a lousy job. But unless you get rid of poor performers, your good performers will think you don't know the difference.

4. Be accessible. Walk around and stick your head into people's offices to ask how they're doing, if they've got any problems and whether they need any help. Show you care about them personally. But don't confuse being there for your people with *always* being there. They need their privacy, too.

5. Demonstrate a sense of humor. Laugh occasionally. This shows that you enjoy your work, and encourages others to feel the same way.

Being allowed to do good work is what attracts creative people to your company and inspires them to do their best.

SECTION 4

Financing and Accounting Strategies for Greater Profits

Small business owners know what's involved in running their businesses. They know how to produce and sell their products or services. And, generally speaking, they know how to deal with their customers, suppliers and employees. But they may have only a limited understanding of what's involved in organizing and structuring a business entity, raising capital for operations or expansion, and keeping track of costs and revenues. "These are things for my accountants, lawyers and bankers to take care of," says the typical business owner.

But these financial decisions and assumptions on which your business is based can be as important as the quality of your products or the efforts of your sales force. That's why it's vital for you at least to know some of the basic finance and accounting concepts.

This section of *The Prentice Hall Small Business Survival Guide* introduces you to the world of corporate law, accounting and finance. This world has its own special language and underlying principles—language and principles you should know to better understand and use your accountant's and lawyer's advice. The time you spend learning these key concepts—and how they can affect your business—will be time well spent.

CHAPTER FOURTEEN

CHOOSING A BUSINESS FORM

One of the first decisions a business owner makes is choosing the business form in which to operate. And even though it's one of your first important decisions, it's not necessarily final. Owners of established businesses should occasionally reevaluate their current operating structures in light of changing tax laws and other considerations.

Here's a look at the main choices: You can operate a business as a *corporation* or as an *unincorporated* entity. The most commonly used unincorporated business forms are *sole proprietorships* and *partnerships*. If you choose to go the corporation route, you can select between a regular C Corporation or a so-called S Corporation. There are other choices: personal service corporations (PSCs), limited partnerships, joint ventures, but the three forms mentioned above—sole proprietorships, partnerships, and corporations—are by far the most common.

CHOOSING WHICH FORM OF BUSINESS IS BEST FOR YOU

There is no one "right" business organization form, just as there is no one right way to run a business. Each one has certain advantages and disadvantages. What's right for your business might not be right for another. The primary differences between the various business forms lie in the areas of taxation, liability for business debts, the fringe benefits available to owners under each form, and how owners participate in profits and losses.

Here's a brief overview of the most common business forms with their similarities and differences:

• **Sole proprietorships:** A sole proprietorship, as the name indicates, is owned and managed by a single individual. It is, relatively speaking, the least complicated way to set up and run a business. The distinguishing feature of a sole proprietorship is that it is not considered a *separate entity* from its owner. For all practical purposes, the owner *is* the sole proprietorship. For example, the owner reports income, expenses and losses from the proprietorship on his own individual tax return.

A key drawback is that the owner has unlimited personal liability for business debts. His or her personal assets are at risk in the event the business runs into problems.

• **Partnerships:** A partnership is the combination of two or more business people who contribute their money, equipment and/or skills for the common purpose of operating a business. The partners share in the profit or loss of the business according to an agreed-upon formula (it doesn't have to be equal), and different items may be divided up in different ways (for example, capital gains vs. ordinary income).

A partnership is similar to a sole proprietorship in that the partners report income, expenses and losses of the partnership on their individual tax returns. In addition, the partners are exposed to unlimited personal liability for obligations of the partnership.

• **Corporations:** A regular or so-called C Corporation is treated as a separate entity from its shareholder/owners from both tax and personal liability standpoints. The C Corporation reports business income, expenses and losses on its own tax return.

A key drawback is that business profits may face double taxation— once at the corporate level and again at the shareholder level when the profits are distributed as dividends, a shareholder sells his or her stock, or the corporation is liquidated. Note, however, that this double taxation problem is avoided by using an S Corporation (discussed below). Avoidance of double taxation is one of the primary advantages of the S Corporation form.

The most important non-tax benefit of the corporate form is that the owner/shareholders have only *limited liability* for corporate debts. Their liability is limited to the amount they've invested in the company. In other words, their personal assets are not at risk.

• **S Corporation:** An S Corporation is sort of a hybrid—a cross between a regular C Corporation and a partnership. For personal liability purposes, an S Corporation is treated like a C Corporation: The owner/shareholders' liability is limited to their investment in the business.

For federal income tax purposes, however, an S Corporation is basically treated like a partnership. The owner/shareholders report the income, expenses or losses of the corporation on their own tax returns. (Note that a number of states do not recognize S Corporations for state income tax purposes; see Figure 14.1. These states require S Corporations to pay tax on their income and don't allow the income to "pass through" to the shareholders.)

Figure 14.1
STATE TAXATION OF S CORPORATIONS

State	Tax Treatment	Election	Restrictions and Conditions
Alabama	Exempt	Federal	Nonresident shareholders must file consent to report—pay Ala. tax on income by date corporate return due.
Alaska	Exempt	Federal	Corporation must file information returns.
Arizona	Exempt	Federal	Nonresident shareholders must pay tax.
Arkansas	Exempt	State	Nonresident shareholders must pay state tax.
California	Taxable	—	—
Colorado	Exempt	Federal	—
Connecticut	Taxable	—	—
Delaware	Exempt	Federal	Corp. taxed on shares allocable to nonresident shareholder.

State	Tax Treatment	Election	Restrictions and Conditions
District of Columbia	Taxable	—	Nonresident shareholder not subject to tax.
Florida	Exempt	Federal	—
Georgia	Exempt	Federal	All GA shareholders and nonresident shareholders must pay state tax.
Hawaii	Exempt	Federal	Certain elderly shareholders must pay state tax.
Idaho	Exempt	Federal	Corp. taxed on compensation dividends not reported by nonresident shareholders.
Illinois	Exempt	Federal	Corp. subject to state replacement income tax.
Indiana	Exempt	State	Corp. taxed on certain capital gains. Nonresident shareholders must pay state tax.
Iowa	Exempt	Federal	Nonresident shareholders must pay state tax.
Kansas	Exempt	Federal	Nonresident shareholders must pay state tax.
Kentucky	Exempt	Federal	Corp. taxed on capital gains over $25,000.
Louisiana	Taxable	—	—
Maine	Exempt	Federal	—
Maryland	Exempt	Federal	Corp. must withhold tax on distributions to nonresident shareholders.
Massachusetts	Exempt	Federal	—
Michigan	Taxable	—	—
Minnesota	Exempt	Federal	Corp. must withhold tax on distributions to shareholders.
Mississippi	Exempt	State	Information return required. Nonresident shareholders must pay state tax.
Missouri	Exempt	Federal	Nonresident shareholder must pay state tax.

Figure 14.1, continued

State	Tax Treatment	Election	Restrictions and Conditions
Montana	Exempt	Federal	Corp. must file copy of federal election. Shareholders must pay tax.
Nebraska	Exempt	Federal	Nonresident shareholders must pay state tax or Corp. must remit 10% of its distributive share.
Nevada	—	—	Nevada has no state income tax.
New Hampshire	Taxable	—	—
New Jersey	Taxable	—	—
New Mexico	Exempt	Federal	—
New York	Exempt	State	Nonresident shareholders must pay state tax.
North Carolina	Taxable	—	—
North Dakota	Exempt	Federal	Nonresident shareholders must pay state tax.
Ohio	Exempt	Federal	File federal election. Shareholders pay tax.
Oklahoma	Exempt	Federal	Nonresident shareholders must pay state tax.
Oregon	Exempt	Federal	—
Pennsylvania	Exempt	State	Election is optional. Corp. must file information return.
Rhode Island	Exempt	Federal	Nonresident shareholders must pay state tax.
South Carolina	Exempt	Federal	Nonresident shareholders must pay tax.
South Dakota	—	—	S.D. has no state income tax.
Tennessee	Taxable	—	—
Texas	—	—	Texas has no state income tax.
Utah	Exempt	Federal	Corp. can elect to be taxed on ratio of stock owned by nonresidents or withhold tax from nonresidents' share of earnings

Figure 14.1, continued

State	Tax Treatment	Election	Restrictions and Conditions
Vermont	Taxable	—	Corp. taxed only on stock allocable to nonresident shareholders.
Virginia	Exempt	Federal	Nonresident shareholders must pay state tax.
Washington	—	—	Wash. has no state income tax.
West Virginia	Exempt	Federal	Corp. must file information return.
Wisconsin	Exempt	State	Nonresident shareholders must pay state tax.
Wyoming	—	—	Wyoming has no state income tax.

Figure 14.1, continued

Owners of partnerships and S Corporations face an annual limit on the deductibility of their business losses. However, they can carry forward their unused losses.

Here's a closer look at the key issues involved in choosing a form for doing business:

PROTECTING YOURSELF FROM PERSONAL LIABILITY

Perhaps the key consideration in selecting the corporate form of doing business is protecting the owner's personal and other nonbusiness assets against the claims of business creditors. This is not to say that taxes—and tax savings—are not an important factor. But saving even thousands of dollars in taxes pales in comparison to the threat of losing one's home and other assets in the event the business folds or the company loses a multimillion-dollar lawsuit to a pedestrian hit by a company car.

You get personal liability protection through the corporate form of doing business—either as a C Corporation or an S Corporation. Going the sole proprietorship or partnership route exposes you to unlimited personal liability for business obligations. What's more, with a general partnership, you can be held personally liable for obligations incurred by fellow partners on behalf of the business.

Business insurance generally can be taken out to protect you and your business against casualty losses and the risks of business-related lawsuits. But for some businesses—especially manufacturers exposed to product liability lawsuits—liability insurance may be too costly, coverage too limited—or insurance may be unavailable. For such businesses, incorporation in one form or another is strongly recommended. The extra costs involved in incorporating a business generally are more than offset by the protection you get from the corporate "shield" against personal liability.

In many cases, a supplier or lender will require an owner/shareholder to personally guarantee a corporation's obligation—say on a line of credit or a loan. If that's the case, all bets are off. A shareholder who signs the guarantee can be held personally liable if the corporation can't repay the debt.

• **Professionals are treated differently.** State laws generally provide that professionals, such as lawyers, doctors, accountants and engineers, can't escape personal liability for their own malpractice by incorporating. (Needless to say, malpractice insurance is a must for professionals.) Nevertheless, incorporating can still be beneficial; in most states, incorporating will shield a professional from personal liability for malpractice committed by *another* member of the firm or practice. And depending on the state, the corporate form may shield the professional from non-malpractice obligations of the business (for example, rent, supplies, or practice-related personal injury lawsuits).

IDENTIFYING TAX FACTORS

• **Income taxes.** Generally, sole proprietorships, partnerships and S Corporations do not pay federal income tax (although an S Corporation may be taxed on certain items, such as long-term capital gain and investment income). Instead, the business owners—the sole proprietor, the partners or the S Corporation shareholders—report business income, losses, expenses, credits, etc. on their own individual tax returns.

All items of business income or loss are, in effect, "passed through" to the individual owners and retain the same character they had in the business (for example, capital gain or ordinary income). Partnerships and S Corporations file their own returns in order to determine the amount of items that are being passed through to the owners.

The owners pay income tax on the business's profits, regardless of whether the profits are distributed by or retained in the proprietorship, partnership or S Corporation. On the other hand, business losses can be used to offset the owner's income, including income from other, nonbusiness sources (dividends, interest, etc.).

A regular C Corporation reports business income, expenses and losses on its own tax return. There is no automatic "pass through" of income or losses to the business owners as there is with the other common business forms. Accordingly, C Corporation shareholders aren't taxed on profits that are retained by the corporation. However, there are limits on how much profit a corporation can retain before it's hit with a so-called "accumulated earnings tax."

Just as there's no pass through of income to C Corporation shareholders, there's no pass through of losses either. Shareholders can't use business losses to offset their income from the corporation or other sources. Instead, the corporation has to carry back or carry forward losses to offset income from other years.

The treatment of losses is especially important to new businesses. Many businesses lose money in their first few years of operation. An owner's ability to immediately deduct business losses against other income is a big plus in favor of an unincorporated business or S Corporation. (Keep in mind, however, that there are annual limits on such deductions for owners of partnerships and S Corporations.)

Owners of corporations may receive payments in two ways:

- *Dividend* payouts in their capacity as shareholders, and
- *Salary* in their capacity as employees of the corporation.

Amounts paid as salary are reported as income by the owner and deducted by the corporation as a business expense. However, it's a different story with dividend payments. Amounts distributed to shareholders as dividends are, in effect, subject to two taxes: one at the corporate level at corporate tax rates and again at the individual shareholder level at the individual's tax rate. In addition, if an officer/shareholder's salary is too high, the IRS may reclassify part of the salary (which is deductible by the corporation) as a dividend (which isn't deductible as a business expense).

- **Income tax rates.** Individuals will pay income tax at either a 15%, 28%, or 31% tax rate.

A C Corporation generally pays an income tax of 15% on the first $50,000 of income, 25% from $50,000–$75,000, and 34% for income above $75,000. A special 5% surtax is added in for income from

$100,000–$335,000. Personal service corporations (PSCs), a corporate form used by many professionals, now pay tax at a flat rate of 34%.

There's no one "best" business form from a strictly income tax standpoint. It all depends on your specific situation and the marginal tax rate paid on each dollar you or the business earn.

For example, you come out ahead using a C Corporation setup if business income that you, as an individual, would otherwise pay tax on at a 31% rate is left in the corporation and taxed at 15%. On the other hand, dividend income you receive from a C Corporation is subject to double taxation.

Another factor is that the highest individual tax rate (31%) currently is lower than the highest corporate income tax rate (34%). So, for businesses generating significant income, the C Corporation setup will not be an income-tax saver. And owner/shareholders of personal service corporations (or business people thinking about setting up PSCs) should consider going another route—perhaps an S Corporation—in light of the flat 34% tax rate on PSC income.

• **Tax-year elections.** Partnerships, S Corporations and PSCs generally are required to use a calendar tax year. The tax law requires them to conform their tax years to that of their owners. (However, see below for some exceptions.) C Corporations, on the other hand, can elect either a fiscal or calendar tax year.

This flexibility in selecting a tax year allows owners of C Corporations to defer compensation income for maximum tax advantage. A fiscal year ending January 31 is commonly used by cash-basis S Corporations. This allows the owner/shareholders to have the corporation pay them a bonus either in December or January, depending on when the payment will do the most tax good.

Some partnerships, PSCs and S Corporations can use a fiscal tax year if they get IRS approval. They must demonstrate a valid business purpose for having a different tax year from their owners (for example, a natural business cycle), and the deferral period generally can be no longer than three months.

However, the business entity generally will have to make additional estimated tax payments based on the amount of tax deferral benefit the owners receive as a result of being on the calendar-year basis. And PSCs are required to make minimum distributions to their shareholders in order to avoid penalties. Generally speaking, these required deposits offset any benefits you may gain through the deferral of income tax by using a fiscal tax year.

PROVIDING RETIREMENT BENEFITS

There's no longer any significant difference between retirement plan setups available to owners of incorporated and unincorporated businesses. Owners of partnerships, proprietorships, C and S Corporations can put in place retirement plans—profit sharing or pension plans, Keogh or corporate plans—that provide for similar contributions, benefits and deductions.

One difference is that shareholders of C Corporations can take out loans from qualified retirement plans, as can employees of S Corporations, partnerships and sole proprietorships. However, the law prohibits such loans to *owners* of S Corporations, partnerships and sole proprietorships.

OFFERING FRINGE BENEFITS

A C Corporation can provide its employees—including owner/shareholders—with a number of fringe benefits that are tax-free to its employees and deductible by the corporation. These benefits include a limited amount of group-term life insurance, accident and health plans (including medical, dental and disability plans) and cafeteria plans.

If a sole proprietorship, partnership or S Corporation provides similar benefits to its owner/employees (in the case of S Corporations, individuals who own more than 2% of the S Corporation's stock), the value of the benefits generally is taxable to the recipients. This can be an important consideration to company owners who draw a lot of fringe benefits from the business.

On the other hand, owners of sole proprietorships and partnerships and owner/employees of S Corporations can deduct 25% of the cost of health insurance premiums for themselves, their spouses and dependents if health insurance is provided to other employees of the business.

C Corporations clearly have an edge over the other forms of doing business when it comes to fringe benefits.

OTHER CONSIDERATIONS

A sole proprietorship has a limited life span. When the owner dies or retires, the business ceases to exist. A partnership theoretically has the same basic limitation. The partnership dissolves when a partner dies, retires, withdraws or is expelled from the partnership. However, the matter of continuity—what happens to the business when a partner dies or withdraws—can be dealt with in the partnership agreement.

The corporate form of doing business—either as a C Corporation or an S Corporation—makes it easier to continue operations of the business following the death or withdrawal of one of the owners. In addition, it's easier to transfer ownership interests in a corporation than in an unincorporated business.

In theory, shareholders of a corporation are free to transfer or sell their stock to anyone. But as a practical matter, most small or family corporations place restrictions on an owner/shareholder's right to sell or transfer his or her stock. This often takes the form of an option of first refusal in favor of the corporation or fellow shareholders. Partnership agreements generally include similar restrictions on the partners' right to sell or transfer their interests to outsiders.

MAKING THE CHOICE

This brief discussion of the pros and cons of common business forms doesn't attempt to answer the question of which form is the right one for you and your company. Again, there's no hard and fast answer. Your choice must be made on the basis of many factors that are unique to you and your business. And to the extent that your decision is based on tax considerations, keep in mind that the law can—and does— change. So you need to stay abreast of the latest tax law changes and react accordingly.

For example, there no longer are significant differences between sole proprietorships, partnerships, C Corporations and S Corporations when it comes to retirement plans and payroll taxes.

There are differences in tax rates between a C Corporation and the other business forms, but there's no clear advantage either way. Generally speaking, a C Corporation pays tax at a lower rate on income below $75,000. On the other hand, C Corporations also have the problem of double taxation.

Experts say that S Corporations will be the predominant choice of small business people (especially those starting a new business) in coming years. An S Corporation combines the advantages of the corporate shield against personal liability with new tax benefits thanks to recent changes in the tax law. Plus, an S Corporation allows an owner to immediately write off business losses against his or her other income. This combination, according to many experts, should make an S Corporation election the norm unless there are compelling reasons against it.

Note, however, that the tax law says an S Corporation can have only 35 shareholders, and that none of the shareholders may be partnerships or corporations. This limitation shouldn't be a problem for most small businesses. One restriction that may pose a problem in the early years of a business (when it may not be making much money) is the so-called passive income restriction. That is, no more than 25% of an S Corp's income may be passive income, such as interest income or dividends.

You should consult an attorney who's familiar with you and your business plans before making your choice. If you decide to form a partnership or corporation, an attorney should be used to draft an agreement and file the necessary papers. It's not a do-it-yourself job.

The comparison chart in Figure 14.2 will help you better understand the differences between C Corporations, partnerships and S Corporations.

Figure 14.2
Comparison Chart

Points to Consider	C Corporation	Partnership	S Corporation
I. General Characteristics			
1. Separate entity versus conduit (flow through) concept	*Entity:* Corporation is treated as a separate tax-paying entity apart from the shareholders. If income is distributed to shareholders in the form of dividends, the shareholders are subject to a second tax on such amounts.	*Modified conduit:* Partners report their distributive share of partnership ordinary income and separately stated items on their individual returns. Most elections, e.g., depreciation methods, accounting period, are made at the partnership level.	*Modified conduit:* Similar to partnership form of organization. However, the S Corporation may be subject to tax at corporate level on excess net passive income, long-term capital gains, or built-in gains under special circumstances.
2. Period of existence	Continues until dissolution; not affected by disaffiliation of shareholders or sale of their shares.	Termination can occur by agreement, or on partner's death, retirement, or disaffiliation.	Same as for C Corporation, except that period of existence may be affected by share transfer to ineligible shareholder.

Points to Consider	C Corporation	Partnership	S Corporation
3. Transferability of interest	Readily and easily marketable by transfer of certificate of stock; corporation may retain right to buy back shares.	Addition of new partner or transfer of partner's interest generally requires approval of other partners.	Same as for C Corporation, except that sale of shares to partnership, corporation, certain trusts, or nonresident aliens terminates election.
4. Liability exposure	Except in rare circumstances, shareholders generally only liable for capital contributions.	General partners are personally, jointly, and severally liable for partnership obligations. Limited partners usually liable for capital contributions only.	Same as for C Corporation.
5. Management responsibility	No requirement for shareholder participation in management. Shareholders may be part of management or may hire outside management.	All general partners participate in management and share joint responsibility. Limited partners generally do not participate.	No requirement for shareholder participation in management. But, because of limited number of shareholders, shareholders usually are part of management.
II. Restrictions			
1. Restrictions on: a. Type of owners	No restriction.	No restriction.	Limited to individuals, estates, and certain kinds of trusts.
b. Number of owners	No restriction.	No restriction.	Limited to 35 shareholders.
c. Investments made by entity	No restriction.	No restriction.	S Corporation must own less than 80% of the voting power and 80% of the value of a second corporation.

Figure 14.2, continued

Points to Consider	C Corporation	Partnership	S Corporation
d. Capital structure	No restriction. Sale of multiple classes of stock or other securities to unlimited number of individuals, corporations, or partnerships permitted.	No restriction. Contribution by general or limited partners, with unlimited number of partners permitted.	Limited to a single class of stock that is outstanding. Differences in voting rights are permitted. Special "safe harbor" rules are available.
e. Passive interest income	No restriction.	No restriction.	Passive investment income can't exceed 25% of gross receipts for three consecutive tax years when the corporation also has Subchapter C E&P at the end of year.
III. Elections			
1. Election and shareholder consent	No election required.	No election required.	Election can be made during preceding tax year or first 2½ months of the tax year. Shareholders must consent to election.
2. Termination of election	Not applicable.	Partnership can terminate if it doesn't carry on any business, financial operation, or venture, or if a sale or exchange of at least 50% of the profits or capital interests occurs within a 12-month period.	Occurs if one of the requirements is failed after the election is first effective or if passive investment income test is failed for three consecutive tax years.

Figure 14.2, continued

Points to Consider	C Corporation	Partnership	S Corporation
3. Revocation of election	Not applicable.	Not applicable.	Election may be revoked only by shareholders owning more than one-half of the stock. Must be made in first 2½ months of tax year or on a prospective basis.
IV. Accounting Periods			
1. Tax year	Calendar year or fiscal year is permitted. Corporation's tax year does not have to match shareholder's tax year. Personal service corporations are restricted to a calendar year unless approval is obtained to use a fiscal year. A special election is available to use a fiscal year resulting in not more than a 3-month income deferral if a series of minimum distribution requirements are met.	Generally use tax year of majority or principal partners. Otherwise a calendar year is required. May use a fiscal year if business purpose is shown for which IRS approval is obtained. A partnership may elect to use a fiscal year resulting in not more than a 3-month income deferral if additional required payments are made.	Same as for a partnership except that majority or principal partner rules do not apply.
2. Accounting methods	Elected by corporation. Cash method of accounting is restricted for certain personal service corporations and C Corporations having $5,000,000 or more gross receipts.	Elected by partnership. Restrictions on the use of cash method of accounting apply to partnerships having a C Corporation as a partner or that are tax shelters.	Elected by S Corporation. Restrictions on the use of the cash method of accounting apply to S Corporations that are tax shelters.

Figure 14.2, continued

Points to Consider	C Corporation	Partnership	S Corporation
V. Tax Treatment of Income, Taxes and Deductions			
1. Treatment of income and losses	All corporate income taxed at corporate level and again taxed at shareholder level when distributed as dividends. Some C Corporations taxed as personal holding companies and can be taxed on excess accumulated income.	Partnership income determined at entity level and passed through to each partner and taxed at individual rates. Income and loss items that affect partner's tax liability are separately stated (e.g., charitable contributions, depletion).	Corporate income determined at entity level and passed through to each shareholder and taxed at individual rates. Some S Corps pay tax on certain capital gains, "built-in gains," and "excess net passive income." Income and loss items that affect a shareholder's tax liability are separately stated—e.g., charitable contributions, depletion.
2. Maximum tax rate for earnings	15% on the first $50,000; 25% from $50,000 to $75,000; 34% above $75,000. A 5% surtax applies to taxable income from $100,000 to $335,000. Special rules apply to controlled groups. Personal service corporations are taxed at a flat 34% rate.	Rates of tax applicable to individual partners from 15% through 31% are levied on the income from the business. C Corporation rates apply to corporate partners.	Same as partnership except for certain special situations where a special corporate tax applies to the S Corporation.
3. Alternative minimum tax	Applies at corporate level. Book income adjustment.	Applies only at partner level. No book income adjustment.	Applies only at shareholder level. No book income adjustment.
4. Liquidation of business	"Double tax" on corporate and shareholder levels.	No tax at partnership level.	No tax at corporate level (except for built-in gains).

Figure 14.2, continued

Points to Consider	C Corporation	Partnership	S Corporation
5. Net operating losses	Deductible only by the corporation in a year which it has offsetting income. Losses may be carried back 3 years or forward 15 years.	Losses pass through to partners at end of the partnership tax year. Losses may be carried back 3 years or forward 15 years.	Losses pass through to shareholders and are deductible to the extent of their stock and debt basis. Losses may be carried back 3 years or forward 15 years.
6. Tax-exempt income	Tax-exempt income increases corporate earnings and profits and is not taxed at corporate level. If distributed to shareholders as dividends, it is subject to tax.	Tax exempt income of partnership retains its character when passed through to partners. It increases partners' bases in entity.	Tax-exempt income of corporation retains its character when passed through to shareholders. It increases shareholder's basis in stock.
7. Capital gains	Capital and Sec. 1231 gains taxed at regular corporate rate or a maximum rate of 34%.	Capital and Sec. 1231 gains pass through to partners and retain their character.	Capital and Sec. 1231 gains pass through to shareholders and retain their character at shareholder level. Rules for taxing S Corps. on capital gains depend on whether S Corp. election was made after 1986 or before 1987.
8. Capital losses	Capital losses deducted at corporate level only to the extent of capital gains. Losses may be carried back 3 years or forward 5 years.	Capital losses pass through to partners and retain their character. Losses offset capital gains and then up to $3,000 of ordinary income. May be carried forward indefinitely.	Capital losses pass through to shareholders and retain their character at the shareholder level. Losses offset capital gains and then up to $3,000 of ordinary income. May be carried forward indefinitely.

Figure 14.2, continued

Points to Consider	C Corporation	Partnership	S Corporation
9. Accumulated earnings	Corps. may accumulate income for reasonable business needs. Up to $150,000 for personal service corporations and $250,000 for other C Corps. may be accumulated without question. Unreasonable accumulations subject to tax.	All income taxed to partners whether distributed or not.	All income is passed through and taxed at shareholder level. S Corps. with carryover C Corp. earnings and profits are subject to corporate tax on excess passive income and distributions of accumulated earnings and profits taxed as dividend income.
10. Distributions and income allocations	Distributions taxed as ordinary income and allocated on basis of shareholders. C Corp. will generally recognize gain on sale or distribution of appreciated property.	Distributions tax-free unless they exceed partner's basis in stock and partnership debt. Distributive income shares may be allocated by agreement of the partners. Partnership does not recognize gain on distribution of appreciated property.	Distributions tax-free unless they exceed a shareholder's basis in stock and debts. Corporation recognizes gain on distribution of appreciated property. Income may only be allocated in proportion to shareholdings.
11. Investment interest deduction	No limitation.	Partner may deduct share of partnership's interest up to the extent of net investment income limitation.	Shareholder deducts share of the S Corp.'s investment interest to the extent of net investment income limitation.
12. Dividends received	C Corp can deduct 70% (80% if dividends received from 20%-or-more owned corp.) of dividends received from domestic corporations.	Income passes through to partners.	Income passes through to shareholders.

Figure 14.2, continued

Points to Consider	C Corporation	Partnership	S Corporation
13. FICA taxes	Tax payable by the corporation and its employees.	Self-employment tax applies to salary and drawings.	Tax payable by the corporation and its employees.
VI. Other Special Items			
1. Fringe benefits	Shareholder-employees may receive tax-qualified fringe benefits, including employer-provided health care, meals and lodging and group term life insurance, without restriction. Owner-employees may be treated as employees for Social Security tax and corporate fringe benefit purposes.	A partner is not considered an employee of the business. Corporate fringe benefits such as group term life insurance are not available (i.e., the premiums are not deductible by the business and are not excludable from the proprietor's income). Self-employed persons may deduct 25% of health insurance premiums for themselves, their spouses, and dependents if health insurance is provided to partnership's employees.	Corporate fringe benefits generally are not available to 2%-or-more owners of S Corp. shares. Deduction for 25% of health insurance premiums available to S corp. shareholders.
2. Retirement plans	C Corp. can provide a broad variety of defined benefit and defined-contribution plans, including those involving the corporation's own stock.	Keogh plans are generally subject to the same limits on contributions and benefits that apply to qualified corporate retirement plans, but Keogh plans can't involve employer stock since there isn't any.	Although generally the same rules and limitations apply to S Corps. as to C Corps., an S Corp. can't have a retirement plan that holds its own stock in trust for employees, and loans to shareholders are prohibited.

Figure 14.2, continued

Points to Consider	C Corporation	Partnership	S Corporation
3. Income splitting between family members	Only possible when earnings are distributed to shareholder. Dividends received by shareholder under age 14 taxed at parents' marginal tax rate.	Transfer of partnership interest by gift allows income splitting. Subject to special rules when family members paid reasonable compensation for capital and services. Income received by partner under age 14 taxed at parents' marginal tax rate.	Transfer of S Corp. interest by gift allows income splitting. Special rules apply when family members paid reasonable compensation for capital and services. Income received by shareholder under age 14 taxed at parents' marginal tax rate.
VII. Tax Return Items			
1. Tax return	Form 1120 or 1120A	Form 1065, Information Return.	Form 1120S, Information Return.
2. Due date	March 15 for calendar-year C Corporation.	April 15 for calendar-year partnership.	March 15 for calendar-year S Corporation.
3. Extensions of time permitted	6 months.	4 months.	6 months.
4. Estimated tax payments required	Yes—April 15, June 15, September 15, and December 15 for calendar-year C Corporation.	No—estimated taxes required of partners for passed through income, etc.	Yes—for 1990 and later tax years. Applies only to built-in gains tax, excessive passive income tax, and investment tax credit recapture amount.

Figure 14.2

MAKING THE MOST OF AN S CORPORATION

HOW TO SAFEGUARD A FAMILY S CORPORATION

S Corporations are popular vehicles for operating family businesses. But as the founding family members get older, the problem arises as to how to turn over the corporation to the next generation while ensuring continued family control of the business.

In you are dealing with a C Corporation, the owner/shareholders could issue different classes of stock with various rights and restrictions. But S Corporation owners face an additional problem: An S Corporation may not have more than one class of stock issued and outstanding. S Corporations are permitted to have outstanding common stock with different voting rights without violating this one-class-of-stock rule. But when it comes to other differences in shareholder rights, S Corporations must tread carefully.

Despite that limitation, there is an IRS-approved way for S Corporation owners to impose restrictions and conditions on the shares they transfer to other family members. By carefully following the IRS guidelines, you can impose transfer restrictions and forced redemption conditions on some shares without creating a second class of stock.

Case Example

Amos Barker is the sole shareholder of Barker, Inc., an S Corporation. Barker, Inc. currently has two kinds of stock outstanding: Class A common with all the voting rights and nonvoting Class B common. Amos plans to leave the company stock to his three children and to a valued company employee. But he plans to give his oldest daughter, Beth, control of the company—and it he wants to keep it that way.

Amos' will provides that half the nonvoting Class B common and all of the voting Class A common will go to Beth at his death. Beth's stock will be unrestricted. The remainder of the Class B common will go to his other two children and the company employee. Neither of these children nor the employee will be permitted to sell or otherwise dispose of their stock. But they may have the company redeem the stock, with the payments made in installments over a number of years. The employee's stock will be subject to additional conditions requiring redemption of his stock if he leaves the company and forfeiture if he violates a noncompetition clause.

The IRS says that Amos' will would not create a second class of stock. The reason is that the restrictions imposed by the will would not affect the shareholders' rights in the profits and assets of the corporation.

Other restrictions

The IRS has approved some other devices that might be used to keep an S Corporation in the family. For example, the IRS has ruled that the following restrictions or conditions did not create a second class of stock:

- A restriction preventing the holder of nonvoting common from transferring his shares without consent of the voting common shareholders.

- A provision giving the corporation or the other S shareholders the right to buy all the shares of a 2%-or-more shareholder/ employee whose employment is terminated.

- A requirement that a deceased shareholder's personal representative sell all of that shareholder's stock to the corporation.

- A provision giving the corporation the right to redeem stock of key employees at any time, where the practice had been to redeem the stock on death, retirement or termination of employment.

- A condition requiring some shareholders to sell their stock to the corporation whenever the board determines a sale is in the best interests of the corporation.

HOW TO GET TOP TAX WRITEOFFS WHEN RAISING MONEY FOR YOUR S CORP

There are many tax advantages to operating your business as an S Corporation. For example, there's no double taxation (once at the corporate level and again at the shareholder level) when earnings are distributed. They're taxed directly to the shareholder.

However, if the corporation has a loss, the shareholders may not be able to deduct the loss on their returns. Shareholders of an S Corporation generally cannot claim tax losses in excess of their investment in the corporation. For this purpose, a shareholder's investment includes cash and property contributed to the corporation and direct loans made to the corporation. However, a shareholder's investment *does not* include his or her share of the corporation's debt—even if *personally guaranteed* by the shareholder.

Case Example

Russell and five others formed an S Corporation. Russell initially contributed $10,000 and loaned another $5,000 (investment = $15,000). The S Corporation then borrowed over $1.5 million, which Russell and the others guaranteed to repay if the S Corporation defaulted. Russell treated his personal guarantee of the corporate debt as an investment in the S Corporation, increasing his total investment to about $350,000. He then wrote off $52,000, representing his share of the S Corporation's net losses for the year.

According to the Tax Court, since Russell's guarantee of payment did not require any capital outlay, it was not an equity investment. And it was also not a loan by Russell to the corporation. The guarantee of payment did not increase his investment in the S Corporation, and Russell was denied all writeoffs in excess of his actual investment ($15,000) in the S Corporation.

If your S Corporation needs money and you don't want to provide the funds out of your own pocket, you should borrow the money from a bank or lender directly, and then lend it to the S Corporation. The corporation can repay you and then you can repay the bank. By handling things this way, the debt will count toward your investment and can be used to increase any loss writeoffs from the S Corporation.

HOW TO SAFEGUARD THE CORPORATE S ELECTION WHEN ANOTHER CORPORATION IS ACQUIRED

Although S Corporations are technically "small business corporations," in many cases the word "small" may be a misnomer. The shift in corporate and individual tax rates made by the 1986 Tax Reform

Act has made S Corporation status attractive for many corporations, regardless of size. What's more, many S Corporations are growing even larger as a result of corporate acquisitions.

Buyer beware. If a corporate acquisition isn't structured properly, a company could lose its S election. And a company whose S election is terminated won't be able to re-elect S status for five years, unless it can convince the Internal Revenue Service (IRS) that the termination was inadvertent.

An S Corporation can acquire the stock or assets of another corporation in any number of taxable or nontaxable transactions. Regardless of how the deal is set up, here are some pitfalls to avoid.

• **Ineligible stockholders.** A corporation's S election will be terminated if its stock is held by ineligible shareholders. Only individuals (other than nonresident aliens), estates and qualifying trusts are eligible to hold stock in an S Corporation. Partnerships, corporations, and nonqualifying trusts are ineligible shareholders.

Even a deal as simple as a taxable purchase of a target corporation's assets can cost a company its election if part of the consideration is stock in the corporation, and that stock winds up in the wrong hands.

Nontaxable reorganizations are particularly likely to present ineligible stockholder problems. For example, in a "C" reorganization, the acquiring S Corporation typically issues its stock to the target corporation in exchange for the target assets, followed by a liquidation of the target corporation and distribution of the S Corporation stock to the target shareholders. Here, however, the IRS may let the S Corporation off the hook. Although the target corporation is technically an ineligible shareholder, the IRS has okayed this type of acquisition. The Service says that an S Corporation won't lose its S status merely because it has a *momentary* corporate shareholder in the course of a reorganization.

• **Too many shareholders.** A corporation also can lose its S election if it has more than 35 shareholders at any given time. Therefore, corporations should be particularly cautious in any acquisition that involves the use of corporate stock as consideration.

For example, in the "C" reorganization described above, the acquiring S Corporation's election would be in jeopardy if the target corporation shareholders who will receive the S Corporation stock on liquidation of the target will put it over the 35-shareholder limit.

• **Too much target stock.** An S election will also be terminated if the S Corporation becomes an "ineligible corporation." Among those corporations ineligible to make or continue an S election are members of an affiliated group of corporations. As a practical matter, the affiliated-group restriction prevents an S Corporation from owning 80% or more of another corporation, regardless of whether the two corporations file consolidated returns.

This pitfall is most likely to be encountered when an S Corporation acquires a target corporation by means of a taxable or nontaxable stock acquisition. This is because the S Corporation will generally acquire enough stock in the target for the two corporations to become members of an affiliated group.

In many such acquisitions, the target corporation will be immediately liquidated into the S Corporation. It is possible that the IRS might ignore the transitory stock acquisition—just as it ignores the momentary corporate stockholder in a "C" reorganization. But the IRS has not ruled on this issue, so there's no guarantee that the IRS would not treat the stock acquisition and the liquidation as separate transactions.

Although the affiliated group problem is of greatest concern in stock acquisitions, S Corporations undertaking asset acquisitions should be wary as well. If the acquired assets include stock of a subsidiary corporation, the S Corporation and its new sub could be considered affiliated corporations, and the S election could be terminated.

- **Two classes of stock.** An S Corporation is permitted to have only one class of issued and outstanding stock. While this obviously prevents an S Corporation from issuing a second class of stock to effect an acquisition, an S Corporation may unwittingly violate this rule if it issues *notes* as consideration for an acquisition.

A "straight debt" instrument generally won't be treated as a second class of stock as long as interest and payment dates aren't tied to corporate profits, the instrument isn't convertible into stock, and the holder is eligible to hold S Corporation stock. But debt that falls outside this safe harbor could jeopardize the corporation's S election.

If all else fails, a company can consider a reverse acquisition. A reverse acquisition in which the target corporation is the surviving corporation may permit a new or continued S election by the target. Similarly, the acquiring S Corporation and the target could be merged into a new entity, which can then make a new S election.

CHAPTER FIFTEEN

HOW TO RAISE CAPITAL FOR YOUR BUSINESS

At one time or another, every business needs an infusion of capital to exploit a new opportunity, expand the current line, consolidate ownership in fewer hands or, sometimes, just to survive.*

In an ongoing business, some of these capital needs can be met from your internal resources: retained earnings, profits on investments or funds set aside for specific ventures. But no matter how well a firm is run, internal resources may not be enough. Short-term financing—six months to five years—may be needed to cover operating expenses, buy more inventory, back up a big sale or cover work-in-progress. Longer-term financing may be required to support a buyout, expand current operations or launch a new venture.

Particularly when your company is growing rapidly, your need for capital is likely to outstrip your cash flow and retained earnings. That's when your ability to raise capital can be most crucial—and the right financing package becomes the key to your company's success.

This section was written by Everett Slosman, president of Slosman & Associates, an industrial and economic development consulting and research firm located in Bedford, New Hampshire.

This chapter gives you an overview of the basic methods of financing available to small business owners, explains how to use borrowing as a business tool and tells you how to control your debt load. We'll look at:

- the types of financing available,
- the best financing options for meeting your specific needs,
- private and public sources of capital,
- how to use your suppliers as resources,
- how to plan and forecast your capital needs,
- how to prepare and present proposals to bankers and investors,
- how to meet particular financing needs—for example, buyouts,
- special capital requirements for startup companies, and
- how to manage your capital for top return.

HOW TO FIND THE KIND OF FINANCING THAT IS RIGHT FOR YOU

Selecting the right funding for your company's needs requires an understanding of the different kinds of financing available and the ramifications of your choices. Here's a look at the four basic categories:

- **Interim financing.** At certain times, particularly in startup situations, you'll need financing before a new business activity is actually underway. The expenses you need to pay for may include preliminary research studies, legal fees, accounting fees, licenses or site location and preparation.

The funding used to meet these expenses is called interim financing. Because outside lenders or investors will generally want to see a record of solid or promising results from an ongoing activity, interim startup financing often requires the business owner to dip into his or her personal resources: drawing on the proceeds of another enterprise or taking out a personal or homeowner's loan, for example.

Some business owners hope to get the interim financing they provide their companies back in a hurry by taking out short-term loans against their businesses and paying themselves back out of the proceeds. Not only are lenders leery of extending these so-called payback or "takeout" loans, but the IRS may object if the company tries to write off the interest payments to you.

The IRS may regard your loan to the company as an equity investment and the money you get back as nondeductible dividends. Generally, it's advisable to treat any interim financing you put up as your equity in the business. If you want to recapture the investment, take it back from the business when it is generating sufficient cash flow to repay you.

You should never try to use interim financing to subsidize operations that will not start producing within a six-month period. Investments that go beyond that are poor financing choices.

• **Short-term financing.** This is money that is used to buy inventory, cover initial operating costs and get a startup off the ground. In the case of ongoing operations, short-term funds provide the extra operating capital that can mean survival during economic downturns.

Unfortunately, during these times, your company won't be the only one that needs short-term help. The pressure such demand places on the capital markets drives interest rates up. That's why it's important to negotiate a line-of-credit arrangement with a bank or some other lending institution. Prudent short-term borrowing during good times, managed properly, will help you develop this relationship.

Examples of short-term loans include: personal and character loans, and installment loans.

Always use short-term money to cover only short-term requirements. Don't consider this "bailout financing." There are too many strings attached.

> **IMPORTANT.** Never use short-term money to purchase machinery and other hard assets. Often, repayment schedules don't provide enough time to generate a profit from this type of asset. Also, be wary of short-term starter loans with balloon payments at the end. These can lead to an "upside down" situation (where you owe more than you're taking in). They're especially dangerous if you have to refinance and have insufficient collateral.

Short-term notes usually run from six months to five years. Since these funds are turned around in a short period of time, the interest charged on such loans should not be as high as on other loans. It's usually fairly close to the current prime. Naturally, however, the rate you are charged will reflect the lender's perception of the risk involved.

Treat short-term debt as a monthly payable and handle it just like any other account payable. Repayment comes from your operating profits, not from assets.

Just as you use interim financing to fund startups until longer-term asset financing is available, short-term borrowing can be used as interim financing for construction projects if you are certain you can later secure long-term takeout loans. But be careful: This strategy can get you in big trouble if your project is never completed. For example, many condominium and office developers have relied on a combination of short-term financing and sales to bankroll projects. These developers used money generated by sales as collateral to take out additional construction financing loans. When the market softened, they were left with unsold units and loans coming due.

As a result, many such projects have gone bankrupt and lenders have been stuck with half-finished projects. The fundamental mistake was using short-term financing to leverage construction. This made the payback dependent on short-term economic conditions. The guarantee of long-term financing so vital to successful real estate ventures was missing.

• **Medium-term financing.** There are certain elements of a business that require slightly longer-term funding. These include purchasing computers and other technology-sensitive equipment, joint ventures and buying assets with medium-length depreciation schedules.

Medium-term financing runs from five to ten years and has as its collateral assets with an expected usable life expectancy of at least the term of the loan.

• **Long-term financing.** As your business grows, you will need expansion capital. Without it, the company can stagnate.

Expansion requires both short and long-term financing. In the case of long-term financing, you are dealing with money borrowed for five or more years and collateralized by hard assets. You would use it to buy machinery, equipment, or real estate—assets that generate depreciation that can contribute to your cash flow. They also represent a significant portion of the company's equity.

Some lenders, such as venture capital companies, are more interested in furnishing long-term financing than others. So getting expansion financing means developing a project package that can appeal to a variety of different lenders and investors. Each will have an opportunity to participate with the kind of financing that it knows best.

Long-term debt is repaid from gross profits and represents a lien on your future success. It also provides a good measure of how the financial community views your new firm.

> **IMPORTANT:** Don't use long-term financing to meet short-term needs. When you do this, you again can find yourself "upside down"—owing more, because of depreciation, than items such as computers or cars may be worth on the open market.

DISTINGUISHING BETWEEN THE TWO BASIC TYPES OF CAPITAL

In deciding where to go for financing, it's important to distinguish between the two basic types of capital: debt and equity. Debt is borrowed money, repaid with interest on a scheduled basis and secured by collateral (assets) that the lender may convert into cash in the event of a default.

Equity, on the other hand, is an investment that earns dividends, taken from your firm's yearly profits. The equity investor's principal is recouped only when the investor's shares or interest are sold. Equity investors look for dividend payments and an increase in your company's per-share value due to growth.

Lenders are concerned with your ability to repay the loan; investors with your ability to generate a good rate of return on their money. Both lenders and investors will look closely at the internal resources you commit to a proposed venture. They take into consideration the percentage of financing you're willing to put up; and they will also judge the quality of your noncapital commitments, such as project personnel, space allocations and in-kind support.

CHOOSING A LOAN THAT MEETS YOUR NEEDS

Business financing is a world of conflicting loan lengths, collateral requirements, multiple repayment terms and limited availability. Your ability to secure business loans depends on the confidence that lenders and investors have in you—your character, capacity and capital.

"Character" means your integrity as a borrower and the reputation you have built for meeting obligations and overcoming business adversities. "Capacity" refers to your ability to use the financing wisely as reflected by your firm's earnings record and standing in the community and the industry. "Capital" represents an objective evaluation of your fiscal strength and the amount of your own money you are willing to risk on the venture.

Do your capital commitment and collateral compare favorably with the risks involved?

Once you've met the three C's test, you can begin to evaluate your financing options by examining the available loan vehicles. Most of these loans are collateralized by your business assets. However, there are a few notable exceptions. Here's a review of your options:

• **Personal and character loans.** Usually, these types of loans are the result of long personal relationships between customer and lender and are secured by good faith and strong credit ratings. But character and friendship aside, you still may be required to execute a personal guarantee. You may also be required to restructure your company's debt load by refinancing or selling off assets.

Personal and character loans typically finance small family firms with long track records and solid physical resources. For example, a family produce business may want to buy a small pickup truck to support its door-to-door sales activities. The truck will need some modifications to make it an efficient business vehicle. Even though the "book" value of the vehicle is far less than the value of the loan, character and capacity win over capital.

With this type of loan, the lender places his own credibility on the line. Today, personal and character loans are found mainly in rural communities where the lender works with tradition and family relationships. Occasionally they're used to help a startup venture or to buy commercial real estate for future development.

There are two drawbacks associated with these loans: (1) lenders willing to make them demand a higher interest rate as a hedge against default, and (2) they will probably require personal guarantees that may place all of your assets at risk. Depending on the laws in your state, your home, furniture, car and other possessions could become subject to the collection process in the event of default.

These loans will almost always be short-term loans. They may contain a "balloon payment" clause. There may also be a penalty for prepayment.

• **Installment loans.** Occasionally, installment loans are used as primary capital funding to back startups. Their main use, however, is for purchasing vehicles, office machinery and other small-ticket items. When cash reserves are low, installment loans become a logical way for a firm to finance such purchases.

Look beyond the bank. There's a tendency to think of installment credit as only bank financing. However, many suppliers offer monthly payment plans to their dealers at reasonable interest rates and without a discounted note.

Beware of the "discounted" installment note. It works against your best interest. With this tactic, the lender deducts the interest *before* the loan is made. It sounds attractive because you pay back only the net. However, because the interest you pay is calculated on the gross amount, this kind of note actually works to your disadvantage. For example, look at the net proceeds of a $10,000 discounted loan at 10% annual interest. The interest for one year is $1,000, so the net value is $9,000. On a two-year note, the value is only $8,000; for four years, just $6,000. Discounting sends the true interest rate into orbit: it's 11.1% for one year, 25.0% for two years, and a whopping 66.7% for four years!

Despite the obvious problems, many lenders still push discounted installment loans to small companies—often at several percentage points over prime, but at rates less than the going consumer rate.

Be careful. Not only does installment interest run higher than for other commercial loans, but your collateral won't be released until the entire loan is paid off. And when it comes to building equity, installment loans are a bust. They seldom generate net asset value for your balance sheet, yet almost always produce liabilities that eat into your firm's net worth.

A big disadvantage of installment loans is the treatment of collateral. Your entire collateral secures the note until it is paid off. Even though your debt is reduced as the loan is paid off, the lender has a lien on the entire asset. The only way you can obtain any additional financing using that asset is to refinance the entire loan.

At one time, tax considerations made installment loans attractive. But since the Tax Reform Act of 1986, their positive impact on a company's tax liability has lessened. So check with your accountant before using installment financing for your business.

• **Home equity loans.** Home equity borrowing offers an acceptable way to tap your personal net worth for business capital when you're in a startup situation or you need to make a personal investment in your business. Using the proceeds of such loans to relend at a higher interest rate to your company is a form of "arbitraging"—the tactic of raising funds at a lower price in one market and selling them for a higher price in a second market.

A home equity loan or line of credit places a second mortgage on your property. That means it carries with it the cost of making application, having your property appraised, closing costs, and, in some cases, even paying the points (usually one percent or more of the loan amount) for making the loan.

However, since home equity loans can be arranged early in your planning process, you can avoid operating on an emergency basis. If you think you may want to use this financing option, start your application now. With a home equity line of credit, you won't have any debt liability until you actually withdraw the money.

A key drawback is that your home is your collateral. Until the loan is repaid, your property is at risk. In the event of a recession or a drop in appraised value, the mortgage holders may require faster repayment schedules or extra collateral. The extent of risk depends on the mortgage terms and real property laws in your state. That's why it's important to check with a lawyer who specializes in real estate before you sign.

Another factor to consider is your obligation to protect the lenders from casualty losses. Your current insurance policy may not provide adequate coverage. Lenders may require an umbrella policy to supplement your standard homeowner's protection.

There are some real benefits to tapping the equity you have built up in your home. The equity continues to grow as the mortgages are paid down, and the interest is tax-deductible on up to $100,000 in home equity borrowing.

The tax deductions are what make this type of financing especially attractive. Borrowing from your home's equity and relending the money to your company accomplishes two things: (1) You can deduct the interest on your home equity loan from your personal taxes. That will offset part of the interest income you get from your company. (2) The company can deduct the interest as a business expense.

Of course, you can invest the money in your company rather than lend it. But investing means that you'll have to wait for a return of your money from the sale of company assets or dividends.

HOW TO TURN YOUR INVENTORY AND SALES ORDERS INTO READY CASH

There are several ways to draw on the value of your current operations:

• **Factoring.** Factoring is a form of short-term financing that involves making loans against the opportunity to buy so-called "soft" assets such as inventory or receivables at discounted prices. Factoring raises capital in a hurry—but at the expense of realizing the full value of your goods or services.

Sometimes, a factor furnishes financing before goods are produced and gets out after they are sold, taking a percentage of the resale value. In the garment industry, for instance, a factor might receive as much as 75% of the proceeds.

In other cases, factors buy receivables and collect directly from the account. An example of this is when an item is bought on an installment plan. The merchant resells the installment contract to a third party (the factor) who then collects from the customer. The merchant is paid by the factor at the time the installment loan is purchased. The customer sends payments to that factor until the repayment schedule is complete.

Credit card sales are a simple form of factoring. Credit card companies pay retailers 95 cents on the dollar for their charge slips. In turn, the credit card companies collect at full value from the cardholders.

• **Receivables financing.** This is a form of borrowing in which you use a percentage of your company's accounts receivables as collateral. The loan is paid down as the receivables are paid off or through monthly payments. Naturally, the amount of the loan is as much as 50 percent less than the value of your receivables.

Lenders prefer to finance current receivables only. They have no interest in receivables over 45 days old. These can be sold instead to a factor.

Lending valuations run from 50% to 60% percent on newer receivables to 25% percent on older transactions. Banks are not collection agencies and are fussy about the *quality* of the collateral that backs the loan. Some contracts require you to make good any bad collections.

• **Inventory/warehouse receipt loans.** Like factoring, the object of taking inventory and warehouse receipt loans is to convert your inventory equity into ready cash. Two critical requirements for this financing are: (1) verification of the inventory through an on-site inspection by an independent organization and (2) auditing at the lender's discretion. These are both done at your expense.

The loan is paid off as the receivables come in. This is arranged through a lock-box where the lender holds the receivables and applies them against your company's note. An alternative is for your firm to continue collecting the receivables and then arrange regular payments to the lender.

The amount of the loan is based on wholesale market values. If the collateral value slips below the present loan value, the lender can call the loan or require additional collateral. The entire loan may also be called if you do not pay down the loan portion related to the sale of any collateral. In other words, you must maintain the collateral-to-loan ratio initially contracted. Thus, if you sell off units from inventory, the loan must be reduced proportionately.

In the case of a default, the lender has the legal right to foreclose, take possession of the collateral and sell it to satisfy the debt. Your only recourse is to cure the default by paying the amount in arrears and any additional interest or penalties incurred.

The lender also has the right to hold your company liable for any shortfall resulting from the sale of the foreclosed property. That's why you often see inventory and warehouse receipt loans coupled with a personal guarantee—to make it easier for the lender to collect in the event of default.

HOW TO RAISE EXPANSION CAPITAL USING YOUR REAL ESTATE FOR LEVERAGE

Expansion capital for your company's present facility or production line should come, in part, from a real estate loan. Lenders will look favorably on your proposals if they involve real estate as collateral. They like "hard" assets that can be appraised according to standards and, if necessary, sold on an open market to pay off a loan.

Real estate collateral affords a variety of financing options, including first, second, and third long-term mortgage positions. It can also be used as a lever to subordinate public funding to your bank's loan position or as evidence of your participation in a project that depends on a Small Business Administration guarantee.

Flexible financing

With real estate as collateral, you can mix and match. Have your real estate back up a first mortgage with a machinery and equipment (M&E) loan covering a second position. Or use it as a third position participation and fill in any shortfall of capital with economic development financing like an Urban Development Action Grant.

Real estate equity is elastic. It stretches to finance several projects at once or in sequence. This is because developed land appreciates in value even as the amount you owe on the loan decreases. The spread can be readily converted into more financing.

How developer incentives and proper maintenance pay off

If your firm acquires property in an industrial park or an office condominium, the developer may offer you attractive incentives. Low interest rates, build-to-suit, leasebacks, free utility hookups and gap financing are only some of the creative options. These are not only part of the finance package, they also increase the value of the real estate and thus add to your leveraging potential.

And keep in mind that properly maintained and upgraded buildings increase in value as collateral assets. This makes upkeep an investment rather than an expense.

> **IMPORTANT:** Have your real estate appraised every few years. This gives you some idea of what your facility is worth and how much it can contribute to a loan package.

HOW NOT TO LET LACK OF CAPITAL PREVENT YOU FROM BUYING NEEDED MACHINERY AND EQUIPMENT

Almost every business needs machinery and equipment to produce its product or deliver its service. As the business grows, bigger, newer, better equipment is often essential for boosting production or improving quality to meet customer demands.

Failure to invest in new equipment at the critical time can cost you orders and customers if your competitors beat you to the punch. But production machinery and other such hard assets can be costly and you may not have the capital available when you need it most.

Luckily, machinery and equipment loans are relatively easy to come by, particularly when your business involves state-of-the-art manufacturing and production processes. Lenders seem willing to lend you more money on high-technology items than on garden variety, low-tech equipment. The equipment serves as its own collateral, and some lenders also allow you to factor in shipping and installation costs as part of the overall loan package.

Machinery and equipment loans are a form of long-term financing that carries flexible, negotiated terms—a result of having something tangible to negotiate over. Loans for new M&E typically provide from 80%–100% of purchase price. Used and reconditioned units have loan values ranging from 50%–90%.

IMPORTANT: It's a good idea to have an appraisal done on any used machinery you plan to buy. The terms of your loan will depend on this evaluation and your lender's perception of the used equipment market.

Don't expect to negotiate a second loan based on any equity you may have built up in your current equipment. The perceived value just isn't there. Even if the book value can support a loan, lenders will not buy a second-position loan.

WHERE TO GO FOR FUNDS

In today's tight credit market, you'll probably have to go to several sources to negotiate the most favorable financing agreements. So it's important to know something about the philosophies that govern the various lenders and potential investors. The ones you're most likely to encounter are discussed here.

Banks and financial institutions

Before the deregulation of financial services in the early 1980s, borrowing capital from a bank or other lending institution was a fairly straightforward process. You sat down with a loan officer, laid out your project and got a decision.

There were fewer lenders involved in small business financing and loan officers developed personal relations with their commercial clients. Obtaining a business loan depended on your credit and your needs. Interest rates were stable and other loan terms were fairly standard arrangements between friends.

Today, it's a more complex matter. Banks that are owned by out-of-state holding companies may divert investment capital out of your community. This can reduce the money available for small business loans and can push up interest rates. Savings and loans, mutual banks and credit unions are now part of the commercial picture. But in today's tough economy, many small companies are having a hard time finding willing lenders. This adds to the amount of time you must devote to looking for funds.

There are also more restrictions on lending today. Most banks will want to hold their loans to 50%–60% of the project cost and will require more collateral and larger personal loan guarantees than before. They may even ask for a first-mortgage position on company assets not connected with the project. However, you may be able to get better terms if your firm's credit rating and the project's merits make a sufficiently attractive package.

Remember, banks are in the business of selling money. So, if your loan officer expresses interest in your project, you should let him or her know you're willing to negotiate.

Despite today's credit crunch, the diligent business owner should still be able to find a financial institution that will support a business finance package, but only if you're willing to take a small, heavily-collateralized short-term loan. Financial institutions tend to be hesitant about taking the lead position on a project unless you offer a string of guarantees. An institution's better customers will need to furnish at least 10% of the financing themselves. Less-favored customers may be required to put up as much as 35%.

Institutional investors

Most institutional investors such as foundations, charitable trusts, pension plans and foreign investment pools have the financial strength to underwrite large financings. And since most institutional investors (with the exception of insurance companies) are unregulated, they're prepared to take higher risks than banks.

The points institutional investors look for in a proposal are:

- a well-thought-out plan,
- strong documentation,
- participation by other lenders,
- a reasonable repayment schedule,
- adequate collateral,
- evidence of your competence as an executive, and
- your willingness to invest your firm's own funds.

Institutional investors are comfortable with big numbers. As a matter of fact, they may not even look at your project unless your company needs at least $500,000. And because they prefer joint ventures with split-collateral positions, they can provide the financing you may need to plug any gaps in your funding.

A major drawback is that institutional investors require more time than banks to come to a decision. But, even though their initial review process will probably take longer, it will probably take you less time to finalize the deal once they've agreed to back your project.

Venture capital firms

When you're seeking financing for a high-tech venture, pay close attention to the potential of venture capital lenders. They understand the risks and rewards associated with state-of-the-art projects and think of themselves as sophisticated investors rather than mere money-lenders.

Best of all, the deals venture capital firms cut are based more on your product's potential in the marketplace and the future value of your company's shares than on your firm's available collateral. This doesn't mean their motives are altruistic. To obtain good financing, you will still have to give up a significant part of your company as security. However, you can usually negotiate a fixed-price repurchase agreement that takes effect after you repay the loan.

What's more, venture capital lenders are willing to take so-called letter stock—a form of stock that can't be traded on the stock market, is highly restrictive and carries few rights. The value of letter stock is that it entitles investors to an entrepreneurial ownership in your firm.

Letter stock can be converted to ordinary stock through a complicated legal process. Venture capitalists often prefer to convert the letter stock and sell their shares at market price rather than sell for a fixed price. An alternative is to dispose of it through a "private treaty sale." This is nothing more than a negotiation between the lender and another party for the purchase of all the stock. A private treaty becomes an opportunity for you to reenter the bidding arena and buy back your stock.

Venture capital companies prefer to finance small aggressive firms with long track records. However, as long as you offer something viable—even a proposed startup—they will listen to your pitch.

Private investors

This is a capital market run by private deals, personal negotiations and "old chum" networks. Frequently you can gain access to this market through the technical and business assistance centers run by universities and colleges.

Private investors look for opportunities other lenders miss or ignore. Although they're interested in technology, they don't limit themselves to this area. It's possible to stir up some interest among private investors even if your firm is a conservative operation in a stodgy industry.

The majority of these investors are wealthy individuals whose primary motivation is to be successful in negotiating mutually satisfactory deals. When you tap this source, you may find yourself dealing with investors who have big egos and enjoy manipulating small companies in a real-life version of Monopoly.

Private investors are also interested in making money, however. They study proposals hoping to find opportunities that others may have overlooked, and their evaluations combine knowledge and intuition. Like other unregulated sources of capital, they're willing to trade a greater degree of risk for a higher potential return.

Suppliers

Suppliers are a potential source of financing that shouldn't be overlooked. They know your company and the industry better than any other lender, and are sometimes in a position to offer terms other financing sources can't afford.

Check with your suppliers to see if they offer any special deals to increase your cash flow, such as allowing you to place an order for delivery in 90 days and taking up to 180 days to pay for the shipment. In this way, you can gain inventory and sales benefits for six months before you have to settle. In reality, it's an unsecured, interest-free loan.

You may also want to consider supplier financing through joint ventures where the supplier provides the funding, you add the operational controls and you both share the profits. Keep in mind: A cash-rich supplier has a direct interest in your success and so may give you better terms than traditional lending institutions.

> **IMPORTANT:** Almost all lenders will take your investment into consideration in deciding whether to commit their funds. So you must be prepared to provide anywhere from 10%–35% of the funding yourself—regardless of your outside financing source.

HOW THE GOVERNMENT CAN HELP YOU RAISE MONEY

Despite cutbacks in certain types of federal financial aid to small businesses, several federal agencies can still play important roles in helping small companies raise business capital. Two of the largest players are the Small Business Administration (SBA) and the Farmer's Home Administration (FmHA).

• **SBA programs.** The SBA's Section 7(a) loan guarantee program is designed to encourage lenders to make commercial loans to small businesses by providing federal payment guarantees. Under this program, SBA will guarantee up to 80% of a loan made to you by a financial institution at a mutually acceptable interest rate—usually around three points over prime.

One drawback is that SBA programs impose a lot of paperwork. For example, you must do the legwork and obtain a loan rejection letter from your bank. In effect, what the bank says is that it is unable to make a loan without the federal government guaranteeing it.

Under Section 504, the SBA also licenses certified development companies (CDCs). CDCs provide equity to small businesses that can be leveraged with SBA matching funds.

Yet another program sponsored by the SBA is the Small Business Investment Corporations (SBIC) program. These corporations act as second-mortgage lenders primarily to support growing companies and finance projects that will lead to job creation. SBA also provides loans for minority businesses, women-owned businesses and victims of natural disasters, often at below-market rates.

You can use SBA financing to develop a multiple-participation package. A typical participation would begin with your primary lender taking 50% of your project with an SBA guarantee and a first mortgage on the real estate, machinery and equipment.

The second participation might be drawn from your state's economic development fund, covering up to 40% of your financing. The rest of your capital would be raised from your firm or another resource willing to take third position.

• **FmHA programs.** Companies involved in agriculture, food processing or forest products may be able to tap the FmHA business loan program. In the past, FmHA has provided low-cost, long-term financing for thousands of rural business projects. Talk to your county agent for more information.

• **State business development programs.** State business loan programs vary from state to state. But they all come under the department of economic, industrial or business development. Some of the sponsoring agencies require you to create new jobs or stabilize your existing employment before obtaining funding. Others create capital by abating real estate and sales taxes, offering employment or training credits that you can apply against your corporate taxes or allowing you to apply for money from a pool created to help small businesses expand.

For example, say you decide to locate your facility on land earmarked for redevelopment. The state economic development agency will compute the difference between the land's current undeveloped tax value and its projected value after development. Then the agency will lend you the difference. This is called tax-increment financing.

 • **Local development corporations.** Local development corporations are organizations that promote the economic growth of the community. Often, they operate revolving loan funds, take participations in business projects and provide incentives like low-cost sites, property-tax abatements and federal grant money.

These agencies can be helpful in putting together all the available resources to fund your project. Because of the amount of paperwork involved, the process of raising capital can seem like an exercise in frustration. Fortunately, the local development corporation is on your side. Its board of directors is made up of business people and its professional staff can help get you around the bureaucratic roadblocks.

HOW TO SECURE FINANCING

The search for financing begins with a carefully written plan that spells out how much you need, what you're going to do with the money, the collateral you can pledge and how your company can make the loan payments.

DEVELOPING AN EFFECTIVE FINANCING PLAN

There's no special methodology for developing a financing plan. You can use an abstract of your current business plan or draw up a new document that spells out your goals for long-term growth. Show the role the financing will play in increasing profits. Lenders want to hear about your company's potential and how, by providing the financing package, they will earn a tidy profit. Write your plan carefully, using the third person formal voice. Stress short, hard-hitting paragraphs that accent your company's goals and objectives. Don't brag and don't beg.

If financing will improve production, detail the technical requirements. Talk about modernization, the increased value of your plant and the added flexibility you will gain. Describe projects that involve your warehousing and inventory in terms of how they increase your material-handling efficiency and make the most of your investment in finished goods.

For financing that covers operations or expanding into new markets, you will need a statement of project goals and objectives that shows how the changes fit into your company's operations and meet market needs. Usually, a simple written presentation is enough. And if you are redefining your target markets, discuss how this will contribute to profits and increase your company's overall share.

Big plans require big proposals

When you're embarking on a completely new venture, major facilities expansion or you need reorganization capital, lenders will insist on a comprehensive business plan with supporting documents. An expansion requires an analysis of the real estate involved, machinery and equipment specifications and cost factors as well as a feasibility study and payback projections. To finance a reorganization, you will have to provide an in-depth discussion of the proposed use of working capital, forecasts of additional capital requirements and an analysis of the potential for success.

You will also score points for including the expected positions and loan percentages of different participation options. Computer spreadsheets make short work of preparing these projections and formatting them properly.

HOW TO FORECAST YOUR CAPITAL REQUIREMENTS USING PRO-FORMAS

A *pro-forma* is a three-year estimate widely used in forecasting capital requirements. In its simplest form, it shows income and expenses projected for a specific time period and the results expected.

All *pro-formas* rest on a set of critical assumptions: (1) the proposed project is valid, (2) there is outside financing available to support the proposal, and (3) your company has the ability to carry out the project. *Pro-formas* work best when they incorporate three forecasts: best case, worst case and most probable scenario. Using these analyses, you establish your project's limits while explaining the financing proposal in terms of cause and effect. The key is to avoid overly optimistic projections.

As a starting point for developing participations, review your company's current three-year *pro-formas*. Do some "what-if" modeling to see what happens when you change certain factors and assumptions. For example:

- Add in the project debt you will incur and see what the effect of new financing does to your business.

- Lower your sales estimate while holding costs steady to see what happens.

- Project what a prolonged recession, rampant inflation, sporadic economic growth and stagnation will do to your *pro-formas*. Add a multiplier to take care of inflation. The multiplier makes an assumption about the inflation rate and is applied yearly. Also add a 10% contingency to cover the variation on Murphy's law that goes: "If it's possible for your project to cost more money, it will." Then fine-tune your numbers and produce the best-case, worst-case and most-probable-case *pro-formas*.

Lenders prefer the three-case presentation. It offers insight into your firm's management style, your expectations and the benchmarks to apply in judging the project.

Use the most-probable-case pro-forma to show financing options and select your most cost-effective approach. It's relatively easy to manipulate the *pro-formas* with a desktop computer. And lenders will appreciate your efforts to be realistic. Most proposals revert to glowing fantasies unsupported by facts. Candor and a willingness to consider all aspects of the funding will lend yours credibility.

- **Pay attention to forecast accuracy.** The old saying, "garbage in, garbage out," is especially true when working with *pro-formas*. Be careful to use sound data. And, when extrapolating information from outside data, be sure to cite the source. Lenders want to know how you applied the extrapolations and where these data can be found. Citations lend credibility to the forecasts.

- **Don't forget the boilerplate.** "Boilerplate" is a buzzword for all the statistical and additional data found at the back of your proposal. It provides the reader with citations and data analyses to justify assumptions.

The difference between narrative and boilerplate lies in the way you use the material. If you include a persuasive statement of facts or a discussion of your assumptions, then it's narrative. Everything else that strengthens the proposal becomes boilerplate.

If available, include your financial statements for the last five years to dramatically underscore your company's growth and ability to survive. If you include government funds, project the interest rates and the average consolidated interest cost. They will affect your project's viability.

Month-by-month repayment schedules are also an important part of your funding request. They provide insight into your ability to pay back the debt without refinancing and demonstrate how much of a base you are building for future expansion.

If you're proposing a startup, include your personal financial statements and those of others involved with the management or ownership of the project. Your objective is to demonstrate your financial acumen and ability to manage money.

• **How to handle collateral.** Along with your business plan and projections, prepare a list of the collateral you propose using. You should indicate whether the collateral is new or used, what it cost you, any depreciation already taken, existing liens or clouds on your title, the current condition, its remaining life and the appraised value. Your list should also contain serial or identification numbers, locations and any other information that describes the collateral.

The format of your collateral list doesn't matter. Nor does it matter if the list is included in your narrative or added to the boilerplate.

• **Pay attention to details.** There is no right or wrong way to format your proposal. It's a matter of personal choice. However, remember that the format reflects your managerial style and the care you have taken to prepare the document.

Make enough copies to cover all the presentations you intend to do and place them in individual binders. Your presentation should match your firm's image. Be as businesslike as possible. Keep in mind that when you're chasing investors and lenders, positive perceptions count.

THREE CREATIVE WAYS TO RAISE CAPITAL FOR YOUR COMPANY

1. Break the deal up into smaller parts

If you're having trouble raising cash for your business, consider breaking large projects down into smaller, multiple-participation units so that you can raise capital separately for each unit. This means less exposure for potential lenders and investors and allows you to stop part of a project at any point without jeopardizing the rest and without lowering your firm's credit rating.

The best way to divide a project is to make sure each segment can survive without the others. The typical enterprise can be broken into three or four parts.

Occasionally, however, a project can't be divided into viable segments. In these cases, your alternatives are to arrange for pre-payments or work-in-progress financing. These provide additional capital infusions as the project reaches specific markers.

The attraction for investors in all these methods is that backers can see results before closing out all their capital commitments. However, these tactics have serious deficiencies because a backer may decide, for any number of reasons, to pull out before the commitment is complete.

To protect yourself, your funding agreement should contain a penalty clause that keeps the capital infusions flowing. For example, the penalty clause might deny a seat on your board of directors to any backer who has not met its funding commitment. Or you might refuse to return funds until replacement capital is obtained.

2. Set up a new company to finance the project

So-called limited stock issues are another creative funding technique that works well for financing larger projects. The basic technique is to back the project with a separate corporation in which your parent company holds at least 60% of the stock. The second corporation can be a "small stock company," with fewer than 25 stockholders and fewer than 10,000 shares outstanding.

A similar setup can be put together to promote your firm's bonds or commercial paper. Make these issues convertible to cash or stock in your company at your discretion. Plan to fold them back into your company or buy out the other shareholders at your convenience.

> **IMPORTANT:** Requirements for small semi-stock companies vary throughout the states. So have your attorney set up any offerings. Also discuss the plan with your accountant to see what the ramifications are from an accounting perspective.

3. Create a limited partnership

If your project involves a large amount of real estate, you can generate capital through a limited partnership.

In a limited partnership, the investors share in the profits and losses but, as general partner, you retain total control. Unlike traditional partnerships, the other partners have no say in the daily operations of the firm. If dissatisfied, their only recourse is to sell back their interests or take legal action.

However, limited partnerships don't do as well in the manufacturing and service sectors. Before trying this one, be sure to consult both your attorney and your CPA.

HOW TO USE EQUITY INVESTING TO MULTIPLY THE VALUE OF A LOAN

Occasionally, you'll come across creative opportunities for leveraging your capital by backing internal projects unrelated to your original borrowing. For example, instead of using short-term money you've borrowed to cover a customer's purchase order, you may want to purchase some inventory with it. This would involve "borrowing" from yourself because you used money from your project's capital fund.

Three elements must be in place to use equity investing successfully:

1. The "borrowing" must have a short-term cycle.
2. Repayment must be guaranteed.
3. The rate differential between the return on these investments and the original cost of the funds must be significant.

This form of borrowing is practiced frequently. However, many capital funding agreements forbid it. So, when you start raising capital, it's in your interest to negotiate an internal investment clause. (Note, however, that this will be impossible if the financing comes from government sources.)

HOW TO USE LETTERS OF CREDIT—THE ULTIMATE CORPORATE CREDIT CARD

Letters of credit take two different forms. One is a pre-approved line of credit from a lending institution. The other is a document used to make payments in a foreign country.

The pre-approved letter of credit comes from your financial backers and states that a specified sum of money is available to cover transactions. The document functions as both a purchasing tool and a bargaining chip.

A letter of credit is the ultimate corporate credit card. For example, a letter of credit can be used to bind over real estate transactions until suitable financing is arranged, or to purchase machinery for your plant. The letter guarantees the seller's bank can settle with your bank for the agreed-upon amount so long as it doesn't exceed the credit level shown.

A letter of credit is also useful as a letter of reference or introduction. Say, for example, you come to a community on business and want to reassure people you are negotiating in good faith. The letter of credit is the best way to do it. It often opens up an instant relationship with local banks.

On the international front, a letter of credit acts as payment for goods purchased or services rendered. For example, when you ship your products to a foreign company, release of title is predicated on presentation of an irrevocable letter of credit to your bank. Your bank will deposit the money in your firm's account, converted into the currency required by the terms of the purchase agreement. You then have the option of using those funds to conduct more business in the foreign country or repatriating the money in dollars.

With the changes that took place in the European Economic Community in 1992, your company may have an opportunity to break into international trade or expand your sales to common market countries. Letters of credit can be used to facilitate the transfer of loans or investment funds from foreign sources. Your bank's international department can give you up-to-date information on specific transactions.

HOW TO USE LEASING TO MAKE YOUR COMPANY'S MONEY GO FARTHER

Three types of leasing work to stretch your company's capital: the straight lease, the lease with option to buy and leasebacks. Each is worth considering when you're searching for building and equipment capital. In essence, leases are a way to reduce your cash outlays and shift a portion of the risk to another party.

Straight leasing

You may decide, for example, to lease a new photocopier rather than buy one. This way, you can avoid an immediate cash outlay and also reduce maintenance costs if the vendor agrees to service the unit. The lease ends when the equipment reverts to the vendor.

Of course, leasing costs more than buying the product outright over the long term since you are paying the full ticket price plus a hefty interest rate. However, if your business is cash-starved, leasing makes sense because it spreads your cost over a period of time.

Leasing with option to buy

This is almost identical to a straight lease. The difference is that you can keep the equipment at the end of the lease by paying a previously agreed-on price.

Be careful. Technological advances can diminish the value of the option to buy. You should make the choice between a straight lease and a lease with option on a cost-plus-utility basis, not on the basis of upfront costs alone.

Don't forget the role "barter" can play in stretching your capital. If your company sells furniture, for example, you might provide some desks free to a computer firm willing to give you a break on its PCs or service your existing equipment. Or, if you're in a startup, you might locate your offices in one of the so-called business incubators springing up around the country in order to benefit from reduced rental costs and free secretarial, computer and cleaning services as part of the contract.

Leasebacks

Here's how these work. You need a new plant but want to avoid adding more long-term debt. So, instead, you find a leaseback partner. After you've built the facility using a construction loan, your partner purchases the building and gives you a fixed-rental lease. This agreement in turn becomes part of the security for his financing while you use the sale proceeds to pay off your original construction loan. Your partner ends up with the income from your lease agreement and you have use of the building plus an option to buy back the facility at a previously agreed-on price when the lease ends.

Leasebacks work best with real estate or where there's some other long-term asset to leverage. And there's a real disadvantage if you should decide not to exercise your repurchase option when the lease expires. Unless your partner is willing to negotiate a lease renewal, you lose the use of the facility. This puts the owner in a power position.

However, the arrangement has the advantage of reducing your debt load because the building or other asset is converted into ready cash while you continue to use it. It also switches the debt repayment schedule from a long-term balance sheet liability (such as a construction loan) to an operating expense (rent).

HOW TO RAISE STARTUP CAPITAL

Startup companies have some unique considerations. They often require a combination of short-term, medium-term and long-term capital. Yet it's often difficult to interest lenders or investors in backing an unproven company.

The solution to this problem begins with the business format you choose. A sole proprietorship is the easiest one to establish. You simply file your business papers with the proper authorities. An alternative is to create a partnership by entering into an agreement to share the risks and rewards equally with another backer.

However, lenders are leery of financing either sole proprietorships or partnerships due to the high incidence of failure. On the other hand, they may be willing to consider a small, closely held corporation because the corporate form gives them more legal protection in the event of a failure. The new firm can be set up as a small corporation according to the laws of your state, with a limited number of shares issued to a small number of stockholders. Your attorney will be able to advise you on this matter.

Since startups rarely break even in the first few years, your capital needs should be projected for at least three years. As your business grows, you will need more capital. An approved line of credit will help.

Expect to pay higher interest rates for capital until your company is well-established. The percentage of your own capital required for the business will range from 20%–35% unless you can obtain a loan from a local development corporation.

No matter what kind of financing you're looking for, do your homework before you begin your search. Many good projects remain uncapitalized because of poor organization or slipshod presentations to potential lenders or investors. First, you must believe in your business plan enough to do whatever's necessary to obtain the capital you need. Then you've got to convince your backers that they were right to trust your business judgment. If you can do that, the next time you need financing a few phone calls may do.

CHAPTER SIXTEEN

WHAT YOU NEED TO KNOW ABOUT ACCOUNTING

Accounting and tax rules often seem complicated and mysterious to nonaccountants, yet they play an important role in all aspects of business. For instance, imagine trying to get a loan without financial statements. Or trying to pay your company's taxes without a complete and accurate set of books.

It may be tempting to leave these matters to your accountant. But that is *not* a sound business practice. When it comes to tax and accounting matters, your accountant should present the issues and options—and *you* should be involved in the decision-making. At stake are real dollars and cents. If you don't understand some basic accounting issues and concepts, you will be totally reliant on *someone else's* judgment to make important decisions about *your* business.

You can't make sound, informed decisions about running your business if you don't understand the information presented to you in your financial statements. And you can't read and analyze your financial statements if you don't understand basic accounting and tax principles.

This chapter deals with some tax and accounting basics. It covers such things as tax and accounting principles and methods and how

405

to determine how much profit or loss your business is generating. You'll also get some practical advice on preparing financial statements and internal reports—how to make them clear, concise and easy to understand.

BASIC ACCOUNTING PRINCIPLES

Underlying the complex array of financial accounting rules are just a few basic accounting principles. These are known as "generally accepted accounting principles" (or GAAP). We will discuss some of these below—and how they relate to a business's financial statements—as well as some other fundamental accounting concepts.

UNDERSTANDING THE BALANCE SHEET

You probably have seen a balance sheet and know that its purpose is to show the financial condition of a business at a particular point in time. A balance sheet has three sections: assets, liabilities and owners' equity.

Assets

Assets represent economic resources that the business owns. Assets can be acquired in several ways: as the result of the sales activities of the business, by borrowing, by purchase, or by people or entities investing in the business in return for a share in ownership.

Examples of assets include cash, accounts receivable, machinery and equipment. In general, assets are accounted for on the basis of how much it cost to acquire them—referred to as "historical cost." This is one of the generally accepted accounting principles, known as the *cost principle*. (It also applies to liabilities, equity and expenses.)

However, some items—inventory, marketable securities—may be valued at the lower of historical cost or market value. This follows the accounting principle of *conservatism*—i.e., choose the alternative that has the least favorable impact on your financial statements. Using the lower of historical cost or market value does this by showing a lower value for your assets. For instance, if you paid $10,000 for some securities that are now worth only $9,000, you would write them down on your balance sheet using their lower market value.

Liabilities

Liabilities are the obligations of a business. They represent claims by third parties against the business's assets. For example, you borrow $5,000 from the bank so you can invest in new equipment. You increase your assets—equipment and cash—but you also owe the bank $5,000. This would appear as a note payable on your balance sheet. Another example is your accounts payable—bills you owe for supplies, services, etc., that you haven't paid yet.

Equity

Equity represents business assets remaining after creditors have been paid. It is made up of the following:

- Assets invested in the business by its owners (capital contributions), and

- Net earnings that have not been paid out to the owners as dividends or capital distributions.

Accountants sometimes refer to the "balance sheet equation" to illustrate that if the business were liquidated, all the assets would be allocable to either the owners (equity interests) or creditors (liabilities). In other words: Assets = Liabilities + Owners' Equity. Liabilities plus owners' equity is also known as a business's capital.

Obviously, the more your company's capital is made up of equity, as opposed to debt, the stronger its financial condition. That's because, unlike debt, owners' equity does not have to be repaid (except upon dissolution of the business).

UNDERSTANDING THE INCOME STATEMENT

Another key financial statement is the income statement. In simple terms, this statement shows the income, or revenue, the business has earned and the costs, or expenses, it has incurred over an accounting period. The accounting period generally is one year.

Revenue

Revenue is made up of the assets—generally cash and receivables—that flow into the business as a result of sales. Not all assets coming into the business are revenues. For example, money that's borrowed is not revenue. The key difference is that revenue *increases owners' equity*. When you borrow money, you create a liability; you don't increase the business's equity.

When do you recognize revenues? Suppose you sell ten widgets to a customer, on account, in December 1993, but the customer doesn't pay you until January 1994. Which year is the year of sale? You have revenue in 1993, the year the sale occurs. An accounting rule, known as the *realization concept*, is the determining factor.

For financial accounting purposes, revenue is realized—and therefore may be recognized—when an exchange has taken place and the earnings process is essentially complete. For example, when you go into a store and exchange your money for merchandise, the store has realized income and may recognize it in its accounting records.

There are special rules for recognizing income for certain businesses. These special rules are designed to account for revenue in a way that most clearly reflects income. Examples include the installment method (for sales where payment is not made in full at the time of the initial sale) and the percentage-of-completion method (for long-term construction contracts).

Expenses

Expenses represent costs incurred or assets consumed in order to produce revenues. While revenues increase owners' equity, expenses decrease it.

However, not all asset expenditures constitute expenses. For instance, if you buy a machine, you're really just exchanging one asset (cash) for another (machinery). Or if you lend money to someone, you're simply substituting one asset (cash) for another by creating an account receivable.

Dividends also reduce owners' equity, but they aren't expenses. Why? Because dividends don't help generate revenues. Instead, they're simply a distribution of a portion of a business's capital back to its owners.

The concept that expenses generate revenues leads to another important generally accepted accounting principle—the *matching concept.*

Expenses incurred to generate revenue should be reported *in the same period* in which the revenues are reported. For instance, suppose you sell 20 widgets in 1993, earning $20. In 1992 you paid $10 to purchase the materials to make those widgets. Is that $10 you spent on materials an expense of 1992 or 1993?

Under the matching concept, you would *defer* deducting the $10 from income until 1993—when you would also report the related revenue. Until then, it would be carried on your balance sheet as an asset, in a raw materials inventory account.

Bad debts

Another example is the allowance for bad debts. Suppose you have sales of $50,000 in 1993—all on account. Unless you're extremely lucky, some of those accounts will turn out to be uncollectible. Those bad debts are expenses incurred in generating that $50,000 of revenue—just like labor or raw materials costs. The problem from an accounting standpoint is that you may not know the dollar amount of this bad debt expense until years later.

To follow the matching principle, you must estimate the bad debts likely to occur in later years that are related to this year's revenue. You deduct this amount from the current year's revenues to arrive at net income. This is referred to as the "reserve" method of accounting for bad debts. If you don't use this method, you overstate the current year's income.

There are various methods you can use to estimate. Some common ones are: aging your receivables; using your business's history of uncollectibles in prior years; referring to industry averages; or a combination of methods. Your accountant can help you decide on a reasonable approach in your particular case. (Note: Since 1987, most businesses may not use the reserve method of accounting for bad debts on their tax returns. You must charge off specific debts as they become worthless.)

Profitability and liquidity

A business that is showing a comfortable profit on its income statement may still have trouble paying its bills. How is this possible? There's a significant difference between *profitability* and *liquidity*. Profitability simply refers to the size of your business's income, measured according to certain accounting rules or formulas. Liquidity is often considered a more meaningful concept in terms of the day-to-day operations of a business. It measures the amount of cash or assets readily convertible to cash you have on hand to pay your bills or reinvest in your business. For example, suppose you have 1993 sales of $50,000 and expenses of $10,000, for a profit of $40,000. You should be in good shape, right? Not necessarily.

Here's the potential pitfall: Suppose half your sales are cash and half are on account. You take the cash portion and buy new equipment so you can expand your promising new business. Now it comes time to pay your bills. But—you have no cash! Your assets are tied up in plant and equipment or in receivables that either aren't yet due or aren't being paid on time. Your creditors are demanding payment or they will stop supplying you. You may be profitable, but you have no cash.

Keep enough of your assets in liquid form—cash, readily marketable securities, or short-term receivables (for example, 10 days)—to meet at least your near-term obligations plus provide a cushion for unexpected expenses.

TAX VS. FINANCIAL ACCOUNTING

The "net income" figure you see on the income statement your accountant prepares to show you how your business is doing may not be the same amount you see on your tax return for that same year. Why? Financial accounting rules—the generally accepted accounting principles we've been discussing—are different from the rules set out in the tax laws.

The many differences between tax and financial accounting can be boiled down to two basic differences: timing and amount.

For instance, an expense may be deducted in one year on your tax return, but must be recorded in another year—in whole or in part—on your financial statements. Some examples are product warranty expenses and bad debts. Or, some financial accounting income may never be taxable, such as interest income from most municipal bonds.

These differences can be either:

- Permanent, meaning they will never "turn around" (i.e., reverse) or

- Temporary, or timing differences, meaning they will turn around in one or more future periods and the net result on income over the long term will wash out to zero.

An example of a permanent difference is the premiums paid on officers' life insurance, if the corporation is a beneficiary. These premiums are deductible on your financial accounting income statement in the year paid or owed, but are never deductible on your tax return.

A common example of a temporary or timing difference has to do with depreciation. Sometimes a company will use straight-line depreciation for financial accounting purposes while using an accelerated method when preparing its tax return. This is done to maximize net income reported on the financial statements (smaller depreciation expense) and lower the tax bill (higher depreciation expense) up front.

For example, suppose you buy a computer for $7,000 that you expect to last for 15 years. You depreciate it using straight-line depreciation on your books. For tax purposes, though, you use cost recovery that allows you to write off 20% of its cost in the first year using an accelerated method. Income is $10,000 and all other expenses are $5,000. Here are your results:

	Financial Accounting	Tax Accounting
Income	$10,000	$10,000
Expenses	5,000	5,000
Depreciation (6.7% for accounting, 20% for tax)	469	1,400
Taxable income	4,531	3,600
Tax rate	× 15%	× 15%
Tax	$ 680	$ 540

You save $140 in taxes by taking advantage of the accelerated depreciation method. Meanwhile, the profit on your financial statements is $791 higher ($931 difference in depreciation offset by the $140 higher tax).

However, this is only a timing difference. By the end of 15 years, the same *total* amount of depreciation will have been taken for both tax and book—$7,000. Also, when you dispose of the asset you may have to "recapture" (i.e., pay back to the IRS) some of the tax savings you realized by using accelerated depreciation. However, you may end up ahead by taking larger deductions in earlier years due to the time value of money.

The difference between the "book" tax expense (that is, the tax on financial accounting income) and the amount you actually pay to the IRS will be carried on your balance sheet in a special account. This account is known as a "deferred tax" account. In many cases, this account will be a liability account. This just means that you took larger deductions (or recognized less income) on your tax return than on your books. You're acknowledging that someday you will have to "make up" this difference—pay taxes on it when the timing differences turn around.

SELECTING AN ACCOUNTING METHOD

There are two main accounting methods:

- The "cash" basis: With this method, you generally recognize income in the year it is received, and recognize as expenses any deductible disbursements made during the year.

- The "accrual" basis: Here, you recognize income as it is earned—which may not be the same as when it is received. And you deduct expenses as the liabilities are incurred—whether or not funds are actually paid out in that year. Income is accruable when events that fix the right to receive it have occurred and the amount of income can be reasonably estimated. (If an estimate is reasonable and the exact amount turns out to be different, an adjustment can be made—even if it's in a later year.)

There are other methods of accounting that are tailored to the special needs of certain types of businesses such as: the installment method, the long-term contract method, and the crop-basis method. Your accountant should be able to advise you on the method best suited to the particular needs of your business.

Use of the cash basis is not in accordance with generally accepted accounting principles. So, if you need to have your financial statements certified, you must keep your books on the accrual basis. Here are several points to keep in mind about the cash basis:

Suppose that on December 30, 1993, a customer, Mr. Heath, orders six caseloads of your product. You arrange to have Joe, one of your employees, deliver the merchandise that day. Before sending him out, you call Mr. Heath to tell him the exact cost of the goods, including delivery charge.

Mr. Heath is willing to give Joe a check when he arrives. However, Joe tends to be a little careless with money, so you ask Mr. Heath to mail you the check. The check arrives January 4, 1994. Assume you keep your books on a cash basis: In which year should you recognize the income?

Under the rule of *constructive receipt*, you would have to recognize this income in 1993. You can't shift income to another year simply by deciding not to accept a payment that has been offered to you.

> **IMPORTANT:** If income has been properly offered to you, or is for all intents and purposes truly within your control, it is income to you *even if* you're on a cash basis of accounting *and* you have not actually received the income yet.

Even if you keep your books on a cash basis, there still may be certain items that must be accounted for on the accrual basis. Two common examples are inventories and fixed assets (i.e., plant, property and equipment). Your accountant should be aware of the applicable rules for both tax and financial accounting purposes.

The method of accounting you use should be the one that most clearly reflects the income of your business, both for tax and accounting purposes.

Since 1986, most corporations have been required to use the accrual method for tax purposes. The cash basis generally is limited to corporations that elect to be taxed as partnerships (so-called S corporations), sole proprietorships, corporations and partnerships with gross receipts of $5 million or less, and personal service corporations (e.g., a doctor's professional corporation).

Not all personal service corporations can use the cash basis. However, if your business is a personal service corporation involved in the fields of health, law, accounting, performing arts or a similar field, check with your accountant to see if you qualify and if it would be beneficial to you.

If the method you use to keep your books gives a fair picture of your income, generally you must use the same method to prepare your tax return. If you have no consistent method of keeping your books or if the method does not fairly show your income, the IRS will compute your taxable income for you. One more point: The IRS will allow you to use a combination of accounting methods under certain circumstances, provided your methods clearly reflect income and are used consistently. And if you run several distinct businesses and keep separate books and records for each, you can use a different accounting method for each business.

CHANGING YOUR ACCOUNTING METHOD

There may be circumstances under which it would be advantageous to change your accounting method, either overall, or for a particular item or type of item. For example, you may find that it's easier to keep records under one method than under another. Or the nature of your business or the environment in which you operate may change, so that a switch in accounting method would yield a truer picture of how your business is doing.

A change in accounting method is either:

- A change in the overall method of keeping your books (for example, from cash basis to accrual basis); or

- A change in the way you account for a material item (for example, how you value inventories or how you account for bad debts).

Certain kinds of accounting changes are not considered to be changes in *accounting method*. For example, correcting mathematical errors, adjustments that don't affect the *timing* of income or expenses, changes in estimates (for example, adjustments to the useful life of fixed assets), and adjustments related to a change in fact.

For instance, assume that for the past three years you've been depreciating an asset over a 10-year period. You now decide that 15 years is more realistic. Or perhaps you discover that last year no depreciation was taken on office furniture, and that you deducted an amount for supplies that was really an interest expense. In cases such as these, you can just make the changes or corrections—they aren't changes in accounting method and don't require any special treatment.

How to handle a change in tax accounting methods

For tax purposes, you'll generally need to obtain IRS consent for a change in accounting method. To get this consent, you file Form 3115. Depending on the kind of change, there are different rules regarding when to file and other specifics. Generally, the form is due within 180 days after the year of change begins. But you can get up to nine months in which to file if you can show good cause for delay.

You can generally count on IRS consent for most accounting changes if you agree to make any resulting adjustments over an appropriate period not exceeding 10 years (usually six tax years). Attach a copy of the Form 3115 you sent to the IRS to your tax return when you file it. It's also a good idea to send it registered mail so you'll have proof that the IRS received it.

Making adjustments

When you change your accounting method, you will need to make a "catch up" adjustment to avoid duplicating or omitting items of income or expense.

Generally, you must make these adjustments over more than one tax year. Tax rules stipulate different adjustment periods for different types of changes.

> **IMPORTANT:** Don't assume that a change in accounting method for tax purposes is also considered one for accounting purposes (although more likely than not the two will be in agreement). Also, in some cases you may be allowed—or required—to change your method of accounting for tax purposes but not for financial accounting purposes.

Accounting treatment for a change in method

First of all, accounting rules stipulate that such a change must be to a "preferable" accounting method—one that improves financial reporting. In most cases, you must compute the cumulative effect of the change and take it into income, in full, *in the year of change.* However, the adjustment is shown separately—after income from operations—to highlight the fact that it's a nonrecurring accounting phenomenon rather than the result of the normal operations of the business.

Say, for instance, you've been depreciating a machine using double declining balance (DDB) and you decide to change to straight line. The machine is three years old. Depreciation to date for the three-year period under DDB is $20,000 more than it would have been had you used straight line. The $20,000 cumulative effect is shown on your current income statement as an "adjustment due to change in accounting principle."

Restating prior results

You need to be able to compare your current year's financial statements to prior years to help you understand trends, improvements, problems, etc. But if this year's statements are prepared using different accounting methods than in prior years, how can you make any valid or meaningful comparisons?

Consistency counts. In order to compare one statement to another, they have to have been prepared using accounting methods that were applied on a *consistent basis.* This, in fact, is another generally accepted accounting principle.

When you change accounting methods, you may be *required* to restate your prior years' financial statements according to the financial accounting rules you are using currently. In other cases, you may want to restate your internal financial statements to make them more useful to you.

When is restatement required? The accounting rules specifically list the types of changes for which restatement is required:

- Change from LIFO to another inventory method;
- Change in the method of accounting for long-term construction-type contracts;
- Change in the method of accounting for development costs in the extractive industries (e.g., recovery of natural resources such as coal mining or oil drilling);

- Change in reporting entity (for example, change in members of a consolidated group); or

- Change from one acceptable accounting method to another for closely-held companies issuing financial statements to the public for the first time.

CHOOSING AN ACCOUNTING PERIOD

When financial statements or tax returns are prepared, the information presented covers a particular time period, generally one year. Your annual accounting period may be either a calendar year (ends on December 31) or a fiscal year (ends on the last day of any month other than December or is a 52/53-week accounting period). Generally an accounting period may not cover more than a full 12-month period.

Your natural inclination might be to assume that it would be most convenient to keep your books on a calendar-year basis. Upon further consideration, however, you might realize that some other accounting period might be a better choice.

Suppose, for instance, that you own a children's shoe store. You do the most business, by far, in August and early September—when parents buy their children new shoes for school—and around holidays. Things are generally pretty slow in June and July.

For this business it might be more convenient to have a June 30 or July 31 close to your accounting year—a time when you're not as busy running your business. This would be referred to as following your "natural business year."

You don't need permission from the IRS to file a *newly formed* C corporation's return on a fiscal-year basis. Just be sure to keep your books on that basis before the close of the first fiscal year.

For other types of business entities, however, there are some constraints in the tax rules (also, see Chapter 14 for more information on various business forms).

- *Sole proprietors* may not use different tax years for different sources of income. So, if you are a sole proprietor and file your individual return on a calendar-year basis, the business may not be operated (for tax purposes anyway) on a fiscal-year basis.

- *Partnerships, S corporations* (i.e., corporations that are taxed like partnerships) and *personal service corporations* must conform their tax years to those of their owners. You can get an exception, however, if: (1) you can convince the IRS that there's a good business purpose for adopting a different tax year for the business; (2) the resulting deferral is three months or less; and (3) the entity makes certain required payments (in the case of partnerships and S corporations) or minimum distributions (PSC's) to employee-owners. Personal service corporations and partnerships whose partners don't have the same tax years generally have to adopt a calendar year.

Some businesses adopt a fiscal year that may vary from 52 to 53 weeks. If you keep your books on the basis of this type of fiscal year, your accounting period always ends on the *same day of the week* that occurs either: (1) for the last time in that month (for example, the last Wednesday in June), or (2) nearest to the end of the calendar month. This is a common practice in some industries. For example, retail businesses often use a 52/53-week fiscal year.

The IRS makes it easy to adopt a 52/53-week year for tax return purposes. Just attach an election statement to the return for the year in which you're making the switch. Show the day of the week and the calendar month you're choosing as well as which of the two approaches mentioned above you're using.

CHANGING YOUR ACCOUNTING PERIOD

What if, after operating your business for several years, you decide that it would be more convenient to have a different accounting year? For instance, suppose that when you began your business—let's say you sell snow plows—you picked a December 31 year end. A few years later, however, you realize that you are very busy during the winter and don't want to be bothered with accounting paperwork. You would prefer a June 30 year end—a time when business is very slow for you.

As you've probably guessed, there are specific procedures to follow to make the change:

For a corporation: You may be able to change your accounting period just by attaching a statement to your tax return because, in certain cases, prior IRS approval is not required. This is the case if:

- You haven't changed your accounting period in the last 10 calendar years,

- You are not creating a short period (see following) with a net operating loss, and

- Short-period annualized taxable income is at least 80% of the preceding year's taxable income.

The statement you attach to your return should show that you meet these necessary conditions.

If you do not meet these conditions, you need to file Form 1128. This form should be filed on or before the 15th day of the second calendar month following the end of the short tax year.

Usually, the change will be approved if there's a substantial reason for it (such as, in our example, to follow the natural business year). It will generally *not* be approved if it will substantially lower your tax liability by shifting income or deductions to another year or to another taxpayer. For instance, suppose you change your tax year from a fiscal year to a calendar year. As a result, a great deal of income gets shifted to a later year with the income becoming subject to lower tax rates. The IRS would most likely disapprove this change. The IRS also frowns on changes that create a short tax year with a substantial net operating loss.

Short period returns

When you change your accounting period, you will end up with one period that covers less than 12 months. This is referred to as a "short period." A short period may also result when you start or end a business entity. When you file the return for a short-period tax year, you have to annualize income and deductions. However, if you are filing a short-period return because it's your business's first or final return, you would not annualize or prorate income, deductions, tax credits, and so on.

Special rules apply to changes in accounting periods involving 52/53-week years, partners and partnerships and some other organizations. Your accountant should know how to deal with these.

DETERMINING BUSINESS INCOME

To prepare the end-of-period returns and financial statements, you need a systematic method of keeping a record of your business transactions. This must be an ongoing activity. You must keep track of every transaction that occurs every day. You have to set up an accounting system—the "books and records" of the business. This system generally involves a three-step process: record, classify and summarize.

• **Record:** Based upon various documents (receipts, invoices, etc.), each business transaction is recorded in journals. Journals are sometimes called the books of original entry. A business can have a general journal and also specialized ones for transactions of a similar type (for example, sales, payroll, cash receipts, cash disbursements, etc.).

• **Classify:** The journal entries are "posted" to the *general ledger* on a regular basis—monthly, weekly or daily depending on the volume of transactions. The ledger is essentially just a listing and summary of all of the system's accounts.

• **Summarize:** At regular intervals, financial statements are prepared using the amounts accumulated in the general ledger accounts (after adjustments for accruals, corrections, etc.). If they are final—rather than interim—statements, the ledger is "closed out" and a new set of books is begun for the next accounting period.

To prepare your end-of-period financial statements and tax returns, your underlying accounting records have to be complete and accurate. If they are not and the IRS believes that you have underreported taxable income, it has the authority to recompute it using whatever method the agency deems appropriate.

When preparing financial statements, there are two generally accepted accounting principles that are particularly relevant—full disclosure and objectivity.

• **Full disclosure:** Financial statements should completely disclose, in an understandable manner, all significant financial information of the business. This should be accomplished by footnotes, explanations, etc., if the basic financial statements themselves are not sufficient.

• **Objectivity:** The information presented should be unbiased and, when possible, verifiable by independent third parties.

HOW TO DETERMINE NET PROFIT

Generally, to figure net profit of your business, compute the gross profit and then deduct business operating expenses. Gross profit equals: (1) Receipts (net of returns and allowances) (2) less the cost of goods sold (3) plus miscellaneous income. The cost of goods sold equals opening inventory plus materials and supplies purchased during the year and other related costs (such as labor, freight, and overhead), less closing inventory.

For example, Wonder Widget Co. shows receipts of $30,000 ($31,500 gross sales less $1,500 returns and allowances); inventory of goods at beginning of the year—$3,700; inventory of goods at the end of the year—$3,000; cost of merchandise bought during the year for sale—$15,000. Costs incurred during the year in the purchase and production of goods for sale include: labor—$7,500; materials and supplies—$600; other costs—$200. Wonder Widget's gross profit is $6,000, computed as follows:

Net sales (total receipts of $31,500 less returns and allowances of $1,500)		$30,000
Cost of goods sold—		
Beginning inventory	$ 3,700	
Plus: Purchases	15,000	
Labor	7,500	
Materials and supplies	600	
Other	200	
Cost of goods available for sale	$27,000	
Less: Ending inventory	3,000	
Cost of goods sold (total)		24,000
Gross profit		$ 6,000

Net profit or loss is gross profit less operating expenses not included in cost of goods sold. Say, for example, that Wonder Widget incurred the following "other expenses" during the year:

Salaries (not included in cost of goods)	$1,200
Interest on business debt	150
Taxes on business and business property	150
Bad debts arising from sales	200
Depreciation, obsolescence, and depletion	250
Rent, repairs, and other expenses	750
Total	$2,700

Gross profit (from above)	$6,000
Total of "other business deductions"	–2,700
Net profit (or loss)	$3,300

While it's clearly better to show a profit, you can also derive some "benefit" from a net operating loss (NOL). Such losses can be "carried" back or forward to eliminate or reduce taxable income in other years. This results in tax refunds (in the case of carrybacks) or reductions (in the case of carryforwards). Most corporations can carry losses back three years and forward 15 years.

- To *carry back* a NOL, file an amended return for the year(s) to which the NOL is being applied. File Form 1139 (for a corporation) for a "quickie" refund. This form must be filed after the return for the NOL year, but no later than one year from the NOL year end. Otherwise, you can carry back the loss by filing an amended return for the affected prior year(s).

- To *carry forward* a NOL, you enter it on the appropriate line of Form 1120 (or other appropriate return, depending on your business's form).

> **IMPORTANT:** Eliminating or reducing taxable income by carrying losses forward or back may also eliminate tax liability against which you could claim *tax credits*. And if you don't generate sufficient taxable income to use those credits in subsequent or prior years, they will expire unused. Some common tax credits include the foreign tax credit, investment tax credit, the research and development credit, and the targeted jobs tax credit. While most tax credits were repealed by the 1986 Tax Reform Act, unused credits from prior years may still be carried forward or back.

ACCOUNTING FOR INVENTORY

When you think of inventory, you usually think of the supply of finished goods that a business has on hand for sale to customers. And you would be correct—a business's stock of merchandise is its inventory. However, when we talk about inventory in terms of determining a business's gross profit, we sometimes have to think in broader terms.

The narrower concept of inventory is generally appropriate in the case of merchandisers, such as a retail merchant. A merchandiser buys a finished product from a supplier and essentially sells it to customers as is. In this case, determining inventory costs is a relatively simple procedure—basically it's the invoice price, less any discounts plus freight paid to obtain the goods.

A manufacturer, on the other hand, creates products for sale from supplies and raw materials. Materials may relate to several different products on hand in various stages of production: not yet begun (raw materials), partially completed (known as work in progress) and completed in full (finished goods).

The manufacturer has employees who work solely on production, partially or indirectly on production or not at all on production. It has overhead costs for operating the building where both production and nonproduction activities take place.

Cost accounting

How can the manufacturer ever hope to arrive at a fair and reasonable estimate of what it costs to make a unit of each product, and then determine how much of those costs should be inventoried or expensed?

The process by which production costs—direct and indirect—are allocated to units produced is known as "cost accounting." Cost accounting allows you to determine the proper values for inventory and cost of goods sold.

Inventory consists of all materials, labor and other costs involved in the production of goods for sale to customers—regardless of where they are in the production process. Since these costs relate to units that will be sold, they're considered assets. When the units are sold—which may not occur in the current accounting period—the related "inventoried costs" can be deducted as cost of goods sold (the matching principle at work again). On the other hand, production costs that don't have to be inventoried are generally deducted when incurred. Thus, you can see why the issue of which costs can and cannot be included in inventory is so crucial.

For example, take the salary of someone who earns $25,000 a year. If that person works in the accounting department, his or her salary is probably deductible in full as an operating expense. But, if that same $25,000 is paid to someone who works on the production line, part of it is likely to be allocated to inventory (finished or unfinished) that's still on hand at the end of the year. Result: That portion of the salary cannot be deducted until a subsequent year.

Here's just a small sample of the types of costs that may or may not be inventorial, depending on individual facts and circumstances:

- Depreciation and depletion,
- Data processing costs,
- Various salaries,
- Utilities, and
- Professional fees.

For tax purposes, you would generally want to inventory as few costs as possible to lower your taxable income. For accounting purposes, on the other hand, you'd want to inventory as many costs as possible to maximize net income.

Tax rules aim to make sure that businesses don't improperly deduct costs that should be inventoried. Accounting rules aim to ensure that financial statements don't show costs as part of inventory when they should be deducted currently.

A special set of rules—known as the uniform capitalization rules, or UNICAP—determines which costs must be inventoried for tax purposes. These rules apply to retailers, wholesalers and manufacturers and can differ dramatically from the financial accounting inventory rules. For instance, certain indirect costs may have to be inventoried for tax purposes that are currently deductible for financial accounting. Examples: depreciation, repairs and maintenance, data processing costs, various salaries, costs of purchasing, storage, handling, processing, assembly and repackaging, administrative costs, and interest. You may need to keep two separate sets of inventory records—one for financial accounting and one for tax purposes.

The accrual method

If your business uses inventory, you must use the accrual method to account for purchases and sales. This is true for both tax and accounting purposes.

If you are organizing a new business and are adopting an accounting method, consider using an accrual method even though inventories are not required at the start. In the event that later developments make inventories necessary, there will be no need to apply for permission to change accounting methods.

Goods are included in inventory if you answer "yes" to the following two questions:

1. Do you have title to the goods or materials?
2. What is the intended use? Were the items acquired either for resale or to physically become a part of merchandise intended for resale?

For example, goods out on consignment are part of the consignor's inventory since he still has title. Wood purchased to make benches that you hope to sell to customers is part of your inventory; if the benches will be used in an employee lounge, the wood is not included in your inventory.

Valuing inventories

Assigning a dollar value to your inventory involves two steps: identification and valuation. Keep in mind that the method you use to value your inventory should follow the best accounting practice in the industry and should fairly state your income.

• *Identifying inventory:* The methods most commonly used to identify inventory are FIFO (first in, first out) and LIFO (last in, first out). There are other, less commonly used methods as well, such as the specific identification method.

FIFO assumes that you sell your inventory in the same order in which you acquire or manufacture it. LIFO, on the other hand, assumes that you sell your most recently acquired or produced goods first.

Which method is more appropriate? Proponents of FIFO say that it gives a more realistic picture of the physical flow of a business's inventory. LIFO, they argue, is distorting because it assumes your inventory is always composed of your oldest goods. Proponents of LIFO, on the other hand, claim that LIFO gives a truer picture of your net income by matching your most recent costs against your current revenues.

For example, suppose that during your first year in business you buy the following items for resale to customers: 100 cases of gadgets at $10 per case in January, 100 cases at $12 per case in May, and 100 cases at $14 per case in September. On December 31 you have 50 cases left unsold. What's the value of that inventory and what's your cost of goods sold for the year?

Using FIFO, you would assume that your ending inventory is composed of the most recently purchased items. Thus, you'd value your 50 cases left at $14 each, for a total of $700. The cost of goods sold would be $2,900, computed as follows:

100 cases at $10 each	=	$1,000
100 cases at $12 each	=	1,200
50 cases at $14 each	=	700
250 cases sold		$2,900

Now let's see how these figures change if we use the LIFO assumption. In that case, ending inventory would be presumed to come from the oldest goods. Thus it would be valued at $10 a case, for a total of $500—$200 less than under the FIFO method. So the asset side of your balance sheet would show a lower value with LIFO. The cost of goods sold, on the other hand, would be:

100 cases at $14 each	=	$1,400
100 cases at $12 each	=	1,200
50 cases at $10 each	=	500
250 cases sold		$3,100

The $3,100 cost of goods sold under the LIFO method is $200 *more* than what was computed under the FIFO method. So you would show $200 less of profit on your income statement with LIFO—a benefit for tax purposes, but not when applying for a loan.

IMPORTANT: Using the LIFO method may be desirable from a tax standpoint in a period of *rising prices*. It produces a smaller income than the FIFO method by deducting from income the higher priced items you most recently put into inventory. Conversely, in a period of *declining prices*, LIFO will produce a lower cost of goods sold by expensing the most recent (lower) costs against revenues. As a result, you have a higher taxable income than under FIFO.

A new business may generally adopt either FIFO or LIFO. The IRS may allow you to use different valuation methods for different segments of your inventory, such as LIFO for raw materials and FIFO for work in progress and finished goods. Switching from one method to another for tax purposes requires IRS consent. Also, the IRS requires conformity—you must use LIFO for accounting purposes if you use it for tax purposes.

• *Physical inventories:* Inventory may be verified by actually taking a "physical" inventory as of the balance sheet date. This is required for financial accounting purposes if your financial statements are being audited. It's also required by the tax regulations.

• *Valuing inventories:* After identifying the inventory, you must select a method by which to value it. Two common methods are: (1) cost and (2) the lower-of-cost-or-market value.

To determine "market" value for purposes of making the lower-of-cost-or-market comparison, you generally use the current replacement cost on the date of inventory as if the inventory was purchased from your usual suppliers in the usual amounts. This is generally done for each item of inventory, rather than for total inventory as a whole.

Once you apply the lower-of-cost-or-market method to "write down" (reduce the value of) your inventory, the written down value becomes "cost" for purposes of future lower-of-cost-or-market calculations. Thus, once inventory has been written down to market, you generally may not write it back up to its original cost basis later—even if its market value rises again.

> **IMPORTANT:** The lower-of-cost-or-market method is considered a conservative accounting method from a financial accounting standpoint. It is not necessarily so for income tax purposes. Any reduction in income for the year in which inventory is reduced to market is offset by a comparable decrease in the cost of goods sold in the next year. Before adopting this method, you should consider the risk of falling into a higher tax bracket in a subsequent year. This might increase your total tax over a two-year period.

• *Unsalable or damaged goods:* Goods that can't be sold at normal prices or that are unusable in the normal way because of damage, imperfections, shop wear, changes of style, odd or broken lots, or other similar causes—including second-hand goods taken in exchange—should be valued at "bona fide selling prices" less direct costs of disposition. This rule applies whether the inventory is taken at cost or at cost or market. "Bona fide selling price" is the actual offering price of the goods during a period ending not later than 30 days after the inventory date.

• *Valuing inventory under LIFO:* If you use the LIFO method, you must value your inventory at *cost* for tax purposes. This is not so for financial accounting.

If you switch to LIFO, you have to restate your opening inventory at cost if it was previously written down to market or because of damaged goods or other factors. The income this creates can be spread out over three years (the election year and the two subsequent years).

HOW TO PREPARE BETTER FINANCIAL STATEMENTS

Financial statements are generally prepared for one of two potential sets of users. They may be prepared for *external* use—shareholders, creditors, or regulatory agencies—or for *internal* use—by management. The same basic statement may be prepared differently as to format or detail depending upon whether it's intended for an internal or external audience. (Chapter 17 discusses reading and analyzing financial statements in greater detail.)

You will probably want your internal financial reports to provide much more detail than you need to disclose in your external financial reports. You may also find that having financial reports tailored to the needs of the user can make the reports easier to understand and better serve the decision-making process for which the reports have been prepared. So, don't let poorly designed financial reports hide information that could help you manage your business.

Frequency is important. Having clear, informative financial reports is not necessarily enough. If they aren't prepared frequently enough, you may not be receiving important information on a timely basis. Suppose expenses are escalating in one area. If your statements are prepared every six months, these expenses may be way out of hand before you are even aware that you need to take some action.

PREPARING THE INCOME STATEMENT

Figure 16.1 illustrates the basic form of the income (or profit and loss) statement.

COMPANY NAME
INCOME STATEMENT

For: (specify period)

Net Sales		$_____
Less Cost of Goods Sold		_____
Gross Profit		_____
Less Operating Expenses:		
Rent	_____	
Salaries and wages	_____	
Payroll taxes	_____	
Utilities and telephone	_____	
Office supplies	_____	
Advertising	_____	
Printing	_____	
Postage	_____	
Repairs	_____	
Legal and professional services	_____	
Insurance	_____	
Interest expense	_____	
Depreciation	_____	
Dues and publications	_____	
Bank charges	_____	
Miscellaneous	_____	
Total Operating Expenses		_____
Operating Profit		_____
Other Income:		
	_____	
	_____	
Total Other Income		_____
Total Income Before Taxes		_____
Less Provision for Taxes		_____
Net Income From Operations		_____

Figure 16.1

Other items may sometimes appear after the net income line. There may be a line called *extraordinary items*. This line is used for unusual items specifically mentioned in the accounting literature as requiring special treatment (e.g., tax benefits related to a net operating loss that's carried forward from a prior year). The intent is to alert the reader to the fact that these items are not the results of normal, recurring operations.

To provide more useful data, your internal income statements might include comparisons of the operations of the current month and the year-to-date with the same periods in the prior year. They also might include budgeted projections. If you have reliable cost standards, it may even be useful to consider statements comparing actual results to the standards.

Show the percent to net sales of all items, also on a comparative basis, to provide more information than is available from dollar amounts alone. For all statements prepared on a comparative basis, you should try to include explanations of major variances, usually in a footnote or supplementary schedule. Also, if a major change in a particular item was expected but did not occur, an explanation of the reason would be in order.

Use supplementary schedules to provide greater detail for any line item—for example, selling expense—that is either large in amount or significant in any other way to your operation. This allows you to study important items in greater detail without cluttering up the basic income statement.

As your company grows, you can expand your statement by providing separate reports for each product line and tying them into the overall income statement. You can do the same for operating divisions.

It may also be useful to prepare an analysis of some important phase of operations. Such reports often point up trends, opportunities for growth or expansion, or weaknesses of which you were not aware. Again, the point is to provide more useful information to help you to better manage your business.

PREPARING THE BALANCE SHEET

The standard balance sheet that's prepared for external reports is divided into two sides. On the left side (or the top) it lists assets. Current assets (such as cash, receivables, inventory and marketable securities) are listed first, followed by assets such as plant, property and equipment, and goodwill.

The other side of the balance sheet lists liabilities and owners' equity. Current liabilities (for example, accounts payable) are followed by long-term liabilities (such as long-term notes payable). The equity section shows the owners' capital investment (for example, common stock for a corporation) and any retained earnings.

"Current" means maturing or turning over within one operating cycle, generally one year. "Long-term" means having a longer maturity—for example, debt that will be outstanding for five years.

For internal reporting purposes, a report form such as the sample shown in Figure 16.2 may be more useful.

Balance Sheet
December 31, 19—

Current assets	$249,000
Less current liabilities	123,500
Working capital	$125,500
Fixed assets	300,000
	$425,500
Less long-term debt	120,000
Stockholders' equity	$305,500
Stockholders' equity:	
Common stock	204,500
Retained earnings	101,000
Stockholders' equity	$305,500

Figure 16.2

How to make the balance sheet more useful

Show comparative data on balance sheets. This may include comparisons with the previous month and/or with the previous year-end. Use an increase and decrease column, showing variances as either percentages or dollar amounts, to highlight significant or material changes. Explanations of variances should be provided by the preparer of the balance sheet (usually in a footnote).

Another way to make your internal balance sheet more informative is to provide more detail of selected accounts than is provided in your external financial statements. For example, you would probably want more detail for accounts that are large in dollar value, significant to your business by their nature (such as inventory for a merchandiser) or much larger or smaller than expected or than in previous periods. This detail should generally be provided in supplementary schedules rather than in the body of the balance sheet.

PREPARING THE STATEMENT OF CHANGES IN RETAINED EARNINGS

This statement analyzes changes in retained earnings (net income or loss, dividends, and so on) between two balance sheet dates. Your external financial reports should include this information.

Sometimes this information is presented as part of a statement showing changes in all the capital accounts. This statement, called "Statement of Stockholders' Equity," is particularly useful when there has been a significant change in capital, such as the issuance of more common stock or the purchase of treasury stock by the company (company buys back outstanding shares of its own stock).

PREPARING THE STATEMENT OF SOURCE AND APPLICATION OF FUNDS

Earlier in this chapter we discussed the difference between profitability and liquidity. We explained how a business might have net income yet still be unable to pay its bills. The statement of source and application of funds—also known as the *funds-flow statement*—provides information regarding cash and/or other net current assets. Because of the value of such information, the funds-flow statement is appearing more and more frequently in annual reports. Management, shareholders, creditors and lenders can use the data to make evaluations of the business's ability to retire debt, maintain dividends, finance expansion or any other activity for which cash is a requirement.

The funds-flow statement shows the inflow and outflow of cash or working capital over a particular period of time. "Working capital" is simply current assets less current liabilities. The statement is intended to be a measure of cash and assets easily convertible into cash that you would have on hand if you had to pay off all your short-term obligations—in other words, net readily available financial resources.

Objectives of a funds-flow statement

A properly prepared funds-flow statement provides answers to such questions as the following:

- Why is working capital down and net income up?
- How could the net current assets increase despite the net loss for the period?
- How were the net earnings absorbed?

- How were the additions to plant and equipment financed?
- How was the retirement of debt financed?
- How were the proceeds of a capital stock issue used?
- If the cash flow exceeded the cost of new plant facilities, why was expansion financed with borrowed money?
- How was the increase in capital financed?

When extending credit to customers, you may find it useful to look at their funds-flow statements. The reason is that some of them may be stretching their capital pretty thin. They may be expanding too rapidly into new product lines, or adding too many fixed assets.

Others, in their eagerness to do as much business as they can, may become imprudent in extending credit to *their* customers. What you want to know is whether an account can be depended upon to generate enough money from its own operations to pay back what it owes you.

HOW TO COMPUTE AND REPORT EARNINGS PER SHARE

Most companies report earnings on a per-share basis, commonly referred to as "EPS." In fact, if your statements are audited, your accountant will require you to present this information in your financial statements. Here's how EPS is determined:

- **Simplest case:** When only common stock is outstanding and the company has no convertible debt, the earnings per share calculation is easy: Divide net income by the number of shares outstanding. (This assumes the same number of shares has been outstanding all year.)

For example, if your after-tax income is $2 million and there are 4 million common shares outstanding, earnings are 50¢ per share.

If there is a material, nonrecurring item—say the gain on the sale of a building—this should be shown as a separate per share amount.

- **When you have a complex capital structure:** Companies sometimes issue instruments that are not common stock but may be converted into stock. If your company has issued convertible debt or other instruments with the potential to "dilute" earnings per common share, you must present two per-share amounts: primary EPS and fully diluted EPS.

Primary earnings per share is based on common shares outstanding plus common stock equivalents. A common stock equivalent is a security that's convertible into common stock and whose cash yield when issued is less than two-thirds of the prevailing prime rate. Essentially, these are the convertible securities that are most likely to be converted into common stock.

Fully diluted earnings per share is based on common shares outstanding, common stock equivalents and all other convertible securities. It shows the maximum potential dilution of EPS if *all* securities with conversion features were exercised. In essence, it shows the maximum potential downside risk to the per share value of the shares held by your current common stockholders.

• **When preferred stock is outstanding:** In the ordinary case, preferred stock dividends are first deducted from after-tax net income. The remaining net income is divided by the common shares outstanding to obtain the earnings per share. In this case, the formula for determining earnings per share of common stock is to subtract preferred stock dividends from net income and then follow the procedures explained above.

It's done this way because dividends on preferred stock are not discretionary; dividends on common stock are. The corporation has an obligation to distribute these funds to the preferred shareholders. Common shareholders do not participate in this portion of earnings, so it would be misleading to include them as earnings per common share.

Where the preferred stock is cumulative, and dividends are in arrears, the same formula is used. The amount required to meet the current and accumulated unpaid preferred dividends is subtracted from net income to calculate the amount available for distribution to holders of common stock.

• **Change in outstanding shares:** In computing earnings per share, you should use the number of common shares outstanding at the end of the year unless a significant change has occurred (new shares issued or shares retired). To take such a change into account, the computation should be based on a weighted average.

For example, ABC Company has sold a new issue of 1 million shares on July 1. Previously, 3 million shares were outstanding. Earnings for the year were $950,000. Here's how EPS would be computed:

3 million shares outstanding 12 months	36 million
1 million shares outstanding 6 months	6 million
Total	42 million

42 million shares ÷ 12 months = 3.5 million. This is the weighted average number of shares. $950,000 ÷ 3,500,000 shares = 27¢ earnings per share.

• **Stock split or dividend:** If the change in shares outstanding is due to a stock dividend or stock split, the computation should be based on the number of shares at the end of the year and per-share earnings for prior years should be restated in terms that allow a fair comparison to be made. In cases like this, you can avoid misinterpretations by explaining the basis for the computation.

HOW TO REPORT CONTINGENT LIABILITIES

Suppose your company is involved in a lawsuit. A customer sues you for injuries sustained while using your product. Any future damage award or monetary settlement in the case could have a material, adverse effect on your financial position.

When it's time to prepare your year-end financial statements, do you disclose this pending litigation? If so, how should you treat it?

This is an example of a contingent liability: a potential liability arising from events that occurred before the end of the accounting period but whose outcome won't be known until some future date. A contingent liability must be disclosed. This is generally accomplished by a footnote.

HOW TO DETERMINE IF YOUR EXTERNAL FINANCIAL STATEMENTS SHOULD BE CERTIFIED

Why would any company spend money to have its financial statements audited if it didn't have to? If a company's stock is not publicly traded, it's not required to be audited.

However, suppose your company needed to raise money to finance an expansion plan. You could either borrow the money or sell an equity interest in the company. Either way, creditors or investors will want to see audited financial statements before they agree to put their money into your company.

Audited financial statements give investors more confidence in your business. The auditor provides an objective, unbiased viewpoint when examining your books and financial statements. An audit is meant to provide independent verification of the information that management presents in its external financial reports.

The accounting profession sets certain rules that auditors must follow to maintain independence both in fact and in appearance. The rules bar auditors from owning an interest in or lending money to a client, from serving as a director or officer of a client company, and other possible conflicts of interest.

An audit can help you to better manage your company. Let's take a closer look at what an auditor does:

• An auditor's review of internal controls is an integral part of the audit. It enables the auditor to make recommendations and correct improper procedures, and to suggest controls where none may exist. The auditor will study, test and evaluate the system.

A good system of internal controls provides a degree of assurance that the financial data provided by your accounting system is essentially reliable, that your assets and records are secure, and that your system is organized to make efficient use of labor and other resources.

• The auditor's analysis of accounts gives management an important tool for evaluating the reliability of the information produced by the accounting system. To perform this type of analysis, the auditor obtains various types of evidence: physical observation (e.g., inventories), confirmation (e.g., receivables), tests of mechanical accuracy, inquiry, documentation, and reasonableness.

The greater the auditor's confidence in your system of internal controls, the less direct testing of the accounts he or she will perform.

• The auditor should obtain an understanding of the industry in which you operate and should become familiar with your particular business early in the audit. An experienced auditor can recommend ways of improving your accounting system and other beneficial changes in your business.

For instance, suppose you're considering automating your payroll system. Your auditor should be able to tell you about the experiences and mistakes of other clients who have gone through similar processes. This can help you choose, design and implement your system.

> **IMPORTANT:** All accountants aren't equal. Not all accountants are certified public accountants (CPAs). CPAs must meet certain educational requirements and pass a rigorous examination to become licensed. An auditor or accountant who is not a CPA may be competent and knowledgeable, but cannot certify your financial statements.

Although there's so much to be gained by having an objective outside accountant auditing the books and records, many companies don't have their financial statements certified. They are concerned that it costs too much.

This may or may not be true in each case. The cost of the audit has to be balanced against the savings that may result from an auditor's suggestions for improving efficiency and control systems. In any case, by cooperating with your auditors, you can reduce the cost of an audit.

When you engage an auditor, tell him or her at the outset that you want to cooperate to hold audit costs down. Arrange to have your own staff prepare many of the working papers and schedules that the auditors will need—and have them ready at the appointed time.

CHAPTER SEVENTEEN

HOW TO READ AND ANALYZE FINANCIAL STATEMENTS

Business owners need to know how to analyze financial statements for many of the different roles they play:

- *Investor*: Financial statements can help you make investment decisions about a company's expected future profitability.

- *Creditor*: As a business owner, you want to extend credit only to customers who will be able to pay you back. You can obtain a lot of information about customers' creditworthiness from their financial statements. (See Chapter 5 For more on credit policies.)

- *Manager*: Your company's financial statements can help you assess your business's performance and can alert you to problems such as escalating expenses and declining revenues.

Financial statements often contain so much information that they appear to be more confusing than helpful. You need to know how to analyze what's reported to find the most usable information about the financial condition of the business—either yours or your customers'.

This chapter offers some tips on what to look for when analyzing financial statements. It will give you some ideas on how to look beyond the numbers to learn more about a company's financial condition. You'll also learn about some analytical tools you can use to make an informed evaluation of how well the company is managed.

The term "financial statements" here refers to all the information contained in a company's external reports. This includes items such as footnotes, supplementary schedules, and management's analysis in addition to the basic statements (such as the balance sheet and income statement).

When analysts evaluate financial statements, they often compute various ratios. While these ratios can be useful, they are at best a limited tool.

Ratios are calculated based upon accounting data. So, you need to understand what's behind the data—the accounting principles used, assumptions and estimates—to understand the ratios. Also, a ratio may be subject to various interpretations. For example, a "high" dividend-payout ratio may indicate a good return on a stockholder's investment. It may also indicate that the company is not retaining enough of its earnings for future reinvestment and long-term growth.

It may be helpful to categorize commonly used types of ratios on the basis of the different types of information they give us about a business:

- Liquidity—ability to meet short-term obligations;
- Leverage—how much of the entity's assets are financed by debt;
- Activity—how efficiently resources are used; and
- Profitability—overall evaluation of the returns on sales and investments.

A ratio in and of itself does not have much meaning. You need to look at it in relation to other information. Two relevant points of comparison are other time periods and other companies in the industry.

• *Trend analysis*: You should never look at just one time period. Compare the current period to several others—preferably 5 to 10 years—to get the full picture of the direction in which the company is headed, to highlight unusual situations, and so forth.

• *Industry norms*: It's helpful to compare a business's ratios to the norm for that industry to get a better idea of whether it's a stellar or mediocre performer. But don't assume that a company is a poor performer just because its ratios deviate from the industry norm. Every company is unique and there may be good business reasons why that company operates differently. So don't take the numbers at face value. You need to dig deeper to find out what they mean.

EVALUATING REPORTED EARNINGS

When you look at a company's income statement, you should be interested in more than just the dollar amount of reported earnings. Almost more important than the amount of earnings is the *quality* of earnings. Quality refers to the following:

- Accuracy: Do the numbers present a realistic picture of how the company performed?

- Composition: What are the components (items of revenue and expense) that make up the reported bottom line, and what can they tell you about how well the entity is doing?

- Stability: Do the numbers indicate that the company consistently performs at or around a certain level of profitability and efficiency?

Can you really determine all of this from looking at an income statement? The following section explains how an informed analysis of the income statement can answer many of these questions.

EXAMINING THE "REVENUE BASE"

This is the foundation upon which the company expects to earn a profit. There are a number of questions you should ask in this area. For example:

- Does the company have a diverse product line or does it rely on one product or type of product for the bulk of its revenue? In general, more diversity of product line implies more stable earnings.

- Are any of the products heavily dependent upon factors beyond the company's control? For example, what about a farmer whose harvest can be made or broken by weather conditions.

- Are earnings derived from products for which there is elastic or inelastic demand? Demand for a product is said to be elastic if it's greatly affected by price changes, even minor ones. Inelastic demand means that even wide price fluctuations will have a relatively limited effect on consumer demand for the product.

  Take, for example, batteries or light bulbs. Chances are that even with a large increase in price, demand would not decline very much. People would still buy light bulbs or batteries to replace used up or broken ones. Demand for a candy bar, on the other hand, might fluctuate sharply with a change in price, even a small one. So, you would say demand for batteries and light bulbs is inelastic while demand for candy bars is elastic.

Products that have inelastic demand enhance earnings quality. Ask the following questions:

- Are the types of products inherently more or less stable ones? Stable goods generally produce less variable earnings streams than novelty items, fad items, luxury goods or heavy goods (such as machinery and equipment). Products subject to seasonal demand (for example, suntan lotion) should be balanced out by other items with different seasonal peaks (for example, ski boots). New, unproven products, or products in the declining phase of their life cycles, do not contribute to the stability of the earnings stream.

- What is the company's experience with respect to sales and/or dealer returns? A decreasing trend in the ratio of returns to sales—or at least no increase in the ratio—is generally regarded as favorable.

- Are there other characteristics of the product that add or detract from its ability to enhance the quality of earnings? For example, are there sales tie-ins? Sometimes the initial sale of a product leads to subsequent sales of other goods or services. For instance, Kodak sells cameras, film and processing and developing services. Another example would be a company that sells equipment and derives further revenue from repair and maintenance of that equipment. In general, it's advantageous for a company to have products that generate revenue beyond the initial sale.

When a new, innovative product comes out for which there is initial high demand, it is said to be in an opportunistic market. In other words, there is a danger that the initial high demand will evaporate once consumers tire of the product or competition sets in. This type of revenue is, obviously, highly unstable. The negative aspects of an opportunistic market can be partially offset if the company can obtain a patent on the product *and* the patent is not one that competitors can "get around" with simple, minor changes.

THE RELATIONSHIP BETWEEN RISK AND DIVERSIFICATION

Almost everyone is familiar with the old cliché about not putting all your eggs in one basket. As trite as it may sound, the underlying principle is a sound one for adding stability to a company's earnings.

Let's take a simple example. Say you sell bricks and all your customers are contractors in the residential housing market. Then, for various reasons, there's a slump in the market and new housing starts to fall off sharply. Your business, in turn, is adversely affected because your only customers have a drastically reduced need for your product.

Suppose, however, you also have a fairly strong customer base among commercial building contractors. Let's say that this sector of the industry experiences only a mild downturn. As a result, your business falls off a little but the effect isn't devastating. By diversifying your customer base, you have minimized your risk.

The concept of diversification carries through to many aspects of a business. In analyzing a company's earnings, you should ask the following:

- Does it have a diverse mix of products? Do the products appeal to different markets or have different seasonal peaks? Are different products at different points in the product life cycle?

- Does the company have many customers or just one major customer? Are customers concentrated in one industry or spread among several industries?

- Is the company dependent upon one source for supplies or is it accustomed to using various sources for supplies?

- Is the company geographically diverse, with respect to both customers and suppliers? For instance, if a certain country put a ban on all imports, would the company lose a significant number of customers?

MAKING SURE THE COMPANY'S COSTS ARE FLEXIBLE

To be more efficient and profitable, a company should have a good degree of flexibility in controlling its costs. In other words, if revenues drop, a company should be able to cut costs to recoup at least some of the losses.

If a cost can't be controlled or altered over a given time period, it's considered a fixed cost. Examples include rent, salaries for essential personnel and depreciation.

If a cost fluctuates in direct proportion to sales or production volume, it's a variable cost; for example, direct labor and materials. (Some costs are a combination of fixed and variable.)

A lower proportion of fixed costs to total costs or fixed costs to net income indicates a higher quality of earnings. Variable costs can be controlled and cut back when business slacks off; fixed costs cannot. The key idea here is flexibility.

Operating leverage is another measure of cost flexibility

The extent to which fixed costs play a role in a company's cost structure is also known as "operating leverage." A high degree of operating leverage—that is, greater proportion of fixed to total costs—results in large swings in net income caused by relatively small changes in volume. Obviously, this leaves the company vulnerable: When sales fall slightly, the effect on the bottom line may be severe.

Case Example

Firm A and Firm B both sell the same product for $2 per unit. Their cost structures are very different, however. Firm A has fixed costs of $20,000 and variable costs of $1.50 per unit. Firm B has fixed costs of $60,000 and variable costs of $1.00 per unit.

At 80,000 units, both firms have $160,000 of revenue. Firm A's costs are $140,000 ($20,000 fixed + $120,000 variable), for a $20,000 profit. Firm B also spends $140,000 ($60,000 fixed + $80,000 variable), for a $20,000 profit. If sales drop to 60,000 units or $120,000 of revenue, Firm A's profits drop by $10,000 ($20,000 fixed + $90,000 variable, or total costs of $110,000) leaving a $10,000 profit. Firm B's profits, however, *drop to zero* because its total costs are $120,000 ($60,000 fixed + $60,000 variable).

Discretionary costs

A discretionary cost is one that fluctuates according to the choices of management. The two most common examples are advertising and research and development costs. Another cost that may be discretionary is repair work on fixed assets.

Look at the trend of discretionary costs over several years and see if there's a year in which the relative amount seems out of line. You can look at total dollar amounts, discretionary costs as a percentage of net sales (such as advertising to sales) or the ratio of discretionary costs to related assets (for example, repair expenses relative to gross fixed assets).

Discretionary expenditures are often the first to be cut when a business has financial problems. Watch out for companies that do this to improve short-term earnings at the expense of long-term growth. For instance, you should be wary of the long-term earnings prospects of a pharmaceutical company that severely curtails its R&D expenditures.

Discretionary costs may also be cut or increased to smooth out earnings. Carefully evaluate years in which the ratio of discretionary costs to sales is unusually high or low, compared to other years. Note, however, that an "unusual" ratio in one or more years might be a deliberate management strategy with a legitimate purpose (for example, discontinuing R&D on a major project that's proven fruitless).

Look at the gross profit percentage. A high ratio of gross profit to net sales is favorable. It indicates that management has good control over its cost of sales. Look for a steady or increasing gross profit percentage.

Can you count on the company's ability to meet its financing costs? Assets that support earnings need to be funded. When you evaluate the soundness of a company's earnings, scrutinize its ability to meet its funding (or financing) costs, as well as other fixed costs.

For instance, look at the company's fixed charges such as bond interest expense, preferred stock dividends or lease commitments. Earnings from operations should be adequate to cover these nondiscretionary costs.

HOW ACCOUNTING POLICIES AFFECT EARNINGS

Accounting is not a precise science. Accountants often have some latitude as to how to reflect transactions in the financial statements. The choice of an accounting policy can have a material effect on reported earnings.

Much of accounting is based on estimates and judgment. For example, the useful life of a fixed asset or the proportion of receivables that will prove uncollectible is anybody's guess. In analyzing a company's income statement, keep in mind the following issues:

• **Conservatism:** Accountants generally prepare conservative financial reports, meaning they choose the accounting treatment that produces the *least* favorable impact on earnings. The intent is to avoid

overstating earnings. Generally, this produces an earnings number of
a higher quality.

Beware of conservatism carried to an extreme, however. This can
be just as distorting as using accounting policies that are too liberal.
A good benchmark is to compare the firm's accounting policies to that
of other firms in the industry to get an idea of whether the company's
policies are too liberal or conservative. For example, one company
may depreciate its production equipment over 10 years, while most
other firms in the industry use a 15-year depreciation period. Note
that while companies still have some leeway in choosing the length
of depreciation periods for financial accounting purposes, these are
generally set by law for tax return purposes. The notes to the financial
statements should outline the significant accounting policies used in
preparing the company's statements.

• **Consistency:** It can't be overemphasized that you need to look
at earnings trends over several years rather than at one time period in
isolation. However, comparisons will not be meaningful if the same
accounting policies are not applied in each period.

Another point to consider is the reason for any accounting change.
In the absence of a well-founded reason (such as a change in the nature
of the business itself), an accounting policy change may signal an
attempt to smooth or otherwise distort earnings.

Changes in significant accounting policies should be disclosed
somewhere in the financial statements. For certain types of changes,
the accounting rules require a restatement of previous years' figures.
This makes multi-year comparisons possible.

Also, in some cases, a business is required to show the cumulative
effect of the change in accounting policy right on the face of the income
statement. The results due to the accounting change are clearly distin-
guishable from the results of normal operations.

• **Realistic:** How accurate is the picture of earnings presented by
the chosen accounting policies? Again, one good basis for comparison
is industry practice. For instance, if a company defers recognition of
a certain type of income, see if that practice is followed by other firms
in the industry. Deferral may be acceptable from a GAAP point of
view, but may not be realistic. Make this evaluation in light of other
information provided in the company's financial report.

For instance, suppose that a few years ago the company was acquired and, as a result, shows goodwill as an asset. This goodwill is
being amortized over a 40-year period. In reading this year's financial
statements, however, you notice quite a significant increase in sales

returns. You also read in one of the footnotes that there is a product liability suit pending against the company.

You may conclude that the goodwill has essentially evaporated and that the amortization expense on the income statement is grossly understated. In this case, writing off the remaining balance of the goodwill account would probably give a much more realistic picture of earnings.

- **Timing considerations:** You should also consider issues such as:
  - Does the timing of revenue recognition seem appropriate?
  - Are there reversals of previously recorded income, write-offs or expenses?
  - Does the company show a pattern of under- or over-accruing expenses?

From examining the treatment of these items you can sometimes get an idea of whether or not management is trying to smooth earnings or distort the true picture.

The difference between book and taxable income

Accounting rules differ from tax rules. So, book income will generally not be the same as the income reported on a business's tax return. Look out for the following instances:

- A company reports a comfortable amount of book income coupled with a tax loss, or
- The difference between book and tax income is increasing out of proportion to the increase in earnings.

Such situations could signal an overstatement of book earnings. Or they could signal an understatement of taxable income. This may mean a future audit by the IRS and an adjustment of taxable income— plus interest and penalties.

To more completely analyze the situation, look at the *tax footnote*. The information presented there will tell you what the material differences are between book and tax income. From there you can begin to evaluate the legitimacy of the differences.

How much of reported earnings is based on estimates?

Some items of income and expense are fairly straightforward. For example, there usually isn't much judgment involved in computing rent expenses for the year.

However, many components of net income aren't that easily calculated. Perhaps the most common examples are the different types of reserves and deferrals that are set up for accounting purposes: depreciation, bad debt, product warranties, etc. The more that estimates are used to determine net income, the less reliable the reported earnings.

You can, however, get a general sense of whether management is "in the ball park" with its accounting estimates. If so, you can have greater confidence in the quality of the earnings. Things to look for include the following:

- Do reserve provisions appear to be continually understated, or are actual expenses over time pretty close to the amount provided?

- When assets are disposed of, are very large gains or losses routinely recognized? This may imply that management is not adept at estimating the appropriate depreciation of assets.

- Does a high percentage of total assets require estimates?

- Are cash and near-cash items more significant than noncash items? Noncash items frequently require estimates. Cash and near-cash items do not. A higher percentage of noncash items may imply more uncertain earnings.

- Look for significant estimated or contingent liabilities.

How does inflation affect reported earnings? When a company reports an increase in earnings, how much of that increase is due to improvements in operations (such as growth in sales volume) and how much is attributable to inflation?

Accounting rules require many companies to publish current cost financial statements as a supplement to the regular (historical cost) statements. These supplements are designed to differentiate inflationary profits from real earnings.

Compare current cost net income to historical cost net income. Look at the ratio of adjusted earnings to reported earnings over time. If adjusted earnings increase more than reported earnings over time, the company's earnings probably aren't growing much in real terms—management is mistaking price-level changes for real growth in income.

Distinguish "one shot deals" from factors that support long-term earnings growth. Items such as income from discontinued operations or extraordinary items (for example, the tax benefit of a net operating loss carryforward) should not be evaluated as part of the results of normal business operations. Such nonrecurring events are not, in and of themselves, good predictors of the firm's long-range earnings potential.

Sometimes, however, a nonrecurring item has an important story to tell. Take, for example, income from discontinued operations. The fact that it appears on the income statement may indicate that management is unburdening itself of a major headache and will have more time and funds to devote to profitable lines of business. Or it could signal the start of a general contraction of a business in severe financial trouble.

Other factors "beyond the numbers"

Any number of qualitative factors can influence your evaluation of a company's reported earnings. For instance, you might try to ascertain if changes in senior management are occurring or looming. If so, you need to make a judgment as to new management's competency to run the organization.

Also, does management change often? If so, the company may be in a constant state of turmoil and uncertainty. Long-range planning may be meaningless or nonexistent in such an environment. The earnings of such a company would be considered of low quality and highly unstable.

If, on the other hand, management has been in place for a long time, some of the key players may be nearing retirement. Does there appear to be some planning with respect to a chain of succession? If not, the company's future could suddenly become very uncertain.

Also, take a look at the company's labor pool. Is it highly dependent on unions? If so, do these unions strike often, or do they have a record of reaching compromises with management? Does the company's location afford an ample supply of trained labor?

Take a look at insurance expenses. Are they decreasing while the pool of assets requiring insurance is increasing? Insurance should be adequate to ensure the minimum possible interruption of the earnings stream should assets become damaged or destroyed.

Has the company fired its auditor due to a disagreement over a change in accounting policy? If so, this must be disclosed in the financial statements, and the net income must be reported without the change (assuming the new auditor agrees to the change). If net income is materially higher after the change than before it, you may question the quality of earnings reported under the new method. Frequent changes in auditors may also indicate a tendency by management to shop for auditors who will agree to more liberal accounting practices.

Some useful calculations

You might find it helpful to look at the trend of certain profitability measurements over time. Remember to find out the industry norms for these measurements to get a meaningful sense of how any single firm is doing.

- *Is the company growing?* Look at the change in earnings from prior years relative to current-year earnings or to stockholders' equity.
- *Is the company "profitable"?* There are various measures of profitability:

$$\text{Profit margin} = \text{Net income after taxes} \div \text{Sales}$$

A low profit margin means a company's prices are too low or its costs are too high relative to the revenues it's earning.

$$\text{Return on net worth} = \text{Net profit after taxes} \div \text{Net worth.}$$

Net worth is the firm's equity capital base. A low return on net worth indicates a poor return on the stockholder's investment.

- *Is the firm efficient?* Fixed asset turnover tells you whether or not the capacity of the fixed plant is being adequately used. It's computed as sales divided by net fixed assets.

Total asset turnover tells you whether or not the volume of business is sufficient to justify the size of a company's investment in its assets. Total asset turnover is stated as sales divided by total assets. A low total asset turnover means a company should increase sales and/or reduce or restructure its asset base.

Return on investment

This is an overall measure of return on the business's invested capital. The return that a business realizes on its invested capital is dependent upon: (1) how well costs are controlled (i.e., the profit margin on sales) and (2) how efficiently assets are used (i.e., the asset turnover). This is a key indicator of how well the business is managed.

Efficiency and profitability interact to produce return on investment. Management often performs well in one area but not in the other. To maximize return on investment, management must maximize both efficiency and profitability. Return on investment or ROI (also called return on total assets) can be calculated as:

$$\frac{\text{Sales}}{\text{Total assets}} \times \frac{\text{Net income}}{\text{Sales}} \quad \text{or} \quad \frac{\text{Net income}}{\text{Total assets}}$$

EXAMINING THE BALANCE SHEET

The assets and liabilities on a company's balance sheet generate the revenues and expenses that make up earnings. Thus, the balance sheet can provide insights into the earnings potential of the business. As with the values given on the income statement, the numbers on the balance sheet may require adjustment to provide an accurate picture of the company's condition.

Say, for example, a company reports total assets of $12.5 million. It claims $375,000 in goodwill as an asset account, although a footnote indicates that the company faces legal action for selling defective merchandise. The true value of the goodwill may be closer to zero, and the true asset value of the business lower than what's stated on the balance sheet.

IDENTIFYING RISK

When you rely on balance sheet values, you are running the risk that an asset could not be converted into cash at its stated value (i.e., so-called "realization risk"). Earnings quality decreases as the proportion of high-risk assets increases. Examples of high-risk assets include machinery and equipment, goodwill, and receivables that are past due.

It's wise for a business to keep some assets in the form of cash or near-cash for liquidity purposes. However, there is also a risk/return tradeoff. Keeping an excess of cash is likely to reduce the company's return on assets. The proper balance between liquid and illiquid assets is a judgment that must be made on the basis of each business's particular set of circumstances at any given point in time.

Cash

Even cash is not necessarily a low-risk asset. In some instances, a company's access to the cash may be restricted. For example, the cash may be deposited in a foreign country that restricts its movement out of the country.

Receivables

Receivables can be very low-risk assets, depending upon the credit-worthiness of the business's customers. If a large proportion of the company's credit sales are to customers in a financially troubled industry, the receivables' risk increases. A diversified customer base reduces the risk.

Sometimes a company offers liberal credit terms to encourage customers to buy a product. For instance, the company may be trying to push a new product line. This is acceptable as long as the product is useful and of high quality. If unneeded or poorly made merchandise is being pushed with easy credit, however, there may be a problem collecting the receivables.

You can detect this kind of problem by looking at quarterly statements. A large increase in sales in one quarter followed by a significant drop in sales or large sales returns in the next quarter may signal a problem.

The collection period

Analysts often compute the "average collection period" as a very rough indicator of whether a company is having problems realizing its receivables. The computation is:

$$\frac{\text{Annual Sales}}{360} = \text{Average daily sales}$$

$$\frac{\text{Receivables}}{\text{Average daily sales}} = \text{Average collection period}$$

If the company's average collection period is 60 days, and credit terms in the industry generally call for payment within 30 days, the company's customers are probably taking too long to pay their bills.

A shorter collection period generally means better quality receivables. On the other hand, credit policies that are too stringent may discourage sales that would ultimately prove to be collectible. Receivables should be analyzed in conjunction with the related bad debt reserve.

If you notice a steady increase in the average collection period or the ratio of receivables to sales, it's fair to conclude that the quality of the receivables is declining. As a result, you would expect the ratio of bad debts to sales and bad debts to receivables to increase.

Also, be alert to any use of the bad debt provision to smooth income. Look out for sudden increases in the provision to adjust for prior year understatements or a history of reversing prior year provisions for overstatements.

Inventories

Inventories that aren't maintained at the proper level may carry a significant realization risk. It takes considerable judgment to strike the right balance between carrying too much and too little inventory. Overstocking carries with it the risk of obsolescence and deterioration, as well as the costs associated with carrying the inventory (such as storage and financing). Excess inventory is a capital investment with close to zero return. On the other hand, an inadequate inventory may result in lost sales if the company is unable to meet customer demand on a timely basis.

So, what's the proper level of inventory? One measure is the "inventory turnover" ratio, computed as:

$$\frac{\text{Sales}}{\text{Inventory}} \quad = \quad \text{Inventory turnover}$$

The ratio is generally favorable if it's at or around the industry norm over time. An unusually low turnover should alert you to overstocking, obsolete goods or other problems.

Of course, there may be legitimate business reasons or explanations for a sluggish inventory turnover. Examples would include a buildup in anticipation of future price increases (for nonperishable goods) or anticipation of a large increase in demand (for seasonal items).

Certain types of inventory are considered to be especially risky: perishable goods, fad items, specialized or custom-made goods, luxury items, secured inventory, and inventory that's not adequately insured. Raw materials are less risky than work-in-progress or finished goods because they have more alternative uses.

If manufacturing a product involves a complicated process, chances are that costing the inventory involves numerous assumptions and cost estimates. So, the inventory value is more likely to be over- or under-stated than goods produced by a more simple production process. You should also question stated inventory valuations if the company has a history of write-offs. On the other hand, the value of inventory carried at the lower of cost or market may be understated.

Securities

Investment securities are generally regarded as easily convertible to cash at their stated value. However, you still need to compare carrying value to market value; the portfolios may be under- or overvalued. There are other key issues:

- What is the composition of the investment portfolio?
- Are the securities volatile, low-risk or combined to achieve a diversified portfolio?
- Has the company acquired a large chunk of stock in another entity? If so, it may be considering an acquisition. This may increase or decrease the riskiness of the investment portfolio, depending upon the financial soundness of the potential target.

Fixed assets

In analyzing fixed assets (plant, property and equipment), you should be concerned primarily about capacity and maintenance. You also need to evaluate the related depreciation accounts.

• Capacity: Is the rate of return on fixed assets adequate to justify the investment? The question once again is one of balance: to find the middle ground between excess capacity and under-capitalization. Too much capacity means that the business isn't fully utilizing its fixed assets, and so isn't getting the maximum return on invested capital. A business that is "underinvested" in fixed assets, on the other hand, may be losing out on revenues because it's unable to meet demand. Return on investment might be improved by taking capital out of other lower-return assets and investing it in fixed plant instead.

One way to evaluate the benefits generated by a company's investment in its fixed plant is to calculate the rate of return on fixed assets. This is the ratio of sales or net income to fixed assets (also known as "fixed asset turnover"). If the rate of return is too low, then the benefits gained from the company's fixed assets are insufficient to justify the investment. The business's capital should be deployed to other assets that can generate a higher return on investment.

However, a decreasing return on fixed assets is not always a negative sign. The company may have added fixed assets to manufacture a new product that has not yet begun to generate sales. If the product is innovative and well-made, subsequent increases in return on total assets could more than make up for the downturn during the product development phase.

• Maintenance: Future earnings can be adversely affected when existing fixed assets aren't properly maintained, or when obsolete ones are not replaced. To get an idea of the adequacy of asset maintenance and replacement effects, look at the ratio of repairs to fixed assets over time. It should be fairly constant and in line with the industry norm.

Also look at the level of fixed asset acquisitions compared to gross fixed assets. In certain industries, it's particularly important for fixed plant to be state-of-the-art. However, such equipment may be prone to rapid obsolescence.

• Depreciation: A depreciation policy that most accurately reflects the decline in the asset's ability to generate income produces the truest measure of earnings. Look at the trend in the ratio of depreciation to sales and fixed assets. It should remain fairly steady. Also, a small increase in depreciation when there has been a substantial increase in fixed assets may signal an inadequate depreciation policy.

Also, be alert to instances where a firm has been using one method of depreciation for a class of assets and switches to another (either for existing assets or new acquisitions). If there isn't an adequate justification for the switch, you should be suspect of the level of earnings calculated under the new depreciation method.

Intangible assets and deferred costs

Intangible assets and deferred costs generally carry a relatively high degree of realization risk. For example, does stated goodwill still truly exist when there has been an increase in sales returns (which could indicate customer dissatisfaction)? Is the amortization period realistic? The 40-year maximum amortization period permitted by accounting rules is probably excessive in many cases. A significant increase in intangibles may indicate that costs are being inappropriately capitalized (i.e., put on the balance sheet as amortizable assets) instead of being written off currently.

Intangibles may also be *undervalued* on a balance sheet. For example, a patent may be worth much more than the amount spent to produce or purchase it. Yet the patent would be listed on a company's balance sheet at that historical cost. On the other hand, a patent could be overvalued if it will expire soon or can be easily infringed with minor changes.

Goodwill is recorded on the books only when one company is purchased by another entity. Goodwill that a company develops on its own as a result of superior performance can't be shown on the books because there's no objective way to value it. However, this type of goodwill definitely enhances a firm's earnings potential.

HOW TO EVALUATE LIABILITIES

The counterpart to the concept of asset realization risk is the possibility that an obligation will have to be satisfied in the very near future. This calls into question the company's ability to meet the obligation on a timely basis. In other words, once again, how liquid is the business?

FINDING THE CURRENT RATIO

To determine the current ratio, divide current assets by current liabilities. This will tell you, roughly, the extent to which a company's short-term obligations are covered by assets that can be readily converted into cash.

For example, if current assets are $300,000, and current liabilities are $100,000, the current ratio is 3. This means a company could liquidate its current assets at only 33% of book value and still generate enough cash to pay off its current liabilities.

A variation called the "quick ratio" deducts inventory from current assets before computing the current ratio. This is done because inventory is generally the most difficult current asset to liquidate—and the most susceptible to liquidation losses.

Another consideration is the proportion of current liabilities to total liabilities and to sales. If this proportion is increasing, it may indicate that the company is stretching its short-term credit too thin.

Don't forget to look for liabilities that you don't see disclosed on the balance sheet, such as contingent liabilities. As you know, business transactions don't always conveniently resolve themselves before it's time to close the books for the accounting period. Sometimes there's a possibility that the company will incur a liability sometime in the future as a result of a pending matter. Often, however, there is no way to reasonably estimate the amount of the potential future obligation or when it will become due.

Because there's no objective way to value these "contingent liabilities," they can't be recorded in the balance sheet. They should, however, be disclosed in a note to the financial statements; for example, pending litigation.

ANALYZING LONG-TERM DEBT

When you analyze the long-term debt section of a balance sheet, you should be concerned with two issues:

- Solvency, and
- The cost and nature of the way the business is obtaining its long-term financing.

Solvency can be thought of as the long-term equivalent of liquidity. That is, a business is solvent if its long-term assets are adequate to cover its long-term debt. Be careful. It's dangerous for a business to fund long-term assets with short-term debt.

- Short-term debt is riskier because the company may not be able to renew short-term debt when it needs to. If a lender insists on repayment when the company is strapped for cash (for example, during a downturn in the business cycle), the company may be forced to liquidate assets it needs to generate future sales.

- When a company uses a higher percentage of long-term debt, its interest costs are more stable over time. This helps the budgeting and planning process.

There are, however, situations in which short-term debt may be the best choice because it offers these advantages:

- Short-term debt is usually cheaper. That's because a company is tying up the lender's money for a shorter period of time. If interest rates rise, the lender can reap the benefit sooner than if they're locked into a long range commitment at old (lower) rates.

- Short-term debt is more flexible. If a company thinks it will require financing for only a limited period of time, it may as well take advantage of obtaining cheaper money.

How to assess solvency

You need to be concerned with the realizability (convertibility into cash) of the long-term assets. Certain ratios can also help you make this evaluation.

$$\text{Long-term debt/equity ratio} \ = \ \frac{\text{Long-term liabilities}}{\text{Stockholders' equity}}$$

The higher this ratio, the riskier the company's capital structure. That's because payments on debt financing must be met on schedule, unlike equity financing.

A variation of this ratio is total debt ÷ stockholders' equity or total debt ÷ total assets. All three ratios have the same purpose: To show the proportion of the business's financing that comes from debt (creditors) relative to equity (shareholders).

The concept of leverage

The basic principle underlying the concept of leverage is really quite simple: It pays to borrow money if you can earn more with the loan proceeds than the lender charges. If the profit a company is making on borrowed funds exceeds its borrowing costs, its return on equity increases the more it borrows—as opposed to the company raising cash by selling equity interests. This positive effect is due to the fact that interest paid on debt is tax deductible, while dividend payments to equity owners are not.

However, it works both ways. That is, return on equity drops more rapidly when return on assets drops if there is a large proportion of debt financing. Thus, a highly leveraged company faces significant downside risk as well as upside potential.

Increasing the proportion of debt in a company's capital structure can be highly profitable. It can also be very risky. It's important to keep this in mind when evaluating a company's financial soundness and stability.

Check outstanding loans

If possible, you should evaluate the particulars of the company's loan agreements. Look for restrictions, compensating balance requirements, acceleration clauses, and collateral pledged against the loan. All of these provide important information about a company's financial vulnerability. Consider the following issues:

- Do any of the loans carry adjustable interest rates? If so, what does this mean for the firm's future cost of capital in light of expected movements in interest rates?

- Does the company have access to adequate, reasonably priced revolving credit lines? Can it issue commercial paper, which is cheaper than other short-term financing? If so, this is a good sign—only financially strong firms are able to obtain funds in the commercial paper market.

Shareholders' equity

Finally, scrutinize the shareholders' equity section of the balance sheet. The following calculations can give you an idea of whether equity investors are realizing a satisfactory return on their investment:

$$\frac{\text{Return on stockholders' equity}}{(\text{Also called } return\ on\ net\ worth)} = \frac{\text{Net income after tax}}{\text{Stockholders' equity}}$$

Index